Medieval Syria and the Onset of the Crusades

Edinburgh Studies in Classical Islamic History and Culture
Series Editor: Carole Hillenbrand

A particular feature of medieval Islamic civilization was its wide horizons. The Muslims fell heir not only to the Graeco-Roman world of the Mediterranean, but also to that of the ancient Near East, to the empires of Assyria, Babylon and the Persians; and beyond that, they were in frequent contact with India and China to the east and with black Africa to the south. This intellectual openness can be sensed in many inter-related fields of Muslim thought, and it impacted powerfully on trade and on the networks that made it possible. Books in this series reflect this openness and cover a wide range of topics, periods and geographical areas.

Titles in the series include:

The Body in Arabic Love Poetry: The 'Udhri Tradition
Jokha Alharthi

Arabian Drugs in Early Medieval Mediterranean Medicine
Zohar Amar and Efraim Lev

Towards a History of Libraries in Yemen
Hassan Ansari and Sabine Schmidtke

The Abbasid Caliphate of Cairo, 1261–1517: Out of the Shadows
Mustafa Banister

The Medieval Western Maghrib: Cities, Patronage and Power
Amira K. Bennison

Christian Monastic Life in Early Islam
Bradley Bowman

Keeping the Peace in Premodern Islam: Diplomacy under the Mamluk Sultanate, 1250–1517
Malika Dekkiche

Queens, Concubines and Eunuchs in Medieval Islam
Taef El-Azhari

Islamic Political Thought in the Mamluk Period
Mohamad El Merheb

The Kharijites in Early Islamic Historical Tradition: Heroes and Villains
Hannah-Lena Hagemann

Classical Islam: Collected Essays
Carole Hillenbrand

Islam and the Crusades: Collected Essays
Carole Hillenbrand

The Medieval Turks: Collected Essays
Carole Hillenbrand

Medieval Damascus: Plurality and Diversity in an Arabic Library – The Ashrafīya Library Catalogue
Konrad Hirschler

A Monument to Medieval Syrian Book Culture: The Library of Ibn ʿAbd al-Hādī
Konrad Hirschler

The Popularisation of Sufism in Ayyubid and Mamluk Egypt: State and Society, 1173–1325
Nathan Hofer

Defining Anthropomorphism: The Challenge of Islamic Traditionalism
Livnat Holtzman

Making Mongol History: Rashid al-Din and the Jamiʿ al-Tawarikh
Stefan Kamola

Lyrics of Life: Saʿdi on Love, Cosmopolitanism and Care of the Self
Fatemeh Keshavarz

Art, Allegory and the Rise of Shiism in Iran, 1487–1565
Chad Kia

The Administration of Justice in Medieval Egypt: From the 7th to the 12th Century
Yaacov Lev

Zoroastrians in Early Islamic History: Accommodation and Memory
Andrew D. Magnusson

A History of Herat: From Chingiz Khan to Tamerlane
Shivan Mahendrarajah

The Queen of Sheba's Gift: A History of the True Balsam of Matarea
Marcus Milwright

Ruling from a Red Canopy: Political Authority in the Medieval Islamic World, From Anatolia to South Asia
Colin P. Mitchell

Islam, Christianity and the Realms of the Miraculous: A Comparative Exploration
Ian Richard Netton

The Poetics of Spiritual Instruction: Farid al-Din ʿAttar and Persian Sufi Didacticism
Austin O'Malley

Sacred Place and Sacred Time in the Medieval Islamic Middle East: An Historical Perspective
Daniella Talmon-Heller

Conquered Populations in Early Islam: Non-Arabs, Slaves and the Sons of Slave Mothers
Elizabeth Urban

Owning Books and Preserving Documents in Medieval Jerusalem: The Library of Burhan al-Din
Said Aljoumani and Konrad Hirschler

Medieval Syria and the Onset of the Crusades: The Political World of Bilad al-sham, 1050–1128
James Wilson

edinburghuniversitypress.com/series/escihc

Medieval Syria and the Onset of the Crusades

The Political World of *Bilad al-sham* 1050–1128

James Wilson

EDINBURGH
University Press

For Marianne and Frederick

Edinburgh University Press is one of the leading university presses in the UK. We publish academic books and journals in our selected subject areas across the humanities and social sciences, combining cutting-edge scholarship with high editorial and production values to produce academic works of lasting importance. For more information visit our website: edinburghuniversitypress.com

© James Wilson, 2023, 2024

Edinburgh University Press Ltd
13 Infirmary Street, Edinburgh, EH1 1LT

First published in hardback by Edinburgh University Press 2023

Typeset in 11/15 EB Garamond by
Cheshire Typesetting Ltd, Cuddington, Cheshire

A CIP record for this book is available from the British Library

ISBN 978 1 3995 0317 4 (hardback)
ISBN 978 1 3995 0318 1 (paperback)
ISBN 978 1 3995 0319 8 (webready PDF)
ISBN 978 1 3995 0320 4 (epub)

The right of James Wilson to be identified as author of this work has been asserted in accordance with the Copyright, Designs and Patents Act 1988 and the Copyright and Related Rights Regulations 2003 (SI No. 2498).

Contents

List of Figures	viii
Note on Names, Transliteration and Abbreviations	ix
Abbreviations	x
Principal Historical Figures, Dynasties and Terminology	xiii
Acknowledgements	xx

Introduction: Defining and Exploring the Political World of *Bilad al-sham*	1
Historiographical Overview	4
The Primary Sources	7
The Scope of this Book	16
Notes	17

Part I Historical Sketch of *Bilad al-sham*

Part I Introduction	33
The System of Autonomous Lordships in Syria	33
Byzantine, Fatimid and Seljuq Syria	35
Notes	37

1 The Byzantine Empire	**39**
Byzantine *Bilad al-sham*	39
The Antiochene–Aleppan Balance of Power	43
The Byzantine Political Footprint in the Face of Seljuq Incursions	50
Byzantine Interactions with Local Rulers in *Bilad al-sham*	54
Conclusion: The Break-up of Byzantine *Bilad al-sham*	59
Notes	60

2 The Fatimid Caliphate — 70
Fatimid *Bilad al-sham* — 70
The Fatimid Political Footprint in Northern Syria:
442–63/1050–71 — 73
The Fatimid Collapse in Southern Syria and Palestine — 80
Fatimid Interactions with Local Rulers in *Bilad al-sham* — 85
Conclusion: The Fatimids as 'the Other' in *Bilad al-sham*? — 89
Notes — 90

3 The Great Seljuq Sultanate — 98
Seljuq *Bilad al-sham* — 98
The Sultan in *Bilad al-sham* — 102
Syrian Campaigns Instigated by Malik Shah — 107
The Seljuq Perpetuation of the System of Autonomous Lordships
 in Syria — 111
Seljuq *Bilad al-sham* in the Sixth/Twelfth Century — 123
The Türkmen in Syria — 126
Conclusion: Reassessing Seljuq *Bilad al-sham* — 132
Notes — 133

Part II Countering the Crusades?

Part II Introduction — 149

4 The Reactions of Seljuq, Fatimid and Syrian Elites — 151
The 'Counter-Crusade' and *'la maqam'* Paradigms — 151
The Seljuq Counter-Crusade — 154
The Fatimid Counter-Crusade — 158
Alliance Networks among Syrian Elites in the Early Crusading Era — 168
Notes — 174

5 The Notables and Frontiers of Aleppo — 184
The Empowerment of Syrian Notables — 185
Appeals for Assistance — 193
The Frontiers of *Bilad halab* — 203

Revisiting Baldwin II's Siege of Aleppo   213
Conclusion: Aleppan Notables and the Threat of Frankish Rule   220
Notes   221

Conclusion: Situating the Crusades in Syrian History   235

Appendix I: Chronology of Events   238
Appendix II: Regnal Dates in Bilad al-sham   240
Appendix III: Aleppo under Siege   244
Appendix IV: Damascus under Siege   251
Bibliography   253
Index   292

Figures

I.1	Ibn Hawqal and al-Muqaddasi's definition of *bilad al-sham*	2
1.1	Key Antiochene settlements on the River Orontes	41
2.1	Typical Fatimid marching route to Aleppo: 440–52/1048–60	77
2.2	Fatimid campaign of 482/1090	83
5.1	Occasions Aleppo and Damascus were besieged: 439–522/1047–1128	187
5.2	Siege events at Aleppo and Damascus: 439–522/1047–1128	190
5.3	Frontiers of *bilad halab*: 442–522/1050–1128	204
5.4	The strategic importance of 'Azaz	207
5.5	Approaches to Aleppo taken by Baldwin II's forces in 518/1124	215

Note on Names, Transliteration and Abbreviations

This book relies upon a number of sources written in a wide variety of languages, which present certain challenges in offering consistent spellings of place names and individuals. All names relating to places and people are given in English, and the Arabic terms *ibn* (son) and *bint* (daughter) are both abbreviated to b. when placed in the middle of a name. This book does not employ Arabic–English transliteration, with the exception of the Arabic letters ʿ and ʾ which represent *ʿayn* and *hamza*, for which there are no equivalents in English.

Dates are provided in both the Hirja (AH) and Common Era (CE) format. For instance, the First Crusaders captured Jerusalem at the end of the fifth/eleventh century in the year 492/1099. In addition, this book has used abbreviations in the notes. The most common abbreviations are listed in the section below.

Abbreviations

AA	Albert of Aachen, *Historia Hierosolymitana*, ed. and trans. Susan B. Edgington (Oxford: Clarendon, 2007).
al-ʿAzimi	Muhammad b. ʿAli al-ʿAzimi, *Taʾrikh halab*, ed. Ibrahim Zaʾrur (Damascus: s.n., 1984).
al-Maqrizi	Taqi al-Din al-Maqrizi, *Ittiʾaz al-hunafaʾ bi-akhbar al-aʾimma al-fatimiyyin al-khulafaʾ*, 3 vols (Cairo: al-Lajnat Ihyaʾ al-Turath al-Islami, 1967–73), vol. I ed. Jamal al-Din al-Shayyal (1967), vols II and III ed. Muhammad H. M. Ahmad (1971–3).
Asbridge, *Creation*	Thomas S. Asbridge, *The Creation of the Principality of Antioch 1098–1130* (Woodbridge: Boydell, 2000).
Beihammer, *Byzantium*	Alexander D. Beihammer, *Byzantium and the Emergence of Muslim-Turkish Anatolia ca. 1040–1130* (Abingdon: Routledge, 2017).
Bianquis, *Damas*	Thierry Bianquis, *Damas et la Syrie sous la domination Fatimide*, 2 vols (Damascus: Institut français de Damas, 1986–9).
Brett, *Empire*	Michael Brett, *The Fatimid Empire* (Edinburgh: Edinburgh University Press, 2017).
Cahen, *Syrie*	Claude Cahen, *La Syrie du nord à l'époque des croisades et la Principauté Franque d'Antioche* (Paris: Librairie Orientaliste Paul Geuthner, 1940).
El-Azhari, *Saljuqs*	Taef K. El-Azhari, *The Saljuqs of Syria During the Crusades 463–549 A.H./1070–1154 A.D.* (Berlin: Klaus Schwarz, 1997).

FC	Fulcher of Chartres, *Fulcheri carnoetensis, Historia Hierosolymitana*, ed. Heinrich Hagenmeyer (Heidelberg: Carl Winters Universitatsbuchhandlung, 1913).
FC trans.	Fulcher of Chartres, *A History of the Expedition to Jerusalem*, trans. Frances R. Ryan, ed. Harold S. Fink (Knoxville: University of Tennessee Press, 1969).
GF	Anonymous, *Gesta Francorum et aliorum Hierosolimitanorum*, ed. and trans. Rosalind M. Hill (London: T. Nelson, 1962).
Hillenbrand, *Crusades*	Carole Hillenbrand: *The Crusades: Islamic Perspectives* (Edinburgh: Edinburgh University Press, 1999).
IAD BH	Kamal al-Din Ibn al-'Adim, *Bughyat al-talab fi ta'rikh halab*, ed. Suhayl Zakkar, 12 vols (Beirut: Dar al-Fikr, 1988).
IAD ZH	Kamal al-Din Ibn al-'Adim, *Zubdat al-halab min ta'rikh halab*, ed. Sami Dahan, 3 vols (Damascus: Institut français de Damas, 1951–68).
IATH	'Izz al-Din 'Ali Ibn al-Athir, *al-Kamil fi'l ta'rikh*, ed. Carolus J. Tornberg, 12 vols (Beirut: Dar Sadir, 1965–7).
IM	Taj al-Din Ibn Muyassar, *Akhbar Misr*, ed. Ayman F. Sayyid (Cairo: Institut français d'Archéologie Orientale, 1981).
IQ	Abu Ya'la Ibn al-Qalanisi, *Dhayl ta'rikh Dimashq*, ed. Suhayl Zakkar (Damascus: Dar Hassan, 1983).
Köhler, *Alliances*	Michael A. Köhler, *Alliances and Treaties between Frankish and Muslim Rulers in the Middle East* (Leiden: Brill, 2013).
ME	Matthew of Edessa, *Armenia and the Crusades, Tenth to Twelfth Centuries: the Chronicle of Matthew of Edessa*, trans. Ara E. Dostourian (London: University Press of America, 1993).

MS	Michael the Syrian, *The Syriac Chronicle of Michael Rabo (the Great): a Universal History from the Creation*, trans. Matti Moosa (Teaneck: Beth Antioch Press, 2014).
Peacock, *Empire*	Andrew C. S. Peacock, *The Great Seljuk Empire* (Edinburgh: Edinburgh University Press, 2015).
RC	Ralph of Caen, 'Gesta Tancredi in Expeditione Hierosolymitana', *Recueil des historiens des croisades, Historiens occidentaux*, 5 vols (Paris: Imprimerie Royale, 1844–95), vol. III (1866), pp. 587–716.
RC trans.	Ralph of Caen, *The Gesta Tancredi of Ralph of Caen*, ed. and trans. Bernard S. Bachrach and David S. Bachrach (Farnham: Ashgate, 2005).
SJ	Yusuf Qizoglu Sibt b. al-Jawzi, *Mi'rat al-zaman fi ta'rikh al-aʿyan*, ed. Kamil S. Al-Jabouri et al., 23 vols (Beirut: Dar al-Kutub al-ʿIlmiyah, 2013).
WC	Walter the Chancellor, *Galterii Cancelarii bella antiochena*, ed. Heinrich Hagenmeyer (Innsbruck: s.n., 1896).
WC trans.	Walter the Chancellor, *Walter the Chancellor's The Antiochene Wars: a Translation and Commentary*, ed. and trans. Thomas Asbridge and Susan B. Edgington (Aldershot: Ashgate, 1999).
WT	William of Tyre, *Willelmi Tyremsos archiepiscopi Chronicon*, ed. Robert B. C. Huygens, Corpus Christianorum Continuatio Mediaevalis 63–63a, 2 vols (Turnhout: Brepols, 1986).
WT trans.	William of Tyre, *William of Tyre: a History of Deeds Done beyond the Sea*, ed. and trans. Emily A. Babcock and August C. Krey, 2 vols (New York: Octagon, 1976).
Zakkar, *Emirate*	Suhayl Zakkar, *The Emirate of Aleppo 1004–1094* (Beirut: Dar al-Amanah, 1971).

Principal Historical Figures, Dynasties and Terminology

Abbasid Caliphate	Sunni dynasty of caliphs, who established their capital in Baghdad in the second/eighth century. They remained nominal heads of the Sunni Islamic world until the Mongol invasions of the seventh/thirteenth century.
Ahdath	Local urban militias who occasionally took an active part in military engagements.
Ahmad Shah	The leader of a group of Türkmen who were in the employ of the Mirdasid dynasty of Aleppo in the late 460s/1070s (d. 471/1078).
Al-Afdal b. Badr al-Jamali	Fatimid vizier (r. 487–515/1094–1121), essentially the most powerful political and military figure in Egypt at the time of the First Crusade.
Al-'Azimi	Aleppan chronicler (d. after 556/1161).
Al-Mustansir	Fatimid caliph (r. 427–87/1036–94).
Alp Arslan	Seljuq sultan (r. 455–65/1063–73) who led a military campaign in northern Syria in 463/1071.
Aqsunqur	Qasim al-Dawla, ruler of Aleppo (r. 480–7/1087–95), father of Zengi and grandfather to Nur al-Din.
Aqsunqur al-Bursuqi	Ruler of Mosul and Aleppo (r. 518–21/1125–7) and close ally of the Seljuq Sultan Muhammad I b. Malik Shah.
Artuqids	A Turkish dynasty, who initially emerged in Syria during the late fifth/eleventh century, before later establishing a power-base in the Jazira based around Mardin.

Atabeg	A Turkish term (a literal translation would be father-ruler), used to designate political figures who took guardianship of under-aged rulers and potential heirs of Turkish potentates. *Atabeg*s occasionally married the widows of former rulers.
'Atiyya b. Salih	Mirdasid ruler of Aleppo (r. 454–7/1062–5).
Atsiz b. Uvaq	Leader of a nomadic Türkmen group named the Nawakiya, who captured Jerusalem and Damascus (r. 467–71/1075–8).
Ayyubids	A Kurdish dynasty, based in Cairo and Damascus established by Saladin (d. 589/1193). The Ayyubids ruled much of the Near East in the first half of the seventh/thirteenth century, before being overthrown by the Mamluks.
Badr al-Jamali	Fatimid vizier (r. 467–87/1074–94), of Armenian heritage. His appointment signalled the empowerment of the vizier over the caliph in the Fatimid system, and he became the most influential political and military figure in Egypt.
Baldwin	A common name for Frankish rulers of Edessa and Jerusalem. During the period covered in this book, it refers to Baldwin I (r. 493–512/1100–18) and Baldwin II (r. 512–25/1118–31) of Jerusalem.
Banu Kilab, Kalb, Munqidh, Numayr and Uqayl/ Uqaylids	A literal translation of the Arabic (*Banu*) is sons of. Generally used to designate Arab tribal groups or leading notable families in the major urban centres. The Banu Kilab, Kalb, Munqidh, Numayr and Uqaylid were tribal groups of Bedouin origin, who were active in Syria and the Jazira between the third and sixth/ninth and twelfth centuries.
Bedouin	Nomadic Arab tribes and peoples who became increasingly influential in Arabia, Palestine, Syria and the Jazira from the fourth/ninth century onwards.
Berkyaruq b. Malik Shah	Seljuq sultan (r. 487–98/1094–1105) when the Franks arrived in the Levant.

HISTORICAL FIGURES, DYNASTIES AND TERMINOLOGY | XV

Bilad al-sham	A geographical area encompassing much of the Levant, stretching from southern Anatolia in the north, the borders of Egypt in the south and the River Euphrates in the east.
Bohemond	A common name for Frankish rulers of Antioch. During this period, it refers to the famous First Crusader and ruler of Antioch Bohemond I (r. 491–504/1098–1111).
Byzantine Empire	A Greek-speaking Orthodox Christian dynasty and empire based in Constantinople, successors to the eastern Roman Empire. A key player in the eastern Mediterranean throughout the Middle Ages.
Danishmendids	A Türkmen dynasty who ruled parts of Anatolia during the late fifth/eleventh and early sixth/twelfth century.
Dinar	A gold coin, the highest value currency circulating in Syria during the fifth/eleventh and sixth/twelfth centuries
Duqaq b. Tutush	Son of Tutush, ruler of Damascus (r. 488–97/1095–1104).
Fatimid Caliphate	A Shi'i Isma'ili dynasty based in Cairo, whose trading networks and territories stretched across the Mediterranean, encompassing much of North Africa, Sicily and the Syrian littoral.
Franks	(*Franj/Ifranj*) Arabic term derived from the western term Franks. Used to designate the western European Crusaders and settlers in the Near East during the sixth/twelfth and seventh/thirteenth centuries.
Great Seljuq Sultanate	Originally a coalition of Turkic tribes who migrated westwards from the Eurasian steppe into Iran and Iraq in the mid-fifth/eleventh century, thereafter becoming the major Sunni Muslim power in the Islamic Near East. Their capital was initially based in Baghdad, and later Isfahan.

Hudna	A peace treaty negotiated between two or more parties.
Ibn al-'Adim	Aleppan historian (d. 660/1262).
Ibn al-Athir	Mosul-born historian (d. 630/1233).
Ibn Khan	A leader of a group of Türkmen who were in the employ of the Mirdasid dynasty of Aleppo during the 450s/1060s and 460s/1070s (d. 462/1069–70).
Ibn al-Qalanisi	Damascene-born politician and historian (d. 555/1160).
Il-Ghazi	Najm al-Din, member of the Aqrtuqid dynasty who ruled Aleppo (r. 512–16/1117–22).
Iqta'	A Persian bureaucratic mechanism, used by the Seljuqs to allocate land tax revenues from specific territories to individuals.
Joscelyn	A common name for Frankish rulers of Edessa. During the period covered in this book, it refers to Joscelyn I of Tell Bashir and Edessa (r. 513–25/1119–31).
Kerbogha	Ruler of Mosul (r. 489–95/1096–1101) and leading commander of the Syrian armies that were defeated by the armies of the First Crusade outside Antioch in 491/1098.
Khidma	*Khidma* has multiple possible interpretations. A literal translation would be 'service'. Chroniclers use the term to describe allegiances formed between political elites.
Khutba	The *khutba* is the sermon given in mosques prior to midday prayers on Friday. The naming of a caliph and or sultan at the start of the sermon denoted an acknowledgement of their sovereignty and legitimacy over that settlement.
Mahmud b. Nasr	Mirdasid ruler of Aleppo (r. 452–53/1060–1 and 457–68/1065–76) during initial Seljuq incursions into northern Syria.

HISTORICAL FIGURES, DYNASTIES AND TERMINOLOGY | xvii

Malik Shah	Seljuq sultan (r. 465–85/1073–92) who led a military campaign into northern Syria in the winter months of 479/1086–7.
Mamluks	Sunni dynasty of Turkic slave soldiers, who ruled much of the Near East between the seventh/thirteenth and ninth/fifteenth centuries.
Mawdud	Ruler of Mosul (r. 502–7/1108–13).
Mirdasids	Arab dynasty who ruled Aleppo for much of the fifth/eleventh century. Had strong ties to the Banu Kilab and Numayr tribal groups.
Muhammad I b. Malik Shah	Seljuq sultan (r. 498–511/1105–18).
Muslim b. Quraysh	Sharaf al-Dawla Muslim b. Quraysh, Uqaylid ruler of Mosul and Aleppo (r. 472–80/1080–7).
Nawakiya	A term used by the Arabic chronicler Sibt b. al-Jawzi to designate a series of Türkmen groups who operated in Syria and Anatolia in the late fifth/eleventh and early sixth/twelfth centuries.
Nizam al-Mulk	Vizier to the Seljuq sultans Alp Arslan and Malik Shah. Probably the most influential figure in fifth/eleventh century Seljuq politics.
Notables	The urban elites in the major settlements (*al-aʿyan*) who tended to play central roles in the day-to-day administration of the towns and cities.
Nur al-Din	Son of Zengi, grandson of Aqsunqur. The second leader of the Sunni *jihad* movement against the Franks during the sixth/twelfth century. Ruler of Mosul, Aleppo, Damascus and, briefly, Egypt (d. 569/1174).
Philaretos Brachamios	An Armenian rebel, general and Byzantine governor of Edessa and Antioch, who later converted to Sunni Islam.
Qadi	A religious judge, usually drawn from the social elite of the major urban centres.
Raʾis	Leader of a local urban militia (see *ahdath* above).

Ridwan b. Tutush	Son of Tutush and ruler of Aleppo (r. 488–507/1095–1104) during the early Crusading period.
Roger of Salerno	Frankish ruler of Antioch (r. 506–13/1112–19), killed while fighting an Aleppan force at the battle of the Field of Blood in 513/1119.
Romanos Diogenes IV	Byzantine emperor (r. 460–3/1068–71) who campaigned in Syria in 461/1068–9, and was defeated by Seljuq forces at the battle of Manzikert in 463/1071.
Saladin	Legendary figure (d. 589/1193), best known for recovering Jerusalem from Frankish possession in 583/1187. The third leader of the sixth/twelfth-century Sunni *jihad* movement against the Franks. Ruler of Egypt, Damascus, Aleppo, and the key figure in the rise of the Ayyubid dynasty.
Sibt b. al-Jawzi	A preacher and historian. Born in Baghdad, he spent most of his adult life in Syria.
Sultan	A literal translation into English would be 'power'. During the period covered in this book, it is generally used to refer to the ruler, 'sultan', of the Great Seljuq Sultanate.
Sulayman b. Qutlumush	Cousin to the Sultan Malik Shah and Tutush of Damascus. Ruler of several territories in Anatolia and Antioch (r. 476–8/1076–8).
Tancred	Frankish ruler of Antioch (r. 504–6/1110–12).
Thimal b. Salih	Mirdasid ruler of Aleppo (r. 433–49/1042–57 and 453–4/1061–2).
Tughtegin	Ruler of Damascus during the early Crusading period (r. 497–522/1104–28).
Türkmen	Nomadic herds people and warriors who began to migrate from the Eurasian steppe to Syria and adjacent lands from the mid-fifth/eleventh century onwards.
Tutush b. Alp Arslan	Ruler of Damascus (r. 471–88/1078–95) and later Aleppo. Son of Seljuq Sultan Alp Arslan, and brother to Sultan Malik Shah.

Umayyads	Sunni dynasty of caliphs who established their capital in Damascus during the first/seventh and early second/eighth centuries.
Usama b. Munqidh	Member of the Banu Munqidh (d. 584/1188) dynasty, based at Shayzar in northern Syria. Usama was a poet and writer who migrated between most of the major Muslim courts of the Near East during the sixth/twelfth century.
Vizier	(*Wazir*) chief minister or adviser to secular and religious rulers in the medieval Islamic world.
Yaghi-Siyan	Ruler of Antioch (480–91/1087–98), who commanded the garrison against the First Crusaders during the siege of Antioch.
Zangi	Son of Aqsunqur and father to Nur al-Din. The first of the three leaders of the Sunni *jihad* movement against the Franks during the sixth/twelfth century. Ruler of Mosul, Aleppo and Edessa (d. 541/1146).

Acknowledgements

This book began as a PhD thesis submitted to the School of History at Queen Mary, University of London. However, my interest in Crusader-era Syria began during my Bachelor's degree, when I first came across Carole Hillenbrand's hugely influential *The Crusades: Islamic Perspectives*. As this project comes to an end, there are a number of people I want to thank.

First, I would like to gratefully acknowledge my PhD supervisor Tom Asbridge, who guided me through the process of researching and writing an academic monograph. His candid feedback and helpful advice have shaped how I think about history and vastly improved this book.

I have also benefited greatly from the invaluable feedback generously given by historians and scholars in the field. These include Andrew Buck, Rory Cox, Susan Edgington, Yvonne Friedman, Belinda Guthrie, Carole Hillenbrand, Andrew Jotischky, Nicholas Morton, Lauren Mulholland, Yossef Rapoport, Miri Rubin, Stephen Spencer, Claire Taylor, Ian Wilson and the anonymous reviewers of the book manuscript. Moreover, I was very fortunate to develop my Arabic language skills under the patient and expert tutelage of Samir Jabal. This book has also been significantly enhanced by the collaborative research environments provided by Trier College for the Medieval and Early Modern Period, University of Trier, and the Zukunftskolleg and Department of History, University of Konstanz. In addition, I am thankful to the excellent editorial and copy-editing staff at Edinburgh University Press.

Finally, I would like to thank my family. To my late mother who helped to support me during my studies. To my wife, Magdalena, who proofread various drafts of the thesis. This book simply would not exist without her unwavering support and loving encouragement. And to our wonderful children, who make it all worth it, and to whom this book is dedicated.

Introduction: Defining and Exploring the Political World of *Bilad al-sham*

Throughout 442–522/1050–1128, *bilad al-sham* (Syria) was subjected to a series of military incursions from the east and west by the nomadic Seljuq Turks and European Crusaders. These invasions complicated the power dynamics in a frontier zone already beset by multiple conflicts fought along several ethno-cultural and religious contours. Most historical studies of this period place special emphasis on the unprecedented arrival of the Frankish Crusaders from 490/1097 onwards. Rather than adopting the traditional approach of western historiography, namely, of analysing this era through the lens of the Crusades, this book seeks to place the First Crusade and the formation of the Latin east within the broader framework of Syrian history.

It does so by reinterpreting the broad strategic picture in late fifth/eleventh- and early sixth/twelfth-century Syria; contending that the urban centres of Damascus and Aleppo should be seen as politically diverse, and subject to local dynastic forces that cut across wider Byzantine, Fatimid and Seljuq polities. This new model is then used to contextualise the initial reactions of Syria's ruling elite to the foundation of the Crusader states.

The Arabic term *bilad al-sham* is most commonly translated as 'Syria'. Yet for most Arabic chroniclers writing between the fifth and seventh centuries (eleventh and thirteenth centuries), *al-sham*'s geographical delineations were far more extensive. The definitions provided by the fourth/tenth-century geographers Ibn Hawqal (d. after 367/978) and al-Muqaddasi (d. 381/991) were adopted in most of the surviving chronicles.[1] Ibn Hawqal provided the clearest textual (and cartographical, see the cover image) representation of the physical boundaries of *al-sham* during this period:

Figure I.1 Ibn Hawqal and al-Muqaddasi's definition of *bilad al-sham*

on the west is the *bahr al-rum* [Mediterranean Sea], on the east the desert from Ailah to the Euphrates, and along this river to *bilad al-rum* [country of the Romans, meaning Byzantium or Anatolia] the northern frontier (*al-thugur*) is *bilad al-rum*, and the southern frontier is Egypt.[2]

This description provides the definition of *bilad al-sham* used in this book, with particular emphasis placed on northern *al-sham* and the environs of Aleppo. In addition to *bilad al-sham*, various other geographical labels can be found in the medieval Arabic source materials. These include appellations such as *bilad al-rum* (the country of the Romans or Byzantines), generally used to refer to Anatolia, *bilad antakiya* (the country of Antioch) and, most pertinently, *bilad halab* (the country of Aleppo).[3] Although the meaning of these terms could fluctuate depending upon the context in which they were used, they typically refer to major settlements and the attendant rural areas that had traditionally fallen under the dominion of specific city-states or empires.[4]

Bilad al-sham encompassed an extensive and diverse territorial area, inhabited by a polyglot population drawn from a broad range of ethno-cultural and confessionally diverse backgrounds. This included Arab, Armenian and Syriac peoples of varying devotional beliefs, comprising Sunni Muslims, Syrian Orthodox and Melkite Christians, Jewish communities, and Shi'i groups such as the Twelver Shi'i inhabitants of Aleppo and the Nizari Isma'ili sect often labelled the 'Assassins'.

Between the second/eighth and fifth/eleventh centuries, Syria had experienced a prolonged period of neglect following the demise of the Umayyad dynasty and the relocation of the Sunni Abbasid Caliphate from Damascus to Baghdad in 132/750.[5] As a consequence, Iraq enjoyed centuries of financial prosperity while Syria's influence dwindled.[6] This was perhaps best represented by the absence of any newly constructed notable Muslim monuments in the region between 132 and 483/750 and 1090, indicative of a pronounced regional decline which had clear political ramifications.

The subsequent disintegration of Abbasid authority in the first half of the fourth/tenth century resulted in the development of the 'Muslim Commonwealth' throughout the Islamic Near East.[7] In northern Syria, the Abbasid power vacuum was initially filled by the northern Syrian branch of the Shi'i Arab Hamdanid dynasty (r. Aleppo 336–94/948–1003). The catastrophic sack of Aleppo by Byzantine forces in 351/962 is viewed as the starting point of an extended period of regional 'anarchy' and decline, which marked the nadir of Aleppan autonomy.[8] Afterwards, the Hamdanids and their successors in Aleppo, the Mirdasids (from 415/1024), were reduced to minor players in the larger struggle between Byzantium to the north and west, and the emerging Fatimid Caliphate to the south, who captured much of Palestine and southern Syria in a series of successful military campaigns in the late fourth/tenth century.[9]

The ensuing collapse of Byzantine and Fatimid influence and their ties to local rulers of Arab, Armenian and Syriac descent from the mid-fifth/eleventh century produced a fissiparous political environment in *bilad al-sham*. From 453/1062 onwards, Syria was ruled by a patchwork of small city-states and lordships with varying allegiances to the assorted ethno-religious groups and factions who held strategic interests in the region. The following fifty years saw successive invasions by the nomadic Seljuq Turks and the Frankish Crusaders insert a series of new military elites into this complex frontier zone.

In recent decades, this final, destabilising series of events and the complex power dynamics they provoked have proved to be a compelling subject for historical enquiry. This book provides a reinterpretation of the underlying political situation in *bilad al-sham* during one of the most turbulent periods in the region's history.

Historiographical Overview

Crusader studies do not exist in isolation, and there is a wealth of excellent historical research on the political situation in Syria and Palestine between 442 and 522/1050 and 1128. Aside from Crusade historiography, there are several perspectives from which historians have traditionally approached the political world of *bilad al-sham* during this time frame. Chief among them are the fields of Islamic history, Byzantine history and the study of native Christian and Jewish communities of the Near East. One of the main challenges of writing this book has been uniting these diverse historiographical branches.

The main foundation for any research in the area remains the scholarship of Claude Cahen, especially his seminal 1940 study of northern Syria at the time of the Crusades.[10] The comprehensive nature of the work – covering Arabic and Latin source material, topography, archaeology and secular society, in addition to providing an analysis of the social and political history of the region from the late fifth/eleventh century to the end of the seventh/thirteenth century – has ensured it retains an important place in modern scholarship. Cahen also stressed the need to place the Crusades within their regional context, a determination central to this book's approach.[11]

Aside from Cahen, the most recent study of northern Syria during this period is that of Taef El-Azhari.[12] El-Azhari provided a detailed historical narrative of events between 463 and 549/1070 and 1154, while also outlining why members of the Seljuq dynasty failed to retain control of Aleppo and Damascus. Suhayl Zakkar's *The Emirate of Aleppo*, published in 1971, provides the most comprehensive account of fifth/eleventh century-Aleppan political history. Similar to El-Azhari, Zakkar placed emphasis on reconstructing a thorough chronology of events.[13]

Another way historians have approached the subject is through cross-cultural diplomacy. Michael Köhler's detailed treatment of regional diplomatic contacts during the sixth/twelfth century is perhaps the most significant of these works.[14] The central thesis of Köhler's work is that the fractured political environment provoked by the arrival of Seljuq rulers in Syria from 463/1071, which was then compounded between 485 and 488/1092 and 1095 by a protracted Seljuq succession crisis, enabled the newly established Frankish polities to quickly assimilate themselves into the regional alliance system.

Carole Hillenbrand's influential research on the Islamic perspectives of the Crusades is also hugely significant, providing a comprehensive overview of the diverse Islamic experiences of the Crusades in the eastern Mediterranean.[15] Hillenbrand dated the period of crisis which struck the Islamic Near East to a series of untimely deaths among the Fatimid and Seljuq ruling elite between 485 and 487/1092 and 1094, but largely agreed with Köhler's argument for the swift integration of Frankish potentates into the political world of *bilad al-sham*.[16] The extent to which Köhler, Hillenbrand and El-Azhari were able to demonstrate the importance of developments in the fifth/eleventh century to the early Crusader period has influenced how this book is structured.

Major urban settlements in Syria have also been the focus of detailed historical enquiry. Damascus is extremely popular in this regard, with no less than three separate modern studies of this period by Thierry Bianquis, Mariam Yared-Riachi and Jean-Michel Mouton.[17] Aside from Zakkar's work, Aleppo has also received attention from Ross Burns, who has published a broad history of the city, whilst Jean Sauvaget, Nikita Elisséeff, Eugen Gaube and Heinz Wirth have also published work focusing on the northern Syrian metropolis.[18] Stefan Heidemann has examined the urban and economic development of Raqqa and Harran.[19]

In addition to individual cities, historical studies have also focused on the political and religious factions and groups operating within Syria and the surrounding areas. Research by Stefan Heidemann, John France and Nicholas Morton has looked to highlight the important role played by Arab dynasties during the fifth/eleventh and early sixth/twelfth centuries.[20] These important works have established the influence wielded by the Syrian-based Arab tribes prior to and following the First Crusade.

There is also a long historiographical tradition surrounding the Great Seljuq Sultanate.[21] Although Seljuq history is currently undergoing a minor resurgence, best represented by Andrew Peacock's *The Great Seljuk Empire*, the most recent scholarship focusing on the situation in Syria remains the work of El-Azhari mentioned above. Alexander Beihammer's work on Anatolia during the late fifth/eleventh and early sixth/twelfth centuries, which also touched upon events in northern Syria, is another significant contribution to the field.[22]

There are additional historiographical branches centred upon other major factions and groups operating in the region. The Fatimid Caliphate, Byzantine Empire, Armenian Cilicia and the Nizari Isma'ili Assassins have all been the subject of intense historical research.[23] With the exception of the work of Bianquis and Beihammer, developments in Syria remain a minority field of inquiry in Fatimid and Byzantine historiography, with most studies focusing on their respective power bases in Cairo and Constantinople.[24]

The Frankish polities founded at the end of the fifth/eleventh century, normally labelled the 'Crusader states', were the final political group active in the region during this period.[25] Perhaps the most popular of the subsidiary historiographical fields, historians of the Near Eastern Crusading movement have also relegated northern Syria to a peripheral role, with the majority of research concentrating on Jerusalem and Palestine. The work of Thomas Asbridge, particularly his study of the Principality of Antioch in the early sixth/twelfth century, provides insight into the Antiochene perspective.[26]

Since the publication of Hillenbrand's hugely influential work, the Islamic perspectives of the Crusades have become integrated into the mainstream of Crusader historiography. Although there were attempts to analyse the conflict from Muslim viewpoints before Hillenbrand, particularly by Cahen, Sivan and Köhler, it has become an increasingly popular research subject.[27] There has also been extensive research on the history of the Crusader states in Arabic by scholars from the Arabophone world.[28] The final areas of historiographical discussion are frontiers in the Middle Ages, cross-cultural contacts in Sicily and Iberia, in addition to archaeological and topographical research on Syria and Palestine.[29]

The Primary Sources

This book relies upon source materials written in a diverse range of languages. Although the principal focus will be placed on Arabic literary sources dating from the fifth/eleventh to ninth/fifteenth centuries, translations of Greek, Syriac, Persian, Latin and Armenian sources will be utilised to supplement the Arabic texts.

Arabic Sources

Annalistic chronicles or universal histories, *ta'rikh* in Arabic, are one of the most valuable sources of information for developments in *bilad al-sham* during this period. The customary format adopted in these chronicles was to provide yearly entries, usually dating from the foundation of Islam or the time of Creation.

The earliest Arabic source utilised in this book is that of Yahya b. Sa'id al-Antaki. Yahya b. Sa'id al-Antaki (d. 425/1034) was a Melikite Christian historian who was born around the year 370/980 and died shortly after his chronicle breaks off in 425/1034.[30] In the early part of his career he was attached to the Fatimid court, but was forced to flee Egypt following the persecution of Christian groups by the Caliph al-Hakim (r. 386–411/996–1021) in the early fifth/eleventh century. Thereafter, al-Antaki moved to Byzantine-held Antioch in 405/1014–15.[31] His chronicle focuses on events in Syria, Egypt and the Byzantine Empire, and utilised Greek and local Christian sources in addition to works in Arabic.[32] This assimilation of material from different linguistic traditions, combined with al-Antaki's presence in Antioch, grants the author unique insights into cross-cultural entanglements in northern Syria during the early fifth/eleventh century.

Further details about Syria during this period are provided by the writings of Al-Mu'ayyad fi'l-Din al-Shirazi (d. 470/1078), a Persian Isma'ili administrator who also served as a courtier at the Fatimid court in Cairo. Between 446 and 450/1054 and 1058, Al-Mu'ayyad fi'l-Din was dispatched to Aleppo on a diplomatic mission by the Fatimid Caliph al-Mustansir. Al-Mu'ayyad was tasked with persuading various Arab and Kurdish polities in Syria and Mesopotamia to form a coalition against the then nascent threat posed by the Seljuq Turks.[33] Al-Mu'ayyad fi'l-Din, who died in 470/1078, provides the sole

Fatimid perspective on events in Syria between 442 and 522/1050 and 1128. Another early Egyptian source is the *History of the Patriarchs of Alexandria*, a collection of Coptic and Arabic historiographical writing that reports on the lives of the Coptic patriarchs of Alexandria, and the information they received through their religious and political networks, from the first to the seventh/thirteenth centuries.[34] Throughout the sections covering this time frame, the authors make repeated references to important events in Egypt, and occasionally in Syria.

Chronologically, the next literary source are the sermons of the Damascene scholar and preacher 'Ali ibn Tahir al-Sulami (d. 500/1106), which were recorded in the *kitab al-jihad*.[35] Al-Sulami provides the earliest Syrian-based reaction to the arrival of the Franks, and although the work is a theoretical treatise on the concept of *jihad*, the date of composition and the focus of the work make it a valuable source.[36]

Abu Ya'la Ibn al-Qalanisi's (d. 555/1160) *Dhayl ta'rikh Dimashq* is one of the most important historical sources for this project. As Niall Christie has outlined, modern historians know relatively little about Ibn al-Qalanisi, aside from his reputation as a man of literature and political skill, having held the position of *ra'is* of Damascus on two occasions.[37] This political experience lends authority to his writing, whilst his occupation of such a high-ranking position meant that he would have had access to a wide variety of official source material relating to the history of the city.[38] Ibn al-Qalanisi provided 'the oldest extant Arabic account of the First and Second Crusades'.[39] This, combined with its relatively early translation into English and French, has ensured that Ibn al-Qalanisi's chronicle is a vital source for historians of Syria during the first half of the sixth/twelfth century.[40] However, there are several problematic aspects relating to the chronicle, namely, that Ibn al-Qalanisi does not quote his sources directly, and that he frequently displays a partiality for the Burid dynasty (ruled Damascus 497–549/1104–1154) in his writing.

Muhammad b. al-'Azimi (d. after 556/1161) wrote the earliest extant Aleppan chronicle for this time frame.[41] Despite a partial French translation by Frédéric Monot of the years 518–38/1124–44, and a more recent English translation of the early Crusading period by Alex Mallett, the source is widely under-utilised in modern historiography.[42] Unfortunately, even less is known about al-'Azimi than Ibn al-Qalanisi. It is probable that he lived until after

556/1161, because extracts of his non-extant *History of Aleppo* have been found for this date in later sources, whilst al-'Azimi provided a birth date of 483/1090–1 for himself in his universal chronicle.⁴³ He taught in an Aleppan *madrasa* and was the son of a *ra'is*, having been born into the influential al-Tanukhi family of Aleppo.⁴⁴ The annual entries in his surviving work tend to be brief, whilst the lack of citation of the author's sources is a further concern, necessitating careful handling. Despite the dearth of information about the author and concerns about the text, it is a vital source for historians of this period.

Ali Ibn al-Hasan Ibn 'Asakir (d. 571/1176) belonged to the prominent Banu 'Asakir family of Damascus, who produced a succession of Shafi'i scholars between 470 ad 660/1077 and 1261.⁴⁵ Ibn 'Asakir spent some years travelling in the east and made a pilgrimage to Mecca, but spent the majority of his career in Damascus, where he entered the orbit of prominent figures such as Nur al-Din, and was present for Saladin's entry into his home town in 570/1174.⁴⁶ Nur al-Din encouraged Ibn 'Asakir to complete his great biographical dictionary, which records all the people of note who inhabited or visited Damascus, in addition to prominent individuals from Aleppo, Ba'albek and Ramla.

Ahmad b. Yusuf Ibn al-Azraq al-Fariqi (d. after 572/1176–7) was employed in the service of Timurtash b. Il-ghazi, the second Artuqid ruler of Mayyafariqin, and the Georgian King Dimitri.⁴⁷ During his life he spent time in Amid, Mosul, Baghdad and Damascus. Whilst in the employ of these rulers, he would in all probability have had access to official records and chancery documents.⁴⁸ His *Ta'rikh al-Mayyafariqin wa-Amid* was written in two phases, the first in 560/1164–5 and the second before his death in 572/1176–7.⁴⁹

Usama b. Murshid b. 'Ali (d. 584/1188), better known as Usama b. Munqidh, was a member of the Banu Munqidh family, who were based in the fortress of Shayzar in northern Syria during the late fifth/eleventh and early sixth/twelfth centuries. The strategic importance of Shayzar, with the castle controlling access to one of the few bridges that crossed the River Orontes, enabled the Banu Munqidh to play a significant role in northern Syrian politics, until an earthquake in 552/1157 destroyed the castle and killed the majority of the family.⁵⁰ Usama b. Munqidh wrote two literary anthologies that are of particular importance to this book. The first was the *Kitab al-I'tibar*, or 'book of contemplation', and the second the *Lubab al-Adab*, or 'gateway to literature', in which he sporadically remarked upon important political events, such as the arrival of the First Crusaders.[51] Like Ibn 'Asakir, Usama b. Munqidh moved in exalted circles. During his career he entered into the service of Imad al-Din Zangi, his son Nur al-Din, the Burids of Damascus and the Fatimids in Egypt.[52] Although his work is valued for its insights into social interactions between Muslim and Frankish elites in the sixth/twelfth century, its importance to this book lies in the insight Usama provides into the Banu Munqidh and the culture of Near Eastern court life in general.

The Baghdadi scholar, teacher, preacher and historian Ibn al-Jawzi's (d. 597/1200) universal history, *al-Muntazam fi ta'rikh al-muluk wa'l-umam*, is another important source.[53] Ibn al-Jawzi was a highly prominent Hanbali member of the twelfth-century *'ulama'* in Baghdad, who received the patronage of several caliphs and viziers. At the height of his power, he directed five *madrasa*s and regularly provided sermons for several caliphs.[54] His universal history provided more detailed coverage of the deaths of scholars and preachers than political events, making it feel like a biographical dictionary.[55] Although his chronicle does not offer as broad an overview as that of his grandson Sibt b. al-Jawzi, it still occasionally grants insight into events in northern Syria, connecting them to events in Baghdad in a way that differentiates him from his contemporaries based in Syria and Mesopotamia.

Ibn al-Athir's (d. 630/1233) universal chronicle, *al-Kamil fi'l ta'rikh*, is perhaps the best known and most widely utilised source for events in Middle East during the fifth/eleventh and sixth/twelfth centuries.[56] This has been facilitated by two factors: the early and reliable translations of the text, and the widely acknowledged historical bona fides of the author. There was an early translation of sections of the chronicle covering the sixth/twelfth century into French in the *Recueil des historiens des croisades* and a more recent translation into English by Donald Richards, which covers the entire time frame of this book.[57] Ibn al-Athir was born into a leading Mosuli family of scholars who were in service to the Zangid rulers of the town, but he also enjoyed good relations with the Ayyubids, participating in several diplomatic missions on their behalf.[58]

Al-Kamil fi'l ta'rikh has a wide geographical focus, providing yearly updates from the time of Creation to 628/1230–1 for the whole of the *dar al-islam*, encompassing Spain, Sicily, North Africa, Egypt, Palestine, Syria and

Mesopotamia, providing a true Muslim global history. Carole Hillenbrand glowingly described Ibn al-Athir as possessing 'the instincts of a true historian' who was 'capable of interpreting events as well as recording them',[59] whilst his universal history has been described as 'one of the most impressive achievements of pre-modern historiography in any culture'[60] and 'the high point of Muslim annalistic historiography'.[61] The only criticism of Ibn al-Athir's methodology is that he often failed to cite the sources of his information.

Despite this high praise, his coverage of the events in *bilad al-sham* during the fifth/eleventh and early sixth/twelfth centuries is far from comprehensive. Additionally, Ibn al-Athir's 'analysis' of the success of the First Crusade is heavily influenced by the reduced status of the Franks at the time he composed his work in the early seventh/thirteenth century. Ibn al-Athir's exemplary history of the Zangids, *al-Ta'rikh al-bahir fi'l-dawlat al-atabakiyya*, is also of interest to this project.[62]

Sibt b. al-Jawzi's (d. 654/1256) *Mi'rat al-zaman fi ta'rikh al-a'yan* is another key source for this period, mainly due the detailed reports it provides about developments in fifth/eleventh-century *bilad al-sham*.[63] Sibt b. al-Jawzi's chronicle is modelled on the work of his maternal grandfather Ibn al-Jawzi, following the same formula of delivering long accounts about the careers of deceased intellectuals, in addition to an annual overview of political events. In a style comparable with his grandfather, Sibt b. al-Jawzi offered insight into how events in Syria were linked to developments in Baghdad and vice versa. Sibt b. al-Jawzi was born in Baghdad around 582/1186, and remained there until he moved to Damascus following his grandfather's death in 597/1201.[64] Renowned during his lifetime for his rhetorical skills, Sibt b. al-Jawzi held the title *wa'iz al-sham* (the [best] preacher in *al-sham*), and held teaching positions at various *madrasas*.[65] Sibt b. al-Jawzi also participated in diplomatic missions for various Ayyubid rulers of Damascus to Aleppo, went on several pilgrimages to Mecca, and visited scholars in Mosul and Jerusalem.[66]

His *Mi'rat al-zaman fi ta'rikh al-a'yan* has a complicated manuscript history, which Cahen attributed to the author's failure to produce a definitive copy of his notes prior to his death. One set of manuscripts contained large gaps between accounts, whilst a second, more comprehensive, group of manuscripts created by Qutb al-Din al-Yunini at the beginning of the eighth/fourteenth century includes additions made by al-Yunini himself.[67] This has meant that until Kamil S. Al-Jabouri produced the new edition cited above, historians of this period had to rely either on one of the problematic manuscript groups, or the partial editions from Ali Sevim, who selected events about the Seljuqs and covering the years 448–80/1056–88, or that of James R. Jewett, who relied on a faulty manuscript and covered the years 495–654/1101–1256.[68] The existence of a new comprehensive edition, affords us a greater insight into a truly vital source for this period of Syrian history.

Yet another vital basis of information for this project are Ibn al-ʿAdim's (d. 660/1262) biographical dictionary and chronicle.[69] Born in 588/1192 into the powerful Banu Abi Jarada family of Aleppo, Ibn al-ʿAdim never occupied the prominent political positions of *qadi* or vizier. He was appointed in 616/1220 to various *madrasa*s in Aleppo, and later founded a *madrasa* in Aleppo in 639/1241.[70] However, his real political influence lay in the diplomatic missions that he undertook between 634 and 657/1236 and 1259 on behalf of various Ayyubid rulers of Aleppo and Damascus to ʿAyntab, Anatolia, Jazira, Egypt and Baghdad, whilst he enjoyed a comfortable lifestyle due to his family's possession of various landed estates and properties in the purlieus of Aleppo.[71]

Ibn al-ʿAdim's biographical dictionary, *Bughyat al-talab fi ta'rikh halab*, originally consisted of forty volumes, of which just ten survive. The first volume includes a geographical description of Aleppo and the surrounding area. The subsequent volumes are dedicated to individuals, providing a list of their achievements, usually academic for the *'ulama'* and military for political figures, in addition to their family background and anecdotes when possible. Ibn al-ʿAdim regularly named his sources in the *Bughyat*. Through an analysis of citations in his work, Anne-Marie Eddé has concluded that he consulted 'more than 500 books, not counting those with unknown titles' in addition to a 'large number of contemporary oral testimonies'.[72]

The rigour and care taken by Ibn al-ʿAdim whilst compiling the *Bughyat al-talab fi ta'rikh halab* underlines its value to historians in the field. His chronicle of Aleppo, *Zubdat al-halab min ta'rikh halab*, is an equally vital source for this project, although it lacks the clear citation of sources present in the *Bughyat*. Eddé has argued that Ibn al-ʿAdim used the sources from his biographical dictionary to write his chronicle and suggested it is possible to correlate the sources used in *Zubdat* with those in *Bughyat* through careful reading of both sources.[73]

Indeed, Zakkar has shown it is possible to discern at least some of the non-extant fifth/eleventh- and sixth/twelfth-century sources that Ibn al-'Adim used for the *Bughyat* and the *Zubdat*.[74] The non-extant fifth/eleventh-century Arabic sources include Abu Ghalib Hammam al-Muhadhdhad, who lived during the reigns of the Mirdasid rulers Thimal b. Salih, 'Atiyya b. Salih and Mahmud b. Nasr;[75] Abu'l Khayr al-Mubarak, a Christian physician who departed Aleppo for Antioch during the reign of Ridwan b. Tutush; and Mansur b. Tamim al-Zankal, a poet from Sarmin who passed judgement on the final Mirdasid ruler of Aleppo, Sabiq b. Mahmud.[76] For the sixth/twelfth century, Ibn al-'Adim used the work of Hamdan b. 'Abd al-Rahim al-Atharibi (d. 541/1147),[77] a physician, poet, administrator and diplomat who held land on the frontier between Antioch and Aleppo, although Paul Cobb has raised doubts about the notion that Hamdan al-Atharibi was a Frankish 'vassal'.[78] Historians in this field have long lamented the loss of Hamdan's chronicle.[79]

Ibn al-'Adim's *Zubdat* is ordered chronologically, and focuses almost exclusively on Aleppo and the outlying areas. This means that events in other important power-centres such as Baghdad, Damascus and Jerusalem are often overlooked, contributing to the *Zubdat* being labelled 'concise'.[80] Yet Ibn al-'Adim often provides far greater detail and insight than other historians on events in and around Aleppo, particularly during the fifth/eleventh century.

Ibn Muyassar (d. 677/1278), was an Egyptian historian of Tunisian origin whose ancestor had served as an amir for the Fatimids.[81] His chronicle covered the years 439–522/1047–1128, and provides a great deal of original information on the Fatimids, due to Ibn Muyassar's access to official documents relating to them. Aside from Ibn Muyassar, arguably the most important Egyptian source for this period is that of Taqi al-Din al-Maqrizi (d. 845/1442). His *Itti'az al-hunafa' bi-akhbar al-a'imma al-fatimiyyin al-khulafa'* is the only separate history of the Fatimids written by a Sunni writer, and includes material from non-extant sources.[82] During his lifetime al-Maqrizi held various positions in the academic, theological and legal fields.[83] The major problem with this work is the date of composition, which was completed nearly 250 years after the starting point of this book.

Other important later sources include the universal histories of Ibn Kathir (d.774/1373)[84] and Ibn Taghribirdi (d. 874/1470).[85] Ibn Kathir held various administrative and academic positions in several mosques and *madrasa*s under the Bahri Mamluk dynasty in Damascus.[86] Ibn Taghribirdi was a high-ranking member of the ninth/fifteenth-century Mamluk court, who rose to the rank of commander in chief of the Egyptian armies and viceroy of Damascus.[87]

Konrad Hirschler and Michael Brett have outlined three separate regional Arabic historiographical traditions in Syria, Mesopotamia and Egypt.[88] While it is clear that many of the later chroniclers utilised the work of those who came before them, access to different sources of localised information meant that certain authors provided more detailed accounts of events than earlier writers. For example, it would be difficult to write a comprehensive history of the Fatimid activities in Syria in the fifth/eleventh century without consulting the seventh/thirteenth-century work of Ibn Muyassar.

One of the main methodological issues with this book is that, with the exception of the *History of the Patriarchs of Alexandria*, there are no extant Arabic chronicles written between 432 and 534/1040 and 1140. The value of Arabic primary source material to research on the Crusades and the wider Islamic Near East has long been a subject of contention. In his formative study on the Crusades, Steven Runciman disputed the value of Arabic texts for the First Crusade and the early Crusading period.[89] Although the work of Carole Hillenbrand has ensured that Arabic source material remain in the mainstream of the field, criticisms of the source base persist.

Omar Safi and Julie Meisami have questioned the objectivity of Arabic and Persian source material in this period. Meisami claimed that 'the medieval historian's primary interest lay less in recording the "facts" of history than in the construction of meaningful narratives'.[90] Safi has demonstrated how the Seljuqs shaped historical writing to meet certain requirements to legitimise their rule, while Hirschler has established how an author's individual 'agency' could shape the narrative of their accounts.[91]

Ironically, the potential impact of these practices may be slightly reduced by the space of years between when the events took place and the writing of the source material. However, the earlier non-extant sources that the authors drew upon could potentially have been influenced by similar issues. Whilst most of this criticism has been applied to Persian historians and the work produced in the Seljuq power-centres of Baghdad and Isfahan in the east, it signifies the need to use the source material with caution. Regional pride or even bias and the need to praise their ancestors, or the ancestors of their patrons, is a common theme within the source base. However, this is a problem that all historians who write on this subject face, and it can be at least partially mitigated by the use of contemporaneous Latin, Greek, Persian, Syriac and Armenian source material.

Other Sources

The most important Persian and Latin material in relation to this project include Nasir-i Khusraw (d. 465–71/1072–8), a famous poet and Isma'ili philosopher who travelled through Aleppo, Jerusalem and coastal Palestine on route to perform pilgrimage at Mecca in the fifth/eleventh century;[92] the anonymous account of the First Crusade known as the *Gesta Francorum*;[93] the history of the early Crusading period complied in Germany by talking to eye-witness participants of the conflict in *bilad al-sham* attributed to Albert of Aachen (d. after 512/1119);[94] the chronicle of the First Crusade and early Crusading period produced by the chaplain of Baldwin I of Jerusalem, Fulcher of Chartres (d. 521/1127);[95] the complimentary account of the career of Tancred of Antioch by the prominent ecclesiastical figure Ralph of Caen (d. around 513/1120);[96] the detailed description of the Seljuq campaign of 509/1115 and the battle of the Field of Blood and its aftermath provided by Walter the Chancellor (d. unknown), who served as chancellor of Antioch between 507 and 516/1114 and 1122;[97] and the highly influential history of the Latin east provided by William of Tyre (d. 582/1186).[98]

In terms of Armenian and Syriac material, Matthew of Edessa (d. 538/1144)[99] and Michael the Syrian (d. 595/1199) are of most interest to this book.[100] The Armenian Matthew of Edessa's chronicle had a wide focus, covering events in Syria, Mesopotamia and the Caucasus region. His coverage of northern Syria, and particularly Antioch, in the fifth/eleventh century is especially detailed. However, we must be aware of Tara Andrews' argument that Matthew tailored his work, particularly sections concerning the arrival of the Seljuqs and Franks, to fit with Armenian historiographical traditions and prophecies, and it should therefore not be viewed as an 'objective' insight into the early Crusading period or the decades preceding it.[101]

Michael the Syrian was a high-ranking member of the Syriac Church who held several prominent positions in the Near East. His chronicle appears to have been written over a fifty-year period. It remains a vital source, not only for his own observations, but for the material taken from other non-extant texts.[102] Other relevant Syriac narrative sources include the Anonymous Syriac Chronicle of 1234 and the history of Bar Hebraeus (d. 685/1286).[103]

In terms of Greek material, the accounts of Michael Attaleiates (d. 472/1080)[104] and Anna Komnena (d. 548/1153)[105] are of most importance for this period. Michael Attaleiates provided detailed information about Emperor Romanos Diogenes IV's campaign into northern Syria in 461/1068–9, while Anna Komnena is an invaluable source for developments in Anatolia prior to, during and after the First Crusade.

The Scope of this Book

The time frame of this monograph enables detailed analysis of the political situation in Syria in the decades leading up to the First Crusade. These findings are then used to contextualise the formative years of the Crusader era. Beginning in 442/1050, rather than adopting the battle of Manzikert in 463/1071 as a starting point, enables a reassessment of the impact of Seljuq potentates upon the region. As will become clear in the first three chapters, the period 442–63/1050–71 is vital for charting the decline of Byzantine and Fatimid influence in *bilad al-sham*. Correspondingly, 522/1128 provides a clear end-date, marked by the installation of 'Imad al-Din Zangi (d. 541/1146) in Aleppo and the death of Tughtegin (d. 522/1128) of Damascus.

The book is divided into two parts. The first examines how the erosion of centralised Byzantine and Fatimid control over *bilad al-sham* from 453/1062 onwards resulted in the empowerment of local potentates and notables in Aleppo and Damascus. This dynamic was then perpetuated by the fragmentary nature of Seljuq authority in Syria. Granular focus will be placed on contacts between individual polities and a fluctuating farrago of military elites, with special attention paid to struggles over strategically important sites. Chapters 1–3 also explore the ways in which supposedly rigid ethno-cultural and religious hierarchies within the Byzantine, Fatimid and Seljuq spheres of influence were obscured by political realities on the ground in *bilad al-sham*.

The second part of this book explores the diverse responses of Syrian-based Muslim polities to the onset of the Crusades, questioning the extent to which the Frankish 'Crusader states' were 'integrated' into the Syrian political system during the early sixth/twelfth century. Chapter 4 asserts that there was a clearly observable, but unsuccessful, military reaction from the Islamic rulers of Syria to the arrival of the Frankish Crusaders. It also scrutinises the appositeness of applying the 'Counter-Crusade' and *'la maqam'* paradigms prior to 522/1128. Chapter 5 outlines the influential role played by Aleppan notables in the selection of prospective rulers, and defines the territorial frontiers of *bilad halab* (the country of Aleppo).

Notes

1. The best overviews of the geographical works of Ibn Hawqal and al-Muqaddasi are Gerald R. Tibbetts, 'The Balkhi School of Geographers', in *The History of Islamic Cartography, vol. Two, Book One*, ed. J. B. Harley and David Woodward (Chicago: University of Chicago Press, 1992), pp. 108–36; Zayde Antrim, *Mapping the Middle East* (Chicago: University of Chicago Press, 2018), pp. 17–61. For the nuances surrounding the Arabic nomenclature for 'frontiers' in these texts, see Michael Bonner, 'The Naming of the Frontier: 'Awasim, Thughur, and the Arab Geographers', *Bulletin of the School of Oriental and African Studies* 57 (1994): 17–24; Ralph W. Brauer, 'Boundaries and Frontiers in Medieval Muslim Geography', *Transactions of the American Philosophical Society* 85 (1995): 1–73.

2. Abu'l-Qasim Ibn Hawqal, *Kitab Surat al-ard*, ed. Johannes H. Kramers as *Opus Geographicum* (Frankfurt am Main: Institute for the History of Arabic-Islamic Science, 1992), pp. 165–6; Shams al-Din Abu 'Abd Allah Muhammad b. Ahmad b. Abi Bakr al-Bana' al-Shami al-Muqaddasi, *Ahsan al-taqasim fi ma'rifat al-aqalim*, ed. Michael J. de Goeje (Leiden: Brill, 2014), p. 186; André Miquel, 'Ibn Hawkal', *Encyclopaedia of Islam*, 2nd edn (2012) and André Miquel, 'al-Mukaddasi', *Encyclopaedia of Islam*, 2nd edn, ed. Peri Bearman et al. (2012), available at Brill online, last accessed 10 July 2017; Guy Le Strange, *Palestine Under the Moslems: a Description of Syria and the Holy Land from A.D. 650–1500* (London: Alexander P. Watt, 1890), pp. 24–43.

3. See, for e.g., Abu Ya'la Ibn al-Qalanisi, *Dhayl ta'rikh Dimashq*, ed. Suhayl Zakkar (Damascus: Dar Hassan, 1983), pp. 187, 194, 216, 221; Yusuf Qizoglu Sibt b. al-Jawzi, *Mi'rat al-zaman fi ta'rikh al-a'yan*, ed. Kamil S. Al-Jabouri et al., 23 vols (Beirut: Dar al-Kutub al-'Ilmiyah, 2013), XII, 232, 480, XIII, 248, 259; Kamal al-Din Ibn al-'Adim, *Zubdat al-halab min ta'rikh halab*, ed. Sami Dahan, 3 vols (Damascus: Institut français de Damas, 1951–68), I (1951), 265, II (1954), 90, 131. For the term *bilad al-rum*, see Koray Durak, 'Who are the

Romans? The Definition of *Bilad al-Rum* (Land of the Romans) in Medieval Islamic Geographies', *Journal of Intercultural Studies* 31 (2010): 285–98.

4. For more background on how the motives of the authors could influence the delineations of the territories they described in their texts, see Zayde Antrim, *Routes and Realms* (Oxford: Oxford University Press, 2012), pp. 1–8, 110–25, 144; Zayde Antrim, 'Ibn 'Asakir's Representations of Syria and Damascus in the introduction to the Ta'rikh Madinat Dimashq', *International Journal of Middle Eastern Studies* 38 (2006): 109–29; Zayde Antrim, 'Becoming Syrian: Aleppo in Ibn al-'Adim's *Bughyat al-talab fi ta'rikh Halab*', in *Grounded Identities: Territory and Belonging in the Medieval and Early Modern Mediterranean and Mesopotamia*, ed. Steve Tamari (Leiden: Brill, 2019), pp. 46–71.

5. For Syria under the Umayyad and 'Abbasid caliphates, see Paul Cobb, *White Banners: Contention in 'Abbasid Syria, 750–880* (New York: State University of New York Press, 2001); Antoine Borrut, *Entre mémoire et pouvoir. L'espace syrien sous les derniers Omeyyades et les premiers Abbassides v. 72-193/692-809* (Leiden: Brill, 2011).

6. This period of Syrian decline has been outlined most comprehensively by Hugh Kennedy, although Gideon Anvi has highlighted the important role that local factors played in shaping the chronology of this process, particularly in Palestine. See Hugh Kennedy, 'From Polis to Madina: Urban Change in Late Antique and Early Islamic Syria', *Past and Present* 106 (1985): 3–27; Gideon Anvi, '"From Polis to Madina" Revisited: Urban Change in Byzantine and Early Islamic Palestine', *Journal of the Royal Asiatic Society* 21 (2011): 301–29; Hagit Nol, *Settlement and Urbanization in Early Islamic Palestine, 7th–11th Centuries* (London: Routledge, 2022), pp. 183–289.

7. The term 'Muslim commonwealth' was coined by Garth Fowden, but has also been discussed in detail by Hugh Kennedy, see Garth Fowden, *Empire to Commonwealth: Consequences of Monotheism in Late Antiquity* (Princeton: Princeton University Press, 1994); Hugh Kennedy, *The Prophet and the Age of the Caliphates: the Islamic Near East from the Sixth to the Eleventh Century* (London: Routledge, 2015), pp. 172–81.

8. Jean Sauvaget, 'Halab', *Encyclopaedia of Islam*, 2nd edn, ed. Peri Bearman et al. (2012), available at Brill online, last accessed 31 July 2019; Jean Sauvaget, *Alep Essai sur le développement d'une grande ville Syrienne, des origins au milieu du XIXe siècle*, 2 vols (Paris: Geuthner, 1941), I, 83–108; Nikita Elisséeff, *Nur ad-Din. Un grande prince musulman de Syrie au temps des croisades*, 3 vols

(Damascus: Institut français de Damas, 1967), I, pp. 173–4. For a contrasting view on this period of Aleppan history, see Thierry Bianquis, 'Pouvoirs arabes à Alep aux Xe et XIe siècles', *Revue des mondes musulmans et de la Méditerranée* 62 (1991): 49–59, 53–5.

9. Kennedy, *The Prophet and the Age of the Caliphates*, p. 115.
10. Claude Cahen, *La Syrie du nord à l'époque des croisades et la Principauté Franque d'Antioche* (Paris: Librairie Orientaliste Paul Geuthner, 1940).
11. Claude Cahen, *Orient et Occident au temps des croisades* (Paris: Aubier Montaigne, 1983), pp. 6–7.
12. Taef K. El-Azhari, *The Saljuqs of Syria during the Crusades 463–549 A.H./ 1070–1154 A.D.* (Berlin: Klaus Schwarz, 1997).
13. Suhayl Zakkar, *The Emirate of Aleppo 1004–1094* (Beirut: Dar al-Amanah, 1971).
14. Michael A. Köhler, *Allianzen und Verträge zwischen fränkischen und islamischen Herrschern im Vorderen Orient* (Berlin: De Gruyter, 1991, repr. 2014); Michael A. Köhler, *Alliances and Treaties between Frankish and Muslim Rulers in the Middle East* (Leiden: Brill, 2013).
15. Carole Hillenbrand, *The Crusades: Islamic Perspectives* (Edinburgh: Edinburgh University Press, 1999).
16. Carole Hillenbrand, 'Jihad Propaganda in Syria from the Time of the First Crusade until the Death of Zengi: the Evidence of Monumental Inscriptions', in *The Frankish Wars and their Influence on Palestine: Selected Papers Presented at Birzeit University's International Academic Conference Held in Jerusalem*, ed. Khalil 'Athaminah and Roger Heacock (Birzeit: Birzeit University Publications, 1994) pp. 60–9; Carole Hillenbrand, '1092: A Murderous Year', in *Proceedings of the 14th Congress of Union européene des arabisants et islamisants*, ed. Alexander Fodor (Budapest: Eotvos Loránd University Chair for Arabic Studies: Csoma de Koros Society, 1995), pp. 281–96; Carole Hillenbrand, 'The First Crusade: the Muslim Perspective', in *The First Crusade: Origins and Impact*, ed. Jonathan Phillips (Manchester: Manchester University Press, 1997), pp. 130–41.
17. Theirry Bianquis, *Damas et la Syrie sous la domination Fatimide*, 2 vols (Damascus: Institut français de Damas 1986–9); Mariam Yared-Riachi, *La politique extérieure de la principauté de Damas 468–549/1076–1154* (Damascus: Institut français d'études arabes de Damas 1997); Jean-Michel Mouton, *Damas et sa principauté sous les Saljoukides et les Bourides 468–549/1076–1154* (Cairo: Institut français d'archéologie orientale, 1997).

18. Sauvaget, *Alep*; Elisséeff, *Nur ad-Din*; Heinz Gaube and Eugen Wirth, *Aleppo: historische und geographische Beiträge zur baulichen Gestaltung, zur socialen Organisation und zur wirtschaflichen Dynamic einer vorderasiatischen Fernhandelsmetropole* (Wiesbaden: Reichert, 1984); Ross Burns, *Aleppo: A History* (London: Routledge, 2017), pp. 92–129.
19. Stefan Heidemann, *Die Renaissance der Städte in Nordsyrien und Nordmesopotamien: städtische Entwicklung und wirtschaftliche Bedingungen in ar-Raqqa und Harran von der Zeit der beduinischen Vorherrschaft bis zu den Seldschuken* (Leiden: Brill, 2002).
20. Stefan Heidemann, 'Arab Nomads and the Saljuq Military', in *Shifts and Drifts in Nomad–Sedentary Relations*, ed. Stefan Leder and Bernhard Streck (Wiesbaden: Reichert, 2005), pp. 289–305; Nicholas Morton and John France, 'Arab Muslim Reactions to Turkish Authority in Northern Syria, 1085–1128', in *Warfare, Crusade and Conquest in the Middle Ages*, ed. John France (Farnham: Ashgate, 2014), XV, pp. 1–38. See also Nicholas Morton, *Encountering Islam on the First Crusade* (Cambridge: Cambridge University Press, 2016).
21. Andrew C. S. Peacock, *The Great Seljuk Empire* (Edinburgh: Edinburgh University Press, 2015); Andrew C. S. Peacock, *Early Saljuq History* (London: Routledge, 2010); Ann K. S. Lambton, 'The Internal Structure of the Saljuq Empire', in *The Cambridge History of Iran, vol. V: The Saljuq and Mongol Periods*, ed. J. A. Boyle (Cambridge: Cambridge University Press, 1968), pp. 203–82.
22. Alexander D. Beihammer, *Byzantium and the Emergence of Muslim-Turkish Anatolia ca. 1040–1130* (Abingdon: Routledge, 2017).
23. Carole Hillenbrand, *Turkish Myth and Symbol: the Battle of Manzikert* (Edinburgh: Edinburgh University Press, 2007); Michael Angold, *The Byzantine Empire 1025–1204* (London: Longman, 1997); Paul E. Walker, *Exploring an Islamic Empire: Fatimid History and its Sources* (London: I. B. Tauris, 2001); Paul E. Walker, *Fatimid History and Ismaili Doctrine* (Aldershot: Ashgate, 2008); Yaacov Lev, *State and Society in Fatimid Egypt* (Leiden: Brill, 1990); Seta B. Dadoyan, *The Fatimid Armenians: Cultural and Political Interaction in the Near East* (Leiden: Brill, 1997); Michael Brett, *The Fatimid Empire* (Edinburgh: Edinburgh University Press, 2017), pp. 181–232; Shainool Jiwa, *The Fatimids 1: The Rise of a Muslim Empire* (London: Bloomsbury, 2017); David Bramoullé, 'Les villes maritimes fatimides en Méditerranée orientale (969–1171)', *Histoire urbaine* 19 (2007): 93–116; Heinz Halm, *Die Kalifen von Kairo: Die Fatimiden in Ägypten 973–1074* (Munich: C. H. Beck, 2003); Heinz

Halm, *Kalifen und Assassinen. Ägypten und der Vordere Orient zur Zeit der ersten Kreuzzüge 1074–1171* (Munich: C. H. Beck, 2014); Farhad Daftary, *The Ismaʿilis: Their History and Doctrines* (Cambridge: Cambridge University Press, 2007); Farhad Daftary, *The Assassin Legends: Myths of the Ismaʿilis* (London: I. B. Tauris, 1994); Azat Bozoyan, 'Armenian Political Revival in Cilicia', in *Armenian Cilicia*, ed. Robert Hovannisian and Simon Payaslian (California: Mazda, 2008), pp. 67–78; Gérard Dédéyan, 'The Founding and Coalescence of the Rubenian Principality, 1073–1129', in *Armenian Cilicia*, ed. Robert Hovannisian and Simon Payaslian (California: Mazda, 2008), pp. 79–92; Jacob Ghazarian, *The Armenian Kingdom in Cilicia During the Crusades* (London: Curzons, 2000); Christopher MacEvitt, *The Crusades and the Christian World of the East: Rough Tolerance* (Philadelphia: University of Pennsylvania Press, 2008); Alan Murray, 'The Franks and Indigenous Communities in Palestine and Syria (1099–1187): a Hierarchical Model of Social Interaction in the Principalities of Outremer', in *East Meets West in the Middle Ages and Early Modern Times: Transcultural Experiences in the Premodern World*, ed. Albrecht Classen (Berlin: De Gruyter, 2013), pp. 291–309.

24. See, e.g., Yannis Stouraitis, 'Trapped in the Imperial Narrative? Some Reflections on Warfare and the Provincial Masses in Byzantium (600–1204)', *Byzantine and Modern Greek Studies* 44 (2020): 1–20.

25. William B. Stevenson, *The Crusaders in the East: a Brief History of the Wars of Islam with the Latins in Syria during the Twelfth and Thirteenth Centuries* (Cambridge: Cambridge University Press, 1907); Steven Runciman, *A History of the Crusades*, 3 vols (Harmondsworth: Penguin, 1965); R. C. Smail, *Crusading Warfare 1097–1193* (Cambridge: Cambridge University Press, 1956); Malcolm Barber, *The Crusader States* (New Haven, CT: Yale University Press, 2012); Jonathan Riley-Smith, *The Crusades: a Short History* (London: Athlone, 2001); Christopher Tyerman, *God's War: a New History of the Crusades* (London: Allen Lane, 2006); Jonathan Phillips, *The Crusades: 1095–1204* (Abingdon: Routledge, 2014); Thomas S. Asbridge, *The Crusades: the War for the Holy Land* (London: Simon & Schuster, 2010); Andrew Jotischky, *Crusading and the Crusader States* (London: Routledge, 2017); Steven Tibble, *The Crusader Armies 1099–1187* (New Haven, CT: Yale University Press, 2018); Nicholas Morton, *The Crusader States and their Neighbours: a Military History, 1099–1187* (Oxford: Oxford University Press, 2020).

26. Thomas S. Asbridge, *The Creation of the Principality of Antioch 1098–1130* (Woodbridge: Boydell, 2000); Thomas S. Asbridge, 'How the Crusades Could

Have Been Won: King Baldwin II of Jerusalem's Campaigns against Aleppo 1124–5 and Damascus 1129', *Journal of Medieval Military History* 11 (2013): 73–93; Thomas S. Asbridge, 'The Significance and Causes of the Battle of the Field of Blood', *Journal of Medieval History* 24 (1997): 301–16; Thomas S. Asbridge, 'The 'Crusader Community at Antioch: The Impact of Interaction with Byzantium and Islam', *Transactions of the Royal Historical Society* 10 (1999): 305–25; Andrew D. Buck, *The Principality of Antioch and its Frontiers in the Twelfth Century* (Woodbridge: Boydell, 2017).

27. Emmanuel Sivan, *L'Islam et la Croisade. Idéologie et Propagande dans les Réactions Musulmanes aux Croisades* (Paris: Librairie d'Amérique et d'Orient, 1968); Suleiman A. Mourad and James E. Lindsay, *The Intensification and Reorientation of Sunni Jihad Ideology in the Crusader Period* (Leiden: Brill, 2013); Paul M. Cobb, *The Race for Paradise: An Islamic History of the Crusades* (Oxford: Oxford University Press, 2014); Niall Christie, *Muslims and Crusaders: Christianity's Wars in the Middle East 1095–1382 from the Islamic Sources*, 2nd edn (Abingdon: Routledge, 2020); Alex Mallett, *Popular Muslim Reactions to the Frankish Presence in the Levant: 1097–1291* (Farnham: Ashgate, 2014); Osman Latiff, *The Cutting Edge of the Poet's Sword: Muslim Poetic Responses to the Crusades* (Leiden: Brill, 2017); Kenneth A. Goudie, *Reinventing Jihad: Jihad Ideology from the Conquest of Jerusalem to the End of the Ayyubids* (Leiden: Brill, 2019).

28. For an overview of modern Arabic historiography on the Crusades, see Ahmed M. Sheir, 'Between Peace and War: the Peaceful Memory of the Crusades between the Middle Ages and the Modern Arabic-Egyptian Writings', in *Studies in Peace-building History between East and West through the Middle Ages and Modern Era*, ed. Ali Elsayed, Abdallah Al-Naggar and Ahmed Sheir (Cairo: Sanabil Bookshop, 2019), pp. 145–64; Al-Amin Abouseada, 'Modern Arabic Historical Scholarship on Medieval Europe: a Biographical Study', in *A Handbook of Modern Arabic Historical Scholarship on the Ancient and Medieval Periods*, ed. Amar S. Badaj (Leiden: Brill, 2021), pp. 595–616.

29. Nora Berend, 'Frontiers', in *Palgrave Advances in the Crusades*, ed. Helen Nicholson (Basingstoke: Palgrave Macmillan 2005), pp. 148–71; Ross Burns, 'The Significance of the Frontier in the Middle Ages', in *Medieval Frontier Societies*, ed. Robert Bartlett and Angus MacKay (Oxford: Clarendon, 1996), pp. 307–30; Ronnie Ellenblum, 'Were there Borders and Borderlines in the Middle Ages? The Example of the Latin Kingdom of Jerusalem', in *Medieval Frontiers: Concepts and Practices*, ed. David Abulafia and Nora Berend (Aldershot:

Ashgate, 2002), pp. 105–19; Alex Metcalfe, *Muslims and Christians in Norman Sicily: Arabic Speakers and the End of Islam* (London: RoutledgeCurzon, 2003); Hugh Kennedy, *Muslim Spain and Portugal: a Political History of al-Andalus* (London: Longman, 1996); Richard A. Fletcher, *Moorish Spain* (London: Phoenix, 1992); Julia Gonnella, 'The Citadel of Aleppo: Recent Studies', in *Muslim Military Architecture in Greater Syria: From the Coming of Islam to the Ottoman Period*, ed. Hugh Kennedy (Leiden: Brill, 2006), pp. 165–75; Ross Burns, *The Monuments of Syria: A Guide* (London: I. B. Tauris, 2009); René Dussaud, *Topographie historique de la Syrie antique et médiévale* (Paris: P. Geuthner, 1927); Paul Deschamps, *Les châteaux des croisés. La défense du comté de Tripoli et de la principauté d'Antioche*, 3 vols (Paris: P. Geuthner, 1934–73).

30. Yahya b. Saʿid al-Antaki, *Taʾrikh al-Antaki*, ed. ʿUmar A. Tadmuri (Tripoli: Yarus Burs, 1990). There is some dispute as to whether Yahya b. Saʿid al-Antaki should be identified as the Melkite physician Abu l-Faraj Yahya ibn Saʿid ibn Yahya (d. after 455/1063). For contrasting views on this, see Marius Canard, 'al-Antaki', in *Encyclopaedia of Islam*, 2nd edn, ed. Peri Bearman et al. (2012), available at Brill online, last accessed 10 July 2017; Mark N. Swanson, 'Yahya ibn Saʿid al-Antaki', in *Christian–Muslim Relations 600–1500*, ed. David Thomas (2010), available online, last accessed 19 August 2022.

31. Carole Hillenbrand, 'Sources in Arabic', in *Byzantines and Crusaders in Non-Greek Sources 1025–1204*, ed. Mary Whitby (Oxford: Oxford University Press for the British Academy, 2007), pp. 283–340, 324.

32. Canard, 'al-Antaki'.

33. Hibat Allah al-Muʾayyad fiʾl-Din al-Shirazi, *Diwan al-Muʾayyad fiʾl-Din daʿi al-duʿah*, ed. Muhammad K. Husayn (Cairo: Dar al-Katib al-Misri, 1949); Verena Klemm, *Memoirs of a Mission: the Islamic Scholar, Statesman and Poet al-Muʾayyad fiʾl-Din al-Shirazi* (London: I. B. Tauris, 2003), pp. 78–88; Ismail Poonawala, 'Al-Muʾayyad fiʾl-Din', in *Encyclopaedia of Islam*, 2nd edn, ed. Peri Bearman et al. (2012), available at Brill online, last accessed 10 July 2017; Hillenbrand, 'Sources in Arabic', p. 332.

34. Sawirus ibn al-Muqaffaʿ, *History of the Patriarchs of the Egyptian Church*, vols II/III and III/I, ed. and trans. Aziz Suryal Atiya, Yassa ʿAbd al-Masih and O. H. E. Burmester (Cairo: Société d'archéologie copte, 1959–68). For more detail on this source, see Luke Yarbrough, 'History of the Patriarchs of Alexandria', in *Encyclopedia of the Medieval Chronicle*, ed. Graeme Dunphy and Cristian Bratu (2016), available at Brill online, last accessed 20 August 2022; Alex Mallett and Johannes Den Heijer, 'The History of the Patriarchs of

the Egyptian Church', in *Franks and Crusades in Medieval Eastern Christian Historiography*, ed. Alex Mallett (Turnhout: Brepols, 2021), pp. 283–312.
35. 'Ali Ibn Tahir al-Sulami, *The Book of the Jihad of 'Ali ibn Tahir al-Sulami: Text Translation and Commentary*, ed. and trans. Niall Christie (Farnham: Ashgate, 2015), pp. 1–8.
36. Goudie, *Reinventing Jihad*, pp. 63–118; Kenneth A. Goudie, 'Legitimate Authority in the Kitab al-Jihad of 'Ali b. Tahir al-Sulami', in *Syria in Crusader Times: Conflict and Co-Existence*, ed. Carole Hillenbrand (Edinburgh: Edinburgh University Press, 2019), pp. 21–33.
37. The *ra'is* of Damascus, and most Syrian towns in this period, was responsible for commanding the *ahdath*, the local urban militia. It was a position of great influence, particularly during times of conflict or transition. See 'Ali ibn al-Hasan Ibn 'Asakir, *Ta'rikh madinat Dimashq*, ed. 'Umar Gh. Al- 'Amrawi, 80 vols (Beirut, 1995–8), XV, 191; Niall Christie, 'Ibn al-Qalanisi', in *Medieval Muslim Historians and the Franks in the Levant*, ed. Alex Mallett (Leiden: Brill, 2015), pp. 8–13; Axel Havemann, 'The Vizier and the Ra'is in Saljuq Syria: the Struggle for Urban Self-Representation', *International Journal of Middle East Studies* 21 (1989): 233–42.
38. Claude Cahen, 'Ibn al-Kalanisi', in *Encyclopaedia of Islam*, 2nd edn, ed. Peri Bearman et al. (2012), available at Brill online, last accessed 10 July 2017.
39. Hillenbrand, 'Sources in Arabic', p. 311.
40. The first partial translation of extracts concerning the Crusader states that covered the years 491–555/1096–1160 into English was completed by Hamilton A. R. Gibb, see Ibn al-Qalanisi, *The Damascus Chronicle of the Crusades*, trans. Hamilton A. R. Gibb (London: Luzac, 1932); the second more comprehensive translation into French, covering the years 467–548/1075–1154, was completed by Roger Le Tourneau, see Roger Le Tourneau, *Damas de 1075 à 1154* (Damascus: Institut français de Damas, 1952).
41. Muhammad b. 'Ali al-'Azimi, *Ta'rikh halab*, ed. Ibrahim Za'rur (Damascus: s.n., 1984). For Hamdan al-Atharibi, whose writings pre-dated those of al-'Azimi, see the discussion of Ibn al-'Adim later in this section.
42. Frédéric Monot, 'La chronique abrégée d'al-'Azîmî, années 518–538/1124–1144', *Revue des Études Islamiques* 59 (1991): 101–64; Alex Mallett, 'Al-'Azimi's *Ta'rikh* for the Crusading Period: the Years 489–508/1095–1115', *Crusades* 19 (2020): 1–34.
43. al-'Azimi, p. 355; Claude Cahen, 'al-'Azimi', in *Encyclopaedia of Islam*, 2nd edn, ed. Peri Bearman et al. (2012), available at Brill online, last accessed 10 July 2017.

44. Ibn ʿAsakir, *Taʾrikh madinat Dimashq*, LXXVI, p. 393; Khalil b. Aybak al-Safadi, *Kitab al-Wafiʾ biʾl-wafayat*, 32 vols, ed. Sven Dedering (Wiesbaden: Franz Steiner Verlag, 1974), IV, p. 131; Cahen, *Syrie*, pp. 42–3; Taef El-Azhari, 'al-ʿAzimi', in *Encyclopaedia of Islam: THREE*, ed. Kate Fleet et al. (2020), available at Brill online, last accessed 29 December 2021.
45. Ibn ʿAsakir, *Taʾrikh madinat Dimashq*, 80 vols; Hillenbrand, 'Sources in Arabic', p. 327; Nikita Elisséeff, 'Ibn ʿAsakir', in *Encyclopaedia of Islam*, 2nd edn, ed. Peri Bearman et al. (2012), available at Brill online, last accessed 10 July 2017.
46. Elisséeff, 'Ibn ʿAsakir'.
47. Ahmad b. Yusuf Ibn al-Azraq al-Fariqi, *Taʾrikh al-Fariqi*, ed. and trans. Carole Hillenbrand, *A Muslim Principality in Crusader Times* (Leiden: Brill, 1990); Hillenbrand, 'Sources in Arabic', p. 312.
48. Alex Mallett, 'Ibn al-Azraq', in *Christian–Muslim Relations: a Biographical History, vol. 3: 1050–1200*, ed. David Thomas and Alex Mallett (Leiden: Brill, 2011), pp. 690–4.
49. Hillenbrand, *A Muslim Principality*, pp. 15–19; Mallett, 'Ibn al-Azraq', pp. 692–3.
50. R. Stephen Humphreys, 'Munkidh', in *Encyclopaedia of Islam*, 2nd edn, ed. Peri Bearman et al. (2012), available at Brill online, last accessed 10 July 2017.
51. Usama b. Munqidh b. ʿAli, *Kitab al-Iʿtibar*, ed. Philip K. Hitti (Princeton, NJ: Princeton University Press, 1930); Usama b. Munqidh b. ʿAli, *Lubab al-Adab*, ed. Ahmed M. Shakir (Cairo: Maktabat Luwis Sarkis, 1935).
52. Humphreys, 'Munkidh'.
53. ʿAbd al-Rahman Ibn al-Jawzi, *al-Muntazam fi taʾrikh al-muluk waʾl-umam*, ed. Muhammad A. Ata et al., 18 vols (Beirut: Dar al-Kutub al-ʿIlmiyah, 1992).
54. Henri Laoust, 'Ibn al-Djawzi', in *Encyclopaedia of Islam*, 2nd edn, ed. Peri Bearman et al. (2012), available at Brill online, last accessed 10 July 2017.
55. Hillenbrand, 'Sources in Arabic', p. 313.
56. ʿIzz al-Din ʿAli Ibn al-Athir, *al-Kamil fiʾl taʾrikh*, ed. Carolus J. Tornberg, 12 vols (Beirut: Dar Sadir, 1965–7).
57. ʿIzz al-Din ʿAli Ibn al-Athir, 'Kamel al-tevarykh', in *Recueil des historiens des croisades. Historiens orientaux*, 5 vols (Paris: Imprimerie Royale, 1872–1906), I (1872), pp. 189–714, II/I (1887), pp. 3–180; Donald S. Richards, *The Annals of the Seljuq Turks* (London: RoutledgeCurzon, 2002); Ibn al-Athir, *The Chronicle of the Ibn al-Athir for the Crusading Period from al-Kamil fiʾl-Taʾrikh*, trans. Donald S. Richards, 3 vols (Aldershot: Ashgate, 2005–8).

58. Françoise Micheau, 'Ibn al-Athir', *Medieval Muslim Historians and the Franks in the Levant*, ed. Alex Mallett (Leiden: Brill, 2015), pp. 52–83, 52–3.
59. Hillenbrand, 'Sources in Arabic', pp. 315–16.
60. R. Stephen Humphreys, 'Ta'rikh', in *Encyclopaedia of Islam*, 2nd edn, ed. Peri Bearman et al. (2012), available at Brill online, last accessed 10 July 2017.
61. Franz Rosenthal, 'Ibn al-Athir', in *Encyclopaedia of Islam*, 2nd edn, ed. Peri Bearman et al. (2012), available at Brill online, last accessed 10 July 2017.
62. 'Izz al-Din 'Ali Ibn al-Athir, *al-Ta'rikh al-bahir fi'l-dawlat al-atabakiyya*, ed. Abd al-Qadir A. Tulaymat (Cairo: Dar al-Kutub al-Hadithah, 1963); Hillenbrand, 'Sources in Arabic', p. 316; Micheau, 'Ibn al-Athir', pp. 68–9.
63. This is in large part due to Sibt b. al-Jawzi's reliance on information contained within the now lost work of Muhammad b. Hilal al-Sabi (d. 481/1088), who was held in high regard at the Abbasid court of Baghdad, granting him access to relevant official documents, see Ali b. Yusuf al-Qifti, *Ikhbar al-Ulama Bi Akhbar al-Hukama'*, ed. Julius Lipp (Leipzig: Dieterich'sche Verlagsbuchhandlung, 1902), pp. 110–11; Zakkar, *Emirate*, p. 34.
64. Claude Cahen, 'Ibn al-Djawzi, Shams al-Din Abu'l-Muzaffar Yusuf b. Kizoglu, known as Sibt', in *Encyclopaedia of Islam*, 2nd edn, ed. Peri Bearman et al. (2012), available at Brill online, last accessed 10 July 2017.
65. Alex Mallett, 'Sibt Ibn al-Jawzi', in *Medieval Muslim Historians and the Franks in the Levant*, ed. Alex Mallett (Leiden: Brill, 2015), pp. 84–108, 84–9.
66. Mallett, 'Sibt Ibn al-Jawzi', pp. 90–2.
67. Cahen, 'Ibn al-Djawzi'; Claude Cahen, 'Review of *Mir'at al-zaman fi ta'rikh al-a'yan*, tome VIII by Sibt B. al-Gawzi; *Dhayl Mir'at al-zaman* by al-Yunini', *Arabica* 4 (1957): 191–4.
68. Yusuf Qizoglu Sibt b. al-Jawzi, *Mi'rat al-zaman fi ta'rikh al-a'yan*, ed. Ali Sevim (Ankara: Matba'at al-Jam'iyat al-Tarikhiyah al-Turkiyah, 1968); Yusuf Qizoglu Sibt b. al-Jawzi, *Mi'rat al-zaman fi ta'rikh al-a'yan*, ed. James R. Jewett (Chicago: University of Chicago Press, 1907).
69. Kamal al-Din Ibn al-'Adim, *Bughyat al-talab fi ta'rikh halab*, ed. Suhayl Zakkar, 12 vols (Beirut: Dar al-Fikr, 1988); Kamal al-Din Ibn al-'Adim, *Zubdat al-halab min ta'rikh halab*, ed. Sami Dahan, 3 vols (Damascus, 1951–68).
70. Anne-Marie Eddé, 'Ibn al-'Adim, Kamal al-Din', in *Encyclopaedia of Islam: THREE*, ed. Kate Fleet et al. (2017), available at Brill online, last accessed 10 July 2017.
71. Anne-Marie Eddé, 'Kamal al-Din 'Umar Ibn al-'Adim', in *Medieval Muslim Historians and the Franks in the Levant*, ed. Alex Mallett (Leiden: Brill, 2015),

pp. 109–35, 109–14; David Morray, *An Ayyubid Notable and His World* (Leiden: Brill, 1994), pp. 122–8.
72. Eddé, 'Ibn al-'Adim', p. 118.
73. Eddé, 'Ibn al-'Adim', pp. 124–5.
74. Zakkar, *Emirate*, pp. 15–21. See also Anne-Marie Eddé, 'Sources arabes des XIIe et XIIIe siècles d'après le dictionnaire biographique d'Ibn al-'Adim (Bugyat al-Talab fi Ta'rih Halab)', in *Itinéraires d'Orient. Hommages à Claude Cahen*, ed. Raoul Curiel and Rika Gyselen (Bures-sur-Yvette: Groupe pour l'étude de la civilisation du Moyen-Orient, 1994), pp. 293–307.
75. IAD BH, X, 4442–3, 4486.
76. IAD BH, III, 1299, V, 2331, VIII, 3685, IX, 4080.
77. IAD BH, IV, 1982, V, 2280, VI, 2926–32.
78. Paul M. Cobb, 'Hamdan al-Atharibi's History of the Franks Revisited, Again', in *Syria in Crusader Times Conflict and Co-Existence*, ed. Carole Hillenbrand (Edinburgh: Edinburgh University Press, 2019), pp. 3–20.
79. Cahen, *Syrie*, pp. 41–2, 343–4; Hillenbrand, *Crusades*, pp. 32, 258; Cobb, *Race for Paradise*, pp. 272–4.
80. Hillenbrand, 'Sources in Arabic', p. 318.
81. Taj al-Din Ibn Muyassar, *Akhbar Misr*, ed. Ayman F. Sayyid (Cairo: Institut français d'Archéologie Orientale, 1981); Claude Cahen, 'Ibn Muyassar', in *Encyclopaedia of Islam*, 2nd edn, ed. Peri Bearman et al. (2012), available at Brill online, last accessed 10 July 2017; Fozia Bora, 'Ibn Muyassar', *Encyclopaedia of Islam THREE*, ed. Kate Fleet et al. (2017), available at Brill online, last accessed 10 July 2017.
82. Taqi al-Din al-Maqrizi, *Itti'az al-hunafa' bi-akhbar al-a'imma al-fatimiyyin al-khulafa'*, 3 vols (Cairo: al-Lajnat Ihya' al-Turath al-Islami, 1967–73), I ed. Jamal al-Din al-Shayyal (1967), II and III, ed. Muhammad H. M. Ahmad (1971–3).
83. Franz Rosenthal, 'Al-Makrizi', in *Encyclopaedia of Islam*, 2nd edn, ed. Peri Bearman et al. (2012), available at Brill online, last accessed 10 July 2017; Frédéric Bauden, 'Taqi al-Din Ahmad ibn al-Maqrizi', in *Medieval Muslim Historians and the Franks in the Levant*, ed. Alex Mallett (Leiden: Brill, 2015), pp. 161–200, 161–7.
84. 'Imad al-Din Ibn Kathir, *al-Bidaya wa'l nihaya fi'l ta'rikh*, 14 vols (Beirut: Dar al-Kutub al-'Ilmiyah, 1932–77).
85. Abu'l Mahasin Yusuf Ibn Taghribirdi, *al-Nujum al-zahira fi muluk Misr wa'l-Qahira*, 16 vols (Cairo: Matba'at Dar al-Kutub al-Misriyah, 1929–72).

86. Henri Laoust, 'Ibn Kathir', in *Encyclopaedia of Islam*, 2nd edn, ed. Peri Bearman et al. (2012), available at Brill online, last accessed 10 July 2017.
87. William Popper, 'Ibn Taghribirdi', in *Encyclopaedia of Islam*, 2nd edn, ed. Peri Bearman et al. (2012), available at Brill online, last accessed 10 July 2017; Hillenbrand, 'Sources in Arabic', p. 322.
88. Konrad Hirschler, *Medieval Arabic Historiography: Authors as Actors* (Abingdon: Routledge, 2006); Konrad Hirschler, 'The Jerusalem Conquest of 492/1099 in the Medieval Arabic Historiography of the Crusades: From Regional Plurality to Islamic Narrative', *Crusades* 13 (2014): 37–76; Michael Brett, 'Lingua France in the Mediterranean: John Wansbrough and the Historiography of Medieval Egypt', in *The Historiography of Islamic Egypt*, ed. Hugh Kennedy (Leiden: Brill, 2001), pp. 1–13; Sami Dahan, 'The Origin and Development of the Local Histories of Syria', in *Historians of the Middle East*, ed. Bernard Lewis and Peter Holt (London: Oxford University Press, 1962), pp. 108–17.
89. Runciman, *Crusades*, I, pp. 333–4.
90. Julie S. Meisami, *Persian Historiography* (Edinburgh: Edinburgh University Press, 1999), p. 3.
91. Omar Safi, *The Politics of Knowledge in Premodern Islam* (Chapel Hill: University of North Carolina Press, 2006), pp. 1–105; Hirschler, *Medieval Arabic Historiography*; Konrad Hirschler, 'Studying Mamluk Historiography: From Source-Criticism to the Cultural Turn', in *Ubi sumus? Quo vademus? Mamluk Studies: State of the Art*, ed. Stephan Conermann (Bonn: Bonn University Press, 2013), pp. 159–86. See also Alex Mallett, 'Islamic Historians of the Ayyubid Era and Muslim Rulers from the Early Crusading Period: a Study in the Use of History', *Al-Masaq* 24 (2012): 241–52; Aaron M. Hagler, 'Unity through Omission: Literary Strategies of Recension in Ibn al-Atir's al-Kamil fi l-Ta'rikh', *Arabica* 65 (2018): 285–313; Gowaart Van Den Bossche, 'Narrative Construction, Ideal Rule, and Emotional Discourse in the Biographies of Salah al-Din and Louis IX by Baha' al-Din b. Shaddad and Jean Sire de Joinville', *Al-Masaq* 30 (2018): 133–47.
92. Nasir-i Khusraw, *Naser-e-Khosraw's Book of travels*, trans. Wheeler M. Thackson (New York: State University of New York Press, 1985); Azim Nanji, 'Nasir-i Khusraw', in *Encyclopaedia of Islam*, 2nd edn, ed. Peri Bearman et al. (2012), available at Brill online, last accessed 10 July 2017.
93. Anonymous, *Gesta Francorum et aliorum Hierosolimitanorum*, ed. and trans. Rosalind M. Hill (London: T. Nelson, 1962).

94. Albert of Aachen, *Historia Hierosolymitana*, ed. and trans. Susan B. Edgington (Oxford: Clarendon, 2007).
95. Fulcher of Chartres, *Fulcheri carnoetensis, Historia Hierosolymitana*, ed. Heinrich Hagenmeyer (Heidelberg: Carl Winters Universitatsbuchhandlung, 1913); Fulcher of Chartres, *A History of the Expedition to Jerusalem*, trans. Frances R. Ryan, ed. Harold S. Fink (Knoxville: University of Tennessee Press, 1969).
96. Ralph of Caen, 'Gesta Tancredi in Expeditione Hierosolymitana', *Recueil des historiens des croisades, Historiens occidentaux*, 5 vols (Paris: Imprimerie Royale, 1844–95), III (1866), pp. 587–716; Ralph of Caen, *The Gesta Tancredi of Ralph of Caen*, ed. and trans. Bernard S. Bachrach and David S. Bachrach (Farnham: Ashgate, 2005).
97. Walter the Chancellor, *Galterii Cancelarii bella antiochena*, ed. Heinrich Hagenmeyer (Innsbruck: s.n., 1896); Walter the Chancellor, *Walter the Chancellor's The Antiochene Wars: a Translation and Commentary*, ed. and trans. Thomas Asbridge and Susan B. Edgington (Aldershot: Ashgate, 1999).
98. William of Tyre, *Willelmi Tyremsos archiepiscopi Chronicon*, ed. Robert B. C. Huygens, Corpus Christianorum Continuatio Mediaevalis 63–63a, 2 vols (Turnhout: Brepols, 1986); William of Tyre, *William of Tyre: a History of Deeds Done Beyond the Sea*, ed. and trans. Emily A. Babcock, and August C. Krey, 2 vols (New York: Octagon, 1976).
99. Matthew of Edessa, *Armenia and the Crusades, Tenth to Twelfth Centuries: the Chronicle of Matthew of Edessa*, trans. Ara E. Dostourian (London: University Press of America, 1993).
100. Michael the Syrian, *The Syriac Chronicle of Michael Rabo (the Great): a Universal History from the Creation*, trans. Matti Moosa (Teaneck: Beth Antioch Press, 2014).
101. Tara Andrews, 'The New Age of Prophecy: the Chronicle of Matthew of Edessa and its Place in Armenian Historiography', *Medieval Chronicle* 6 (2009): 105–23; Tara Andrews, 'Matthew of Edessa (Mattʿeos Urhayecʿi)', in *Franks and Crusades in Medieval Eastern Christian Historiography*, ed. Alex Mallett (Turnhout: Brepols, 2021), pp. 153–78; Tim Greenwood, 'Armenian Sources', in *Byzantines and Crusaders in Non-Greek Sources 1025–1204*, ed. Mary Whitby (Oxford: Oxford University Press for the British Academy, 2007), pp. 221–41.
102. Dorothea Weltecke, 'Originality and Function of Formal Structures in the Chronicle of Michael the Great', *Hugoye: Journal of Syriac Studies* 3 (2000): 173–202; Dorothea Weltecke, 'Michael the Great', in *Franks and Crusades*

in Medieval Eastern Christian Historiography, ed. Alex Mallett (Turnhout: Brepols, 2021), pp. 213–43. Witold Witakowski, 'Syriac Historiographical Sources', in *Byzantines and Crusaders in Non-Greek Sources 1025–1204*, ed. Mary Whitby (Oxford: Oxford University Press for the British Academy, 2007), pp. 255–61.

103. Anonymous Syriac Chronicle, pt. 1: 'The First and Second Crusades from an Anonymous Syriac Chronicle', trans. Arthur S. Tritton and Hamilton A. R. Gibb, *Journal of the Royal Asiatic Society* 65 (1933): 69–101; Herman G. B. Teule, 'The Anonymous Syriac Chronicle to the Year 1234', in *Franks and Crusades in Medieval Eastern Christian Historiography*, ed. Alex Mallett (Turnhout: Brepols, 2021), pp. 243–57; Bar Habraeus, *The Chronography of Gregory Abul Faraj Commonly Known as Bar Hebraeus*, trans. Ernest A. W. Budge, 2 vols (London: Oxford University Press, 1932); Marianna Mazzola, 'Gregory Abu l-Faraj Bar 'Ebroyo (Bar Hebraeus)', in *Franks and Crusades in Medieval Eastern Christian Historiography*, ed. Alex Mallett (Turnhout: Brepols, 2021), pp. 257–81.

104. Michael Attaleiates, *The History*, trans. Anthony Kaldellis and Dimitris Krallis (Cambridge, MA: Harvard University Press, 2012).

105. Anna Komnene, *The Alexiad*, trans. Edgar R. A. Sewter, rev. with introduction and notes by Peter Frankopan (London: Penguin, 2009).

PART I
HISTORICAL SKETCH OF *BILAD AL-SHAM*

Part I Introduction

The System of Autonomous Lordships in Syria

Writing 30 years ago, Michael Köhler coined the phrase 'the Syrian system of autonomous lordships (*des systems syrischer Staatswesen*)', to describe how political power was dispersed among a small collection of minor potentates in *bilad al-sham* during the three decades that preceded the First Crusade. Although Köhler did not explicitly define the 'system of autonomous lordships', beyond a shared prioritisation of independent power by minor rulers in Syria, their development was triggered by the advent of Seljuq rule from 463/1071.[1] The following chapters present a new chronology for the development of what should rather be called the system of autonomous lordships in Syria – as this phenomenon was not unique to *bilad al-sham*, with comparable potentates and minor dynasties emerging in the regions across the Mediterranean during this period – with an earlier date, 454/1062, proposed for the formation of the first autonomous lordship in Syria.

It is first necessary to explain what is meant by the term 'autonomous lordship', at least in the context of this book. Simply put, it describes urban-based political elites who were able to pursue their own political agendas, without ceding military or financial resources to regional rivals or the ruling hierarchies in Constantinople, Cairo or Isfahan.[2]

The 'system' refers to the coexistence of multiple 'autonomous lordships' in Syria. Set definitions are difficult to apply universally, and ultimately each autonomous lordship developed in a unique political and temporal context. It is perhaps best to conceive of each individual polity as existing on a constantly fluctuating continuum, with annexation at one end and autonomy at the other. Individual events, such as the death of a ruler or military defeat, could severely alter a lordship's 'autonomous' status.

For much of the early fifth/eleventh century, Byzantine emperors and Fatimid caliphs had been able to directly appoint rulers or governors (*wali*) to rule over key settlements in Syria. However, as the fifth/eleventh century progressed, it become increasingly more difficult for those in Cairo or Constantinople to remotely assign governors to *bilad al-sham*, whilst Seljuq appointees were nearly always accompanied by large armies led in person by the sultan or a coalition of prominent amirs. The Byzantine, Fatimid and Seljuq hierarchies were therefore forced to rely on other martial and diplomatic mechanisms to assert or expand their political influence in Syria. These mechanisms can be broadly divided into three interlocking categories: military activity, symbolic acts of submission and tributary relationships.

Military activity, and the attendant formation of alliances or coalitions, is the most clearly observable of these mechanisms in the literary sources. Military action typically consisted of siege warfare, battles, skirmishes, the occupation of settlements or raiding activity, with the ultimate objective of installing preferred candidates in urban centres or strategically important fortresses.[3]

Conversely, symbolic acts of submission encompassed several ambiguous diplomatic ceremonies and arrangements. For the Byzantines, the granting of titles to Muslim rulers based in Syria (and other territories throughout their empire) was fairly common practice.[4] In the medieval Islamic world, special importance was attached to the interconnected conventions of the *khutba*, *khidma* and the *sikka*. The *khutba* is the sermon given in mosques prior to midday prayers on Fridays. The naming of a caliph or sultan at the start of the sermon signified their sovereignty and legitimacy within that settlement. *Khidma*, literally translated as 'service', had a broader meaning, but has often been compared with the European concept of 'vassalage'.[5] In the chronicles, *khidma* is generally used the refer to personal bonds or allegiances formed between political elites. *Khidma* ties were often reinforced by written correspondence and conquest letters (*fathnama*) which legitimised a ruler's claim to newly captured territory, or the bestowal of robes of honour.[6] *Sikka* was the practice of inscribing the name of individual caliphs or sultans on coinage.[7]

Khidma, the *khutba* and *sikka* were often combined together, as the designation of a specific caliph during Friday prayers, or on coins, were indicators of political allegiance. This was particularly pertinent in *bilad al-sham*, which was subject to competing claims from the Shi'i Isma'ili Fatimid Caliphate of Cairo and the Sunni Abbasid Caliphate of Baghdad. The steady erosion of Fatimid power during the late fifth/eleventh century, and the ensuing emergence of the Seljuqs, forced Syrian-based rulers into a difficult choice between the potential benefits of publicly proclaiming their adherence to the Seljuq–Abbasid cause, and the threat of armed reprisals from Egypt.

Tributary agreements, whereby one settlement, faction or ruler committed to making monetary payments to another, were usually negotiated features of broader peace treaties (*hudna*). Tributary agreements could take the form of one-off fees, or longer-term treaties with an agreed-upon sum payable every year (*kul sina*). Throughout 442–522/1050–1128, the payment of tribute was a key element of cross-cultural diplomatic interactions, with the terms of these tributary arrangements providing important insights into underlying regional power dynamics.[8]

In the abstruse political world of late fifth/eleventh and early sixth/twelfth century *bilad al-sham*, the ability to avoid unfavourable military alliances and tributary agreements, or demand tributary payments from the Syrian-based representatives of the major factions, are the strongest indicators of an autonomous lordship. This is not to minimise the significance attached to ceremonial activities which underpinned relationships between elites, nor the importance attributed to martial success, and both of these factors are taken into consideration when defining autonomous lordships in this book.

Byzantine, Fatimid and Seljuq Syria

The following three chapters survey this complex period of Syrian history from the perspective of the Byzantine Empire, the Fatimid Caliphate and the Great Seljuq Sultanate. Emphasis will be placed on determining how and when autonomous lordships developed in Syria during the late fifth/eleventh century, and the extent to which their existence hindered Fatimid and Seljuq reactions to the onset of the Crusades.

In 442/1050, *bilad al-sham* was the focal point of a power struggle between the Byzantines of Constantinople and Fatimid Cairo. This was a long-standing conflict, dating back to the emergence of the Fatimids as a major regional power eighty years previously. By the mid-fifth/eleventh century, there was little direct warfare between Byzantine and Fatimid forces, and peace treaties were a customary feature of their relationship. Instead, the primary bone of contention was the northern Syrian city of Aleppo, ruled by the Arab Mirdasid dynasty since 415/1024, which both parties sought to absorb into their dominions through a blend of military and meditative measures.

Although this fluid state of affairs occasionally enabled Mirdasid rulers to play the Byzantines off against the Fatimids, and vice versa, for much of the fifth/eleventh century Aleppan rulers were forced to accept many of the diplomatic trappings of political subordination to Constantinople or Cairo, or both simultaneously.[9]

As will be discussed in Chapters 1 and 2, this dynamic changed from 454/1062 onwards, as a sharp decline in Byzantine and Fatimid regional authority led to the emergence of the Mirdasid dynasty as the dominant power in northern Syria. The Mirdasids were militarily reliant upon the Arab tribal groups of the Kilab, Kalb and Numayr, who inhabited pasture lands between Rahba and Aleppo on the River Euphrates. From the 450s/1060s onwards, newly arrived nomadic Türkmen from the Eurasian Steppe, further bolstered Aleppo's military capabilities, enabling the Mirdasids to pursue their own agenda with minimal interference from Constantinople and Cairo.

But this influx of Türkmen groups and Seljuq dynasts throughout the 450s/1060s and 460s/1070s also precipitated a proliferation of Turkish potentates throughout the Levant, most of whom struggled to survive for longer than one or two generations. Chapter 3 outlines how most attempts to impose centralised Seljuq control over *bilad al-sham* from Baghdad and Isfahan were undermined by this constantly changing cast of Arab and Turkish military elites. Constraints inherent to the Seljuq system of governance; such as the fostering of amiral rivalry and the apparent unsuitability of Syria for prolonged Seljuq military campaigns, provided further impediments. As a consequence, the system of autonomous lordships in Syria was able to survive and even thrive, at least until the armies of the First Crusaders arrived outside the walls of Antioch in 491/1097.

Notes

1. Köhler, *Alliances*, pp. 7–20; Köhler, *Allianzen und Verträge*, pp. 1–19.
2. Although it has been argued that the Arab dynasties and their Bedouin tribal allies – who constituted the dominant political force in northern Syria and the Jazira – had wielded a huge degree of autonomy from 401/1011 onwards, the date of 454/1062 applies specifically to the Mirdasids of Aleppo. See Heidemann, 'Arab Nomads and the Saljuq Military', p. 290.
3. Aside from alliances and sieges, the listed military activities follow the definitions provided by Morton. See Morton, *Crusader States and their Neighbours*, pp. 5–9. On siege warfare, see Chapter 5.
4. On the granting of Byzantine titles to Syrian-based rulers, see Liliana Simeonova, 'In the Depths of Tenth-century Byzantine Ceremonial: the Treatment of Arab Prisoners of War at Imperial Banquets', *Byzantine and Modern Greek Studies* 22 (1998): 75–104; Alexander D. Beihammer, 'Muslim Rulers Visiting the Imperial City: Building Alliances and Personal Networks between Constantinople and the Eastern Borderlands (Fourth/Tenth–Fifth/Eleventh Century)', *al-Masaq* 24 (2012): 157–77, 164–71. An analogous example occurred in Sicily during this period, when the Kalbid Amir Ahmad al-Akhal was granted the title of *Magistros* in 426/1035, see Brett, *Empire*, pp. 174–5; Alex Metcalfe, *The Muslims of Medieval Italy* (Edinburgh: Edinburgh University Press, 2009), pp. 70–87; Leonard C. Chiarellia, *A History of Muslim Sicily* (Santa Venera: Midsea Books, 2010), pp. 119–32.
5. For more information on wider definitions of *khidma* in the Islamic world during the Middle Ages, see Michael Chamberlain, *Knowledge and Social Power in Medieval Damascus* (Cambridge: Cambridge University Press, 1994), pp. 116–18; Peacock, *Empire*, p. 158. For the importance attached to kneeling on a carpet during Seljuq *khidma* ceremonies, see Jürgen Paul, '*Khidma* in the Social History of Pre-Mongol Iran', *Journal of Economic and Social History of the Orient* 57 (2014): 392–422, 408–11.
6. For instance, Ibn al-Qalanisi included a copy of a conquest letter written by Sultan Muhammad I in 509/1115–16 to Tughtegin of Damascus, reaffirming the latter's control over territory in *bilad al-sham*, whilst Tutush b. Alp Arslan's *khidma* relationship with the Mirdasid leader Wathab b. Mahmud involved ceremonial kneeling and the granting of robes of honour, see IQ, pp. 308–13; IAD ZH, I, 244. For more detail on conquest or victory letters (*fathnama*) and robes of honour, see Christine Woodhead, 'Fethiname', in *Encyclopaedia of Islam THREE*, ed. Kate Fleet

et al. (2014), available at Brill online, last accessed 29 December 2021; Dominique Sourdel, 'Robes of Honor in 'Abbasid Baghdad during the Eighth to Eleventh Centuries', in *Robes and Honor: the Medieval World of Investiture*, ed. Stewart Gordon (New York: Palgrave Macmillan, 2001), pp. 137–46; Antony Eastmond and Lynn Jones, 'Robing, Power, and Legitimacy in Armenia and Georgia', in *Robes and Honor: the Medieval World of Investiture*, ed. Stewart Gordon (New York: Palgrave Macmillan, 2001), pp. 147–92; Paula Sanders, 'Robes of Honor in Fatimid Egypt', in *Robes and Honor: the Medieval World of Investiture*, ed. Stewart Gordon (New York: Palgrave Macmillan, 2001), pp. 225–39.

7. For more information on the process of *sikka*, see Stefan Heidemann, 'Numismatics', in *The New Cambridge History of Islam, Volume I*, ed. Chase F. Robinson (Cambridge: Cambridge University Press, 2010), pp. 648–63; G. S. P. Freeman-Greenville, 'Sikka', in *Encyclopaedia of Islam*, 2nd edn, ed. Peri Bearman et al. (2012), available at Brill online, last accessed 15 June 2019.

8. Yehoshua Frenkel, 'Muslim Responses to the Frankish Dominion in the Near East, 1098–1291', in *The Crusades and the Near East Cultural Histories*, ed. Conor Kostick (Abingdon: Routledge, 2011), pp. 27–54; Yvonne Friedman, 'Peacemaking: Perceptions and Practices in the Medieval Latin East', in *The Crusades and the Near East: Cultural Histories*, ed. Conor Kostick (Abingdon: Routledge, 2011), pp. 229–57; Nikita Elisséeff, 'The Reaction of the Syrian Muslims after the Foundation of the First Latin Kingdom of Jerusalem', in *The Crusades: The Essential Readings*, ed. Thomas F. Madden (Oxford: Wiley-Blackwell, 2002), pp. 221–33; Hadia Dajani-Shakeel, 'Diplomatic Relations between Muslim and Frankish Rulers 1097–1153 A.D.', in *Crusaders and Muslims in Twelfth-Century Syria*, ed. Maya Shatzmiller (Leiden: Brill, 1993), pp. 190–215; Asbridge, 'Crusader Community at Antioch, pp. 305–25. For more on regional norms surrounding tributary relationships in Syria during this era, see James Wilson, 'The Ransom of High-ranking Captives, Tributary Relationships and the Practice of Diplomacy in Northern Syria 442–522/1050–1128', *Journal of the Royal Asiatic Society* 32 (2022): 635–69.

9. For more background on the Mirdasid dynasty of Aleppo, see Zakkar, *Emirate*, pp. 67–204; Thierry Bianquis and Samir Shamma, 'Mirdas, Banu or Mirdasids', in *Encyclopaedia of Islam*, 2nd edn, ed. Peri Bearman et al. (2012), available at Brill online, last accessed 15 June 2019.

1

The Byzantine Empire

Byzantine *Bilad al-sham*

Control of cities and regions that had historically constituted the Roman *imperium* validated claims made by Byzantium's ruling elite of presiding over the 'New Rome'.[1] Antioch held a particular resonance within Byzantine circles, due to its status as a former capital of the eastern Roman Empire. Antioch, and the rest of northern Syria, had fallen from imperial dominion during the Arab-Islamic conquests of the first/seventh century, before returning to Constantinople's possession in 358/969.

A picturesque description of the Byzantine province of northern Syria at the start of the period covered can be found in the correspondence of Ibn Butlan (d. 456/1064), an Arab Nestorian Christian physician who relocated from Baghdad to Antioch in 440/1048–9:

> We found the region between Aleppo and Antioch to be flourishing, with no evidence of destroyed houses or ruined farmsteads. Instead, the earth was sown with wheat and barley, which grows beneath the olive trees. The villages run continuously, with blooming gardens and waters flowing everywhere, so that the traveller can traverse the area in a relaxed, safe and peaceful manner.[2]

At the time this letter was written, Byzantium's position as a principal player in the political world of *bilad al-sham* was fairly secure. The two fundamental bulwarks of the Byzantine eastern frontier zone, Antioch and Edessa, were firmly under the control of Constantinople. Moreover, successive emperors enjoyed a dominant diplomatic relationship with the Mirdasid dynasty of Aleppo, best demonstrated by the receipt of annual tributary payments from 421/1030 onwards.[3] Barely three and a half decades later Byzantine influence in northern Syria had collapsed. Antioch was removed from their control in 477/1084 and Edessa in 479/1086.

Modern historians have typically viewed the rapid decline of Byzantine influence in northern Syria as one consequence of a wider period of crisis that engulfed the empire during the fifth/eleventh century. The death of the Emperor Basil II (d. 416/1025) provoked a series of internecine civil wars between bureaucratic figureheads in Constantinople and the provincial military magnates of Anatolia. This internal strife, combined with a series of invasions by the Pechenegs in the Danube region, the Normans in Sicily, southern Italy and the Adriatic coast, and the Seljuqs from the east, led to the loss of the eastern territories of Anatolia, Armenia, Mesopotamia and northern Syria.[4] Within this school of thought, the Byzantine defeat at Manzikert in 463/1071, and the capture, ransom and subsequent death of the Emperor Romanos Diogenes IV, are seen as a further source of political turmoil in Constantinople and Anatolia, making it a contributor to this much larger problem, rather than a definitive event.[5]

This wider narrative of crisis and decline helps to explain why events in northern Syria have received limited focus within modern historiography. Greater emphasis has instead been placed on developments in Asia Minor, largely because the Greek source materials provide a more detailed picture of Byzantine activity there. Indeed, the fall of Antioch and Edessa are viewed as a direct consequence of the Türkmen incursions into Anatolia. That Antioch fell in 477/1084 as a result of an attack that was launched from a 'Seljuq' polity in Asia Minor seemingly reinforces this argument.[6] Most assessments of Byzantine activity in Syria rely upon brief discussions of external military campaigns and the state of relations with the Fatimid Caliphate.[7] This has led to the neglect of the political situation at a regional level, where an understanding of the complex interactions between individual Syrian polities is vital for gauging Byzantium's regional authority.

This chapter examines the underlying causes of the rapid decline in diplomatic and territorial consequence experienced by the Byzantine polity of Antioch between 442 and 477/1050 and 1084, with particular attention paid to the agency of the Mirdasids, their Bedouin Arab allies and Türkmen groups with only nominal ties to the Seljuqs. This is followed by a discussion of interactions between the Byzantine ruling hierarchy and Syrian-based potentates from divergent ethnic, cultural and religious backgrounds. These contacts, which became more frequent as centralised imperial power in Syria faded, indicate a willingness on the part of Constantinople's political elite to collaborate across ethno-doctrinal divides, providing important context for similar interactions that occurred during the Crusading era.

Byzantine Governance of the Syrian Frontier

In order to maintain and augment their influence in northern Syria, the Byzantine court used a variety of governing mechanisms, including the appointment of provincial governors, the cultivation of key diplomatic alliances and military expeditions into the region.

Antioch and Edessa were fundamental to Byzantine strategic interests in the east. Control of these settlements, combined with the natural defences provided

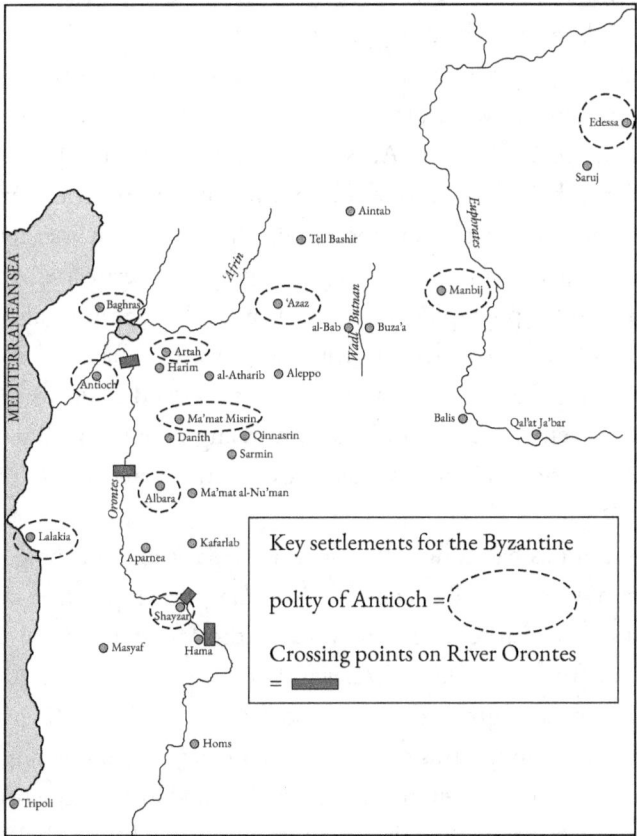

Figure 1.1 Key Antiochene settlements on the River Orontes

by the Taurus Mountains, created a vital defensive shield against incursions by hostile forces into the Byzantine provinces of Anatolia, Armenia and Cilicia. As Michael Decker has succinctly summarised, these cities formed 'the primary nodes of political control, the vertebrae of the Byzantine backbone'.[8]

Traditionally, the region controlled from Antioch stretched southwards from the city from which it took its name, along the coast close to Tripoli, all the way up to Marash and Cilicia, which formed its northern and north-western limits.[9] As Thomas Asbridge has outlined in detail, possession of the settlements of Shayzar and Jisr al-Shugur,[10] situated at two important crossing points on the River Orontes to the south of Antioch, along with Artah, which controlled access to the Jisr al-Hadid (Iron bridge) spanning the same river to the northeast, were vital for defending the city against incursions from the interior of *bilad al-sham*.[11] The port settlement Latakia was also integral, principally for trading reasons, although possession of Latakia also enabled their navy to swiftly deploy troops in northern Syria when necessary.

It is important, however, to not envisage the Byzantine eastern frontier, or any frontier in the Middle Ages, as a clearly delineated boundary, with Byzantium and their allies on one side and hostile actors on the other.[12] Nor was conflict the only form of interaction on this frontier, which actually consisted of several overlapping but distinct geographical territories, with diverse demographic and topographical compositions. This complex amalgamation of people and places provided opportunities for various forms of cross-cultural exchange, ranging from military action, diplomacy and trade, to the development of heterogeneous communities comprising peoples of differing creeds and ethnicities who cohabited villages, towns and sacred spaces over several generations.[13]

The Byzantines had long-standing practices for appointing governors in Antioch, who were typically given the title '*dux*', developed over centuries of commanding vast swathes of territory across the Mediterranean.[14] According to an account from the mid-fifth/eleventh century, the *dux* of Antioch was supported by a rotated group of 4,000 troops dispatched from Constantinople every two years, although this garrison would have been increasingly difficult to maintain as Byzantine regional authority declined in subsequent decades.[15]

However, even prior to the disruption caused by Türkmen raids in Anatolia and northern Syria during the latter half of the fifth/eleventh century, the Byzantine Empire had not always enjoyed an uninterrupted chain of governors in the east appointed by the ruling hierarchy in Constantinople.[16] Most Byzantine appointments on the eastern frontier in the fourth/tenth and fifth/eleventh centuries, were of a temporary nature and subject to moments of rapid change.[17] This is perhaps best demonstrated by the short reigns of the Arab Christian potentates Kulaib and Ubayd Allah in Antioch between 364 and 367/975 and 978, both of whom rose to power without having been directly appointed by the emperor.[18]

Imperial appointees in Antioch were also theoretically bolstered by 'a network of Muslim vassals' along the eastern peripheries of Byzantine territory. These 'vassals' included the Shaddadids based near the River Aras in northeastern Anatolia, the Marwanids of Diyar Bakr, the Uqaylids in Mosul and northern Jazira, the Banu Numayr in Raqqa, and, most importantly, for northern Syria, the Mirdasid dynasty based in Aleppo.[19] In addition to the aforementioned payment of an annual tribute, the impression that the Mirdasids were Byzantine 'vassals' was reinforced by their acceptance of Byzantine titles. The Byzantine Empress Theodora granted Thimal b. Salih (d. 449/1058) the titles of *Magistros* (*makhistrus*) in 433/1042 and *Proedros* (*abridrus*) in 443/1051–2, whilst other prominent family members, such as his brother's widow al-Sayyida al-'Alawiyya (d. unknown) and his nephew Mahmud b. Nasr II (d. 468/1076), were awarded the lesser title of *Patrikos* (*batriqa*).[20]

One interpretation of these conferments would be that Mirdasid rulers of Aleppo held official rank within the Byzantine political hierarchy until at least 468/1076, and therefore acted as 'vassals' until this point. Yet this would not reflect the realities of local power dynamics in northern Syria, with the emergence of Aleppo as the predominant polity in the region exposing the largely symbolic nature of these titles.

The Antiochene–Aleppan Balance of Power

In 442/1050, there was a delicate equilibrium in northern *bilad al-sham*, with power shared between the Byzantine Empire, the Fatimid Caliphate and a series of smaller lordships or city-states with varying degrees of autonomy.[21] According to the northern Syrian chroniclers Yahya al-Antaki and Ibn al-'Adim, the Byzantine emperor received an annual tribute of

500,000 dirhams, or 8,000 dinars, from the Mirdasid ruler Thimal b. Salih. Aleppan delegations were reportedly sent to Constantinople with the requisite funds in 422/1030–1 and 443/1051.[22]

Whilst these annual payments would have augmented the Byzantine imperial treasury, their real significance was symbolic, with the tributary arrangement establishing Antioch as the predominant power in the region. These treaties also provided a premise for regular diplomatic contact, in addition to limiting Mirdasid financial resources and their ability to hire mercenary groups.[23] The Mirdasids also had a similar arrangement with the Fatimid Caliph in Cairo, demonstrating the fluid political dynamics present in northern *bilad al-sham* at this point in time.[24]

Whilst the growing belligerence of Mirdasid and Türkmen forces during the 450s/1060s would ultimately undermine Byzantine interests in northern Syria, the delicate balance of power had already been disturbed by a Byzantine–Fatimid diplomatic dispute during the mid-440s/1050s. This disagreement was triggered by an outbreak of famine and plague in Egypt, caused by low water levels in the River Nile in 446/1054–5. The Fatimid hierarchy reportedly turned to their Byzantine counterparts, requesting a shipment of wheat to alleviate the crisis. Constantinople's failure, or unwillingness, to meet this appeal provoked a sense of animosity in Cairo, which quickly escalated. Military altercations followed, with a failed Egyptian attack against Latakia in 446/1054 prompting an unsuccessful Byzantine siege of Tripoli in 448/1056–7.[25] The dispute also led to symbolic acts at sites of devotional importance. In 447/1055, the Byzantine Empress Theodora, supposedly at the behest of the Seljuq Sultan Tughril Beg, ordered the *khutba* in the mosque of Constantinople to be made in the name of the Abbasid Caliph al-Qa'im, in place of the Fatimid Caliph al-Mustansir.[26] Al-'Azimi and Ibn Muyassar reported that in the same year, al-Mustansir forbade Christians from entering the Church of the Holy Sepulchre in Jerusalem for a short period.[27]

Whilst this relatively intense military and diplomatic activity could be viewed as evidence of the enduring importance of the relationship between the Byzantines and Fatimids, ultimately, they proved to be the final acts of this long-standing conflict. From this point onwards, it was events further inland that would dominate Byzantine attentions and diminish their standing in *bilad al-sham*. As a consequence, interaction between the Byzantine Empire and the

Fatimid Caliphate, the preferred procedure for settling disputes in northern Syria for nearly a century, became largely irrelevant. Instead, both factions were forced to deal with the newly invigorated and emergent potentates at Aleppo and Damascus.

The Nascent Mirdasid and Türkmen Threat

For much of the 440s/1050s, the Byzantine relationship with the Mirdasid dynasty remained fairly stable, with the brief Egyptian annexation of Aleppo between 450 and 452/1057 and 1060 probably marking the end of the yearly remittances to Constantinople.

Following the short-lived Fatimid occupation of Aleppo, Byzantine forces from Antioch attempted to expand their influence in northern Syria by capturing the fortresses of Qastun and ʿAyn al-Tamar in 454/1062.[28] At some point in the same year a dispute arose between Adrien, the Byzantine *dux* of Antioch, and the Mirdasid ruler Thimal of Aleppo over an unspecified fee or tax (*rasm*) owed to the Mirdasids for the fortress of al-Karim Bismiran.[29] This disagreement culminated in a battle at Artah in 454/1062, from which Thimal's army emerged victorious. Mirdasid troops then captured Artah and proceeded to besiege Antioch. Sibt b. al-Jawzi reported that in order to persuade the Aleppan force to withdraw, the Antiochenes paid an unspecified amount, whilst Ibn al-ʿAdim claimed that they also surrendered Maʿrrat Misrin as part of the settlement.[30] This was the first real indication of an alteration in the balance of power between Antioch and Aleppo and marked the point when the Mirdasids ceased to be a member of the Byzantine 'network of Muslim vassals'.

In order to appreciate the significance of this defeat, the strategic importance of Artah needs to be fully understood.[31] Artah was located to the north of the main road between Antioch and Aleppo. Bordering this road on both sides is a difficult-to-traverse limestone range, which forms a natural defensive barrier against any army approaching Antioch from the east. Artah also controlled access to the Jisr al-Hadid (Iron Bridge), one of the few crossing points on the River Orontes, and the quickest route to Antioch from the direction of Aleppo.[32] Put simply, control of Artah was essential to Antioch's security. If Artah fell into enemy possession, hostile forces would be able to assail the town and its environs with relative impunity.

The Mirdasids of Aleppo were not immediately able to capitalise on their success in 454/1062 as they were soon engulfed in a succession crisis. Thimal's death at the end of 454/1062 sparked a dispute between his nephew, Mahmud b. Nasr, and his brother, 'Atiyya b. Salih, which lasted until 457/1065.[33] One of the more significant aspects of this protracted conflict was the involvement of Türkmen troops.[34] Whilst Türkmen groups had been operating in eastern Anatolia since the early 440s/late 1040s, the reported arrival of Ibn Khan's forces at Aleppo in 455/1063 is the earliest reference in the Arabic literary sources to Türkmen activity in northern Syria.[35]

Further conflict with Byzantine forces occurred in the midst of the ongoing Mirdasid succession struggle, when troops under the command of Mahmud's new Türkmen ally Ibn Khan engaged an Antiochene army near Edessa in 457/1064–5.[36] As part of the subsequent peace negotiations with Antioch, Mahmud gave his son as a hostage (*rahina*) in exchange for unspecified territories, robes of honour and all of their limited gold reserves.[37] Again, we can see the *dux* and inhabitants of Antioch being forced to make a payment to the Mirdasids to secure a peace treaty, even if the reported terms of this negotiated settlement seem more equitable.

Presumably, the Byzantines managed to regain control of Artah by the winter of 460/1067–8, as a joint Mirdasid and Türkmen army once again placed the fortress under siege during the winter and spring of 460/1067–8, ultimately returning Artah to Aleppan control after a five-month blockade.[38] Whilst this siege was taking place, a series of raids into Byzantine territory were led by Türkmen troops under Afshin b. Bakji. Initially, Afshin led his troops to Marash, to the north of Aleppo, before wintering in the Amanus Mountains to the north of Antioch. Matthew of Edessa described how the Türkmen 'destroyed all the villages and many monasteries that were located in the region'.[39] Afshin's forces then launched raids upon the region of Antioch itself, perhaps facilitated by the ongoing Mirdasid siege of Artah. The *dux* of Antioch, Nikephoros Botaneiates, was again forced to pay a besieging force to withdraw. On this occasion Afshin received '100,000 dinars and an amount similar to this in silk lined clothing and other instruments'.[40]

Whilst this attack upon Artah in 460/1067–8 could be characterised as an opportunistic venture, it was just one of several Mirdasid attacks against Antioch over a five-year period. Taken together, they represent a marked change in Mirdasid policy towards the Byzantines during the 450s/1060s. Having long played the role of tribute-payer to Constantinople, this decade saw the adaptation of a more aggressive approach by Mirdasid rulers in an attempt to reverse this long-standing dynamic.

As a result, the Byzantine polity of Antioch become increasingly susceptible to direct attacks from both Mirdasid and Türkmen rulers, with the inhabitants of Antioch forced to pay tribute to besieging forces on several occasions. Although indicative of a sharp decline in Byzantine regional authority, Constantinople's capacity to select governors to rule over the provincial peoples of Antioch was contingent upon the emperor's ability to protect the citizens of Antioch from external threats. If these attacks remained unchecked, Antiochene support for the imperial cause would begin to fade.

The Malik al-rum *in* Bilad al-sham

The 460s/1060s saw a Norman siege of Bari, the key Byzantine outpost in southern Italy, and an Oguz Turk raid of the Danube region threaten Byzantium's southwestern and northern frontiers.[41] Yet it was the east, and specifically Syria, that the newly installed Byzantine Emperor (*malik al-rum*) Romanos Diogenes IV (r. 460–3/1068–71) decided to prioritise.

Afshin's attack on the city of Antioch in 460/1067–8 was one of a series of Türkmen and Seljuq raids which infiltrated the Caucasus, Mesopotamia, the Euphrates region, Armenia and Cilicia in the late 450s and early 460s/1060s, laying bare the increasingly porous nature of the Byzantine eastern frontier.[42] The main concern for Constantinople centred upon two invasion routes: the first from the north, through Azerbaijan and the Araxes valley to the upper Euphrates region; and the second to the south through Diyar Bakr, Edessa and Aleppo into Antioch and Cilicia. The Emperor Romanos Diogenes IV led a series of military expeditions in 461/1068–9, 462/1069–70 and 463/1070–1 with the intention to cut off these pathways into Anatolia.

The first campaign in 461/1068–9 targeted the southernmost route leading to Antioch, with the prioritisation of northern Syria providing another indicator of the precarious state of affairs in Antioch at this juncture. Arriving in northern *bilad al-sham* from the direction of Marash and Duluk, Romanos' forces raided the area around Aleppo, before moving to capture Manbij to the east of Aleppo, close to the River Euphrates. After defeating a coalition of

Mirdasid and Türkmen at Manbij, the emperor's army proceeded to raid the vicinity of 'Azaz before crossing the Vale of 'Afrin and expelling the Mirdasid garrison at Artah, recapturing one of the most important settlements in the vicinity of Antioch. Another skirmish occurred at Artah, with Mahmud b. Nasr, the Mirdasid amir of Aleppo, and his nomadic Arab tribesmen allies the Banu Kilab, being defeated a second time.[43]

The strategy of propping up the beleaguered province of Antioch through targeted military campaigns was sound in theory. The recapture of Artah would have reassured the inhabitants of Antioch, and made it more difficult for assailants to attack the territory in the immediate vicinity of the town. This was demonstrated by the raid led by the Türkmen ruler Sunduq al-Turki later in 461/1069–70, shortly after the departure of the emperor's army. Sunduq's Türkmen had arrived in *bilad al-sham* from the direction of Anatolia. Rather than attacking the region of Antioch, the Türkmen remained in central Syria, where they raided Ma'rrat al-Nu'man, Kafartab, Homs, Hama and Rafaniyya during the winter months.[44] While it is probable that Byzantine control of Artah prevented Sunduq's forces from attacking the area around Antioch, it is also quite likely that this region was a less attractive target as it had already been raided in the past twelve months by Afshin's Türkmen.

While the emperor's 461/1068–9 campaign into northern Syria can be characterised as a success, it is also worth noting that the Byzantine's only made limited territorial gains, despite enjoying decisive victories over two separate Mirdasid armies. The capture of Manbij and Artah would have somewhat ameliorated the Byzantine position in the region, enabling the rulers of Antioch to better defend against Aleppan and Türkmen incursions. Yet, even with the emperor personally leading the campaign, his forces were unable to capture other strategically important settlements. For instance, if Romanos' forces had managed to capture 'Azaz, it could have placed significant pressure on the Mirdasids of Aleppo, helping to tip the balance of power in northern Syria back towards Antioch.[45]

Shortly after the departure of the imperial field army the *dux* of Antioch, Khatatourios, captured the fortress of Asfuna, close to Ma'rrat al-Nu'man. This was an attempt to expand Antiochene regional influence and place further pressure on the Mirdasids of Aleppo following the emperor's expedition. Yet any impact proved to be short-lived, as Aleppan forces recaptured Asfuna after a short seven-day siege. Mahmud then concluded a truce with Khatatourios in which the latter agreed to pay the amir of Aleppo 14,000 dinars.[46] This episode reinforced the impression that the Mirdasids remained the ascendant power in the region, while exposing the limited benefits that Antioch derived from the 461/1068–9 Byzantine campaign into northern Syria.

Romanos' approach of targeted military campaigns was then completely undermined by the decisive defeat of a huge Byzantine army at Manzikert, eastern Anatolia in 463/1071.[47] Modern historians generally agree that the defeat at Manzikert was less damaging for Byzantium than the drawn-out succession crisis that it sparked.[48]

Yet it should be noted that Romanos was the only Byzantine emperor with the inclination or means to lead a campaign into *bilad al-sham* in almost a hundred years (421–531/1030–1137). This drawn-out absence was caused by protracted internal conflicts, the need to combat the threat to Byzantium's western and northern frontiers posed by the Normans and Pechenegs, and the dramatic events of the First Crusade, which, ultimately, was launched at the behest of the Byzantine Emperor Alexios Komenenos (r. 473–512/ 1081–1118) in the hopes of restoring Antioch to imperial dominion.[49] Yet, despite these mitigating factors, Romanos' removal from office, which came as a direct consequence of the defeat at Manzikert, deprived the inhabitants of Antioch of the only emperor who actually led a military campaign into northern Syria during this time frame.

In summary, between 442 and 463/1050 and 1071, the ruling elite in Antioch were forced to make several payments to the amirs of Aleppo and Türkmen potentates in order to bring an end to direct assaults upon the town. Instead of making annual tributary payments as a Byzantine 'vassal', the Mirdasids developed into an autonomous polity in northern Syria, able to coerce these payments from Antiochene rulers. Essentially, Aleppo was operating as something resembling an 'autonomous lordship' nearly a decade before the establishment of the first Seljuq rulers in *bilad al-sham*.[50]

Romanos Diogenes III's 461/1068–9 campaign, the sole external attempt to strengthen Byzantine influence in the region prior to 531/1137, made little lasting difference to the political situation in *bilad al-sham*, which had seen a steady reduction in Antiochene influence *vis-à-vis* Aleppo over the preceding decade. A resurgent Mirdasid Aleppo under the rule of Mahmud b. Nasr, bolstered by Türkmen raiders, undermined Byzantine mechanisms of governance, which had historically relied upon military successes sustaining a dominant diplomatic relationship with Aleppo. Constantinople's inability to reassert its authority in northern Syria, even after direct intervention from the emperor, left Antioch isolated and vulnerable.

The Byzantine Political Footprint in the Face of Seljuq Incursions

The establishment of Seljuq potentates in northern Syria from 463/1071 contributed to the further weakening of Byzantium's grip on Antioch. The Seljuq Sultan Alp Arslan's siege of Aleppo in 463/1071, and Sulayman b. Qutlumush's capture of Antioch in 477/1084, are generally viewed as the most significant developments in this deterioration of imperial authority in the region. Yet these events were merely indicative of a broader shift in local power dynamics, as significant damage had already been done to Byzantine standing in *bilad al-sham* by Arab and Turkmen potentates.

Alp Arslan's Siege of Aleppo: 463/1071

Any Antiochene aspirations of re-establishing themselves as the predominant faction in northern Syria dissipated in 463/1071. In Jumada II 463/late March–early April 1071, the Seljuq Sultan Alp Arslan led an army into *bilad al-sham*. After a month-long siege of Aleppo, the sultan reached a negotiated settlement with Mahmud b. Nasr, whereby the Mirdasid ruler was forced to perform the ceremonial act of *khidma*, and to make the *khutba* in Aleppo in the name of the Abbasid Caliph al-Qa'im.[51]

Aside from the implications that Alp Arslan's arrival in *bilad al-sham* had for Seljuq and Fatimid influence in the region, Byzantine historians have viewed this campaign as a key turning point.[52] However, as discussed above, there is persuasive evidence that Aleppo had ceased acting like a 'Muslim vassal' of the Byzantines nearly a decade before Alp Arlsan's siege of Aleppo in 463/1071.

It is also unclear that the switch of the *khutba* in Aleppo actually altered Byzantine strategy in the region in any meaningful way. Historically, Byzantine emperors had been accustomed to sharing influence in the city with the Fatimid Caliphate, with the Mirdasids often making annual tribute payments to both factions simultaneously. Based upon this past precedent, this switch in Aleppo's public allegiance from the Fatimids to the Seljuqs in 463/1071 should not have overly troubled the imperial court in Constantinople.

The Increasing Isolation of Antioch

The *dux* of Antioch Khatatourios made another failed attempt to reverse this downward trend in Byzantine fortunes in 463/1071, leading an attack on Ma'rrat Misrin that Mirdasid forces successfully repulsed.[53] In 464/1072, another Byzantine attempt to capture the strategically vital town of 'Azaz was repelled by a small army led in person by Mahmud b. Nasr.[54]

There are suggestions within one source of an increasing disillusionment with imperial rule within Antioch the following year. According to the Greek historian Nikephoros Byrennios (d. 531/1137), there were widespread riots in Antioch after a failed attempt to assassinate the Byzantine *dux* Isaac Komnenos in 467/1075. In an order to quell the revolt, Isaac Komnenos was forced to call in Byzantine reinforcements from the surrounding settlements.

Then, shortly after violently supressing the rioters, reports reached the *dux* that a Türkmen army would shortly be arriving outside the town walls. When they arrived, Isaac Komnenos elected to lead a sortie against the Türkmen, during the course of which he was taken captive. He was later ransomed by the inhabitants of Antioch for a sum of 20,000 dinars.[55] Sibt b. al-Jawzi confirmed that a Türkmen force, led by an 'Ibn Qutlumush', attacked Antioch and imposed an annual tribute of 20,000 dinars on the town, although this second report does not mention the rioting or the ransom of Isaac Komnenos.[56]

Whilst this ransom payment could be viewed as evidence of residual support for Isaac Komnenos and Byzantine rule within Antioch, in all likelihood this episode only exacerbated pre-existing tensions between the imperial centre and the provincial elites of northern Syria.[57] One potentially revealing feature of Nikephoros Byrennios' account is that it was the inhabitants of Antioch who paid Isaac Komnenos' ransom, but other sources specify that earlier Mirdasid tribute payments had been conveyed directly to Constantinople. Seemingly, the imperial court benefited from any Aleppan tributary agreements, whilst the townspeople of Antioch had to shoulder the costs of paying off enemy forces at times of crisis.

Additionally, Sibt b. al-Jawzi reported that the diplomatic agreement of 467/1075 included a commitment from the Türkmen to protect Antioch from future raids, perhaps demonstrating the growing sense of isolation and vulnerability caused by these repeated attacks. The imposition of an annual tribute would also have been a significant development, as it implied a more permanent relationship between the two parties involved.

Mahmud's successor as Mirdasid ruler of Aleppo was his son Sabiq b. Mahmud. With the support of a new Türkmen commander named Ahmad Shah, Sabiq recaptured Manbij from Byzantine dominion in Safar 468/September–October 1075.[58] In 469/1077, Sabiq again dispatched Ahmad Shah and his Türkmen to attack Byzantine territory. On this occasion the Türkmen besieged Antioch and the new *dux*, Philaretos Brachamios, was forced to pay the huge sum of 100,000 dinars to get them to withdraw.[59] This reinforces the impression that Mirdasid rulers were increasingly coming to view Antioch as a source of potential income through the payment of tribute.

Antioch suffered further raiding by Türkmen in 472/1079. This nomadic Turkish force, led by Afshin b. Bakji, first raided settlements further east, such as Hisn al-Jisr, Qastun, Rafaniyya, Sarmin, Maʿrrat al-Nuʿman and Maʿratah, before approaching Antioch and besieging the town. The *dux* Philaretos Brachamios reportedly made another payment of 30,000 dinars to secure Antioch's safety.[60] This raid, launched in conjunction with similar expeditions conducted by Arslan Tash and Tutush b. Alp Arslan to the east and south, interrupted trade and agricultural production, provoking a severe famine throughout northern Syria. 'Security of life did not exist in Antioch, in the whole country of Cilicia up to Tarsus, in the country around Marash, in Duluk, and in all their surrounding regions' noted Matthew of Edessa, giving the impression of a lack of Antiochene control over the northern areas of the province.[61]

Further evidence that Antioch was becoming increasingly isolated from the region it traditionally governed, not only to the north and west, but also to the south, can be found in the loss of Shayzar and Hisn al-Jisr. According to several Arabic sources, the bishop of Albara effectively sold the fortress of Shayzar to Sadid al-Mulk ʿAli of the Banu Munqidh for an unspecified sum in 474/1081–2.[62] By 475/1082–3 the ruler of Damascus, Tutush b. Alp Arslan, was using the Jisr al-Hadid (Iron Bridge) as his base of operations to launch raids into the area around Aleppo.⁶³ This indicates that Byzantine Antioch no longer controlled territory in the immediate vicinity of Antioch. Coupled with the occupation of Shayzar and Hisn al-Jisr by the Banu Munqidh, Byzantine rulers would have found it difficult to launch offensive campaigns beyond the River Orontes or defend against attacks from the interior of Syria after 475/1082–3. Effectively, the Byzantine province of Antioch was confined to the immediate vicinity of the town from this point onwards.

The Annual Tributary Relationship

Any semblance of an autonomous lordship at Antioch came to an end in 475/1082. In 475/1082, the Uqaylid ruler of Mosul and Aleppo, Sharaf al-Dawla Muslim b. Quraysh,⁶⁴ imposed an annual tribute of 20,000 dinars on the Byzantine *dux* Philaretos Brachamios.⁶⁵ It seems likely that this agreement lasted until the fall of the town from Byzantine control two years later, as Sharaf al-Dawla demanded that Philaretos' successor continue paying the tribute after 477/1084.⁶⁶ According to Sibt b. al-Jawzi, the treaty was triggered by negotiations undertaken without an attack being made upon the city of Antioch.

This annual tributary agreement was the culmination of an aggressive policy by successive Aleppan rulers, who had extracted several payments from Antioch over the preceding twenty years, whilst Türkmen raids had further exacerbated the situation. When placed alongside the territorial losses outlined above, this agreement was a natural consequence of the steady decline of Byzantine regional influence. After Philaretos entered into this agreement in 475/1082, the people of Antioch looked to Sharaf al-Dawla Muslim b. Quraysh and the Seljuq Sultan Malik Shah to protect them from assailants and provide military assistance, rather than to Constantinople.

Antioch fell to Sulayman b. Qutlumush, a distant relation of the Sultan Malik Shah, in Sha'ban 477/December 1084. Sulayman approached the city from the direction of Anatolia, where he had carved out a zone of control that included Nicaea and parts of Cilicia.⁶⁷ Just two years later, in 479/1086, Edessa surrendered to the Seljuq Sultan Malik Shah during his first and only campaign into the Euphrates region.⁶⁸

Throughout 454–77/1062–84, the traditional Byzantine strategy of maintaining a strong polity at Antioch capable of containing the threat posed by Aleppo was undermined by incessant Türkmen attacks and the increasingly hostile northern Syrian Mirdasid and Uqaylid potentates. Although internal succession crises and the collapse of Byzantine control in Anatolia, the Danube and southern Italy hindered any potential attempt to maintain Byzantine influence in *bilad al-sham*, much of the damage to their interests at a regional level was inflicted by local Arab rulers based in Aleppo. The Byzantine frontier within Syria had been eroded long before Antioch and Edessa actually fell from Byzantine dominion. This casts doubt on the notion that Seljuq rulers were a decisive factor in the decline of Byzantine authority in *bilad al-sham*. Alp Arslan's campaign of 463/1071 had little substantive impact on Constantinople's strategy in the region, whilst Sulayman b. Qutlumush's conquest of Antioch in Sha'ban 477/December 1084 was largely symbolic, as it had effectively become a 'vassal' of Aleppo two years earlier.

Byzantine Interactions with Local Rulers in *Bilad al-sham*

Successive Byzantine emperors and their representatives in northern Syria employed a variety of diplomatic strategies to compliment more conspicuous military methods. As Türkmen leaders established themselves in *bilad al-sham* and Anatolia, it became common practice for approaches to be made to these emerging potentates, whilst the decline of imperial control over Armenia and Anatolia necessitated the empowerment or toleration of former rebels, or individuals who held only loose ties to the ruling elite of Constantinople.

The Mirdasids of Aleppo

The leaders of the Mirdasid dynasty, and those in their entourage, were the most frequent targets of Byzantine diplomatic overtures in northern Syria. Byzantine relations with the Mirdasids of Aleppo dated back to the early fifth/eleventh century. The strength of this association is perhaps best represented by the ambassadors that the Byzantines sent to the Fatimid court to intercede on the Mirdasid's behalf in 440/1048–9.[69] For much of his reign, the Mirdasid ruler of Aleppo Thimal b. Salih navigated a careful diplomatic course, simultaneously recognising the suzerainty of both Constantinople and Cairo. With Thimal's death in 454/1062, Byzantium lost a key ally in *bilad al-sham*.

His nephew and ultimate successor in Aleppo, Mahmud b. Nasr, proved to be far more difficult for Constantinople to cultivate as an ally. As outlined above, Mahmud had received the title of *Patrikos* in 433/1042, and also accepted financial support from Byzantium in 452/1060 to fund the succession conflict against his rival claimant and uncle ʿAtiyya b. Salih.[70] But ultimately this investment failed to provide any political dividends, as Mahmud spent much of his life leading military attacks which severely damaged Byzantine interests in *bilad al-sham*.

Once this became apparent to the Byzantine court, a decision was taken to start backing Mahmud's uncle and rival ʿAtiyya b. Salih instead. In 463/1071, Antiochene forces commanded by the *dux* of Antioch Khatatourios, supported by ʿAtiyya and members of the Arab Banu Kilab tribe loyal to ʿAtiyya, launched a failed attack on Maʿrrat Misrin. ʿAtiyya died in Constantinople a year later whilst lobbying for further support against his nephew.[71]

As the Byzantine Empire had long-standing precedents for diplomatic interactions with the Mirdasids, and other non-Byzantine groups and peoples, these approaches were not indicative of their eroding influence in northern Syria. Yet these diplomatic missteps with Mirdasid rulers did contribute to the deterioration of Byzantine power in northern Syria.

Seljuq and Türkmen Rulers: Ibn Khan and Sulayman b. Qutlumush

Byzantium also approached Türkmen rulers who emerged as key players in the political world of *bilad al-sham*. Ibn Khan was one of the first such individuals solicited by the Byzantines. Ibn al-ʿAdim claimed that two separate approaches were made. The first came when Ibn Khan was in the employ of the Marwanids of Diyar Bakr, prior to his arrival in northern Syria.[72] The second was made in 460/1068, when a Byzantine army descended on Artah. The Byzantines reportedly attempted to persuade Ibn Khan, who was in charge of the settlement's defence, to surrender Artah and other neighbouring settlements, but the Türkmen leader refused.[73]

It is likely that this rejection was motivated by superior offers made by the Mirdasid dynasty. Ibn Khan played a huge role in nearly all Aleppan military activities during his time in their service, and Mahmud rewarded Ibn Khan with control of the key settlement of Maʿrrat al-Nuʿman.[74] Had the Byzantines managed to place ʿAtiyya in charge of Aleppo, or persuade Mahmud and Ibn

Khan to assist the polity of Antioch, rather than follow aggressive policies that severely damaged it, the Byzantine Empire would have been better able to retain its influence in northern Syria.

Sulayman b. Qutlumush was another Türkmen or Seljuq ruler who successfully navigated the murky power dynamics of the eastern Byzantine frontier, carving out a series of lordships stretching from Anatolia and Cilicia to northern Syria. Partly as a result of this success, Peter Frankopan has described Sulayman as being an 'agent' of the Byzantine Emperor Alexios I Komnenos.[75] Yet this ignores the significance of Sulayman's ancestry, and the complexity of the situation on the ground in northern Syria and Anatolia, where the political spheres of the Great Seljuq Sultanate and the Byzantine Empire overlapped.

Sulayman was the grandson of the eldest son of Seljuq, the eponym of the Seljuq dynasty. This not only made him a prominent member of the Seljuq family, but also granted him a relatively good claim to the sultanate and strong support among the Türkmen.[76] While Sulayman evidently had ties to Alexios and held territories in Anatolia with the emperor's acquiescence, he also attempted to integrate his lordships into Seljuq domains by applying for legitimisation from the Sultan Malik Shah.[77]

The entangled nature of the ethno-cultural and religious sentiments during this period is best summarised by Bar Habraeus' description of how 'the inhabitants of Antioch were very much more pleased with him [Sulayman b. Qutlumush] than with Philaretos, who was nominally a Christian'.[78] In essence, Sulayman, like many other individuals, found it beneficial to his territorial ambitions to concurrently adopt two separate identities, both as a Byzantine 'vassal' and as a prominent member of the Seljuq dynasty.[79]

Philaretos Brachamios and his 'Byzantine' Contemporaries

The ruling hierarchy of the Byzantine Empire also fostered diplomatic contacts with rulers of Armenian heritage. The most prominent Armenian figure in the context of Byzantine northern Syria was Philaretos Brachamios. Philaretos has received a great deal of attention from historians, as he briefly declared himself emperor during a rebellion against the Byzantine Emperor Michael VII in the 460s/1070s, before later converting to Islam to gain the support of the Seljuq sultan.[80]

Philaretos established himself in northern Syria from 464/1072 onwards, capturing Marash, Lykandos, Sumaysat and Melitene, while he received titles for accepting the authority of the Byzantine emperors Nikephoros III and Alexios I Komnenos in around 470/1078.[81] He took control of Edessa in 475/1083–4 courtesy of a dispute between rival Armenian families. Iskkhan of the Arjk't'onk family rebelled against the *dux* Smbat and handed control of the city to Philaretos.[82] Antioch came under Philaretos' control in 469/1076–7, following a call for aid from the populace following the death of the previous Armenian *dux* Vasak. Shortly after arriving in Antioch, Philaretos gathered together 'all the perfidious and apostate Romans, as many as 700 men', led them to a village called Ap'shun and had them all killed.[83]

Philaretos' ability to seize control of the two most important settlements on the Byzantine eastern frontier without being appointed by the emperor in Constantinople could be viewed as another symptom of Byzantium's waning influence. However, Holmes has demonstrated how there was an existing precedent for local rulers, particularly those of Arab-Christian descent, to seize control in these settlements during the fourth/tenth centuries.[84] Nevertheless, the way in which Philaretos took control of Antioch and Edessa indicates that he was not strongly aligned to the ruling hierarchy of Constantinople.

Arabic, Armenian, Syriac and Greek sources all concur that Philaretos converted to Islam in around 478/1085, following Sulayman b. Qutlumush's capture of Antioch a year previously.[85] This act of apostasy colours the narrative of Philaretos' career provided by the chroniclers. This is most clearly observable in the Armenian and Syriac traditions, where Philaretos is universally depicted as a rapacious and amoral tyrant, equally despised by political rivals and the people he ruled over.

Yet, despite the controversy surrounding Philaretos' conduct, there are suggestions that his predecessors in Antioch and Edessa also took steps to integrate themselves into Seljuq political structures. For instance, the Aleppan chronicler al-'Azimi reported that as part of a peace treaty agreed between the Mirdasid ruler of Aleppo Mahmud b. Nasr and Antioch in 464/1071–2, the *dux* agreed to 'accept the rule of the Sultan of Iraq'.[86] Presumably, this meant that the *khutba* in Antioch was switched to recognise the authority of the Seljuq sultan and the Abbasid caliph, matching the *khutba* in Constantinople, which been changed to the Abbasids as early as 447/1055.

The authority of the Uqaylid ruler of Aleppo and Mosul Sharaf al-Dawla Muslim b. Quraysh, the Abbasid caliph and the Seljuqs had also been recognised by 'Byzantine' rulers of Edessa prior to the settlement's surrender to the Sultan Malik Shah in 479/1086. Sibt b. al-Jawzi claimed that in 474/1081–2 Muslim b. Quraysh sent to Baghdad informing the sultan and the caliph that 'the lord of Edessa obeyed him and that he engraved his name on his coins'. Both the sultan and the caliph wrote back approving Muslim b. Quraysh's claim to Edessa and ordered him to arrange for their names to be read from the *minbar* in the mosque.[87]

These examples indicate that Philaretos' conversion to Islam was not inconsistent with the behaviour of other Byzantine rulers in Syria. Although it is probable that Philaretos undertook this action to curry favour with Malik Shah, this should be viewed against the backdrop of similar attempts by his 'Byzantine' contemporaries to assimilate themselves into the political structures of the Great Seljuq Sultanate.

A Failure in Byzantine Diplomacy?

Byzantium's increasing reliance upon local actors in *bilad al-sham* is yet another indication of the progressively restricted influence they wielded in the region. It is also apparent that doctrinal and ethno-cultural differences were not an issue for the Byzantine rulers in Syria or Constantinople, as they were willing to approach local Christian or Muslim rulers and those of Arab, Armenian or Turkish heritage. However, unlike their erstwhile Fatimid rivals in Cairo, Byzantine attempts to realise their strategic goals through interactions with Syrian-based rulers proved to be largely unsuccessful.[88]

These activities also provide a useful frame of reference for similar contacts during the early sixth/twelfth century. If contacts across set religious or ethnic barriers were a common feature of political interactions in *bilad al-sham* throughout the latter half of the fifth/eleventh century, then alliances and treaties made during the early Crusading period should not be viewed as a unique product of the advent of Seljuq rule, or the process of early Frankish settlement. Instead, they were an ingrained feature of diplomatic and military interactions in *bilad al-sham* throughout this period.

Conclusion: The Break-up of Byzantine *Bilad al-sham*

Between 454/1062 and Sulayman b. Qutlumush's capture of Antioch in 477/1084–5, Byzantine influence and territorial holdings in northern Syria collapsed. This chapter has highlighted the damage done to the Byzantine polity of Antioch by Mirdasid and Türkmen rulers during this twenty-two-year time frame. Whilst Byzantine internal conflicts and the loss of territory in Anatolia, southern Italy and the Danube region severely inhibited Constantinople's ability to respond to developments on the ground in northern Syria, much of the damage to their influence was inflicted by local rulers in *bilad al-sham* before Byzantium suffered major territorial losses in Anatolia in the 470s/1080s and early 480s/1090s.[89]

This chapter has set out a different chronology for the decline of Byzantine authority in northern Syria. The Mirdasids of Aleppo ceased acting as a Byzantine vassal in 454/1062, nearly a decade prior to the arrival of the first Seljuq campaign into *bilad al-sham* in 463/1071. It would be possible to argue that this occurred in 450/1057, when the Fatimids occupied Aleppo and the tributary relationship came to an end. Then again, the Mirdasid attack on Antioch in 454/1062 is more representative of Aleppo's transition from a submissive tribute payer, to an aggressive imposer of tribute. From this point on, there was an increasing frequency of tributary payments made by Antioch to Aleppo, culminating in annual payments from 475/1082–3 onwards.

The year 454/1062 also marked the point at which Mirdasid Aleppo developed into an autonomous lordship, at least in relation to Byzantium. This signifies that 'autonomous lordships' were not a by-product of the establishment of Seljuq polities or a period of unprecedented crisis and instability, but rather a feature of the political world of *bilad al-sham* which both pre-dated 442/1050, and extended beyond 522/1128.

Finally, Byzantine emperors and their regional delegates attempted to foster relationships with 'local actors' in order to extend Byzantium's influence in northern Syria. Although approaches were extended to individuals from a range of religious and ethno-cultural backgrounds, this key feature of Byzantine diplomatic policy proved to be largely inefficacious. Consequently, Byzantium's failure to navigate the shifting political sands of late fifth/eleventh-century northern Syria was as much a result of diplomatic missteps as it was military failures. These contacts also indicate that there was an established precedent for treaties and alliances that spanned fixed ethno-cultural boundaries in *bilad al-sham*, particularly between Muslim and Christian polities, which long pre-dated the dramatic events of the First Crusade.

Notes

1. Stouraitis, 'Trapped in the Imperial Narrative?' pp. 3–4.
2. Ibn Butlan's description of northern Syria is taken from a letter he wrote to an acquaintance in Baghdad, following his relocation to Antioch. It is therefore possible that the author gave an overly positive report of the 'frontier' province to an acquaintance or friend living in the metropolis of the Islamic Near East. Extracts of the letter were preserved in Yaqut al-Hamawi's chronicle, *Kitab Muʻajam al-Buldan* (dictionary of the countries). See Yaqut al-Hamawi, *Kitab Muʻajam al-Buldan*, 5 vols (Beirut: Dar Sadir, 1977), I, pp. 266–7; Le Strange, *Palestine Under the Moslems*, pp. 370–1.
3. Both Yahya al-Antaki and Ibn al-ʻAdim reported tribute payments by the Mirdasids from 422/1030–1 onwards, see al-Antaki, *Taʼrikh al-Antaki*, pp. 422, 435; IAD ZH, I, 247, 262–3, 268.
4. Speros Vryonis, *The Decline of Medieval Hellenism in Asia Minor and the Process of Islamization from Eleventh through Fifteenth Century* (Berkeley: University California Press, 1971), pp. 68, 70–80.
5. Jean-Claude Cheynet, 'Manzikert: un désastre militaire?', *Byzantion* 50 (1980): 410–38; Jean-Claude Cheynet, 'La résistance aux Turcs en Asie Mineure entre Manzikert et la Première Croisade', in *Eupsykhia: Mélanges offerts à Hélène Ahrweiler*, 2 vols (Paris: Publications de la Sorbonne, 1998), I, pp. 131–47; Clive Foss, 'The Defences of Asia Minor against the Turks', *Greek Orthodox Theological Review* 27 (1982): 145–205; John Haldon, 'Approaches to an Alternate Military History of the Period ca. 1025–1071', in *The Empire in Crisis(?): Byzantium in the Eleventh Century (1025–1081)*, ed. Vassiliki N. Vlyssidou (Athens: Institute for Byzantine Research, 2003), pp. 45–74; Peter Frankopan, *The First Crusade: The Call of the East* (Cambridge, MA: Belknap Press of Harvard University Press, 2012), pp. 42–71. For discussion of climate change as the underlying cause of these developments, see Ronnie Ellenblum, *The Collapse of the Eastern Mediterranean: Climate Change and the Decline of the East 950–1072* (Cambridge: Cambridge University Press, 2012), pp. 88–146; Johannes Preiser-Kapeller, 'A Collapse of the Eastern Mediterranean: New Results and Theories on Interplay between Climate and Societies in Byzantium and the Near East,

ca. 1000–1200 AD', *Jahrbuch der Österteichischen Byzantinistik* 65 (2015): 195–242.

6. al-'Azimi, p. 352; IATH, X, 138–9; SJ, XIII, 158–9; IAD ZH, II, 86–7.
7. Some notable exceptions would be: Catherine Holmes, 'Byzantium's Eastern Frontier in the Tenth and Eleventh Centuries', in *Medieval Frontiers: Concepts and Practices*, ed. David Abulafia and Nora Berend (Aldershot: Routledge, 2002), pp. 83–105; Jean-Claude Cheynet, 'The Duchy of Antioch during the Second Period of Byzantine Rule', in *East and West in the Medieval Eastern Mediterranean I: Antioch from the Byzantine Reconquest until the End of the Crusader Principality*, ed. Krinja Ciggaar and David M. Metcalf (Leuven: Peeters, 2006), pp. 1–16; Beihammer, *Byzantium*, pp. 133–98, 244–65; Zakkar, *Emirate*, pp. 154–204; Bianquis, *Damas*.
8. Michael Decker, 'Frontier Settlement and Economy in the Byzantine East', *Dumbarton Oaks Papers*, 61 (2007), 234–238, 220.
9. Beihammer, *Byzantium*, pp. 55–6.
10. While it is generally believed that there was no settlement at Jisr al-Shugur during the early Crusading period, Ibn al-'Adim made multiple references to Hisn al-Jisr and Qa'lat al-Jisr during his coverage of the fifth/eleventh century. For instance, Ibn al-'Adim asserted that in 470/1077–8 the Türkmen ruler Ahmad Shah, who was in the employ by the Mirdasid ruler of Aleppo, inhabited 'Hisn al-Jisr'. Ibn al-'Adim also claimed that Sadid al-Mulk 'Ali of the Banu Munqidh 'repaired Qa'lat al-Jisr' in 474/1081 in order to pressure the bishop of Albara to relinquish control of Shayzar, whilst al-'Azimi wrote that the 'Turks captured al-Shugur' in 476/1083–4. This indicated that there was a settlement at Jisr al-Shugur in the late fifth/eleventh century. al-'Azimi, p. 344; IAD ZH, II, 56, 66, 76–8. See also Beihammer, *Byzantium*, pp. 189–91; Humphreys, 'Munkidh'.
11. Asbridge, *Creation*, pp. 42–91; Asbridge, 'Field of Blood', pp. 301–16.
12. For more detail on the complexities and nuances of frontiers during the middle ages, see Burns, 'The Significance of the Frontier', pp. 307–30; David Abulafia, 'Introduction: Seven Types of Ambiguity, c. 1100–1500', in *Medieval Frontiers: Concepts and Practices*, ed. David Abulafia and Nora Berend (Aldershot: Ashgate 2002), pp. 1–34; Ellenblum, 'Were there Borders', pp. 105–19; Berend, 'Frontiers', pp. 148–71.
13. The most detailed consideration of this frontier-zone is A. Asa Eger, *The Islamic Byzantine Frontier* (London: Bloomsbury, 2014). For a discussion of 'shared sacred space', see Benjamin Z. Kedar, 'Studying the "Shared Sacred Spaces" of the

Medieval Levant: Where Historians May Meet Anthropologists', *Al-Masaq* 34 (2022): 111–26.

14. *Duqs/Douq/Doux* (duke or commander) is a Latin title that dates back to the Roman Empire and is most commonly found in the Arabic literary sources. Other Byzantine titles and terms with similar applications, such as *katepano* (senior officer), *themata* (administrative or military district) and *strategoi* (military general appointed for specific campaigns), are also used occasionally in the source material. See Jean-Claude Cheynet, 'Les ducs d'Antioche sous Michel IV et Constantin IX', in *Novum Milennium (sic): Studies on Byzantine History and Culture Dedicated to Paul Speck*, ed. C. Sode and S. Takacs (Aldershot: Routledge, 2000), pp. 53–63.
15. On the garrison, see Yaqut al-Hamawi, *Mu'ajam al-Buldan*, I, 266–7; Le Strange, *Palestine Under the Moslems*, pp. 370–1.
16. For a chronology of Byzantine appointees in Antioch during this period, see Vitalien Laurent, 'La Chronologie des Gouverneurs d'Antioche sous la seconde Domination Byzantine', *Mélanges de l'Université Saint-Joseph* 38 (1962): 221–54.
17. Holmes, 'Byzantium's Eastern Frontier', pp. 89–91.
18. For Kulaib and Ubayd Allah's brief periods in control of Antioch, see al-Antaki, *Ta'rikh al-Antaki*, pp. 162–3, 167–71; Laurent, 'La Chronologie des Gouverneurs d'Antioche', pp. 231–2. For more detail on Philaretos Brachamios, see the section at the end of this chapter dealing with Byzantine interactions with local rulers.
19. Beihammer, *Byzantium*, pp. 53, 57–61; Beihammer, 'Muslim Rulers Visiting the Imperial City', pp. 157–77; Holmes, 'Byzantium's Eastern Frontier', pp. 83–105.
20. IAD ZH, I, 262–3, 268; Beihammer, 'Muslim Rulers Visiting the Imperial City', pp. 164–71. *Magistros* was a title that played the dual role of both loose legitimisation from one side and partial supplication from the other.
21. For more detail on the political situation in Syria prior to 442/1050, see Zakkar, *Emirate*, pp. 67–186; Beihammer, *Byzantium*, pp. 99–102; Bianquis and Shamma, 'Mirdas'.
22. al-Antaki, *Ta'rikh al-Antaki*, pp. 422, 435; IAD ZH, I, 247, 262–3, 268. According to both chroniclers, the Mirdasids paid a regular tribute of 500,000 dirhams 'per annum' to Constantinople. Stefan Heidemann has outlined how the collapse of the Abbasid Empire in the fourth/tenth century led to the silver dirham becoming a 'debased copperish coin with no regulated finance or weight' comparable with the anonymous Byzantine copper coins that were imported

into northern Syria between 359 and 485/970 and 1092. This resulted in payments involving silver dirhams being 'transacted by weighing the coins'. Yahya al-Antaki claimed the final agreement specified that 60 dirhams would equate to one piece of gold, which is consistent with the conversion rate of fifty to sixty-seven Byzantine copper coins per gold dinar outlined by Heidemann. Under these terms 500,000 dirhams would amount to approximately 8,333 gold dinars, similar to the '8,000 pieces of gold' noted by Ibn al-'Adim. See Heidemann, *Die Renaissance der Städte*, pp. 355–435, 446–7; Heidemann, 'Numismatics', pp. 648–779, 661.

23. Beihammer, *Byzantium*, pp. 119–20.
24. The tributary relationship between the Mirdasids of Aleppo and the Fatimid Caliphate is discussed in Chapter 2. See also Wilson, 'The Ransom of High-ranking Captives', pp. 23–8.
25. IM, pp. 13–14; SJ, XII, 267–8; al-Maqrizi, I, 230–1. For more details on this dispute, and discrepancies between the various Arabic and Greek sources, see Mathew Barber, 'Reappraising the Arabic Accounts for the Conflict of 446/1054–5: An Egyptian Perspective on Constantine IX and His Immediate Successors', in *Transmitting and Circulating the Late Antique and Byzantine World*, ed. Mirela Ivanova and Hugh Jeffrey (Leiden: Brill, 2020), pp. 170–98; Beihammer, *Byzantium*, pp. 100–2; Halm, *Die Kalifen von Kairo*, pp. 380–3; Brett, *Empire*, pp. 192–3;
26. On the diplomatic significance attached to 'the mosque of Constantinople', see Glaire D. Anderson, 'Islamic Spaces and Diplomacy in Constantinople (Tenth to Thirteenth Centuries)', *Medieval Encounters* 15 (2009): 86–113, 101–2.
27. al-'Azimi, p. 343; IM, p. 14.
28. IAD ZH, I, 286. The precise location of could not be identified. Qastun/Qastoûn was located on the southern edge of the al-Ghab valley in the region of Jabal al-Summaq, also known as Jabal Zawiya. For more information on Qastun, see Yaqut, *Mu'ajam al-Buldan*, IV, 348; Cahen, *Syrie*, pp. 141, 161, 274, 285; Deschamps, *Les châteaux*, III, pp. 61, 63, 84, 88, 89.
29. The Byzantine commander could also have been Nikephoros Sebastophoros, who according to Laurent, was appointed *dux* of Antioch in 454/1062, see Laurent, 'La Chronologie des Gouverneurs d'Antioche', p. 244.
30. SJ, XII, 398–9; IAD ZH, I, 287. The precise location of al-Karim Bismiran could not be identified. Sibt b. al-Jawzi designated 'Aryah' as the location of the battle. This is probably Artah, as his account specifies that the battle took place 'six parasangs' (approximately 21 miles) away from Aleppo, which roughly corresponds

to Artah's location, while Ibn al-'Adim provides partial corroboration that the Mirdasids captured Artah this year. On the Arabic term Rasm, see Halil Inalcik, 'Resm', in *Encyclopaedia of Islam*, 2nd edn, ed. Peri Bearman et al. (2012), available at Brill online, last accessed 15 June 2019.

31. The strategic importance of Artah is discussed in more detail in Chapter 5 in relation to the frontiers of Aleppo.
32. For more detail on Artah, see 'Izz al-Din Muhammad b. 'Ali Ibn Shaddad, *al-A'laq al-khatira fi dikr umara' al-Sham wa'l-Jazira*, 2 vols, I/I (Damascus: Institut Français de Damas, 1953), ed. Dominique Sourdel, I/II (Damascus: Wizarat al-Thaqafa, 1991), ed. Yahya Zakariya 'Abbara, II (Damascus: Institut Français de Damas, 1956), ed. Sami Dahan, I/I, 15; 'Izz al-Din Ibn Shaddad, *Description de La Syrie du Nord*, trans. Anne-Marie Eddé-Terrasse (Damascus: Institut Français de Damas, 1984), pp. 270–3; Yaqut, *Mu'ajam al-Buldan*, IV, 348; Dussaud, *Topographie historique*, pp. 225–8; Cahen, *Syrie*, pp. 133–6; Deschamps, *Les châteaux*, III, pp. 59–61; Burns, *Monuments of Syria*, p. 168; Asbridge, *Creation*, pp. 47–91; Asbridge, 'Field of Blood', pp. 309–11.
33. For more detail on this Mirdasid succession crisis, see Zakkar, *Emirate*, pp. 165–8; Bianquis, *Damas*, II, pp. 568–88; Bianquis and Shamma, 'Mirdas'.
34. For more detail on Türkmen groups and their complex relationship with the Greater Seljuq Sultanate and the political elite of *bilad al-sham*, see Chapter 3.
35. According to Ibn al-'Adim: 'these were the first Turks to enter *al-sham*'. On the appearance of Ibn Khan in northern Syria, see al-'Azimi, pp. 345–6; IAD ZH, I, 294–5. It is difficult to provide a definitive date for the arrival of Türkmen in northern Syria, but it seems most likely that it was at some point between 452 and 455/1060 and 1063. If Türkmen bands had been present in northern Syria prior to this date, it is probable that Türkmen troops would have participated in the battle between Mirdasid and Fatimid troops at al-Funaydiq in 452/1060, and that this would have been noted in the source material. Although Andrew Peacock and Alexander Beihammer have outlined how the prevalence of pasturelands in eastern Anatolia made the area a more attractive target for nomadic Türkmen than Syria, an additional explanation could be that Seljuq control of northern Iraq remained patchy until Sharaf al-Dawla Muslim b. Quraysh (r. 453–78/1061–85) became ruler of the Banu 'Uqayl in 453/1061. As the Banu Uqayl controlled much of Mesopotamia, their frequently hostile relations with the Seljuq sultans prior to 453/1061 may have limited Türkmen access to northern Syria. On Türkmen activity in Anatolia prior to 455/1063, see Andrew C. S.

Peacock, 'Nomadic Society and the Seljuq Campaigns in Caucasia', *Iran and Caucasus* 9 (2005): 205–30; Jason T. Roche, 'In the Wake of Mantzikert: the First Crusade and the Alexian Reconquest of Western Anatolia', *History* 94 (2009): 135–53; Beihammer, *Byzantium*, pp. 74–80. The earliest references to Türkmen raids upon Syria in Syriac sources were dated to 1066 and 1068, respectively, see Michael the Syrian, *Syriac Chronicle*, p. 610; Bar Habraeus, *Chronography*, p. 218.

36. Ibn Khan had previously been allied to Mahmud's uncle, 'Atiyya b. Salih, before later switching his allegiance to Mahmud. al-'Azimi, pp. 345–6; SJ, XII, 345; IAD ZH, I, 294–7, II, 9. See also Zakkar, *Emirate*, pp. 166–8; Beihammer, *Byzantium*, pp. 110–11, 117–21.

37. IAD ZH, I, 296. Ibn al-'Adim stated that the Antiochenes gave Mahmud '50 dinars a day' and '300 *mithqal*' of gold, amounting to approximately 942 grams, 400 silver dirhams or 7 gold dinars. According to Walther Hinz, who used the writings of the Syrian-based market inspector (*muhtasib*) 'Abd al-Rahman b. Nasr al-Shayzari (d. 589/1193) as a reference, one *mithqal* equated to 3.14 grams or 5/12 of 1 dirham in Syria during this period. See Walther Hinz, *Islamische Masse und Gewichte. Umgerechnet ins Metrische System* (Leiden: Brill, 1970), p. 4; Heidemann, 'Numismatics', p. 656.

38. IAD ZH, II, 12–13.

39. ME, p. 125.

40. IAD, ZH, II, 11–12; Bar Habraeus, *Chronography*, p. 218. Corroboration of the severe impact of this raid can be found in Michael Attaleiates, who as a result of his participation in Romanos Diogenes IV's campaign in Syria the following year was able to provide an emotive, first-hand description of the damage done to rural communities in the region of Antioch during Afshin's attack. See Attaleiates, *The History*, pp. 173–4, 215–19.

41. For more detail, see Angold, *Byzantine Empire*, pp. 16–17, 31–3.

42. For more information on these raids, see Beihammer, *Byzantium*, pp. 104–24, 138; Peacock, *Empire*, pp. 52–9; Peacock, 'Nomadic Society and the Seljuq Campaigns in Caucasia', pp. 205–30.

43. al-'Azimi, p. 347; SJ, XII, 461–2; IAD ZH, II, 13–14; Attaleiates, *The History*, pp. 199–219; MS, p. 609; Bar Habraeus, *Chronography*, p. 218.

44. IAD, II, 16.

45. The strategic importance of 'Azaz, which is to the northwest of Aleppo, is discussed in detail in Chapter 5.

46. IQ, p. 165; IAD ZH, II, 14. For more information on Asfuna/Asfoûna, see

Yaqut, *Mu'ajam al-Buldan*, I, 179; Dussaud, *Topographie historique*, pp. 186, 191; Cahen, *Syrie*, pp. 162–3, 177.
47. al-'Azimi, pp. 347–8; IQ, pp. 166–8; SJ, XII, 481–5; IAD ZH, II, 24–7; Attaleiates, *The History*, pp. 275–303; MS, p. 609; ME, pp. 132–6; Bar Habraeus, *Chronography*, pp. 220–2.
48. For more on the battle of Manzikert and its significance, see Cheynet, 'Manzikert: un désastre militaire?' pp. 410–38; Angold, *Byzantine Empire*, pp. 44–8; Hillenbrand, *Turkish Myth and Symbol*; Beihammer, *Byzantium*, pp. 155–61.
49. For more detail on Byzantium's western and northern frontiers, see Angold, *Byzantine Empire*, pp. 121–3, 129–34. For Byzantine influence upon the First Crusade, see Frankopan, *The First Crusade*.
50. For the definition of autonomous lordship used in this book, see the introductory section of Part I.
51. For more detail on *khidma* and the *khutba*, see the introductory section of Part I. IQ, pp. 165–6; al-'Azimi, p. 343; IATH, X, 64; SJ, XII, 481–2; IAD ZH, II, 16–23.
52. Alp Arslan's campaign is discussed in detail in Chapters 2 and 3. Beihammer argued that Alp Arslan's campaign 'basically dissolved the Byzantine web of Muslim vassals at the outer range of the frontier zone'. Beihammer, *Byzantium*, p. 155.
53. IAD ZH, II, 31. Ma'rrat Misrin is about half way between Antioch and Aleppo, to the north of the Jabal al-Summaq area, see Figure 2.1 and Ibn Shaddad, *al-A'laq al-khatira*, I/I, p. 153; Ibn Shaddad, *Description de La Syrie*, pp. 30–2; IAD BH, I, 133–4; Yaqut, *Mu'ajam al-Buldan*, V, 155–6; Dussaud, *Topographie historique*, pp. 170–2; Cahen, *Syrie*, pp. 153, 156. For more on the involvement of the Banu Kilab and 'Atiyya b. Salih in this failed attack on Ma'rrat Misrin, see the section at the end of this chapter dealing with Byzantine interactions with local rulers.
54. IAD ZH, II, 42.
55. Nikephoros Byrennios, *Nicephori Byrennii Historiarum libri quattuor*, trans. Paul Gautier (Brussels: Byzantion, 1975), pp. 204–6.
56. SJ, XIII, 72–3. Ibn al-'Adim's account of this event differs slightly, as he described a band of Türkmen from Anatolia led by an 'Muhammad b. Dimlaj' arriving in northern Syria on 11 Dhu 'l-Ka'da 468/16 July 1076, see IAD BH, IX, 4078. The sum of 20,000 dinars also matches the ransom paid to Türkmen forces for the *dux* of Edessa, who was taken captive in 458/1066, see Bar Habraeus, *Chronography*, pp. 217–18.

57. On the tensions between the imperial court in Constantinople and the provincial experiences of Byzantine rule, see Stouraitis, 'Trapped in the Imperial Narrative?' pp. 166–92.
58. IAD ZH, II, 46; Bar Habraeus, *Chronography*, p. 225.
59. SJ, XIII, 105.
60. SJ, XII, 120; IAD ZH, II, 56, 67.
61. ME, pp. 143–4.
62. IQ, p. 184; al-'Azimi, p. 351; SJ, XIII, 133; IAD ZH, II, 65–6, 76–7; IAD BH, I, 145–7. The denomination of the 'Bishop of Albara' is not provided in the literary sources. The Banu Munqidh and their occupation of Shayzar is discussed in relation to the frontiers of Aleppo in Chapter 5.
63. SJ, XII, 141.
64. The career of Sharaf al-Dawla Muslim b. Quraysh, and his opaque connection with the Great Seljuq Sultanate, is discussed in Chapter 3.
65. al-'Azimi, p. 352. Only Sibt b. al-Jawzi recorded the terms of the treaty, see SJ, XIII, 139.
66. IATH, X, 139–40; IAD ZH, II, 89–92; Bar Habraeus, *Chronography*, pp. 229–30.
67. al-'Azimi, p. 352; IATH, X, 138–9; SJ, XII, 158–9; IAD ZH, II, 86–7; MS, p. 612; ME, pp. 147–8; Bar Habraeus, *Chronography*, p. 227; Komnene, *The Alexiad*, pp. 169–70. Sulayman b. Qutlumush and his links to the Byzantine Empire are discussed in the section at the end of this chapter focusing on Byzantine interactions with local rulers.
68. SJ, XIII, 179; IAD ZH, II, 100; IATH, X, 162; ME, p. 154.
69. IM, pp. 7–8.
70. IAD ZH, I, 262–3, 268, 281–2, 296.
71. al-'Azimi, p. 348; SJ, XIII, 81; IAD ZH, II, 31. According to the Arabic sources, 'Atiyya, who was supposedly drunk at the time, died in Constantinople when a building collapsed on him. The comic nature of this story is a probably a literary trope, intended to humiliate a Muslim ruler collaborating with Byzantium against Aleppan interests. For context, see Beihammer, 'Muslim Rulers Visiting the Imperial City', pp. 157–77.
72. Ibn al-'Adim noted upon Ibn Khan's arrival in Aleppo that 'the Byzantines had previously tried to get him to enter their service with money'. IAD ZH, I, 294–5.
73. IAD ZH, II, 13.
74. IAD, ZH, I, 295–6, II, 9.
75. Frankopan asserted that after 474/1081 Sulayman became an 'agent' of Alexios I Komnenos, and that Sulayman's capture of Antioch in 477/1084 was part of

the emperor's strategy to remove Philaretos Brachamios. Frankopan, *The First Crusade*, pp. 46–52.
76. Peacock, *Empire*, pp. 131–2.
77. Beihammer, *Byzantium*, pp. 204–34.
78. Bar Habraeus, *Chronography*, p. 229.
79. There were other figures who attempted to bridge similar ethno-cultural divides, such as the 'Seljuq' rulers Atsiz b. Uwaq, Tutush b. Alp Arslan, his son Ridwan b. Tutush, Sharaf al-Dawla Muslim b. Quraysh and Tughtegin, all of whom are discussed in Chapters 2 and 3.
80. Alexander D. Beihammer, 'Defection across the Border of Islam and Christianity: Apostasy and Cross-Cultural Interaction in Byzantine–Seljuk Relations', *Speculum* 86 (2011): 597–691; Alexander D. Beihammer, 'Christian Views of Islam in Early Seljuq Anatolia: Perceptions and Reactions', in *Islam and Christianity in Medieval Anatolia*, ed. Andrew C. S. Peacock, Bruno De Nicola and Sara Nur Yildiz (London: Routledge, 2015), pp. 51–76; C. J. Yarnley, 'Philaretos: Armenian Bandit or Byzantine General?' *Revue des études arméniennes* 9 (1972): 331–53; Gérard Dédéyan, *Les arméniens entre grecs, musulmans et croisés. Étude sur les pouvoirs arméniens dans le Proche-Orient méditerranéen (1068–1150)*, 2 vols (Lisbon: Fundação Calouste Gulbenkian, 2003), I, pp. 287–357; Cheynet, 'The Duchy of Antioch', pp. 13–15.
81. Dédéyan, *Les arméniens entre grecs*, II, p. 32; John H. Pryor and Michael J. Jeffreys, 'Alexius, Bohemond and Byzantium's Euphrates Frontier: a Tale of Two Cretans', *Crusades* 11 (2012): 31–86, 35–8, 83; Beihammer, *Byzantium*, p. 285.
82. ME, pp. 147–8; Bar Habraeus, *Chronography*, p. 229.
83. MS, p. 612; ME, p. 141; Bar Habraeus, *Chronography*, p. 229.
84. Holmes, 'Byzantium's Eastern Frontier', pp. 94–5.
85. IATH, X, 138–9; SJ, XIII, 131; Komnene, *The Alexiad*, pp. 169–70; MS, p. 612; ME, pp. 152–53; Bar Habraeus, *Chronography*, p. 229. In 458/1066 there was a comparable, reportedly 'unwilling' conversion of Armenian troops, led by Aristakis, who like Philaretos, repented and returned to Christianity prior to their deaths, see Bar Habraeus, *Chronography*, p. 218. For additional context, see Frankopan, *The First Crusade*, pp. 46–52; Beihammer, *Byzantium*, pp. 285–90; Yarnley, 'Philaretos: Armenian Bandit or Byzantine General?', pp. 331–53.
86. al-'Azimi, p. 348.
87. SJ, XIII, 131. Philaretos' successor in Melitene also reportedly sent for legitimisation to Baghdad, see MS, pp. 615–16.

88. For more information on Fatimid interaction with local rulers, see Chapter 2.
89. Beihammer has provided the most detailed chronology for Byzantine territorial losses in Anatolia. Beihammer, *Byzantium*, pp. 198–243, 265–303.

2

The Fatimid Caliphate

Fatimid *Bilad al-sham*

Much like the Byzantine Empire, the Fatimid Caliphate had long-standing territorial interests in *bilad al-sham* that dated back to the fourth/tenth century. The Mirdasid dynasty had wrested Aleppo from Fatimid control in 416/1025, and although the Egyptians regained the city briefly between 429 and 433/1038 and 1042, dominion over Aleppo for a sustained period proved to be elusive. Instead, Cairo had to settle for intermittent tribute payments and the *khutba* in Aleppo being made in the name of the Fatimid caliph, which had been common practice in the city since 360/970.[1] The Egypt-based caliphate also maintained control of the coastline settlements in *bilad al-sham* from Tripoli southwards, in addition to Damascus and Jerusalem further inland.

A thirty-five-year period of crisis from 437/1045 resulted in a sharp decline in Fatimid influence in Syria, in addition to significant territorial losses in Sicily, North Africa, Yemen and Arabia. The main causes of this crisis were a combination of severe drought in Egypt as a result of low water levels in the Nile, the outbreak of civil war in Egypt between rival factions of the military, and the declining influence of the bureaucratic class, known broadly as 'the men of the pen', who were replaced by military figures like Badr al-Jamali.[2] Ronnie Ellenblum has pointed to evidence of climate change along the Nile delta and on the Eurasian Steppe as the source of the political turmoil afflicting Egypt and the eastern Mediterranean during this period.[3]

Much of the analysis of events in northern Syria has been framed in the context of this wider Fatimid decline. Michael Brett's comprehensive work on the Fatimid Caliphate, for example, attributed developments in Tyre, Aleppo and the region as a whole to an ongoing 'growth of municipal autonomy' throughout the Mediterranean, rather than anything specific to northern Syria.[4] There has been some research on Fatimid policy in fifth/eleventh-century Syria and Palestine, though Bramoullé and Bianquis, Mouton and Yared-Riachi focused more on Damascus, the coastal settlements of Tyre, Acre and Tripoli, and the Red Sea.[5] To date, Fatimid activity in the northern parts of the region, and in particular their interactions with the emergent 'Seljuq' potentates, has largely been overlooked.[6]

The curtailment of Fatimid influence in *bilad al-sham* during the late fifth/eleventh century has largely been attributed to the arrival of 'Seljuq' rulers from 463/1071 onwards.[7] The first part of this chapter reassesses the chronology and causes of this decline in Fatimid regional authority, highlighting the significance of the defeat suffered by Egyptian forces to the Mirdasids at al-Funaydiq in 452/1060, and the resulting territorial losses.[8] It also details how Fatimid territorial priorities in *bilad al-sham* shifted over time. As Egyptian influence in northern *bilad al-sham* dwindled, their objectives moved further southwards, shifting from Aleppo to Damascus, before eventually moving on to Jerusalem.

The second part discusses evidence of interaction, and even collaboration, between 'Seljuq' figures and the Fatimid Caliphate during the latter half of the fifth/eleventh century. These contacts and alliances provide insight into pragmatic approaches from political actors operating on both sides of what is often portrayed as an irrevocable doctrinal divide. This raises questions about fixed conceptualisations of 'Fatimid' or 'Seljuq' rulers within the political world of *bilad al-sham*. Fatimid readiness to cooperate with Seljuq rulers not only facilitates a nuanced interpretation of the political landscape into which the Frankish Crusaders entered; it also helps to contextualise the strategies employed by the Egyptian hierarchy during the early decades of the sixth/twelfth century.

Cairo's Shifting Territorial Priorities in Bilad al-sham

As with the Byzantine Empire, the Fatimid Caliphate had developed a system of appointing governors that stemmed from several decades of exerting authority over regions as diverse as Sicily, Libya, Arabia, Yemen, Palestine and Syria. In 442/1050, Fatimid appointees governed most of the coastal settlements of *bilad al-sham* with key the port settlements of Acre, Tyre and Tripoli being of principal importance to their trading interests in the region.

Further inland, Fatimid dominion over Jerusalem and Damascus dated back to 359/969 and 372/983, respectively. They were among the first settlements occupied by the Fatimid Caliphate when they emerged as realistic challengers to the Abbasids of Baghdad in the Near East. Fatimid authority in Aleppo was more ambiguous. Egyptian policy in northern Syria was dependent upon maintaining a dominant relationship with the Mirdasid dynasty, which had repeatedly foiled their attempts to permanently annex the settlement to the caliphate. The Fatimids occupied Aleppo briefly between 429 and 433/1038 and 1042, and two attempts to retake the city in 440/1048 and 441/1049 failed.[9]

Aleppo, Damascus and Jerusalem played a key strategic role as a buffer zone, which protected both their lucrative commercial hubs on the coastline, and Egypt itself, from overland incursions. Aleppo was seen as particularly important for keeping Byzantine ambitions in northern Syria in check, and the city often found itself at the epicentre of most military encounters between Cairo and Constantinople. As Egyptian influence in *bilad al-sham* collapsed during the latter half of the fifth/eleventh century, control of settlements inland and the maintenance of this buffer zone remained one of Cairo's main priorities. Consequently, Fatimid ambitions shifted southwards, with control of Damascus, then Jerusalem and, finally, Ascalon, becoming fundamental in order to protect Egypt from the threat of land invasion.

Many of these settlements were also locations of devotional importance. The Aqsa mosque in Jerusalem is widely accepted to have been the scene of Muhammad's night journey (*isra'*) and ascension (*mi'raj*), while Damascus had historically served as the capital of the Umayyad Caliphate.[10] Ascalon also came to take on more religious significance during late fifth/eleventh century, due to the construction of a congregational mosque and shrine for the head of the martyred al-Husayn b. 'Ali b. Abi Talib by the Fatimid Vizier Badr al-Jamali.[11] In comparison, it may seem that Aleppo would have held less religious importance for the Fatimids, but the city was viewed as the key to any future Egyptian invasion of Iraq. One fourth/tenth-century Fatimid commander named Bakjur labelled Aleppo 'the entrance hall of Iraq'.[12] Control, or the impression of control, over these settlements supplemented Fatimid claims of being legitimate challengers to the Abbasid Caliphate in Baghdad. Loss of influence over these settlements not only increased the risk of overland invasion into Egypt, but also damaged Fatimid prestige, calling into question the viability of their *raison d'être*, establishing hegemony over the Abbasids.

The Fatimid Political Footprint in Northern Syria: 442–63/1050–71

Ibn al-ʿAdim reported that in 442/1050 the Mirdasid ruler of Aleppo Thimal b. Salih 'earned the affection of al-Mustansir after he sent him 40,000 dinars from the citadel' in lieu of two years' tribute, before later being confirmed as ruler of Aleppo.[13] The original dispute in 440/1048 had been triggered by Thimal's refusal to pay the customary annual tribute, and return funds that had been in the possession of al-Duzbari, the previous Fatimid governor of Aleppo. Thimal's willingness to recommence these payments in 442/1050 represented a return to Fatimid obedience by Mirdasid Aleppo, even if physical occupation continued to prove elusive for the Egyptian Caliphate.

Al-Muʾayyad fiʾl-Din al-Shirazi and the Fatimid Occupation of Baghdad

Only a few years later in 449/1058, another opportunity for the Fatimids to capture Aleppo presented itself. This came about as part of a wider plan to achieve their ultimate goal: the conquest of Baghdad. The approach of the Seljuq Sultan Tughrul Beg's armies towards Baghdad in 447/1055 had forced the former Buyid commander of the Turkish forces in the city, al-Basasiri, to withdraw westwards. When he reached Rahba on the River Euphrates, he sent an appeal to Cairo for assistance. The Fatimid Vizier al-Yazuri, sensing an opportunity, assented to support him with alacrity. The head of the Egyptian chancery, al-Muʾayyad fiʾl-Din al-Shirazi, was dispatched to northern Syria in 447/1056 with huge financial backing, more than 2 million dinars according to al-Maqrizi, and additional military equipment. Al-Muʾayyad was instructed to establish a coalition, initially formed from the troops of Damascus, the Mirdasids of Aleppo and the Arab tribes of the Banu Kalb and Banu Kilab.[14]

Al-Basasiri managed to capture Baghdad in Shawwal 451/December 1058, achieving the stated aim of the Fatimid Caliphate since its inception, but this proved to be a Pyrrhic victory. The Abbasid Caliph al-Qaʾim remained out of the Fatimids' reach, safely ensconced with a Bedouin leader named

Muharish at Hadithat al-Furat on the River Euphrates. Muharish refused to surrender al-Qa'im to the Fatimids despite being offered large financial incentives to do so. Tughrul Beg recaptured Baghdad a year later and al-Basasiri was again forced to retreat westwards towards the Euphrates, where he was eventually captured and killed in 452/1060. Ultimately, Cairo's decision to back al-Basasiri proved to be hugely risky, expending large quantities of Egyptian military and financial resources for little long-term gain.

The Final Fatimid Occupation of Aleppo: 450–2/1058–60

Whilst the al-Basasiri venture in Baghdad ended in failure, the presence of the Fatimid courtier al-Mu'ayyad fi'l-Din al-Shirazi in northern Syria facilitated the Egyptian occupation of Aleppo in 450/1058. Thimal b. Salih came to an accommodation with al-Mu'ayyad to surrender Aleppo in exchange for Acre, Jubayl, Beirut, Caesarea, Sidon and other settlements on the Palestinian coast in 448/1057, and Ibn Mulhim took up his position as Fatimid governor of Aleppo in Dhu 'l-Qa'da 448/January 1058.[15] Although Suhayl Zakkar has argued that Thimal may have been given only nominal control or the incomes from these settlements, the ceding of these coastal settlements reinforces the importance Cairo placed upon physical control of Aleppo.[16]

Initially, remnant members of the Mirdasid dynasty and their allies in the Arab tribes of the Banu Kilab and Banu Numayr were unable to respond to the loss of Aleppo. This changed with the death of al-Basasiri in 452/1060. In Safar 452/April 1060, 'Atiyya b. Salih, Thimal's brother, captured Rahba and took all the funds, provisions and military equipment that al-Basasiri had stored there.[17] While the loss of Rahba and al-Basasiri's cash reserves would have been a blow to the Fatimids, 'Atiyya also established the *khutba* in the city for the Abbasid caliph and the Seljuq sultan. 'Atiyya even travelled to Baghdad to perform *khidma* according to Sibt b. al-Jawzi.

This was the earliest indication of what would become a growing trend of cooperation and eventual submission to the Seljuqs by members of the Mirdasid dynasty. It also demonstrated how in their determination to occupy Baghdad, the Fatimids had failed to fully appreciate the fragile political situation in northern Syria and the tensions their presence provoked.

The Battle of al-Funaydiq and its Aftermath: 452–62/1060–70

Sensing Fatimid weakness following the fall of Rahba, Mahmud b. Nasr, the nephew of both Thimal and 'Atiyya, managed to briefly seize control of Aleppo with a small force in Jumada I 452/June 1060. However, as Mahmud was unable to take the citadel, he was forced to withdraw from the city shortly afterwards.[18]

This act of aggression provoked an immediate response from Cairo, with the Fatimid governor of Damascus, Nasir al-Dawla Husayn b. Hamdan, ordered to march north to Aleppo to assist Ibn Mulhim and the Egyptian garrison. On 30 Rajab 452/30 August 1060, Fatimid forces engaged Mahmud and the Banu Kilab in battle at al-Funaydiq, a short distance to the south of Aleppo.[19] The Damascene army was defeated, with Nasir al-Dawla wounded and taken captive. After the battle Ibn Mulhim surrendered Aleppo and the citadel to Mahmud.[20]

With his own ambitions now thwarted by his nephew's occupation of Aleppo, 'Atiyya 'reconciled with the lord of Egypt and entered into a treaty with him', according to Sibt b. al-Jawzi.[21] When informed of developments at al-Funaydiq, al-Mustansir pressed Thimal to return to Aleppo and retake control of the settlement as his vassal. Thimal successfully regained control of the city a year later following a short siege, which culminated in the negotiated surrender of Aleppo by Mahmud in 453/1061.[22] Ibn Mulhim would be the last governor in Aleppo directly appointed by the caliph's court in Cairo. Yet again, Fatimid attempts to permanently occupy Aleppo were frustrated by the military resistance of the Mirdasid dynasty and their Arab Bedouin allies.

Events at al-Funaydiq had two long-term implications for Fatimid influence in northern Syria. The first was a fundamental transformation in how the Mirdasids interacted with the Fatimid Caliphate. Although Thimal's return to Aleppo as al-Mustansir's deputy in 453/1061 marked a return to the earlier status quo, Thimal died the following year in 454/1062. A dispute over who should succeed him broke out between his nephew Mahmud and his brother 'Atiyya, from which Mahmud would eventually emerge victorious in Ramadan 458/August 1067.[23]

Al-Mustansir, much like his Byzantine rivals, would come to find Mahmud far less pliable than his uncle Thimal had been. Upon taking control of Aleppo,

Mahmud dispatched a delegation to Baghdad, led by his Türkmen ally Ibn Khan, who soon returned with a letter of legitimisation from the Abbasid caliph.[24] Mahmud also began defying directives from Cairo. Sibt b. al-Jawzi reported that in 459/1067–8, the Fatimid Caliph al-Mustansir sent to Mahmud ordering him 'to pay money into his treasury and to expedite the invasion of neighbouring Byzantine territory'. The message also commanded him to cease any association with Türkmen groups in order to 'refrain from their corruption'. Mahmud promptly refused to pay a tribute to the Fatimids, giving the rather weak excuse that he had no funds available. He also declined to attack the Byzantines as they had lent him money and taken his son hostage to ensure repayment.[25] These same circumstances had not prevented Mahmud from launching raids on Antiochene territory throughout much of his reign.[26] This reported exchange demonstrated the extent to which Fatimid influence over Mirdasid Aleppo had deteriorated in the years after the battle of al-Funaydiq. Mahmud's rise to power had undercut the Fatimid hierarchy's influence in Aleppo, and they were unable to reassert their influence through military expeditions.

Although the prolonged period of famine, plague and civil war engulfing Egypt at this juncture would have severely hampered any attempt to revive Fatimid authority in northern Syria, their inability to campaign in the region was greatly restricted by the second long-term implication of the defeat at al-Funaydiq: the loss of control over all territorial possessions north of Baalbek in the ensuing decade.

Traditionally, Egyptian rulers had used Damascus as a command centre for expeditions into northern Syria.[27] Both the 440/1048 campaign against Aleppo, and the Fatimid forces at al-Funaydiq were led by the Fatimid governor of Damascus, the diplomatic mission led by al-Mu'ayyad fi'l-Din al-Shirazi had absorbed troops from Damascus into his entourage in 447/1056. The Egyptian army that targeted Aleppo in 441/1049, commanded by the Amir Rifq, had also stopped at Damascus. Once in northern *bilad al-sham* these armies tended to take a similar route north, through Baalbek, Homs and Hama, then past Ma'rrat al-Nu'man and Qinnasrin before arriving at Aleppo.[28] For the Fatimids, retaining influence in at least some of these settlements was necessary for any future attempt to exert military pressure on Aleppo.

However, most of these settlements fell to Thimal, Mahmud or 'Atiyya in the decade following the battle of al-Funaydiq in 452/1060. Homs and

THE FATIMID CALIPHATE | 77

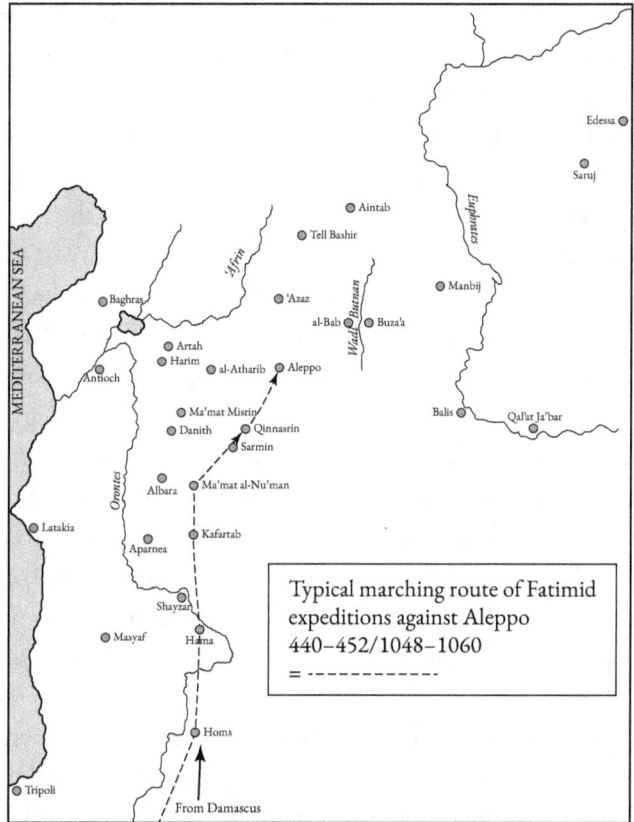

Figure 2.1 Typical Fatimid marching route to Aleppo: 440–52/1048–60

Hama had been captured and their fortifications destroyed by ʿAtiyya prior to the battle at al-Funaydiq. While Nasir al-Dawla and then Thimal had subsequently stayed at Homs on their way north, ʿAtiyya was again residing in the settlement by 458/1065.[29]

Apamea was 'secured' by Mahmud during the course of 452/1060, whilst Thimal took Maʿrrat al-Nuʿman and Qinnasrin in the same year.[30] Al-Atharib, which, according to Ibn al-ʿAdim, the Mirdasids 'had not held since the time before Thimal's reign', was also absorbed into Mahmud's territorial possessions in 457/1065, although it is unclear if the settlement was taken from a Byzantine, Fatimid or independent ruler.[31] The only settlement that the Fatimids gained control of during this period was the fortress of Asfuna close to Maʿrrat al-Nuʿman, which the commander Hussayn b. Kamil b. al-Duh surrendered in 458/1066 to an 'Egyptian garrison'. Ibn al-'Adim asserted that Mahmud managed to recapture the fortress two years later when a 'north African commander' surrendered it to him.[32]

The significance of the battle of al-Funaydiq has been overlooked in the historiography to date. It is only once the loss of these northern Syrian settlements are taken into account that the consequences of the Fatimid defeat at al-Funaydiq can be fully understood. Prior to 452/1060, Cairo could always deploy military deterrents against the Mirdasids. Less than a year after al-Funaydiq, most of the settlements between Damascus and Aleppo were under Mirdasid rule, providing a buffer zone against incursions from the south. This meant that there was no realistic prospect of an Egyptian army threatening the security of Aleppo from this point onwards. From the perspective of territory lost as a consequence of a battle, al-Funaydiq was one of the most consequential military engagements in northern Syria between 442 and 522/1050 and 1128, comparable with events at Antioch in 491/1098 or the battle of the Field of Blood in 513/1119.[33] These Mirdasid territorial gains provide a rationale for Mahmud's refusal to follow direct instructions from al-Mustansir.

Additionally, the simultaneous cessation of tribute payments to both Constantinople and Cairo would have freed up additional funds with which to recruit Türkmen leaders such as Ibn Khan.[34] Indeed, modern historians have argued that the influence of these Türkmen potentates grew in Aleppo to such an extent during this period that Mirdasid rulers were reduced to mere figureheads.[35] Yet at some point during the 450s/1060s, Mahmud was able to expel Ibn Khan, seemingly without much difficulty, following a failed plot on Mahmud's life.[36] This suggests that at least during Mahmud's reign, the Mirdasid's managed to retain their authority within Aleppo. Instead, it seems more likely that Türkmen power became more steadily entrenched during the succession crisis that followed Mahmud's death in Sha'ban 468/March 1076, and the violent death suffered by his son and heir a couple of months later.[37]

Ultimately, Fatimid control in northern Syria was dealt a critical blow at al-Funaydiq in 452/1060, from which they were not able to recover. It also marked the point at which the Amirate of Aleppo became an 'autonomous lordship', freed from the constrains of Fatimid interference.[38]

Alp Arslan's Campaign against Aleppo: 463/1071

Following the defeat at al-Funaydiq, the last semblance of Egyptian influence in Aleppo lay in the *khutba* being made in the name of the al-Mustansir. Even though Mahmud had applied for legitimisation from Baghdad and ceased paying a regular tribute to Cairo, the *khutba* had remained in the name of the Fatimid caliph.

This changed on 19 Shawwal 462/31 July 1070, when al-Mustansir's name in the sermon given in mosques prior to Friday midday prayers was replaced by that of the Abbasid Caliph al-Qa'im.[39] This was seemingly in preparation for the arrival of the Seljuq Sultan Alp Arslan, although both al-'Azimi and Sibt b. al-Jawzi mentioned that the Fatimids persuaded Mahmud to revert the *khutba* to al-Mustansir prior to Alp Arslan's arrival in 463/1071.[40] Alp Arslan's army then besieged Aleppo for a month between Tuesday 17 Jumada II and 23 Rajab 463/22 March and 26 April 1071, before Mahmud surrendered to the sultan.[41] As part of this process Mahmud personally performed *khidma* to the sultan, which he had refused to do before the siege, and again switched the *khutba* to the Abbasids.[42]

This in and of itself would have been a catastrophic development for the Fatimid Caliphate, but Mahmud went a step further. He also 'promised to attack Damascus and the Egyptians there' according to Ibn al-'Adim.[43] Mahmud attempted to make good on this promise almost immediately. He launched an attack on Baalbek in Sha'ban 463/May 1071, but was forced to withdraw northwards in order to repel a Byzantine attack on Ma'rrat Misrin.[44] By making this commitment, Mahmud effectively became a client ruler of the Seljuq sultan.

Not only did the last symbol of Fatimid influence over Mirdasid Aleppo come to an end as a result of Alp Arslan's campaign, Aleppo had now become an openly hostile polity capable of launching military expeditions against Egyptian interests. The arrival of the Seljuqs in Syria has often been identified as the key to this development, and this is certainly accurate with regard to the switching of the *khutba*. However, increasing Mirdasid autonomy, demonstrated by Mahmud's appeal for legitimisation from Baghdad in 458/1067 and his refusal to renew tribute payments or follow al-Mustansir's orders in 459/1067–8, had been growing since the battle of al-Funaydiq in 452/1060.

This loss of Egyptian leverage in Aleppo was a blow to both Fatimid prestige and their ability to achieve their wider strategic aims in the region. It also increased the risk of future attacks against key settlements in southern Syria, Palestine and even Egypt. As a consequence, their focus shifted southwards and towards the coastal settlements.

The Fatimid Collapse in Southern Syria and Palestine

Civil war in Egypt: 460–8/1067–76

The ramifications of sponsoring al-Basasiri's doomed coalition and failing to permanently assimilate Aleppo into the caliphate were not only territorial. These missteps precipitated a period of internal instability in Cairo, prompted and exacerbated by a string of territorial losses in Sicily, North Africa, Arabia and Yemen. The Fatimid Vizier al-Yazuri was dismissed and executed in Rabiʿ I 449/February 1058, before al-Basasiri temporarily seized Baghdad.[45] His successors in the role of vizier were unable to retain their positions for any sustained period, leading to the downfall of the 'men of the pen', who had formed the dominant bureaucratic faction in Cairo for much of the fifth/eleventh century.[46]

Egypt was eventually plunged into a nine-year period of civil war between 460 and 468/1067 and 1076 provoked by a prolonged famine, plague and economic crisis. In 460/1067 conflict (*fitna*) erupted between two contingents of the Egyptian army, the Turks and the Blacks. By 464/1072, the Caliph al-Mustansir's influence was heavily curtailed, as he was effectively imprisoned in his palace and given a stipend of 100 dinars a month on which to live. His main adversary, Nasir al-Dawla, was assassinated in 465/1073, and al-Mustansir seized the opportunity to regain some semblance of his former power by appointing the Armenian governor of Tyre Badr al-Jamali as vizier, ushering in the era of the 'Vizierate of the sword'.[47]

Badr al-Jamali eventually stabilised the situation in Egypt, and by 468/1076 this protracted conflict was brought to an end. While domestic struggles help to explain the lack of Egyptian military activity against Mirdasid Aleppo during the 450s/1060s and 460s/1070s, any attempts to regain a foothold in northern Syria would have been further hampered by a sharp decline in Fatimid influence in southern Syria and Palestine.

Urban Rebellions and the Influx of Türkmen into Southern Bilad al-sham

During the 450s/1060s, cracks were starting to appear in the façade of Fatimid authority in Damascus and along the Syrian coastline. At the onset of this period, many of the major urban centres were governed by experienced military figures. Following his ousting from Aleppo, Ibn Mulhim was reassigned to Acre in 454/1062. Elsewhere, the soon to be Vizier Badr al-Jamali, who at this point in time was an Armenian *ghulam* (slave) who had distinguished himself in the service of the Banu 'Ammar of Tripoli, was made governor of Damascus in 455/1063.[48]

Yet rebellions against Fatimid dominion broke out throughout Palestine and Syria. In 456/1064, Badr al-Jamali was expelled from Damascus following a revolt led by the local notables Haydara b. Manzu and Abu Tahir Haydara.[49] Civil unrest in Damascus was a particularly unwelcome development for the Fatimid court, as Damascus was a key trading and military hub from which they had traditionally administrated *bilad al-sham*. Badr al-Jamali resumed his position as governor of Damascus in Sha'ban 458/July 1066, only to be ejected again and forced to flee to Acre in Ramadan 460/July 1068.[50]

The Fatimids encountered similar issues in the costal towns along the Syrian littoral. The ruler of Tyre, Ibn Abi 'Aqil, declared his independence from Fatimid rule in 455/1063.[51] A separate rebellion took place in Tripoli in 457/1064–5, where an attempt to supress this insurgency by the Fatimid commander of Ramla was stymied by Abu Talib al-Hasan b. 'Ammar, who used the *ahdath* (local urban militia) to hold onto the port-settlement. Afterwards, Ibn 'Ammar retained only nominal links to the Fatimids and the 'people of Tripoli' agreed to pay a fine of 100,000 dinars for their 'disloyalty to the lord of Egypt'.[52]

By accepting partially autonomous rulers in Tripoli and Tyre, the Fatimids demonstrated a certain level of pragmatism. In all probability, the benefits of retaining commercial ties with these cities were seen as more important than direct rule during a period of severe crisis in Egypt. This is reminiscent of their approach towards the Mirdasids of Aleppo, but it also served to emphasise their growing weakness in these vitally important mercantile hubs.

The influx of Türkmen groups into Palestine delivered a further blow to Fatimid territorial ambitions in southern Syria and Palestine. Following his second ejection from Damascus, Badr al-Jamali attempted to recapture Tyre in 462/1070, but was frustrated by a Türkmen force led by a chieftain named Qurlu.[53] Badr al-Jamali then left Acre by ship for Egypt in Jumada I 466/ January 1074 to take up the position of vizier at al-Mustansir's invitation, thereby becoming the most powerful figure in the Fatimid Caliphate.[54] Acre fell shortly after his departure to another Türkmen commander named Shukli in Rabi'I 467/October 1074.[55]

In 463/1071 Atsiz b. Uwaq al-Khwarizmi, yet another Türkmen commander, captured Jerusalem and Ramla. By mid-summer 468/1076, Atsiz's Türkmen had also forced the surrender of Damascus.[56] Although Damascus had largely been outside direct Fatimid control since Badr al-Jamali's expulsion eight years previously, the Egyptians had retained a veneer of influence in the city through the *khutba*, which remained in the name of the Caliph al-Mustansir.[57] After Atsiz changed the *khutba* to include the Abbasid caliph, the sermon prior to Friday prayers in Damascus would never again be made for a Fatimid caliph.

These developments had a hugely detrimental impact upon Fatimid authority in *bilad al-sham*, and exposed Egypt to the possibility of an overland invasion from the direction of Palestine. This threat was realised in late Jumada II 469/January 1077, when Atsiz b. Uwaq al-Khwarizmi led his Türkmen troops in a campaign targeting the Nile delta and Cairo. Badr al-Jamali managed to defeat Atsiz in a battle near Cairo on 22 Rajab 469/19 February 1077, and then launched a counter attack against Atsiz, culminating in a failed siege of Damascus in 471/1078.[58]

During this period, drought, plague and civil war pushed the Fatimid Caliphate to the very brink of survival. Between 456 and 468/1064 and 1076, the Fatimid presence in southern Syria and Palestine was reduced to nominal links with the governors of Tripoli and Tyre, while Damascus, Acre, Jerusalem and Ramla were captured by Türkmen rulers with only loose ties to the Great Seljuq Sultanate.[59] Cairo's strategy of retaining territorial possessions in the interior of *bilad al-sham* had been completely undermined by civil revolts and Türkmen incursions, leaving the Egyptian heartlands vulnerable to invasion.

Fatimid Military Expeditions into the Levant: 482–91/1090–8

For much of the next sixteen years the Fatimids were forced to accept Seljuq and Türkmen dominion over Jerusalem and Acre, and only loose associations with the rulers of Tripoli and Tyre. It was not until 482/1090 that the Fatimids developed a military policy capable of regaining some of their lost influence in *bilad al-sham*. The period between 482 and 491/1090 and 1098 saw a shift in Cairo's priorities, with Jerusalem becoming an increasingly important settlement from the Egyptian perspective.

This change in approach was seemingly triggered by the seizure of Beirut and Sidon by Tutush of Damascus, and the capture of Tyre by 'the Turks' in 482/1090.[60] Later the same year an Egyptian army led by the Amir al-Juyush

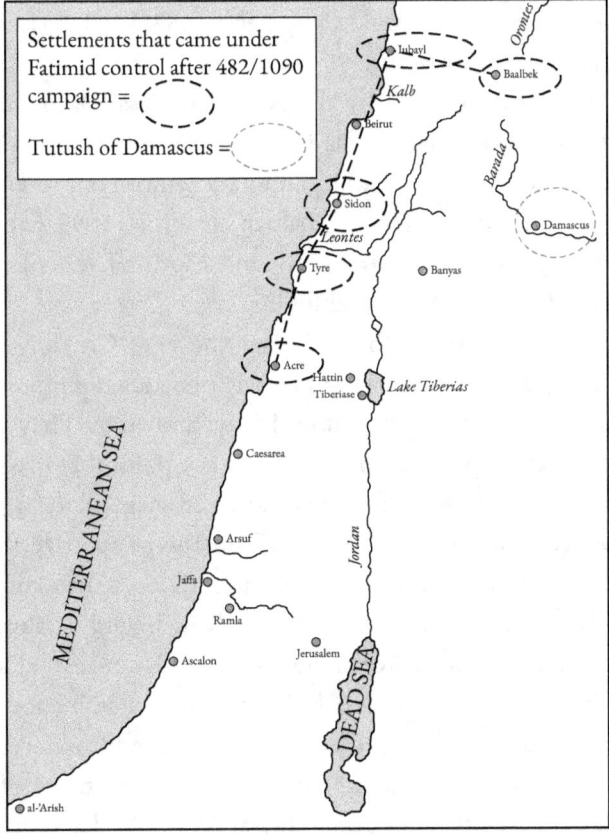

Figure 2.2 Fatimid campaign of 482/1090

(commander of the army) Nasr al-Dawla al-Juyushi conquered Tyre, Sidon, Jubayl and Acre. The Fatimid army then descended on Baalbek 'and Khalaf b. Mulaʿib arrived and promised to make the *khutba* for al-Mustansir' in Homs.[61]

Historians have viewed this campaign as evidence of the importance of the coastal settlements and their commercial potential to Fatimid interests.[62] Yet the occupation of Tyre, Sidon, Jubayl, Acre and Baalbek in addition to Homs aligning with the Fatimids, effectively isolated the Seljuq ruler of Damascus, Tutush b. Alp Arslan from his supposed 'Seljuq' allies in northern Syria and Mesopotamia.[63] Tutush suffered further inconvenience due to the loss of his treasury in Acre, as he lamented in his appeal for assistance to Qasim al-Dawla Aqsunqur of Aleppo and Buzan of Edessa, 'these lands that they have taken had my supplies and funds in them ... and I demand assistance from you both'.[64] While the capture of the coastal settlements was obviously the most important outcome of the Fatimid campaign in 482/1090, it is also increased pressure on Tutush in Damascus.

Further rebellions in Tyre by the Amir Munir al-Dawla al-Juyushi in 486/1093–4 and the *wali* Balkutiyla in 489/1095–6 were brutally repressed by Egyptian forces.[65] The final Fatimid military campaign into *bilad al-sham* before the First Crusade came in Shaʿban 491/July 1098, when al-Afdal departed from Egypt with a large army and captured Jerusalem from the Turkish Aqtuqid amirs Suqman and Il-Ghazi.[66]

In the ten years prior to the arrival of the First Crusade, the Fatimid Caliphate managed to recoup many of their previous dominions along the Syrian coastline, including Tyre, Sidon, Jubayl and Acre. They also tried to expand inland, placing pressure on Damascus at a point that many historians have identified as the height of Seljuq authority in *bilad al-sham*, before later retaking Jerusalem in Rajab 491/July 1098. From this perspective, these military activities were largely successful. That the Fatimids lost control of Jerusalem a year later to the armies of the First Crusade only highlights a failure to achieve the objective of retaining a territorial presence inland, not that it did not exist.

The Fatimid determination to build and regain influence in Aleppo, Damascus and Jerusalem during the latter half of the fifth/eleventh century was driven both by the devotional and strategic importance of the settlements and the prestige that the ruling hierarchy could derive from exerting authority over them. As Egyptian chances of regaining authority in Aleppo and Damascus declined over time, Jerusalem took on increasing importance in Fatimid circles.

Fatimid Interactions with Local Rulers in *Bilad al-sham*

Forging contacts and connections with local rulers were vital elements of Fatimid policy in *bilad al-sham*, which became ever more critical in the aftermath of the prolonged political crisis that convulsed Egypt between 460 and 468/1067 and 1076. Although often driven by necessity, these diplomatic overtures could also be an offensive tool used to expand Egyptian authority, or sow dissention between rival polities. Often these interactions crossed religious and ethnic boundaries, and even those with ties to the Great Seljuq Sultanate were targeted by the Fatimid hierarchy. These contacts also demonstrate how rigid cultural or ideological constructs were distorted by the opaque nature of political entanglements in fifth/eleventh-century *bilad al-sham*.

Badr al-Jamali

At first glance, the most obvious exemplar of this policy would be the Vizier Badr al-Jamali, a former Armenian slave who became the most powerful figure in the Fatimid political hierarchy. Parallels could potentially be drawn with Philaretos Brachamios, the Armenian governor of Antioch with official ties to the Byzantine court.[67] However, this would be a false comparison. Philaretos was part of an influx of Armenian military figures who assumed control over various territories in northern *bilad al-sham* and eastern Anatolia as a result of the sharp decline in Byzantine authority in these regions during the latter half of the fifth/eleventh century. Conversely, Badr al-Jamali was a *ghulam* (slave) who was purchased at a young age to serve the Banu 'Ammar of Tripoli. Badr al-Jamali would most probably have converted to Islam and been absorbed into the Fatimid system at an early age.[68] As Badr al-Jamali rose through the military and governmental ranks of the Egyptian Caliphate, his career is not comparable to that of Philaretos Brachamios.

Individuals like Badr al-Jamali also demonstrate the difficulties that stem from applying broad ethno-cultural labels onto individuals and groups. Where practical, the employment of such terms requires a nuanced understanding of the fluid networks of communication between these different groups. This is well reflected by Seta Dadoyan's use of the term 'Fatimid

Armenians', merging what are often perceived to be two distinct ethnic or ideological categories.⁶⁹

Syrian-based Türkmen and Seljuqs: Atsiz, Tutush and Ridwan

The are several examples of Fatimid rulers making direct diplomatic approaches to Seljuq rulers during the late fifth/eleventh century. These episodes illustrate how even for those operating on opposite sides of the Sunni/Shi'i divide, communication, and even collaboration, was possible under the right conditions.

The earliest instance occurred during Atsiz's failed invasion of Egypt in 469/1077, when the Vizier Badr al-Jamali offered to pay Atsiz 100,000 dinars to withdraw whilst his forces raided the countryside. Although Atsiz rejected this offer, 1,000 Arab horsemen from the Banu Kilab, who were part of Atsiz's forces, agreed to switch allegiance to the Fatimids. Sibt b. al-Jawzi claimed that another unnamed Türkmen commander was able to convince 700 *ghulam*s to do the same due to the 'avarice and injustice' of Atsiz.⁷⁰ While these defections were limited in terms of numbers, they helped to facilitate Atsiz's defeat.⁷¹

Badr al-Jamali also offered his daughter in marriage to the sultan's brother Taj al-Dawla Tutush b. Alp Arslan, in the hope of making a marriage alliance with the Seljuq *malik* of Damascus in 476/1083–4. Although Tutush originally decided to accept the offer, he was subsequently persuaded by Ibn 'Ammar, the semi-independent ruler of Tripoli, to reject the proposal. Sibt b. al-Jawzi reported that after he rebuffed this overture, 'no gifts or friendliness arrived from Egypt' for Tutush.⁷²

This offer made by the most powerful figure in the Fatimid Caliphate to the brother of the Seljuq sultan, and Tutush's initial willingness to accept it, indicated a readiness on both sides to conclude a marriage alliance across a deep doctrinal divide. For Badr al-Jamali, this arrangement would have had the potential to increase Fatimid influence in Damascus, while simultaneously fostering misgivings at the Seljuq court about Tutush's allegiance to the sultan. Tutush could have gained a powerful ally with whom he could collaborate to augment his own territorial dominions.⁷³

It is also important to note 'Ammar, lord of Tripoli's role in reportedly advising Tutush to reject this offer, underlining the complicated nature of the Banu ʿAmmar's relationship with the Fatimid Caliphate.[74] While commercial ties to Egypt were obviously important to Tripoli, Ibn ʿAmmar would not have wanted closer ties between Damascus and Cairo, out of fear that this would impinge upon his autonomy. While nothing concrete came of the proposed marriage, it was the first major Fatimid interaction with a Seljuq ruler appointed by the sultan, which established a precedent for later diplomatic contacts between Cairo and other Turkish rulers of Damascus and Aleppo.

Tutush was again accused of collaborating with the Fatimids in 478/1085–6 by Fakhr al-Dawla Ibn Jahir. Ibn Jahir was the father of the former vizier of the Abbasid Caliph al-Muqtadi, and was granted Diyar Bakr as an *iqtaʿ* in 476/1083–4.[75] In the course of his attempts to lay claim to his new territory, Ibn Jahir came into conflict with Sharaf al-Dawla Muslim b. Quraysh, the Uqaylid ruler of Mosul and Aleppo, while besieging Amid in Rabiʿ I 477/July 1084. During this struggle, Ibn Jahir also had a disagreement with Artuq b. Aksab, who had been ordered by the sultan to assist him.[76]

Sibt b. al-Jawzi reported that Ibn Jahir therefore wrote to the Sultan Malik Shah alleging that Artuq had accepted a financial inducement from Sharaf al-Dawla to allow him to escape the besieged town of Amid, which corresponds well with Ibn al-Athir's account of events. Ibn Jahir also reportedly claimed that both Artuq and Sharaf al-Dawla had come to an agreement with Tutush of Damascus to send an appeal for aid to the Fatimid court. Afterwards, Badr al-Jamali sent his son 'Ibn Maghribi and a group of commanders' to Damascus, but the plot failed because Sharaf al-Dawla was killed before their plans could come to fruition.[77]

Essentially, Ibn Jahir accused the rulers of Damascus and Aleppo of being at the centre of a plot to surrender *bilad al-sham* into Fatimid hands. While there is quite a lot of evidence of a predisposition on Sharaf al-Dawla's part to cooperate militarily with the Fatimids, the only suggestion that Tutush even considered a closer relationship with Egypt came in Badr's proposed marriage alliance discussed above.[78] As Sibt b. al-Jawzi is the only source who reported this claim, it seems likely that Ibn Jahir included Tutush in the accusation only because the latter welcomed Artuq into his entourage after he fled from Amid.[79]

Yet another example of a 'Seljuq' ruler in Syria entertaining overtures from Egypt came when Ridwan b. Tutush changed the *khutba* in Aleppo to include the Fatimid Caliph al-Musta'li in 490/1097–8. There is disagreement in the source material as to which settlements actually made the call to prayer for the Fatimid caliph, and for how long they did so. Ibn al-Qalanisi claimed that the *khutba* was made for al-Musta'li throughout Aleppo for a period of four weeks, before Ridwan was persuaded to switch it back to the Abbasids. In contrast, Ibn al-'Adim stated that the *khutba* remained in the name of the Fatimid caliph until as late as 492/1099–1100, and that this change was made in only four mosques. Ridwan later sent apologies to the Abbasid caliph in Baghdad for his actions.[80]

Most of the more contemporaneous Syrian-based chroniclers agree that an Egyptian messenger made the initial approach to Ridwan. However, the Egyptian historian Ibn Muyassar asserted instead that a messenger from Ridwan arrived in Cairo on 16 Safar 490/2 February 1097 'offering to enter into his (al-Afdal's) obedience and establish the *khutba* for al-Musta'li in *al-sham*' in return for 'Egyptian troops to take Damascus from his brother Duqaq'.[81] It is noteworthy that both regional historiographical branches attributed the first approach to the other side, perhaps indicating the depth of hostility and stigma present beyond the interaction.

Generally modern historians have viewed this episode as an isolated event, driven by Ridwan's inherent opportunism and the uniquely unstable political situation in Syria at this time.[82] Yet when set in the wider context of similar approaches, what is perceived to be an extraordinary incident involving Ridwan, can clearly be seen as part of a wider Fatimid policy of subversive diplomatic contact with Syrian-based Seljuq rulers. The political elite of Cairo pursued this policy to stoke divisions between the rival polities that made up the political landscape in *bilad al-sham* in the hope of extending or maintaining their own influence in the region. This stratagem was reasonably successful, as it enabled them to play a major role in Syrian political affairs while providing only a limited military threat.

These examples also demonstrate how the Fatimids were willing to approach high-ranking individuals in the Seljuq hierarchy in order to achieve their objectives, indicating that ideological differences did not present a significant obstacle to the pursuit of this policy. Similarly, leading members of the

Seljuq dynasty, such as Tutush and Ridwan, were seemingly willing to open diplomatic channels with Egypt, even if this came in the form of temporary arrangements that often led to retractions and apologies sent to Baghdad. This willingness to engage in communications that spanned deep sectarian divides provided a framework for later cross-cultural interactions that took place during the sixth/twelfth century.

Conclusion: The Fatimids as 'the Other' in *Bilad al-sham*?

Writing ninety years ago in the introduction to his English translation of Ibn al-Qalanisi's *Dhayl ta'rikh Dimashq*, Hamilton A. R. Gibb wrote that:

> it would be a serious mistake to assume that the influence of the Fatimids in Syria was entirely dissipated by their ... growing weakness ... they still had a strong following both in the chief cities and the outer districts, and that even the Seljuqid princes and their successors found it expedient to court their favour.[83]

Gibb also maintained that the 'definite breach' between the Fatimids and local rulers in Syria did not occur until the time of Nur al-Din. Yet Gibb provided no evidence to substantiate these conclusions as these thoughts were only briefly articulated in a short contextual introduction.

Throughout the fifth/eleventh century, the Fatimid Caliphate combined a pragmatic diplomatic policy with carefully targeted military campaigns to preserve their influence in *bilad al-sham*. Yet Fatimid power in Aleppo, and northern Syria as a whole, was damaged beyond repair by the defeat at al-Funaydiq in 452/1060 and the resulting territorial losses. This date also marked the point at which Aleppo developed into an autonomous lordship from the perspective of the Fatimid Caliphate.[84]

Fatimid power in southern Syria and Palestine took slightly longer to fade, and the onset of domestic conflicts in Egypt between 460 and 468/1067 and 1076, combined with the incursions by transhumant Türkmen groups and the loss of other regions throughout their trans-Mediterranean empire, were hugely decisive factors in their inability to respond to their declining authority in southern *bilad al-sham*. It should be noted that much of the damage was done by this first wave of Türkmen rulers with only loose ties to the Great Seljuq Sultanate, rather than specific campaigns led by the sultan or prominent members of his family or entourage.

Despite these territorial losses, carefully planned military expeditions launched from Egypt proved to be relatively effective in the last decade of the fifth/eleventh century. These campaigns enabled Cairo to regain control of coastal settlements that were vital to the caliphate's mercantile interests. They were also able to apply some pressure on the Seljuq ruler of Damascus, and to recapture Jerusalem and Ramla. This was part of a wider strategic plan to maintain territorial dominions inland in order to prevent an overland invasion of Egypt.

Fatimid diplomatic efforts were also largely successful, helping to drive divisions between Cairo's political rivals, particularly the Turkish rulers of Syria and the Seljuq sultan's court. The apparent willingness of prominent members of the Seljuq dynasty to enter into diplomatic arrangements with Fatimid Cairo calls into question the notion that dealings between these two parties were driven by bitter political rivalry rooted in ideological antithesis.[85] Even in *bilad al-sham*, supposedly the key battleground of this intense sectarian conflict between the Shi'i Fatimids and Sunni Great Seljuq Sultanate, there remained a readiness on both sides to cooperate for personal gain.

As Gibb noted, the Fatimid Caliphate did not represent an alien 'other' to rulers of Turkish origin during the fifth/eleventh century. Rather, the political reality on the ground in Syria, Palestine and Egypt necessitated contacts that bridged this deep devotional divide.

Notes

1. Bianquis, *Damas*, II, p, 590.
2. See, e.g., Lev, *State and Society*; Jiwa, *The Fatimids*; Halm, *Die Kalifen von Kairo*; Halm, *Kalifen und Assassinen*.
3. Ellenblum, *The Collapse of the Eastern Mediterranean*, pp. 41–122, 147–60. Andrew Peacock, Johannes Preiser-Kapeller and Yehoshua Frenkel have questioned the scientific basis of Ellenblum's thesis regarding the migration of nomadic Seljuq tribal groups from the Eurasian steppe, although Ellenblum's conclusions on Egypt have been partially substantiated by recent research. See Peacock, *Empire*, pp. 287–8; Preiser-Kapeller, 'A Collapse of the Eastern Mediterranean', pp. 209–10, 216; Yehoshua Frenkel, 'The Coming of the Barbarians: Can Climate Explain the Seljuqs' Advance?' in *Socio-Environmental Dynamics along the Historical Silk Road*, ed. Liang Emlyn Yang, Hans-Rudolf

Bork, Xiuqi Fang and Steffen Mischke (Cham: Springer, 2019), pp. 261–74; Leigh Chipman, Gideon Anvi and Ronnie Ellenblum, 'Collapse, Affluence, and Collapse again: Contrasting Climactic Effects in Egypt during the Prolonged Reign of al-Mustansir (1036–1094)', *Mediterranean Historical Review* 36 (2021): 199–215.
4. Brett, *Empire*, pp. 181–232.
5. Bianquis, *Damas*; Mouton, *Damas*; Yared-Riachi, *Damas*; Bianquis, 'Pouvoirs arabes à Alep', pp. 49–59; David Bramoullé, 'Recruiting Crew in the Fatimid Navy 909-1171', *Medieval Encounters* 13 (2007): 4–31; David Bramoullé, 'Les populations littorals du Bilad al-Šam fatimide et la guerre', *Annales islamologiques* 43 (2009): 303–34; David Bramoullé, 'Tyr dans le sources de la période fatimide (969–1171)', in *Sources de l'Histoire de Tyr: Textes de l'Antiquité et du Moyen Âge*, ed. Pierre-Louis Gaitier, Julien Aliquot and Lévon Nordiguian (Beirut: Presses de'Ifpo, 2011), pp. 157–77; David Bramoullé, 'The Fatimids and the Red Sea (969–1171)', in *Navigated Spaces, Connected Places*, ed. Dionisius Agius, John Cooper, Athena Trakadas and Chiara Zazzaro (Oxford: Archaeopress, 2012), pp. 127–36; David Bramoullé, *Les Fatimides et la mer 909–1171* (Leiden: Brill, 2019).
6. Beihammer has discussed Fatimid interactions with Türkmen groups in southern Syria and Palestine in some detail, Beihammer, *Byzantium*, pp. 179–88. See also Claude Cahen, 'La première pénétration turque en Asie Mineure (seconde moitié du XIe siècle)', *Byzantion* 18 (1948): 5–67, 36–8.
7. The foremost proponents of this viewpoint are Carole Hillenbrand and Michael Köhler. See Hillenbrand, *Crusades*, pp. 33–6; Köhler, *Alliances*, pp. 7–20.
8. This chronology closely corresponds to the decline of Byzantine influence in Aleppo from 454/1062 onwards. See Chapter 1.
9. al-'Azimi, pp. 338–40; SJ, XII, 232–3; IAD ZH, I, 251–60, 263–6; IM, pp. 6–7, 9–10; al-Maqrizi, II, 208–10. For more detail, see Zakkar, *Emirate*, pp. 131–7, 141–8.
10. Jennifer Pruitt, 'The Fatimid Holy City: Rebuilding Jerusalem in the Eleventh Century', *Medieval Globe* 3 (2017): 35–58; Uri Rubin, 'Muhammad's Night Journey (*isra'*) to al-Masjid al-Aqsa: Aspects of the Earliest Origins of the Islamic Sanctity of Jerusalem', *Al-Qantara* 29 (2008): 147–64; Bentram Schrieke et al., 'Mi'radj', in *Encyclopaedia of Islam*, 2nd edn, ed. Peri Bearman et al. (2012), available at Brill online, last accessed 15 June 2019.
11. Al-Husayn b. 'Ali b. Abi Talib was one of the sons of 'Ali b. Abi Talib, the fourth Muslim caliph and the first imam in the Isma'ili Shi'i doctrine. The deaths

of 'Ali and his sons played an enormously influential role in the emergence of Shi'ism and therefore held huge significance for the Isma'ili Shi'i Fatimid Caliphate and their followers. For more on the importance of 'Ali and his sons, see Carole Hillenbrand, *Islam: A New Historical Introduction* (London: Thames & Hudson, 2015), pp. 145–64; Najam I. Haider, 'Al-Husayn b. 'Ali b. Abi Talib', in *Encyclopaedia of Islam: THREE*, ed. Kate Fleet et al. (2016), available at Brill online, last accessed 15 June 2019. For more on the religious significance of Ascalon in the late fifth/eleventh and early sixth/twelfth centuries, see Brett, *Empire*, pp. 241–3.
12. Brett, *Empire*, pp. 120–2.
13. IAD ZH, I, 267; al-Maqrizi, II, 208–11.
14. al-Mu'ayyad fi'l-Din, *Diwan al-Mu'ayyad fi'l-Din*, pp. 96–184; IQ, pp. 145–6, 150; al-'Azimi, pp. 342–4; IATH, IX, 625–6, 630–1, 639–50; SJ, XII, 250, 253–4, 261–3, 270–1, 292, 351; IAD ZH, I, 274–5; IM, pp. 14, 18–20; al-Maqrizi, II, 232–4, 252–8. For more detail on al-Mu'ayyad's diplomatic efforts and Fatimid support for al-Basasiri, see Klemm, *Memoirs of a Mission*, pp. 78–88; Peacock, *Empire*, pp. 48–51; Brett, *Empire*, pp. 192–7; Halm, *Die Kalifen von Kairo*, pp. 383–94.
15. IQ, p. 141; SJ, XII, 327; IAD ZH, I, 273–4; IM, p. 15; al-Maqrizi, II, 235.
16. Zakkar, *Emirate*, p. 154.
17. SJ, XII, 374, 377; IAD ZH, I, 275.
18. IQ, pp. 150–1; al-'Azimi, p. 344; IATH, X, 12; SJ, XII, 377–8; IAD ZH, I, 276–7; al-Maqrizi, II, 259.
19. Yaqut al-Hamaqi wrote that al-Funaydiq was renamed Tell al-Sultan by the seventh/thirteenth century, see Yaqut, *Mu'ajam al-Buldan*, II, 42, IV, 278; Dussaud, *Topographie historique*, p. 313; Cahen, *Syrie*, p. 155.
20. al-'Azimi, p. 344; IQ, pp. 150–1; IATH, X, 12; SJ, XII, 377–9; IAD ZH, I, 276–80; IM, pp. 21–2; al-Maqrizi, II, 259–61.
21. SJ, XII, 378.
22. al-'Azimi, p. 345; SJ, XII, 378–9; IAD ZH, I, 286; IM, p. 22; al-Maqrizi, II, 263.
23. IQ, p. 156; al-'Azimi, p. 346; SJ, XII, 435; IAD ZH, II, p. 9.
24. IQ, p. 156; al-'Azimi, p. 346.
25. SJ, XII, 449-50. As discussed in Chapter 1, Ibn al-'Adim claimed that Mahmud gave one of his sons as a hostage to the Byzantines as part of a peace treaty negotiated in 457/1064–5, see IAD ZH, I, 296.
26. See Chapter 1 for a detailed overview of Mirdasid military activity against Byzantine Antioch.

27. Fatimid issues in Damascus between 452 and 468/1060 and 1076 are discussed later in this Chapter.
28. In 452/1060 Nasir al-Dawla also stopped at Apamea on route to Aleppo. IAD ZH, I, 263–6, 272–4, 276–7.
29. IAD ZH, I, 275–6, II, 10.
30. IAD ZH, I, 280–2.
31. IAD ZH, I, 295.
32. IAD ZH, II, 10, 12. For more detail on Asfuna, see Chapter 1, n. 44.
33. Asbridge described the Frankish victory at Antioch in 491/1098 as 'the most important military engagement of the entire expedition (the First Crusade)', while Carole Hillenbrand characterised it as 'probably *the* turning-point of the First Crusade', see Thomas S. Asbridge, *The First Crusade: A New History* (London: Free Press, 2004), p. 239; Hillenbrand, *Crusades*, p. 59. On the battle of the Field of Blood, see Asbridge, 'Field of Blood', pp. 301–16.
34. Beihammer, *Byzantium*, pp. 119–20.
35. Zakkar, *Emirate*, pp. 167–9; El-Azhari, *Seljuqs*, pp. 26–31; Morton and France, 'Arab Muslim Reactions', pp. 3–13.
36. SJ, XII, pp. 472, 481.
37. Ibn al-'Adim described how after Mahmud's death, his son Nasr detained the Türkmen leader Ahmed Shah, and was then killed while leading an attack on a Türkmen encampment outside Aleppo's walls. The Türkmen subsequently attacked the city and freed Ahmed Shah, who promoted another of Mahmud's sons called Sabiq to rule Mirdasid Aleppo. The Banu Kilab backed the claims of a third son, Wathab, which led to a battle between the nomadic Arab and Türkmen forces on 15 Dhu 'l-Ka'da 468/20 July 1076, from which the latter group emerged victorious. Ahmed Shah's selection of Sabiq, ahead of his older brother Wathab, matched the approach of elevating younger client rulers adopted by later Turkish rulers and '*atabegs*' in Syria, the most notable of whom being Tughtikin of Damascus. See IAD BH, III, 1298–9, IX, 4078. The 'symbiotic' relationship that developed between the Mirdasids and some Türkmen groups is discussed in Chapter 3.
38. For the definition of autonomous lordship used in this book, see Introduction to Part I.
39. IQ, pp. 165–6; SJ, XII, 481–2.
40. al-'Azimi, p. 343; SJ, XII, 481–2.
41. IQ, pp. 167–8; al-'Azimi, pp. 348–9; IATH, X, 64; SJ, XII, 480–1; IAD, II, 19–23.

42. For more information of the procedure of *khidma* and its importance, see Chamberlain, *Knowledge and Social Power*, pp. 116–18; Peacock, *Empire*, p. 158; Paul, 'Khidma', pp. 408–11.
43. IAD, II, 22–3.
44. IAD, II, 30–1. Baalbek is situated to the east of Mount Lebanon, in southern Syria, lying on the main route from Aleppo to Damascus. This episode is discussed in more detail in Chapter 1.
45. IATH, X, 61–2; SJ, XII, 295, 427–8, 461, 465–9, XII, 22, 28–9, 36–9, 49, 97; IM, pp. 32–43; al-Maqrizi, II, 236, 238–9.
46. The terms 'men of the pen' (designating the bureaucratic group at the Egyptian court who had occupied the Fatimid vizierate for much of the fifth/eleventh century) and the 'Vizier of the sword' (assigned to the military figures who rose to the position of vizier, starting with Badr al-Jamali) were coined by the medieval Egyptian chroniclers of the Ayyubid and Mamluk eras who wrote most of the extant chronicles covering the Fatimid period. For a better understanding of how Fatimid history was shaped by later historians, see Fozia Bora, *Writing History in the Medieval Islamic World: the Value of Chronicles as Archives* (London: Bloomsbury, 2019); Walker, *Exploring an Islamic Empire*, pp. 152–69. See also Brett, *Empire*, pp. 157–79, 194–5, 198–9; Daftary, *The Isma'ilis*, p. 223.
47. For more detailed information on the crisis and civil war in Egypt between 460 and 468/1067 and 1076, see Brett, *Empire*, pp. 201–6; Lev, *State and Society*, pp. 43–50; Halm, *Die Kalifen von Cairo*, pp. 400–20; Halm, *Kalifen und Assassinen*, pp. 17–22, 35–7, 42–5. For indications that climate-related issues were the root cause of this conflict, see Ellenblum, *The Collapse of the Eastern Mediterranean*, pp. 41–6, 147–60; Preiser-Kapeller, 'A Collapse of the Eastern Mediterranean', pp. 209–10, 216.
48. IQ, pp. 153–5; SJ, XII, 412; IM, p. 28; al-Maqrizi, II, 264–319. The term *ghulam* refers to a person who had been bought as a slave, and could still be a slave or of free status.
49. IQ, pp. 154–5, 182; SJ, XII, 412–13; IM, p. 29; Brett, *Empire*, p. 199.
50. IQ, p. 157; SJ, XII, 446, 455–6; IM, p. 33.
51. Moshe Gil, *A History of Palestine 634–1099* (Cambridge: Cambridge University Press, 1992), p. 419; Bramoullé, 'Tyr dans le sources de la période fatimide', pp. 170–2.
52. SJ, XII, 436. See also Alex Mallett, "Ammar, Banu (Syria)', in *Encyclopaedia of Islam: THREE*, ed. Kate Fleet et al. (2019), available at Brill online, last accessed 2 July 2019.

53. IQ, p. 165; SJ, XII, 472. For more information about Badr al-Jamali's interactions with Türkmen in *bilad al-sham*, see Beihammer, *Byzantium*, pp. 179–88.
54. Badr al-Jamali redefined the position of vizier, assuming political powers comparable with those of the Seljuq sultan. For more discussion on Badr's influence, see Heinz Halm, 'Badr al-Gamali. Wesir oder Militärdiktator', in *Egypt and Syria in the Fatimid, Ayyubid and Mamluk Eras*, 9 vols, ed. Urbain Vermeulen and Kristof D'Hulster (Leuven: Peeters, 2007), V, pp. 79–85; Halm, *Kalifen und Assassinen*, pp. 17–21, 35–42; Brett, *Empire*, pp. 207–15; Michael Brett, 'Badr al-Gamali and the Fatimid Renascence', *Egypt and Syria in the Fatimid, Ayyubid and Mamluk Eras*, 9 vols, ed. Urbain Vermeulen and Kristof D'Hulster (Leuven: Peeters, 2007), V, pp. 61–79; Carole Hillenbrand, 'Nizam al-Mulk: A Maverick Vizier?' in *The Age of the Seljuqs*, ed. Edmund Herzig and Sarah Stewart (London: I. B. Tauris, 2015), pp. 33–4; Paul E. Walker, 'Was the *Amir al-Jayush* actually a *Wazir*?' in *The Fatimid Caliphate: Diversity of Traditions*, ed. Farhad Daftary and Shainool Jiwa (London: I. B. Tauris, 2018), pp. 80–93.
55. SJ, XII, 66–7; IM, p. 41.
56. IQ, pp. 166–7, 174–5; IATH, X, 68, 99–100; SJ, XIII, 30; IM, p. 36, 42–3. Atsiz b. Uwaq al-Khwarizmi and his ties to the Seljuqs are discussed in Chapter 3.
57. For more background on these revolts against Fatimid rule in Damascus, see Bianquis, *Damas*, II, 644–52; Halm, *Kalifen und Assassinen*, pp. 22–8, Brett, *Empire*, pp. 202–6.
58. This Fatimid siege of Damascus is discussed in more detail in Chapter 3. Sawirus ibn al-Muqaffa', *History of the Patriarchs of the Egyptian Church*, II/III, pp. 218–19, 343–4; IQ, pp. 176–83; IATH, X, 103–4, 111; SJ, XIII, 97–8, 119–20; IM, pp. 44–5; al-Maqrizi, II, 319.
59. The relationship between the early Türkmen rulers in *bilad al-sham* and the Seljuq ruling elite are discussed in Chapter 3.
60. Only al-'Azimi mentioned the fall of Tyre into Turkish possession, but Ibn Muyassar stated that Tyre, Sidon, Jubayl and Acre had been under Tutush's control when an Egyptian army arrived in *bilad al-sham* in 482/1090, see al-'Azimi, p. 355; IM, p. 50.
61. Quote taken from SJ, XIII, 195. The Egyptian campaign is also mentioned in the following sources IQ, p. 197; al-'Azimi, p. 355; IM, p. 50; al-Maqrizi, II, 326.
62. Bramoullé asserted that the Fatimid court of Cairo gave up any hope of recovering former territories in Syria or Palestine after Atsiz captured Damascus in 469/1076, see Bramoullé, 'Les villes maritimes fatimides', p. 114. See also Brett, *Empire*, p. 218.

63. The muted response this appeal drew from the Seljuq rulers of *al-sham* is discussed in Chapter 3.
64. This quote is taken from Sibt b. al-Jawzi. SJ, XII, 195; IM, p. 50.
65. IQ, pp. 204–5; al-'Azimi, p. 355; IATH, X, 223; SJ, XIII, 247; IM, p. 51; al-Maqrizi, II, 328.
66. Their father Artuq, who was in *khidma* to Tutush b. Alp Arslan in Damascus, was the eponym of the Artuqid dynasty, who became important political figures during the sixth/twelfth century.
67. Philaretos Brachamios is discussed in Chapter 1.
68. Halm, 'Badr al-Gamali', pp. 79–85; Halm, *Kalifen und Assassinen*, pp. 17–21, 35–42; Brett, *Empire*, pp. 207–15; Brett, 'Badr al-Gamali', pp. 61–79; Seta B. Dadoyan, *The Armenians in the Medieval Islamic World: Paradigms of Interaction Seventh to Fourteenth Centuries*, 2 vols (London: Routledge, 2013), II, pp. 56–9, 77–90.
69. Dadoyan, *The Fatimid Armenians*, II, 107–27.
70. SJ, XIII, 97–8.
71. Peacock minimised the threat that Atsiz's 469/1077 campaign posed to Fatimid Egypt, arguing that Atsiz 'overreached himself with a disastrous campaign'. Peacock, *Empire*, pp. 61–4.
72. SJ, XIII, 149; El-Azhari, *Saljuqs*, pp. 61–2.
73. Tutush b. Alp Arslan and his seemingly problematic relationship with his brother, the Sultan Malikshah, is discussed in detail in Chapter 3.
74. Mallett, "Ammar, Banu (Syria)'.
75. IATH, X, 129. *Iqta'* grants are discussed in more detail in Chapter 3. On the Banu Jahir, see Eric Hanne, 'The Banu Jahir and Their Role in the 'Abbasid and Seljuq Administration', *Al-Masaq* 20 (2008): 29–45.
76. IATH, X, 134–5.
77. SJ, XIII, pp. 166–7.
78. For more on Sharaf al-Dawla Muslim b. Quraysh's interactions with the Fatimids and his relationship with the Great Seljuq Sultanate, see Chapter 3.
79. al-Fariqi, *Ta'rikh al-Fariqi*, p. 148; IATH, X, 147–8; SJ, XIII, 176–7; IAD, II, 97.
80. IQ, p. 217; al-'Azimi, p. 360; IATH, X, 269–70; SJ, XII, 247; IAD, II, 127.
81. IM, p. 64.
82. El-Azhari, *Saljuqs*, pp. 87–90; Köhler, *Alliances*, p. 17; Cobb, *Race for Paradise*, p. 88.
83. Ibn al-Qalanisi, *The Damascus Chronicle*, p. 17.

84. As outlined in Chapter 1, 454/1062 marked the end point of Byzantine influence in Aleppo.
85. Nicholas Morton has made a similar point about the ideological flexibility of the Seljuq ruling elite. See Morton, *Encountering Islam*, pp. 111–90; Nicholas Morton, 'The Saljuq Turks' Conversion to Islam: the Crusading Sources', *al-Masaq* 27 (2015): 109–18.

3

The Great Seljuq Sultanate

Seljuq *Bilad al-sham*

This chapter re-examines the emergence and nature of Seljuq power in *bilad al-sham*. It details how in addition to the difficulties provoked by Malik Shah's death in 485/1092, there were systemic factors inherent to the political structures of the Great Seljuq Sultanate which inhibited efforts to expand their influence within Syria, both before and after 485/1092.

In broad terms, there is unanimity among modern historians about the growth and decline of Seljuq influence in Syria and Palestine between 463 and 492/1071 and 1099. The origins of Seljuq power in *bilad al-sham* is typically traced to the arrival of the Sultan Alp Arslan in Aleppo, and the defeat of the Byzantine army at the battle of Manzikert that same year. Taj al-Dawla Tutush b. Alp Arslan, the brother of the Seljuq Sultan Malik Shah, took control of Damascus in 472/1079–80. This is viewed as another indicator of increasing Seljuq authority in Syria. Malik Shah's campaign of 479/1086–7, which led to the direct appointment of Yaghi Siyan in Antioch, Aqsunqur b. ʿAbd Allah in Aleppo and Buzan in Edessa, marked the apogee of Seljuq control. Later collaborative campaigns by these new governors led to the addition of Homs to the Great Seljuq Sultanate's dominions.

Then, in 485/1092, disaster struck. Malik Shah and his powerful Vizier Nizam al-Mulk died. In the ensuing succession crisis, Tutush, Aqsunqur and Buzan were all killed in various battles in the following three years. Thereafter, conflict erupted between Tutush's sons Ridwan and Duqaq in Syria, who came to control Aleppo and Damascus, respectively. This destabilising series of events brought a new level of autonomy to Syrian-based rulers. In the midst of this ongoing crisis, the armies of the First Crusade arrived in *bilad al-sham* in Dhu 'l-Qaʻda 490/October 1097. The Crusaders and western European settlers took advantage of the continuing regional volatility to establish polities at Antioch, Jerusalem, Edessa and Tripoli.[1]

This chronology feeds into the conception of a linear development and decline of Seljuq regional authority in late fifth/eleventh-century Syria, beginning with Alp Arslan's campaign and culminating in joint military campaigns by those directly appointed by the sultan against Fatimid possessions in *bilad al-sham*, before collapsing in 485/1092 in the aftermath of Malik Shah's death. However, David Durand-Guédy has persuasively argued that modern Seljuq historiography, particularly in relation to Iran, has often conformed to an 'imperial narrative' centred upon 'expansion up to the crisis of 1092, then fragmentation and decline'.[2] As Durand-Guédy has shown through a detailed study of Isfahan, Seljuq authority in any given region was not always tied to the reigns of individual sultans.[3]

This chapter applies this regional approach to Seljuq *bilad al-sham*. While Malik Shah's death and the resulting succession crisis was detrimental to Seljuq authority in Syria and Palestine, there were two issues inherent to the Seljuq system of governance that prevented Seljuq sultans from maintaining a position of dominance in the region between 463 and 522/1071 and 1128. The first of these are logistical and political problems that repeatedly impeded Seljuq military campaigns into northern Syria. The second stemmed from the inveterate autonomy that leading Seljuq amirs enjoyed, which consistently hampered collaborative military actions within Syria during the late fifth/eleventh and early sixth/twelfth centuries.

This chapter also questions the extent to which sectarian concerns influenced the decision-making processes of Seljuq sultans and those they empowered in Syria and Palestine. There is an ongoing debate around how Seljuq sultans fulfilled their role as 'champions of Sunni Islam'. Deborah Tor contended that many of the sultans were highly pious individuals who took this duty extremely seriously, whilst Andrew Peacock has instead highlighted examples of Seljuq 'tolerance' of Shiʻism, hinting at a more pragmatic approach.[4] As *bilad al-sham* formed the focal point of the Seljuq war against the 'heretical' Fatimids, the cross-cultural interactions that took place on this key frontier zone will be closely scrutinised with this debate in mind.

Discussion begins with the campaigns led in person by the sultans Alp Arslan in 463/1071 and Malik Shah in 479/1086–7. This is followed by a reassessment of Seljuq campaigns into *bilad al-sham* ordered by the sultan Malik Shah in the late fifth/eleventh century. The next section explains Malik Shah's attempts to limit the authority of his younger brother Tutush facilitated the preservation of the system of autonomous lordships in Syria, before exploring Seljuq ties to the amirs of *al-sham* during the first three decades of the sixth/twelfth century.[5] The final part considers the impact of Türkmen peoples on the political world of *bilad al-sham*.

Mechanisms of Seljuq Governance in Syria

Both the Byzantine Empire and the Fatimid Caliphate developed the governmental structures they used to administer their territories over several generations. Correspondingly, their shared interest in *bilad al-sham* can be traced back to at least the fourth/tenth century. In contrast, the Seljuqs were newcomers to a region where their influence would fluctuate heavily throughout the late fifth/eleventh and early sixth/twelfth centuries. This makes it more difficult to assess the extent of Seljuq authority at any given time.

The Seljuq political system was a based upon hybrid of traditional ideals from the Eurasian Steppe society, such as shared family rule and the broad-natured Persian revenue distribution system of *iqta'*. In simple terms, collective family rule revolved around the notion that authority was to some extent distributed throughout the dynasty, as most prominent male members of the royal clan could potentially rise to the position of sultan. At least in theory, it was incumbent upon all those with the best claim to the sultanate to challenge for it, thereby ensuring that the best possible candidate became sultan. As a consequence, multiple individuals often contested succession to the sultanate. Those family members who were close relatives of the sultan therefore expected to be granted their own territories to rule over in order to build up their power bases in anticipation of potential future leadership bids.[6]

In order to meet these demands, Seljuq sultans utilised a Persian administrative tool called *iqta'*, which had originally been adopted by their successors in Persia, the Buyid dynasty. An *iqta'* grant provided its holder with the right to collect a portion of the revenues from a specific area, region or settlement. Typically, the terms on which *iqta'* grants were allocated were highly subjective. Moreover, different dynasties employed *iqta'* in distinct ways. Yossef Rapoport's detailed reconstruction of the use of *iqta'* grants in the Egyptian region of the Fayyum during the seventh/thirteenth century, demonstrated how the Ayyubid dynasty systematically distributed the incomes from various tracts of land within the same settlements to different military officers. This was done to ensure that no individual could gain a monopoly over a specific area to use as a power base.[7]

Under the Seljuqs *iqta'* grants tended to be far more indulgent, often allocating revenues from major urban centres, or in some cases large regions, to individuals.[8] This enabled Seljuq appointees to accrue huge incomes and effectively operate as local rulers. Usually, *iqta'* were assigned to senior administrators, high-ranking military figures and prominent members of the Seljuq dynasty.[9] The sultan was therefore obligated to grant large swathes of territory to those best placed to challenge for the sultanate in the future. Even those *iqta'* holders who were not related to the sultan often operated with a large degree of autonomy.

Autonomous amirs were therefore an ingrained feature of the Seljuq system of governance, and affected the sultan's authority in both positive and negative ways. On the one hand, it promoted a political culture of self-interest and rivalry driven by an incessant battle for survival between the amirs, which made collaborative action against external enemies difficult. Conversely, Stefan Heidemann has demonstrated how amiral autonomy actually helped to promote a form of 'Seljuq' culture, as the various regional courts looked to emulate those in Baghdad and Isfahan and adapt their architectural styles. The amirs also had a vested interest in defending, developing and extending the areas on which they depended for survival, which increased the likelihood that the Seljuq sphere of influence would expand further.[10]

These dual concepts help to explain why the Great Seljuq Sultanate held an interest in the political machinations of *bilad al-sham*. Syria and the wealthy cities of Damascus and Aleppo, offered abundant lands to dispense as *iqta'* to family members and other high-ranking figures at the sultan's court. Conversely, *bilad al-sham* also had the potential to cause problems for the sultan, as any family member who managed to establish control over multiple major urban centres, such as Damascus, Aleppo and Antioch, would have the requisite means to launch a bid for the sultanate.

As Seljuq influence in the region grew, it became increasingly important for the sultan to maintain a balance of power in Syria, while the influence of prominent Seljuq family members had to be carefully monitored. As a result, the appointment of rulers in Aleppo with close personal or familial ties to the sultan became more frequent during the reign of the Sultan Malik Shah. Appointees loyal to the sultan in Aleppo could provide a useful check on ambitious potentates in Mosul or Damascus, while also impeding any advances from the west by the Byzantines or the Frankish Crusaders. Yet these attempts to preserve an equilibrium in *bilad al-sham* essentially ensured a more chaotic and conflict-driven state of affairs for Syrian-based Seljuq amirs. This contradicts the widely held view that Malik Shah's reign contributed to the increased centralisation of Seljuq rule within Syria. If anything, some of Malik Shah's decisions actually made it harder for the sultan to control developments on the Syrian frontier.

These choices also provide the framework for a nuanced interpretation of Seljuq–Fatimid relations. On the Seljuqs' arrival in the region, the Fatimid Caliphate had been the dominant force in Syria and Palestine for over a hundred years. Tughrul Beg made a vow to invade Egypt shortly before his accession to the sultanate in 447/1055, and consequently, military successes against the Fatimids bolstered any sultan's credentials as a 'champion of Sunni Islam'.[11] Yet this blueprint of manufactured instability also impeded efforts to combat external enemies, which raises important questions about how integral devotional concerns were to Seljuq policy in *bilad al-sham*.

The Sultan in *Bilad al-sham*

The Seljuq sultans Alp Arslan and Malik Shah led two military expeditions into *bilad al-sham* in 463/1071 and 479/1086–7. The following section will review the historical accounts of these campaigns, examining how some of the problems that the Seljuq forces experienced during these short military operations are indicative of the limitations of Seljuq authority within Syria.[12]

It should first be noted that the modalities by which Seljuq sultans governed their realms underwent significant change during this period. In the traditional model, based upon the careers of Tughril Beg and Alp Arslan, the sultan's influence in any region was directly linked to their personal presence in that area, meaning that they spent much of their reigns moving between the territories under their control. This peripatetic leadership style, stemming from the dynasty's origins on the Eurasian Steppe, ensured the sultan maintained strong personal ties with their various 'vassals' scattered throughout Seljuq dominions.[13]

More recently, David Durand-Guédy and Andrew Peacock have highlighted how Malik Shah and his successors moved away from the role of nomadic chieftain. This was achieved by establishing a capital at Isfahan where later sultans were able to spend a large portion of their time, ruling over the sultanate from the centre of their domains.[14]

Alp Arslan's Campaign: 463/1071

The first Seljuq military expedition was led by the Sultan Alp Arslan, whose army entered *bilad al-sham* in the middle of Rabi' I 463/January 1071.[15] This is widely viewed as the starting point of Seljuq influence in northern Syria, although contacts between the Seljuq court and members of the Mirdasid dynasty had taken place long before this date.[16]

Alp Asrlan's forces placed Aleppo under siege at the end of Jumada II 463/late March–early April 1071. The siege ultimately forced the Mirdasid amir of Aleppo, Mahmud b. Nasr, to personally surrender to the sultan in the beginning of Sha'ban/early May.[17] While returning to Iraq, the sultan was informed that a huge Byzantine army under the command of Emperor Romanos Diogenes IV was advancing upon eastern Anatolia. Alp Arslan marched north and the two armies met in battle at Manzikert, near Lake Van on 27 Dhu 'l-Qa'da 463/26 August 1071, where the Seljuqs secured a famous victory.[18] Alp Arslan was then killed the following year in 465/1072 while campaigning in Transoxiana.[19]

Alp Arslan's campaign of 463/1071 is generally viewed to have been successful, although events at Manzikert are factored into most assessments.[20] Yet, even when discussion is confined to events in northern Syria, there are indications that Seljuq influence grew as a result of the sultan's expedition. The most obvious gain came in the form of Mahmud b. Nasr's submission, a clear indication that Mirdasid Aleppo was being integrated into the Seljuq political sphere. After Alp Arslan's siege in 463/1071, the *khutba* in Aleppo would never again be given in the name of the Fatimid caliph, save for one brief interlude in 490/1096.[21] This was a hugely significant change, as the *khutba* in Aleppo had for been made for the Fatimid caliph since 360/970.[22]

The negotiated surrender also created personal *khidma* ties between Alp Arslan and Mahmud b. Nasr, a fundamental concept that underpinned relationships between Seljuq elites.²³

Despite this, it is also possible to overstate the importance of Alp Arslan's achievements in northern Syria. After all, Aleppo remained under Mirdasid control, and despite a promise to lead a sustained offensive against Fatimid Damascus, Mahmud launched only one unsuccessful attack on Ba'albek in 463/1071.²⁴ It is also significant that Aleppo was not forced to make a financial payment as part of the final diplomatic settlement, especially when previous Mirdasid tribute payments to the Byzantines and Fatimids are taken into consideration.²⁵

Alp Arslan's campaign initially departed from Hamadhan in Dhu 'l-Qa'da 462/August 1070 and got off to a successful start with the capture of the strategically important settlements of Arjish and Manzikert in eastern Anatolia. This was followed by the surrender of the Marwanid ruler of Mayafariqin, Nasr b. Marwan, who also made a payment of '100,000 *dinars* ... for the army' according to Sibt b. al-Jawzi. *Ghulam* troops from the sultan's army also raided the region around Harran, whose inhabitants later agreed an unspecified settlement with the sultan.²⁶

It was at Edessa that Alp Arslan's campaign first began to experience difficulties.²⁷ An intense month-long siege prompted the populace to enter into a diplomatic dialogue with the sultan. In Sibt b. al-Jawzi's version of events, the Edessene leadership offered to pay Alp Arslan '50,000 dinars' to withdraw, but stipulated that they would not make the payment until 'you [Alp Arslan] are deprived of your machines of war by burning them'. Once the siege engines had been burnt, the townspeople sent a messenger informing the sultan that they would no longer be sending the agreed upon sum. Despite being enraged by this deception, Alp Arslan eventually took the advice of his Vizier Nizam al-Mulk and reluctantly ended the siege.²⁸

This setback was followed by a two–three-month period camped around the River Euphrates between Rabi' I-Jumada II 463/January–late March 1071. Two reasons were given for this delay. The first was to wait for a report from a Türkmen commander named Afshin b. Bakji, who had been sent to scout ahead into Byzantine territory. The second was unrest 'from those who were left with him [Alp Arslan] from the Iraqi army of Tughrul Beg'.²⁹

Campaigning in *bilad al-sham* had historically proven to be a problem for Seljuq sultans, largely due to a reluctance to do so from Türkmen troops.[30] Tughrul Beg's attempt to launch a campaign into northern Syria in 447/1055 had run into difficulties when one of his Türkmen commanders refused, reportedly opining of Syria:

> this land is ruined, there is neither food nor fodder here and we have no funds left. We cannot stay indefinitely on the back of our horses. What if our families, horses and beasts come, but our absence becomes drawn out?.[31]

While Sibt b. al-Jawzi did not explicitly state that Türkmen troops were the cause of disturbances in Alp Arslan's camp in the early months of 463/1071, 'the Iraqi army of Tughrul Beg' may be a reference to Türkmen troops that the sultan had inherited from his predecessor. Their patience would have been severely tested by the month-long siege of Edessa which yielded no tangible reward. A further three months spent encamped on the banks of the Euphrates, followed by a siege of Aleppo that culminated in a negotiated surrender, would have provided little if any real prospect of plunder for Türkmen troops in the sultan's army. This may well have dampened enthusiasm for any further campaigning in *bilad al-sham*, especially as by the time Mahmud of Aleppo agreed to surrender in Shaʿban/early May 1071, the sultan had been absent from his eastern provinces for eight months.

A period of four months with little material reward did not correspond well with the 'nomadic chief' leadership style that Alp Arslan typically favoured, which necessitated almost constant movement throughout the sultanate granting territories and plunder to his Türkmen troops and military commanders.[32] These factors help to explain how the Mirdasids were able to negotiate such advantageous terms with the sultan, and raise questions about the sustained impact of Alp Arslan's 463/1071 campaign upon the underlying power dynamics in *bilad al-sham*.

Malik Shah's Campaign: 479/1086–7

Alp Arslan's son and successor, Malik Shah b. Alp Arslan, led his own campaign into northern Syria between 13 Shaʿban and 1 Shawwal 479/23 November 1086 and 9 January 1087. The expedition was triggered by an appeal for help in 478/1085–6 from the besieged populace of Aleppo.[33]

The sultan's army departed Isfahan in Jumada II 479/September–October 1086, capturing Mosul, Harran, Edessa and Qalʿat Jaʿbar on route to occupying Aleppo, where they arrived on 13 Shaʿban 479/23 November 1086. The sultan then spent the next month or so occupying Antioch, which surrendered without resistance, and hunting near Maʿrrat al-Nuʿman. During this period, Nasr b. ʿAli of Shayzar and Ibn Malaʾb of Homs both submitted to the sultan and were confirmed in control of their territories.³⁴ The sultan's army left Aleppo on 1 Shawwal 479/9 January 1087, having celebrated Eid al-Fitr (breaking of the Ramadan fast) in the city. Malik Shah appointed Qasim al-Dawla Aqsunqur b. ʿAbd Allah in control of Aleppo, in addition to Yaghi Siyan in Antioch and Buzan in Edessa during this campaign.³⁵ Malik Shah's departure was triggered by reports of a rebellion by his brother Tekesh in Khurasan, which he returned east to quell.³⁶

Again on the surface, the campaign can be viewed as a marked success. Malik Shah managed to appoint governors with personal ties of loyalty to him in the key settlements of Aleppo, Antioch and Edessa, while also accepting the subjugation of the rulers of Homs and Shayzar.³⁷ His withdrawal marked the high point of Seljuq influence in northern Syria; no sultan would have more direct appointees in the region than during the period between the end of this campaign and Malik Shah's death on 3 Shawwal 485/7 November 1092.

Yet this campaign also ran into difficulties. Sibt b. al-Jawzi detailed how 'a large number of deserters from the army of the sultan came to Tutush' because of high food prices 'due to the absence of supplies'.³⁸ This does seem remarkable given that Malik Shah's army spent just one and a half months in northern Syria, and encountered no sustained opposition, although some explanation is provided by the fact that this expedition took place during the winter months, between 13 Shaʿban and 1 Shawwal 479/6 December 1086 and 9 January 1087.

When this desertion in 479/1086–7 is placed alongside the resistance that Tughrul Beg had encountered when trying to instigate a campaign in 447/1055, and the dissention Alp Arslan experienced during his expedition in 463/1071, a pattern emerges which suggests that Seljuq sultans found it difficult to campaign in northern Syria for prolonged periods of time. This was perhaps due the distance between *bilad al-sham* and the traditional hub of the sultanate further east, Aleppo is situated some 1,400 km northwest of Isfahan.

Sultan-led Campaigns on the Syrian Frontier

> The army of the Sultan began to arrive in *al-sham*, and Taj al-Dawla [Tutush] withdrew from Aleppo, and the Sultan conquered it. He then went to Antioch to take it from the hands of Sulayman's Vizier Hasan, and travelled to al-Suwaydiyya and prayed on the coast to thank Allah for providing him the support to rule from the sea of the east to the sea of the west.[39] He [the Sultan] then returned to Aleppo and celebrated.[40]

This extract, taken from al-ʿAzimi, *Taʾrikh halab* underscores the symbolic value that *bilad al-sham* held for the Sultan Malik Shah. Yet the limited amount of time both Malik Shah and his father Alp Arslan spent in northern Syria signify that it was not high on either sultans' list of priorities.

In total, Alp Arslan spent only four months in *bilad al-sham* between Rabiʿ I-Shaʿban 463/January–early May 1071, nearly three months of which was spent encamped around the River Euphrates, dealing with dissenting troops. Malik Shah only remained in northern Syria for little over a month and a half between 13 Shaʿban and 1 Shawwal 479/23 November 1086 and 9 January 1087. Based on rough estimates, this amounted to just 2.73 per cent of Alp Arslan's reign and 0.64 per cent of Malik Shah's, which contrasts heavily to the 12 and 62 per cent of their reigns they each spent in Isfahan.[41]

Even though Alp Arslan and Malik Shah faced little active opposition while present in the region, their campaigns failed to advance further south than the environs of Aleppo. While both Alp Arslan and Malik Shah's expeditions helped to expand Seljuq influence in the region, dissent among the troops and supply problems were indicative of the systemic issues which repeatedly hindered Seljuq forces campaigning in northern Syria. The persistent problems surrounding Seljuq military expeditions, even those commanded by sultans, were part of a wider trend that would have negative long-term consequences for Seljuq influence in the region.

Syrian Campaigns Instigated by Malik Shah

In addition to the expeditions led by Alp Arslan and Malik Shah, several campaigns in northern Syria were launched at Malik Shah's behest between 471 and 484/1079 and 1091. This section outlines how supply issues and the inability of Seljuq commanders to cooperate, rooted in the political culture of amiral rivalry, regularly impeded attempts to confront external enemies in northern Syria during the late fifth/eleventh century.

Taj al-Dawla Tutush b. Alp Arslan's Campaign: 471–2/1079–80

According to Ibn al-'Adim, Tutush's campaign into northern Syria was initially triggered by an appeal from disgruntled members of the Mirdasid dynasty in Dhu 'l-Hijja 469/July 1077. Wathab b. Mahmud and two companions travelled to the sultan's court to complain about the conduct of his brother, Sabiq b. Mahmud, who had recently become the new Mirdasid ruler of Aleppo.[42]

Seeing an opportunity to expand Seljuq influence in *bilad al-sham*, Malik Shah elected to send his then eleven-year-old brother Tutush on a military expedition into northern Syria. Malik Shah appointed Afshin b. Bakji, Sunduq al-Turki and 'and other Turkish Amirs' to assist Tutush. Aside from Seljuq military figures, individuals from the Arab dynasties and tribal groups of northern Syria and the Jazira also contributed resources to the campaign. The Mirdasid Wathab b. Mahmud, whose approach to the sultan had prompted the campaign, departed for *bilad al-sham* with Tutush, while the Uqaylid ruler of Mosul Sharaf al-Dawla Muslim b. Quraysh, joined up with the Seljuq army upon its arrival at Aleppo.[43]

Tutush's coalition force first targeted Aleppo, placing it under siege at the end of Shawwal 471/early May 1079. But Tutush's siege of Aleppo was ultimately undermined by the Uqaylid ruler Muslim b. Quraysh, who sold supplies to the besieged population before later departing from the Seljuq camp. Muslim b. Quraysh then joined with a coalition force of Arab troops drawn from the tribes of the Banu Numayr, Qushayri, Kilab and Uqayl to ambush a group of 1,000 Türkmen at al-Faya (a village between Manbij and Aleppo) who had been sent to Syria by Malik Shah as reinforcements for Tutush.[44] Muslim b. Quraysh's actions effectively sabotaged any chance Tutush's forces may have had of capturing Aleppo in 471/1079.

Following this setback, Tutush and his commanders led their army east beyond the River Euphrates, but returned to *bilad al-sham* in 472/1079–80, capturing Manbij, Buza'a and 'Azaz to the east and north of Aleppo. Tutush then besieged Aleppo again, but received a call for aid from the Türkmen ruler of Damascus, Atsiz b. Uwaq al-Khwarizmi, which had been placed under siege by a Fatimid army. Tutush and his army called off the siege of Aleppo for a second time and marched south to relieve Damascus. As Tutush approached the city, the besieging Egyptian force withdrew from the area. Tutush then killed Atsiz and assumed control of Damascus and other territories in Palestine under Atsiz's dominion.[45] During Tutush's absence from northern Syria, the Uqaylid ruler of Mosul Muslim b. Quraysh captured Aleppo in 473/1080.[46]

While Tutush's attempts to establish himself in *bilad al-sham* eventually proved to be successful, the events of 471/1079 suggested that, even when acting on the orders of the Sultan Malik Shah, rival amirs struggled to place collective objectives ahead of personal ambition.

Collaborative Seljuq Campaigns against Homs and Tripoli: 483–4/1090–1

The second and third instances when Malik Shah ordered collaborative military action came after the appointments of Qasim al-Dawla Aqsunqur at Aleppo, Yaghi Siyan at Antioch and Buzan in Edessa in 479/1086–7. Both of these joint expeditions were launched against potentates who had ties to the Fatimids, or in reaction to Fatimid campaigns. Yet despite the target of these campaigns being 'Fatimid' rivals, joint military operations requiring cooperation between Seljuq amirs remained problematic.

In 480/1087, Tutush reportedly wrote to his brother Malik Shah requesting that the sultan order the newly appointed rulers of Aleppo and Edessa to support him, as the Fatimids had taken control of the coast and had 'harassed' Damascus. Although Sibt b. al-Jawzi reported that Malik Shah acceded to this request, no concrete steps were taken to combat the Fatimids at this time.[47]

Then, in 482/1089–90 an Egyptian army captured Tyre, Sidon, Jubayl and Acre. The ruler of Homs, Khalaf b. Mula'ib, also switched allegiance to the Fatimids. As discussed in Chapter 2, this campaign placed Damascus under significant threat, cutting the city off from the recently appointed Seljuq amirs to the north. Therefore, Tutush appealed directly to Aqsunqur and Buzan, and although they eventually sent troops to assist Damascus, neither ruler felt the need to lead armies into southern Syria.[48]

The Fatimid campaign in 482/1089–90 did ultimately lead to collaborative Seljuq campaigns against Homs in 483/1090 and Tripoli in 484/1091. However, disputes arose between the Seljuq amirs of Syria even in the course of these short military operations. While the 483/1090 campaign did lead to the capture of Homs, there was a disagreement between Aqsunqur and Tutush over who would take control of the newly captured settlement, resulting in an appeal to Malik Shah to settle the matter. The dispute was resolved when 'the Sultan gave it (Homs) to Taj al-Dawla Tutush' according to Ibn al-'Adim.[49]

One year later in 484/1091, Tutush, Aqsunqur and Buzan launched another joint campaign against Tripoli, where there were further reports of disagreement between Seljuq amirs. Both Ibn al-Athir and Sibt b. al-Jawzi reported that while the settlement was under siege the ruler of Tripoli, Ibn 'Ammar, surreptitiously approached Aqsunqur of Aleppo, sending him documents of investiture from the Sultan Malik Shah. Ibn al-Athir also claimed that Ibn 'Ammar gave Aqsunqur's vizier a payment of 30,000 dinars to further induce Aqsunqur to lift the siege. Aqsunqur then withdrew from the siege, claiming to Tutush that he could not attack an individual possessing such documents, as he viewed it as disobedient to the Sultan Malik Shah. After Aqsunqur departed, Tutush was forced to do so too, 'furious' at this turn of events, according to Ibn al-Athir.[50]

The issues that arose during the course of these campaigns demonstrate how even when participating in military offensives targeting the Fatimids, their supposed ideological enemies in the region, Seljuq amirs struggled to cooperate effectively. This ineptitude provides important context for the failed Seljuq military activity against the Frankish Crusaders and settlers in the early sixth/twelfth century.

The Limitations of Seljuq Military Capabilities in Bilad al-sham: *463–90/1071–97*

Seljuq military campaigns into northern Syria throughout late fifth/eleventh century were consistently disrupted by supply problems, desertion and the inability of rival amirs to place collective objectives ahead of personal gain. These issues, which were intertwined with the autonomy wielded by amirs throughout the Great Seljuq Sultanate, inhibited Seljuq efforts to confront external enemies in Syria, but also contributed significantly to their inability to maintain a position of dominance in the region.

The shortcomings of Seljuq military policy in *bilad al-sham* during the fifth/eleventh century also needs to be factored into any explanation of the success enjoyed by the armies of the First Crusade between 490 and 492/1097 and 1099. In a highly influential article on this subject, Carole Hillenbrand contended that had 'the First Crusade arrived even ten years earlier, it would have met strong, unified resistance from the East under Malikshah'.[51]

In the light of the persistent problems that disrupted Seljuq military expeditions into the region in the late fifth/eleventh century, the assertion that Malik Shah would have led a campaign against or in response to the First Crusade had it occurred while he was alive could be open to question. Between Alp Arslan's campaign of 463/1071 and Malik Shah's death in 485/1092, both Seljuq sultans spent a total of five and a half months in northern Syria over a period of more than twenty years.

Even those campaigns led in person by these sultans encountered significant problems when in Syria. Moreover, Malik Shah did not personally lead an expedition into the region in response to the Fatimid campaign in 482/1090. How can we be sure that Malik Shah would have reacted more vigorously to the arrival of the First Crusade than he had to an incursion by the Seljuq's Shi'i ideological enemies? Even if the Franks had arrived ten years earlier, the issues encountered by Seljuq armies from the east in northern Syria raises doubts that they would have provoked an immediate response from the eastern heartlands of the Great Seljuq Sultanate.

The Seljuq Perpetuation of the System of Autonomous Lordships in Syria

Chapters 1 and 2 detailed how the system of autonomous lordships in Syria pre-dated the arrival of the Seljuqs. Mirdasid Aleppo had thrown off the shackles of Byzantine and Fatimid influence by 454/1062 at the latest, whilst a rebellion by the populace of Damascus successfully expelled the Fatimid representative of the city in 458/1066.

The Seljuq potentates who established themselves in Syria and Palestine after 463/1071 took advantage of the already present system of autonomous lordships in the region, rather than being the root cause of its development.

This places doubt on the widely held perception that the introduction of Seljuq rulers had a hugely destabilising impact upon the political world of *bilad al-sham*.

The following section will examine whether decisions taken by the Sultan Malik Shah to limit the authority of his younger brother Tutush led to the preservation of the system of autonomous lordships in Syria. Particular focus will be placed upon Malik Shah's reported interventions on behalf of the Uqaylid ruler of Aleppo and Mosul, Sharaf al-Dawla Muslim b. Quraysh, and what this may reveal about the sultan's overarching strategy the region. This is followed by a reconsideration of Seljuq influence in *bilad al-sham* under Malik Shah's successors, and the contacts between Syrian-based Seljuq amirs and the sultan's court. Notwithstanding the marked decline in Seljuq authority that followed Malik Shah's death in 485/1092, his descendants managed to retain some semblance of influence with the amirs of Syria during the early sixth/twelfth century.

Tutush: Balancing the Principle of Shared Family Rule against the Threat of Rebellion

A detailed understanding of the relationship between the Sultan Malik Shah and his brother Tutush b. Alp Arslan is fundamental to any assessment of Seljuq influence in *bilad al-sham*. There are numerous indications within the medieval Arabic chronicles that Malik Shah repeatedly intervened in political developments in the region in ways that restricted his brother's territorial dominions.

However, much of the evidence touching upon this fraternal friction is dependent upon reported speech and excerpts from correspondence between Malik Shah, Tutush and other rulers in *bilad al-sham* contained in the chronicles of Sibt b. al-Jawzi and Ibn al-'Adim. The notion that Sibt b. al-Jawzi and Ibn al-'Adim would have had access to this material nearly two hundred years after the events took place is dubious, and these sections therefore need to be treated with caution. Sibt b. al-Jawzi may also have been motivated by a desire to portray his place of birth, Baghdad, or Iraq in general, as more influential in Syrian politics than was actually the case.

However, it should also be noted that Sibt b. al-Jawzi incorporated material from the now lost work of Muhammad b. Hilal al-Sabi (d. 481/1088) in his chronicle. Muhammad b. Hilal al-Sabi was a high-ranking figure at the Abbasid court in Baghdad, which would have granted him access to many pertinent official documents.[52] In addition, Sibt b. al-Jawzi and Ibn al-'Adim provide the fullest accounts of events in *bilad al-sham* during the later fifth/eleventh century, and their evidence deserves to be fully considered.

As discussed above, Tutush b. Alp Arslan's appointment was triggered by an appeal to the Seljuq court by disaffected members of the Mirdasid dynasty in Dhu 'l-Hijja 469/July 1077. In response to their complaint, Malik Shah granted his brother, Taj al-Dawla Tutush b. Alp Arlsan, '*al-sham*' as an *iqta'*.[53]

It is important to appreciate the political dynamics that formed the backdrop to Tutush's appointment. Due to the Seljuq adherence to the principle of shared family rule, Malik Shah was expected to bestow positions of authority upon prominent family members. Yet by granting Tutush *al-sham* as an *iqta'*, the sultan was effectively giving his younger brother *carte blanche* to establish his own power-base in Syria. This meant that this decision came with inevitable risks for Malik Shah. Although Tutush was only thirteen years old upon his arrival in northern Syria in Shawwal 471/early May 1079, his new position furnished him with the chance to establish himself as the dominant ruler in Syria and Palestine with little oversight from his older brother in Isfahan.

Interestingly, Sibt b. al-Jawzi reported that the sultan's vizier 'Nizam al-Mulk had no influence' in Malik Shah's decision to grant Tutush '*al-sham*' as an *iqta'*. Nizam al-Mulk was finely attuned to the dangers of empowering family members in the Seljuq political system.[54] Upon Malik Shah's accession to the sultanate, Nizam al-Mulk had attempted to curtail the influence of the Seljuq royal family, killing and blinding several members of the new sultan's extended family. It therefore seems unlikely that the vizier would have championed Tutush's preferment in *al-sham*.[55]

Malik Shah's first attempt to restrict Tutush's broad brief in '*al-sham*' came during the course of his brother's first campaign in 471/1079. According to Sibt b. al-Jawzi, the ruler of Damascus, Atsiz b. Uwaq al-Khwarizmi, sent to the sultan to complain about Tutush's appointment, prompting Malik Shah to write to his brother warning him 'not to enter into *al-sham* except to pursue the territory around Aleppo'.[56] Despite this injunction from the sultan, Tutush's forces did eventually march to Damascus in response to an appeal for aid from Atsiz, as the city had been placed under siege by a Fatimid army in 472/1079. The Egyptian besieging force withdrew as Tutush's army approached and Tutush had Atsiz arrested and summarily executed in Rabiʿ I 472/September 1079, before seizing control of the territories under Atsiz's control.[57]

This episode bespeaks the limitations of Malik Shah's power in northern Syria. Tutush's killing of Atsiz removed a ruler with ties to the sultan, who could have acted as a check on Tutush in the event that he attempted to challenge for the sultanate. Tutush's disregard for Malik Shah's order to keep out of Damascene affairs, and the lack of punishment he received, laid bare the sultan's inability to assert his authority in *bilad al-sham* from afar.

The Elevation of Muslim b. Quraysh

There are several indications that the Uqaylid ruler of Mosul, Muslim b. Quraysh Sharaf al-Dawla, was earmarked by the sultan to help constrain Tutush's territorial ambitions in *bilad al-sham*. The Uqaylid dynasty, descended from the north Arab Uqayl tribe who had been active in northern Syria and the Jazira from the fourth/tenth century onwards, had ruled Mosul since 380/990.[58]

Although Muslim's father, Quraysh b. Badran (d. 453/1061), had endured a difficult, often antagonistic, relationship with the Seljuq Sultanate, things changed rapidly under his son's rule. Muslim b. Quraysh inherited control of Mosul after his father's death in 453/1061, and the first indications of improved dealings the sultan's court came in 458/1065, when Alp Arslan granted the Uqaylid ruler 'Anbar, Hit, Harba', al-Sinn and Bawazij as an *iqtaʿ*.[59] Another signal of Muslim b. Quraysh's growth in favour came in his marriage to Malik Shah's sister in 462/1070.[60] Further gains would have been made when Muslim b. Quraysh fought alongside Malik Shah's army during the succession crisis that had followed Alp Arslan's death in Shaʿban 465/April 1073.[61] By backing Malik Shah's claim to the sultanate and helping to defeat his uncle Qavurt Beg's army at Hamadhan, Muslim b. Quraysh likely earned the gratitude and trust of the new ruler of the Seljuq world.

This joint history may well have influenced Malik Shah's decision-making regarding northern Syria over the following fifteen years, during which time Muslim b. Quraysh would emerge as a highly influential figure in the region. As has been outlined above, Muslim b. Quraysh had participated in Tutush's first siege of Aleppo in 471/1079, but had actively sabotaged the efforts of the sultan's brother to take the city. Despite this, Malik Shah confirmed Muslim b. Quraysh's right to rule Aleppo when he captured the city in Rabiʿ II 473/ November–December 1080. Ibn al-Athir noted that Muslim b. Quraysh also requested that he 'be assigned the tax of farming revenue (of Aleppo) ... which the Sultan granted'.[62] This appears to have been quite similar to an *iqtaʿ*, which would have granted him a similar level of independence to that enjoyed by the sultan's brother Tutush.

This decision implies that the sultan had a large amount of trust in Muslim b. Quraysh. In combining Aleppo with Mosul, Muslim b. Quraysh effectively became the most influential ruler in the western Seljuq world. Indeed, simultaneous dominion over Aleppo and Mosul was almost unprecedented between 442 and 522/1050 and 1128, with the only comparable examples being Tutush for a short period in the midst of a failed bid for the sultanate in 488/1095, Aqsunqur al-Bursuqi's 22-month reign in Aleppo between 518 and 520/1125 and 1126, and the *atabeg* Imad al-Din Zangi b. Aqsunqur from 522/1128. Why was Muslim b. Quraysh granted this level of authority when Malik Shah had actively impeded Tutush's attempts to capture Aleppo in 471/1079?

The answer perhaps lies in the risk to Malik Shah and his descendants posed by Tutush's appointment in Syria, as only members of the Seljuq dynasty could challenge for the sultanate.[63] As a consequence, even though he was only thirteen or fourteen years old at the time, Tutush presented a far greater potential threat to Malik Shah's position, or the succession of his children, than Sharaf al-Dawla in 473/1080.

Muslim b. Quraysh is a figure who has often been overlooked in modern historiography, probably as he was of 'Arab', not 'Turkish' descent. Sharaf al-Dawla again exemplifies why it is so misleading to apply reductionist ethnic labels, such as Arab and Turk, to multiple individuals. There was no single Arab or Turkish 'identity' in the political arena of *bilad al-sham*, and it is therefore important to judge each figure on an individual basis.

If anything, Muslim b. Quraysh's lack of Turkish heritage helped him to gain the support of the sultan. By the time of his occupation of Aleppo in 473/1080, Muslim b. Quraysh had built up a stable track record with Malik Shah, best illustrated by his marriage alliance with the sultan's sister. Muslim b. Quraysh had no realistic chance of becoming sultan. This made him an ideal candidate to rule Aleppo and potentially hinder any attempts by Tutush to expand his power base in Syria.

Muslim b. Quraysh's Fatimid Connections

Conflict between Tutush and Muslim b. Quraysh was almost inevitable, particularly after Malik Shah granted his brother the entire region of '*al-sham*' as an *iqta'*. The first clash between Tutush and Muslim b. Quraysh occurred in 475/1082–3. At this time, Tutush received appeals for military aid from various rival Arab rulers and Bedouin tribal groups who had lost territory to Muslim b. Quraysh since his acquisition of Aleppo two years previously.

Tutush marched to the Jisr al-Hadid (Iron Bridge), a key crossing on the River Orontes to the northeast of Antioch, and dispatched raiders under his commander Artuq to ravage the area around Aleppo. The Sultan Malik Shah did not look favourably upon Tutush's actions. Sibt b. al-Jawzi claimed that Malik Shah wrote to his brother Tutush, telling him to 'return to Damascus and to not establish himself in the city of Aleppo'. He also supposedly sent a separate message to Artuq ordering him to stop his raiding activity, which the same chronicler tells us 'weakened' their position, although Ibn al-Qalanisi claimed that the siege was not lifted until a relief force arrived from Homs, which was also under Muslim b. Quraysh's control.[64] This alleged intervention by the sultan provides further corroboration that Malik Shah was willing to actively intervene in Syrian affairs in order to curb his brother's influence in *bilad al-sham*.

Malik Shah's intervention is even more surprising given reports that Muslim b. Quraysh was actively courting the support of the Shi'i Fatimid caliph at this time. Sibt b. al-Jawzi detailed how earlier in 475/1082–3, the sultan's court had received a message from the Byzantine *dux* of Antioch, Philaretos Brachamios, informing the sultan of correspondence between Muslim b. Quraysh and the Fatimid caliph, claiming that Muslim b. Quraysh had 'obtained from him [the Fatimid Caliph] robes of honour and money'.[65] Upon receiving this accusation, Malik Shah dispatched his Vizier Nizam al-Mulk 'to censure Muslim b. Quraysh', but the latter vehemently denied having had any contact with Fatimid Cairo.[66]

The sultan's interference enabled Muslim b. Quraysh to rally his forces and launch a counterattack against Tutush, besieging Damascus in Muharram

475/late May 1083.⁶⁷ It appears that Muslim b. Quraysh misled the sultan and his vizier about his contacts with the Fatimid court, as the majority of our sources note that Sharaf al-Dawla fully expected to receive military support for his assault on Damascus in 475/1083, even though the Fatimids ultimately decided against dispatching any troops.⁶⁸ The lack of military support from Egypt, combined with a rebellion against Uqaylid rule in Harran, forced him to lift his siege of Damascus.

It is also worth noting that Malik Shah apparently took no action to intervene in Sharaf al-Dawla's siege of Damascus, despite suggestions that he was conspiring with the sultan's Shi'i ideological enemies. This was in stark contrast to the messages which Sibt b. al-Jawzi claimed the sultan sent to Tutush and Artuq, commanding them to stop raiding Aleppo earlier that same year. This suggests that Malik Shah was willing to intercede in Syrian politics to protect Muslim b. Quraysh's interests, but not those of his brother, probably due to the potential threat Tutush's posed as a member of the Seljuq aristocracy.

Ibn al-'Adim provided details of a second instance when Muslim b. Quraysh attempted to collaborate with the Fatimid Caliphate. Whilst under pressure following a military defeat against Seljuq forces at Amid in Rabi'I 477/July 1084, Muslim b. Quraysh dispatched his uncle Miqbal b. Badran to the Fatimid court 'to request their support, offering them his obedience', while simultaneously sending a messenger to the sultan 'reminding him that he was in *khidma* to him'. Once the sultan learnt of Miqbal b. Badran's presence in Egypt, he summoned Muslim b. Quraysh to explain himself. Supposedly taking Nizam al-Mulk's advice, as the sultan's vizier 'inclined towards Sharaf al-Dawla [Muslim b. Quraysh]' and 'he indicated his good deeds to him and wanted a pardon for him', Malik Shah overlooked Muslim b. Quraysh's indiscretions and confirmed him again in control of all of his territories, including Mosul and Aleppo.⁶⁹ Remarkably, Malik Shah instead 'wrote to his brother Taj al-Dawla [Tutush] that he was not to enter his [Muslim b. Quraysh's] territory, as he had approached it before', presumably alluding to Tutush's attack on Aleppo in 475/1082–3.⁷⁰

Muslim b. Quraysh seemingly made multiple attempts to enter into alliances with the Fatimid Caliphate against other Seljuq rulers, including the sultan's brother Tutush. Despite this, Malik Shah and his Vizier Nizam al-Mulk not only permitted Muslim b. Quraysh to retain a position of great influence in the Seljuq political realm, the sultan actively discouraged Tutush from attacking Muslim b. Quraysh's territory in *bilad al-sham* on two separate occasions.

In return, Muslim b. Quraysh's loyalty to the Sultan Malik Shah, at least in a Seljuq context, seemingly extended beyond the grave. Before going into what would be his final battle in 478/1085 against one of the sultan's cousins, Muslim b. Quraysh, he had advised his deputy in Aleppo, Salim b. Malik al-Uqayli, 'not to surrender except to the Sultan Malik Shah'.[71] A subsequent appeal to the sultan's court from the besieged inhabitants of Aleppo would bring Malik Shah to *bilad al-sham* for the first and only time during his reign as sultan.

Despite being of Arab descent, Muslim b. Quraysh became a hugely authoritative figure in Seljuq circles, both in terms of the territories he controlled and his connections at the sultan's court. His influence stretched from northern Syria and Mesopotamia to Isfahan, where he enjoyed the support of the all-powerful Vizier Nizam al-Mulk. For the sultan, Muslim b. Quraysh seemingly played an important role as a check on Tutush's power in *bilad al-sham*. Muslim b. Quraysh's fulfilment of this duty was seemingly more important to Malik Shah and Nizam al-Mulk than any attempts the Uqaylid ruler made to ally himself to the Fatimids. Their readiness to overlook these contacts with Fatimid Cairo does not sit well the perception of Malik Shah as a 'champion of Sunni Islam'.

Aqsunqur, Yaghi Siyan and Buzan: Further Limitations on Tutush's Power?

This delicate balance of power that Malik Shah had cultivated in *bilad al-sham*, with Tutush confined to the south in Damascus and Palestine and Sharaf al-Dawla holding Mosul and Aleppo, was shattered by 477/1084. This was the year in which Sulayman b. Qutlumush, a distant cousin to Malik Shah and Tutush who controlled a string of other territories in Cilicia and Anatolia, announced his entry onto the Syrian political scene by capturing Antioch in Sha'ban 477/December 1084.[72]

Although Sulayman b. Qutlumush was not a direct family member of the sultan, he was a direct descendant of Arslan Isra'il, the eldest son of Seljuq the eponym of the Seljuq dynasty, giving Sulayman a relatively good claim to the sultanate and strong support from some key Türkmen leaders.[73]

Suddenly, there were two family members operating in Syria who posed a potential threat to Malik Shah's position. This threat increased in Muharram 478/May 1085, when Sulayman b. Qutlumush's troops defeated Muslim b. Quraysh's army in a battle at Qurzahil, near the River 'Afrin to the north of Aleppo, with the sultan's long-term ally in Syria, Muslim b. Quraysh, perishing on the battlefield.[74] This left Tutush and Sulayman to contest control of *bilad al-sham* between themselves, and it was Malik Shah's brother who would emerge victorious after Sulayman was killed in a battle against Tutush's forces at 'Ayn Silim, 3 miles away from Aleppo, on 18 Safar 479/4 June 1086. Tutush's troops subsequently besieged Aleppo, hoping the add the main urban centre of northern Syria to his growing dominions.[75]

The death of Muslim b. Quraysh, followed just a year later by that of Sulayman b. Qutlumush, created a substantial strategic problem for Malik Shah. His younger brother Tutush's path to control of Syria was now unchecked. In response, Malik Shah decided to launch his first and only campaign into *bilad al-sham*, which was nominally in response to a call for aid from notables of Aleppo, whose city had now been placed under siege by Tutush's forces. The sultan's army departed from Isfahan in Jumada II 479/September–October 1086, arrived at Aleppo on 13 Sha'ban 479/23 November 1086, with Tutush returning to Damascus when he received word of the sultan's approach.[76] This relatively short timeline, with the sultan arriving in northern Syria within five months of Sulayman b. Qutlumush's death, combined with credible reports of supply problems, are indicative of a hastily arranged expedition launched in response to Tutush's emergence as the predominant Seljuq ruler in the region.[77]

Upon his return to Damascus, Tutush reportedly wrote to the sultan, requesting reassurance about his position. According to Sibt b. al-Jawzi's account, Tutush asked Malik Shah if 'he would remain in command of his *iqta*' or if he should depart to a place he was safe in?'. This strongly suggests that Tutush saw Malik Shah's sudden arrival in Syria as a direct move against him, leaving the younger brother fearful about his standing and security. The sultan wrote back to Tutush confirming that he could retain control of Damascus as he had a 'good heart'.[78]

This decision not to remove Tutush seemingly contradicts the notion that Malik Shah went to great lengths to restrict his younger brother's influence.

But it should be remembered that one element of the Seljuq political tradition was an expectation that high-ranking family members would be granted territory to rule over. Considering that Tutush had displayed no overt signs of disloyalty to the sultan, had Malik Shah stripped Tutush of his *iqta'* in 479/1086–7, it would have been poorly received at the Seljuq court. It is also not clear that Malik Shah would have had the time to remove Tutush from Damascus, as he remained in northern Syria for less than two months before being forced to return to the east to combat a separate rebellion by another brother.

Nevertheless, Tutush was not placed in control of Aleppo, with that honour given instead to Qasim al-Dawla Aqsunqur b. 'Abd Allah.[79] Malik Shah's 479/1086–7 campaign into northern Syria and the appointment of another potential rival to Tutush in Aleppo are the clearest manifestations of Malik Shah's efforts to limit his younger brother's influence in *bilad al-sham*.[80] Aqsunqur was an amir at Malik Shah's court, and Ibn al-Athir strongly implies that the sultan's Vizier Nizam al-Mulk played a significant role in Aqsunqur's appointment in Aleppo. This was allegedly driven by the vizier's need to 'distance him [Aqsunqur] from the Sultan's service', as Aqsunqur had been granted privileges at the Seljuq court which Nizam al-Mulk deemed to be above his station.[81] Ibn al-'Adim also noted that Aqsunqur had a good relationship with the sultan, writing that 'it is said that he (Aqsunqur) was among the *maliks* of Malik Shah, and it is said that he was close to him', potentially because Aqsunqur's wife had served as the sultan's childhood wet nurse.[82]

Although Aqsunqur was an up-and-coming Turkish commander at the Seljuq court, one generation removed from the Eurasian Steppe, and Muslim b. Quraysh was a member of an Arab dynasty who had ruled Mosul for several generations, they had a lot in common with each other, particularly in terms of their relationship with the Sultan Malik Shah. Both Aqsunqur and Muslim b. Quraysh possessed a military background and were married to women with close personal ties to the sultan. Yet they were not prominent members of the Seljuq dynasty, making it highly improbable that they would make a future claim to the sultanate. Buzan and Yaghi Siyan, who the sultan appointed as rulers of Edessa and Antioch, were also of relatively minor stature in the Seljuq ruling hierarchy.

This triumvirate of Seljuq commanders at Aleppo, Antioch and Edessa would help to derail Tutush's eventual bid for the sultanate, which came after

Malik Shah's death in 485/1092.⁸³ Although initially Aqsunqur, Buzan and Yaghi Siyan all made common cause with Tutush in the war of succession against Malik Shah's eldest son Berkyaruq, this alliance did not survive long. Tutush apparently alienated Aqsunqur and Buzan by failing to properly reward them and showing favouritism to Yaghi-Siyan.⁸⁴ Aqsunqur and Buzan therefore switched sides to join with Malik Shah's son Berkyaruq in 486/1093, throwing Tutush's plans into chaos. Tutush, who had been marching on Iran to confront Berkyaruq's army, was forced to return to Syria to secure his western flank, eventually defeating a coalition force drawn from Antioch and Aleppo in battle near Buza'a, to the east of Aleppo, in 487/1094.⁸⁵ Although Aqsunqur and Buzan were both killed in the aftermath of this battle, their initial betrayal had forced Tutush to return to *bilad al-sham* 486/1093, which enabled Berkyaruq to recover from earlier setbacks and eventually to defeat and kill Tutush in battle near Rayy in 488/1095.⁸⁶

Following Tutush's death, his sons Ridwan and Duqaq seized control over his former dominions in northern Syria, with the former taking Aleppo and the latter Damascus. The way in which Ridwan and Duqaq were able to seize power in Aleppo and Damascus, with little oversight from the sultan, is reminiscent of the way in which Tutush assumed control over Damascus, or Sharaf al-Dawla Aleppo. Within a year of their father's death, a protracted conflict broke out between Ridwan and Duqaq, dominating the Syrian political scene until the armies of the First Crusade arrived outside Antioch in 491/1097.⁸⁷

The Consequences of Preserving the System of Autonomous Lordships in Syria

Modern historians have long accepted that the death of the Sultan Malik Shah and his Vizier Nizam al-Mulk in 485/1092, followed closely by that of Tutush in 488/1095, were hugely disruptive events that undermined the Great Seljuq Sultanate's ability to respond to the onset of the Crusades in 491/1097.⁸⁸ Yet this perhaps overstates both the strength of Tutush's hold upon northern Syria, and the extent to which Malik Shah was able to establish centralised Seljuq control upon the region.

Beginning with the impact of Tutush's death, Ibn al-'Adim reported that Tutush spent a total of just three days in Aleppo after occupying it in 488/1095, while after Tutush's death, the Aleppan notable Aba al-Qasim b. Badi'a seized control of the city. It took Tutush's son Ridwan and his *atabeg* Janah al-Dawla nearly a year to firmly establish themselves in command of Aleppo.[89] This hardly conveys the impression that Tutush established a great deal of authority within Aleppo, and calls into question the significance of Tutush's demise for the region as a whole. Instead, Tutush's death merely re-established the status quo within Syria; whereby power was distributed among a collection of minor local potentates with varying degrees of allegiance to Fatimid Cairo and Seljuq Isfahan.

The perpetuation of this system of autonomous lordships in Seljuq *bilad al-sham* was a direct repercussion of strategic choices made by the Sultan Malik Shah. Although there were some exceptions, such as Malik Shah's attempts to order Seljuq amirs to participate in collaborative military actions against Fatimid rulers in Homs and Tripoli in the 480s/1090s and the subsequent granting of Homs to Tutush, the sultan repeatedly intervened in Syrian political affairs in order to limit the territories under the direct control of his younger brother.[90] These efforts ultimately proved to be successful, as individuals directly appointed by Malik Shah in Syria disrupted Tutush's eventual bid for the sultanate, enabling Malik Shah's sons to succeed him as sultan.

But the ramifications for Syria were severe. Rather than being an inadvertent by-product of the vicissitudes of dynastic politics or the incomplete nature of the Seljuq conquest of Syria, the profound instability that characterised the political world of *bilad al-sham* during the last twenty-five years of the fifth/eleventh century was created by design, an intended consequence of the sultan's attempts to manage the threat posed by Tutush. Essentially, it would be more accurate to characterise this period of Syrian history as centralised chaos, as opposed to centralised Seljuq control. Moreover, this constant state of upheaval would have made it more difficult for Malik Shah to control developments in Syria from Isfahan.

There was also an ideological cost associated with this policy. In purposefully denying Tutush the combined resources of Aleppo and Damascus, the sultan and his Vizier Nizam al-Mulk caused efforts to combat the Shi'i Fatimid Caliphate to become bogged down in internecine disputes and confusion. Another example of the prioritisation of internal political concerns over the doctrinal conflict with the Fatimids were the repeated allowances made for Muslim b. Quraysh, the Uqaylid ruler of Mosul and Aleppo, who attempted to form alliances with the Fatimids against other Seljuq rulers on multiple occasions. The legacy of these decisions would endure even after the arrival of the Frankish Crusaders and settlers, as the inability of Seljuq military leaders to combat external enemies was inherently linked to level of autonomy wielded by Seljuq amirs in Syria.

Seljuq *Bilad al-sham* in the Sixth/Twelfth Century

Seljuq influence in *bilad al-sham* was severely impaired by the deaths of Malik Shah and Nizam al-Mulk in 485/1092 and the resulting series of succession crises.[91] In Syria, Tutush, Aqsunqur and Buzan were all killed in the space of three years (485–8/1092–5), destroying nearly all of the *khidma* networks built up over the preceding twenty-five years. These figures were replaced by a complex patchwork of lordships ruled by individuals of Arab, Turkish, Armenian and Syriac heritage who held only nominal ties to the Seljuqs or the Fatimids.

In the subsequent decades, the sultans Muhammad b. Malik Shah and Mahmud b. Muhammad both attempted to rebuild Seljuq influence in *bilad al-sham*. These efforts were not confined to the failed military campaigns in 505/1111 and 509/1115, with the literary sources providing glimpses of contacts between Syrian-based Seljuq amirs and the sultan's court.[92] These interactions indicate that Seljuq influence in the region persisted into the sixth/twelfth century, at least in nominal form.

The succession crisis fought between Malik Shah's sons Berkyaruq and Muhammad between 491 and 498/1098 and 1105 made the very notion of allegiance to the Seljuq sultan nebulous, as there were two claimants in a conflict to the east in which none of the amirs in *bilad al-sham* played an active role.[93] Communications between the Seljuq court and Turkish amirs in Syria only resurfaced after Muhammad's emergence as the undisputed claimant to the Great Seljuq Sultanate in 498/1105.

Tughtegin of Damascus

Contacts between Sultan Muhammad and Zahir al-Din Tughtegin of Damascus, the former *atabeg* of Duqaq who took control of the city following the latter's death in 497/1104, increased in frequency from Ramadan 501/14 April–13 May 1108 onwards. This was when Tughtegin's son,

Taj al-Muluk Buri, accompanied the ruler of Tripoli, Fakhr al-Mulk ʿAmmar, on a diplomatic mission to Baghdad, where they requested assistance from the Sultan Muhammad to combat the Franks. While in Baghdad, Ibn al-Qalanisi reported that Buri received 'gratifying favours' and 'magnificent robes of honour' from the caliph and sultan.[94]

Ibn al-Qalanisi also recounted how Tughtegin dispatched Fakhr al-Mulk ʿAmmar to Baghdad again in 503/1109, when rumours reached him that the sultan had 'invested' other amirs with the 'governorship of *al-sham*'. The same chronicle tells us that Fakhr al-Mulk ʿAmmar was again well received in Baghdad, where he was told reports that Tughtegin was going to be replaced were 'baseless'. Further comfort was offered by 'a succession of letters' that arrived in Damascus from Baghdad which offered support and reassurance to Tughtegin.[95]

Both the 501/1108 and 503/1109 embassies to Baghdad saw Tughtegin and his son Buri receive some tacit form of approval from the Sultan Muhammad, either in the form of robes of honour or letters of support. This implied that Tughtegin valued these symbolic representations of approval, and that the Seljuq sultan still had some influence over who governed Damascus at this point in time.

The final most comprehensive form of legitimisation for Tughtegin came in Dhu 'l-Qaʿda 509/17 March–15 April 1116. This was when Tughtegin came in person to seek the sultan's support, following his open resistance to the expedition into *bilad al-sham* ordered by Muhammad 509/1115.[96] Tughtegin was well received in Baghdad and was granted a robe of honour, before returning to Damascus with a document that, according to Ibn al-Qalanisi, invested him with 'the tax revenue of *al-sham*, giving him a free hand in disposing of its revenues at his own discretion'.[97] This *iqtaʿ* grant effectively empowered Tughtegin with a level of authority comparable to that enjoyed by Tutush, Muslim b. Quraysh and Aqsunqur in the late fifth/eleventh century.

These communications with the sultan's court were also in keeping with those that took place in the fifth/eleventh century, when political figures in *bilad al-sham* tended to initiate contact with the sultan only under specific circumstances. These included seeking legitimisation for their newly captured territories, asking for aid against external enemies or when threatened by the impending arrival of new rulers appointed by the sultan. For instance, Atsiz contacted Malik Shah in 471/1078–9 when he heard about the appointment of Tutush; Tutush sent messages to Malik Shah in 480/1087 and 482/1090 to ask for assistance against Fatimid incursions against his coastal dominions; and Sulayman b. Qutlumush wrote to the sultan to secure legitimisation for Antioch in Sha'ban 477/December 1084.

'Seljuq' Rulers of Aleppo

Less substantive interactions took place with the Seljuq ruler of Aleppo in 507/1113. Ibn al-'Adim claimed that at this time, the Sultan Muhammad sent a letter to Ridwan's son and successor in Aleppo, Alp Arslan b. Ridwan, to encourage him to move against the Nizari Isma'ili Assassins.[98] Ridwan had allowed the sect to establish themselves in Aleppo during the first decade of the sixth/eleventh century. Alp Arslan b. Ridwan accepted the sultan's request, launching a purge against the Nizari Isma'ili Assassins in the city. This reported contact suggests not only that the sultan implicitly approved of Alp Arslan's right to rule the city following the death of Ridwan, but that Alp Arslan ostensibly valued Muhammad's good opinion.[99]

Muhammad's successor as sultan, his son Mahmud b. Muhammad, also made attempts to restore Seljuq influence in Aleppo by building connections to the city's rulers. One such instance involved Najm al-Din Il-ghazi, who established himself in Aleppo in 512/1118. Ibn al-Athir and Ibn al-Azraq al-Fariqi both claimed that Najm al-Din Il-ghazi sent his son to the sultan's court in 515/1121–2. At this point Il-ghazi was around fifty years old and a veteran of Seljuq politics, who had a chequered past of intermittent conflict with Mahmud's father, the Sultan Muhammad.[100] Il-ghazi's son also presented his father's readiness to 'offer obedience' and to pay a tribute to the sultan. Although discussions were inconclusive, the Sultan Mahmud decided to grant Il-ghazi Mayyafariqin as an *iqta'*.[101] As a result of Mahmud's willingness to overlook Il-ghazi's past, Aleppo was at least partially re-integrated back into the sultan's sphere of influence in 515/1121–2.

Aqsunqur al-Bursuqi's brief period in control of Aleppo from Dhu 'l-Hijja 518 to Dhu 'l-Qa'da 519/January 1125 to November 1126 probably matched the fifth/eleventh-century peak of Seljuq influence in northern Syria's major urban centre.[102] According to Ibn al-'Adim, Aqsunqur al-Bursuqi had been granted Aleppo and Rahba as an *iqta'* by the Sultan Muhammad in

510/1116–17, indicating his high standing at the Seljuq court.[103] If anything, Aqsunqur al-Bursuqi's status with the Sultan Mahmud exceeded that which he had enjoyed with his father, as he helped Mahmud to secure the sultanate ahead of his brother, Mas'ud b. Muhammad in 514/1120.[104] Aqsunqur al-Bursuqi was subsequently reappointed in Mosul in Safar 515/21 April–19 May 1121, which Ibn al-Athir explains was because 'in Sultan Mahmud's service he had been a loyal adviser and constant ally in all his wars'.[105] His influence was further bolstered when the sultan granted him Wasit in Sha'ban 516/October 1122, while Mahmud also sent one of his younger brothers and his mother to be with Aqsunqur in 518/1124–5, effectively elevating him to the position of *atabeg*.[106]

Aqsunqur al-Bursuqi had the closest ties of any Syrian-based Seljuq ruler to a reigning sultan in the sixth/twelfth century. He also fit the prototype set by those appointed in Aleppo by the Sultan Malikshah in the late fifth/eleventh century. Like Muslim b. Quraysh and Aqsunqur, Aqsunqur al-Bursuqi was a military commander outside the sultan's immediate family, who had a personal relationship with the sultan. Ultimately, this period of increased Seljuq influence in Aleppo was brought to an abrupt end by the assassination of Aqsunqur al-Bursuqi in Mosul on 8 Dhu 'l-Qa'da 520/25 November 1126.[107]

The Seljuqs in Syria after the Onset of the Crusades

While the system of autonomous lordships in Syria remained present until 522/1128 and beyond, Seljuq influence in the region endured in at least nominal form during the first three decades of the sixth/twelfth century. It was not completely eroded by the death of Malik Shah in 485/1092. Aqsunqur al-Bursuqi's eventual successor in Mosul and Aleppo, Imad al-Din Zangi, would prove to be far more successful at asserting his independence from the Great Seljuq Sultanate than his predecessors had been.

The Türkmen in Syria

The relationship between Türkmen groups in *bilad al-sham* and the Great Seljuq Sultanate was relatively opaque. Crusade historians have often failed to draw a distinction between 'nomadic' Türkmen and Seljuq rulers and troops of Turkish descent operating in Syria during this period. This section will reconsider the role that Türkmen played in Syrian politics in the light of recent work by David Durand-Guédy and Andrew Peacock, who have highlighted the differences between Türkmen and Seljuq groups in Iran, Iraq, Syria and Anatolia.[108] Discussion begins with an assessment of the impact that Türkmen groups had upon the nature of conflict in Syria, before analysing the relationship between the Seljuq court and the most prominent Syrian-based Türkmen ruler of the fifth/eleventh century, Atsiz b. Uwaq al-Khwarizmi.

Arabs, Bedouin, Seljuqs and Türkmen

Nomadic Türkmen are generally perceived to have had a hugely disruptive influence upon the urban and rural communities of Syria and Palestine, triggering a new form of conflict between nomadic and sedentary groups.[109] Yet it should be acknowledged that the migration of Türkmen groups did not introduce nomadic elements into the political world of *bilad al-sham*. Transhumant Arab tribes had been the dominant political force in Syria since the mid-third/ninth century, long pre-dating the influx of Türkmen groups from 456/1064 onwards.[110] To what extent did conflicts involving Türkmen differ from earlier struggles between Byzantine, Fatimid and nomadic Arab groups?

Distinguishing between varying definitions and forms of the term 'nomad' is a difficult task, and nomadism has been the subject of much debate in medieval Islamic historiography.[111] Michael Rowton's model of 'enclosed' and 'external' or 'Bedouin' nomadism has been used to categorise Syrian-based nomadic Arab tribes in the fifth/eleventh century.[112] According to Rowton's thesis, 'enclosed' nomads are 'integrated tribes' that have some form of 'symbiotic' relationship with neighbouring sedentary societies, while 'external' nomads contain no sedentary elements.

The Arab tribal groups of the Kilab, Kalb, Uqayl and Numayr fit the characterisation of 'enclosed' nomads, as although these groups inhabited grazing zones across northern Syria and the Jazira in the Euphrates area, they remained semi-reliant upon the Mirdasid and Uqaylid rulers of Aleppo, Raqqa, Rahba and Mosul to exert political power and to access the markets in these settlements.[113] In turn, the Uqaylid and Mirdasid dynasties constituted what Rowton labelled 'dimorphic states', whereby autonomous potentates presented themselves as urban, while ruling over and relying upon nomadic military forces residing outside the city walls to secure their position.[114]

Theoretically, the Türkmen should be viewed as 'external' nomads, who came to Syria in order to raid or participate in battles, before moving on to target other areas or return to their herds and tribes.[115] The Türkmen are relatively easy to identify in the sources, as the chroniclers use a small collection of terms to identify them.[116] There are numerous episodes that support the impression that deep tensions existed between the urban populations of Syria and Türkmen troops, with the Aleppan chroniclers including numerous references to widespread fear among the city's inhabitants at the prospect of Türkmen forces entering the city.[117] On one notable occasion in 468/1076, the Mirdasid ruler of Aleppo, Nasr b. Mahmud, was killed by Türkmen troops who had been in his service.[118] There were also two destructive Türkmen raids on Aleppan territory in 461/1069–70 and 467/1075.[119]

These examples support the notion that Türkmen groups should be viewed as 'external' nomads, whose transient status enabled them to raid Syrian territory indiscriminately. Yet there are also indications that Türkmen groups exhibited characteristics of 'enclosed nomadism', who formed 'symbiotic' ties with sedentary communities in *bilad al-sham*.[120] For instance, some of the earliest Türkmen groups, led by individuals named Ibn Khan and Ahmed Shah, entered into the service of the Mirdasid rulers of Aleppo. In return, they were granted territories in northern Syria to rule over or reside in.[121]

Yet even transient 'external' Türkmen, who only remained in Syria for short periods, needed to access markets where they could sell the 'spoils of war' accumulated during their raiding activities. As it would have been impractical for Türkmen groups to transport thousands of captives across the Syrian desert while returning to their herds and families, it was advantageous to refrain from raiding certain areas too extensively in order to maintain amicable relations with certain Syrian urban centres.[122] This dependency was best exemplified by a Türkmen raid on the region of Antioch in the winter months of 460/1067–8, after which 70,000 captives taken from Byzantine territory were sold in the slave markets of Aleppo.[123] One consequence of this dynamic was that, though raids on Aleppan territory were not unheard of, they were less common than those conducted in Antioch during the same period. Therefore, while the nomadic lifestyle of Türkmen in *bilad al-sham* was not 'enclosed' to a specific area, their conduct in the region was constrained by the prosaic need to utilise economic apparatuses that were accessible only through constructive interaction with sedentary communities.

Türkmen raids in *bilad al-sham* decreased in frequency following the instalment of Turkish rulers with ties to the Seljuqs in Aleppo and Damascus.[124] This can be partly explained by Frankish settlement in northern Syria during the sixth/twelfth century. The early Frankish rulers placed strong emphasis on the capture and retention of strategically important sites, which provided far greater obstacles to Türkmen raiding activity than the highly permeable frontiers of their Byzantine predecessors.[125]

Despite this, the formation of the Latin east provided the Türkmen with a new high-value source of revenue, elite Frankish captives. In what became a relatively frequent occurrence during the sixth/twelfth century, high-ranking members of the Frankish aristocracy were captured by Türkmen troops and then ransomed for huge sums by Muslim rulers based in Syria.[126] The only drawback being that the diplomatic procedures surrounding these ransoms typically took several months or even years to be completed, meaning that the Türkmen had to rely upon the Turkish rulers of the Syrian urban centres to negotiate these payments.

Likewise, throughout 442–522/1050–1128 the 'dimorphic' states of Aleppo and Damascus became heavily dependent upon the Türkmen's martial skills. Almost every Seljuq ruler of Aleppo and Damascus during this period utilised Türkmen troops to bolster their military capabilities. Türkmen troops were integral to the Mirdasid dynasty's successful erosion of Byzantine influence in northern *bilad al-sham*, and were frequently involved in civil wars and succession conflicts. They also played active roles in campaigns against the Frankish armies of the Crusader states, starting with the battles of Dorylaeum and Antioch during the First Crusade, up to the battle of the Field of Blood in 513/1119 and beyond.[127] This reliance was perhaps best demonstrated in the summer of 468/1076, when Sabiq, the Mirdasid ruler of Aleppo, paid 10,000 dinars and twenty horses to ransom Ahmed Shah, a Türkmen leader, who had been taken captive by a rival Türkmen group.[128] Essentially, this was a member of a prominent Arab dynasty, ransoming a Türkmen ruler, as his highly skilled nomadic troops gave Sabiq a better chance of retaining his position.

Any assessment of the impact that the Türkmen had upon the underlying political dynamics in Syria also has to consider how and when nomadic Turkish or Seljuq potentates became integrated into the sedentary societies they came to rule. While Michael Rowton contends that a ruler ceased to be a nomad once they took control of an urban settlement, Steven Tibble categorises the period 456–534/1064–1140 as one of 'chaos and infiltration', suggesting that all rulers of Aleppo prior to Nur al-Din were to some extent nomadic.[129]

Yet, even allowing for a certain ambiguity on this point, it is far from certain that the establishment of Türkmen or Seljuq potentates had a debilitating impact upon the urban and rural communities of *bilad al-sham*. For example, Sibt b. al-Jawzi credited unnamed Türkmen operating in Palestine in 464/1071 with improving the fortunes of the uninhabited settlement of Ramla by encouraging peasants to return to the town and tax-farming olive trees in the area.[130] Moreover, many Syrian-based Seljuq potentates pursued policies designed to repopulate the cities of Aleppo and Damascus, and encouraged investment in urban infrastructure to help improve the settlements they governed. The first hospital and *madrassa* were built using the *waqf* endowment system in Damascus in 491/1097–8, while the final stages of the minaret attached to the Great Mosque of Aleppo was commissioned during the reign of Tutush b. Alp Arslan.[131]

Correspondingly, early Seljuq rulers such as Tutush, Qasim al-Dawla and Tughtegin, were praised in the Arabic chronicles for acts of good governance and generally improving the fortunes of the people of Aleppo and Damascus.[132]

Further evidence that Seljuq rulers had a positive impact on settled societies in northern Syria, or at least that their presence overlapped with a period of regional prosperity, can be found in the numismatic evidence. As Stefan Heidemann has demonstrated, the late fifth/eleventh century saw an increased demand for Byzantine copper currencies, particularly in northern Syria, where these 'silver dirhams' were given a greater worth than in other surrounding Byzantine-held territories. Based upon this finding, in combination with the rapid urban expansion seen in towns like Raqqa, Heidemann concluded that the Seljuq rule coincided with an 'urban, political and economic renaissance' in northern Syria and the Jazira in the latter half of the fifth/eleventh and early sixth/twelfth centuries.[133]

As Alexander Beihammer has proposed, it is perhaps best to think of the Türkmen as operating in the 'grey zones' between the nomadic and sedentary spheres.[134] To varying degrees many nomadic Türkmen in Syria, much like their Arab predecessors, developed 'symbiotic relationships' with Syrian urban communities. It is therefore doubtful that their presence fundamentally altered the way in which warfare was conducted between nomadic and sedentary societies. Rather, the arrival of highly mobile Türkmen cavalry from the Eurasian Steppe merely introduced a new, highly effective and dominant military force to the region. The case can also be made that under certain circumstances, transhumant Türkmen groups actually empowered notables in the urban settlements, enabling them to pursue their own agendas.[135]

Was Atsiz a 'Seljuq'?

Atsiz b. Uwaq al-Khwarizmi al-Turkmani was perhaps the best known Türkmen figure active in *bilad al-sham* throughout this period. Leading one of the first Türkmen groups that migrated to Syria, his forces captured Jerusalem and much of Palestine in 463/1071, before subjugating Damascus in the summer of 468/1076 and leading an unsuccessful invasion of Egypt the following year. Atsiz's career has drawn scrutiny from modern historians, who have queried his allegiance to the Great Seljuq Sultanate.[165]

However, the circumstances surrounding Atsiz's initial arrival in *bilad al-sham* underscore his close ties to the Seljuq Sultan Alp Arslan. In Sha'ban 463/May 1071, the Mirdasid ruler Mahmud b. Nasr, who was facing the threat of a Byzantine attack on Aleppan territory, sent an appeal for help to the court of the Seljuq Sultan Alp Arslan. Atsiz b. Uwaq, the 'paternal nephew of the Malik Ibn Khan', who had formerly been in the service of the Mirdasids, descended 'on Mahmud to support him, and they stayed until the Byzantine army broke up'.[137] This implies that before his arrival in Palestine, Atsiz b. Uwaq was a member of the Seljuq court of Alp Arslan, and had in all likelihood participated in his campaign against Aleppo earlier that year.[138]

Despite his long-standing Seljuq pedigree, there were some indications that Atsiz occasionally displayed mixed loyalties to the sultan. Following his capture of Jerusalem and other settlements in Palestine in 463/1071, Atsiz did not write to Baghdad until 466/1073–4 to inform the caliph and sultan that the *khutba* in the town had been established in the name of Abbasid caliph.[139] It seems probable that Atsiz delayed the changing of the call to prayer in Jerusalem due to a general Shi'i inclination among the populace, which he had to respect.[140]

Rather than viewing this reluctance to change the *khutba* in his dominions as a signal of disloyalty to the Seljuqs, Atsiz's actions should be interpreted as an indication of the level of 'religious' pragmatism required to gain influence in the region.[141] Despite this apparent delay, Atsiz still received 3,000 *ghulam* troops 'from the army of Malik Shah' in 467/1074–5.[142] The only other reference to a Seljuq amir receiving reinforcements directly from the Sultan Malik Shah was Tutush during his attempts to take Aleppo in 471/1079.

A letter Atsiz apparently sent to Malik Shah in 471/1078–9, when he learnt that the sultan's brother Tutush b. Alp Arslan had been granted *bilad al-sham* as an *iqta'*, provides further insight into his relationship with the sultan. Sibt b. al-Jawzi recorded how Atsiz complained that he had taken the territories he held on his own without assistance and had remained a 'compliant servant' of the sultan, while sending the treasury '30,000 dinars' a year.[143] This indicates that Atsiz held his territory on very different terms to Tutush, the latter having been granted more autonomy in the form of an *iqta'*. Instead of being granted all tax revenues, Atsiz was apparently obligated to send a tribute back to the sultan in order to maintain control over the settlements he governed.

Although Atsiz did have ties and connections to Malik Shah that extended far beyond other Türkmen rulers, he was still required to pay a tribute to the sultan in order to retain his position. While this agreement meant that Atsiz did not enjoy as much autonomy as other major Seljuq amirs in the region, he was not a prototypical Türkmen ruler either.

Conclusion: Reassessing Seljuq *Bilad al-sham*

Throughout the late fifth/eleventh century, two structural issues ingrained within the Seljuq political system continually undermined the sultanate's authority in *bilad al-sham*, both prior to and following the death of the Sultan Malik Shah in 485/1092. The first was repeated supply and morale problems experienced by Seljuq armies campaigning in Syria, even when led in person by the sultan. The second stemmed from the autonomy wielded by Syrian-based amirs, which often undermined Seljuq attempts to further consolidate their influence in the region or combat external adversaries, including the Shi'i Fatimid Caliphate.

The continuous presence of these issues raises doubts not only about the willingness of any Seljuq sultan to launch sustained military campaigns into the region, but their ability to do so. These difficulties also provide important context for the muted Seljuq response to the formation of the Crusader states. Additionally, the establishment of Seljuq and Türkmen polities failed to have a hugely disruptive impact upon either the nature of conflict in the region, or the underlying power dynamics in Syria and Palestine. Rather, the system of autonomous lordships in Syria, which pre-dated the arrival of the Turkish potentates, was merely preserved by strategic decisions made during Malik Shah's reign, while many nomadic Türkmen groups developed 'symbiotic' relationships with certain Syrian urban centres.

Notes

1. This viewpoint is particularly prominent in the works of Michael Köhler, Carole Hillenbrand, Taef El-Azhari and Alexander Beihammer, who all link Seljuq influence in *bilad al-sham* to this fixed chronology. Köhler, *Alliances*, pp. 31–75; Hillenbrand, 'The First Crusade', pp. 130–41; Hillenbrand, *Crusades*, pp. 31–50; El-Azhari, *Saljuqs*, pp. 24–113; Cobb, *Race for Paradise*, pp. 70–94; Beihammer, *Byzantium*, pp. 133–98, 244–65.
2. David Durand-Guédy, 'New Trends in the Political History of Iran Under the Great Saljuqs (11th–12th Centuries)', *History Compass* 13 (2015): 321–37.
3. See, e.g., David Durand-Guédy, *Iranian Elites and Turkish Rulers: a History of Isfahahan in the Saljuq Period* (London: Routledge, 2010).
4. Deborah Tor, '"Sovereign and Pious": the Religious Life of the Great Seljuq Sultans', in *The Saljuqs: Society, Politics and Culture*, ed. Christian Lange and Songul Mecit (Edinburgh: Edinburgh University Press, 2011), pp. 39–62; Peacock, *Early Saljuq History*, pp. 119–21.
5. Chapters 1 and 2 have outlined how the system of autonomous lordships in Syria was observable from 454/1062 onwards. For the definition of autonomous lordship used in this book, see the introductory section of Part I.
6. Lambton, 'The Internal Structure', pp. 203–82, 218; Hillenbrand, *Crusades*, pp. 33–42; Peacock, *Empire*, pp. 68–71, 128–32.
7. Yossef Rapoport, *Rural Economy and Tribal Society in Islamic Egypt: a Study of al-Nabulusi's 'Villages of the Fayyum'* (Turnhout: Brepols, 2018), pp. 143–70.
8. A copy of a Seljuq-era *iqta'* bestowed upon Tughtegin of Damascus following a visit to Sultan Muhammad's court in 510/116 has been preserved in Ibn al-Qalanisi's sixth/twelfth-century chronicle. The copied document, dated to Muharram 510/May–June 1116, granted Tughtegin 'the tax revenue of

al-sham', lending credence to the view that Seljuq *iqta'* grants were often of a wide-ranging nature, see IQ, pp. 308–13.

9. Ann Lambton placed *iqta'* into five separate overlapping categories: members of the Seljuq dynasty; administrative; military; members of the bureaucracy; and personal *iqta'*. Lambton, 'The Internal Structure', pp. 203–82; Ann K. S. Lambton, *Continuity and Change in Medieval Persia: Aspects of Administrative, Economic and Social History* (Albany, NY: Bibliotheca Persica, 1988), pp. 97–115. See also Heidemann, *Die Renaissance der Städte*, pp. 310–15; Peacock, *Empire*, pp. 79–80.
10. Heidemann, *Die Renaissance der Städte*, pp. 145–75, 440–2.
11. Ibn al-Jawzi, *al-Muntazam fi ta'rikh*, XV, 348–9; IATH, IX, 609; Bar Habraeus, *Chronography*, p. 207; Peacock, *Empire*, p. 49.
12. Both campaigns are generally regarded as key indicators of growing Seljuq influence in the region. See El-Azhari, *Saljuqs*, pp. 26–34, 64–71; Köhler, *Alliances*, pp. 7–20; Beihammer, *Byzantium*, pp. 151–5, 244–50.
13. Lambton, 'The Internal Structure', p. 223.
14. Durand-Guédy has roughly calculated that Malik Shah and his son Muhammad b. Malik Shah spent 60–65 per cent of their reigns in Isfahan. Durand-Guédy, *Iranian Elites*, pp. 75–6, 208, 321–3; Peacock, *Empire*, pp. 171–2.
15. IAD ZH, II, 19–20.
16. As discussed in Chapter 2, 'Atiyya b. Salih briefly made the *khutba* at Rahba in the name of the sultan and the Abbasid caliph in Safar 452/March 1060, while Mahmud b. Nasr had applied for legitimisation from the Seljuq court in Ramadan 458/August 1067. IQ, p. 156; al-'Azimi, p. 346; SJ, XII, 374, 377; IAD ZH, I, 275; Cobb, *Race for Paradise*, p. 78.
17. The dates given here are taken from Ibn al-'Adim's *Zubdat al-halab*. Sawirus ibn al-Muqaffa', *History of the Patriarchs of the Egyptian Church*, II/III, 202, 307; IQ, pp. 167–8; al-'Azimi, pp. 348–9; IATH, X, 64; SJ, XII, 480–1; IAD ZH, II, 22–3; IAD BH, IV, 1971–80.
18. The implications of the battle of Manzikert for Byzantine authority in northern Syria, and the wider significance of events at Manzikert, are discussed in Chapter 1.
19. IQ, pp. 169–70; al-'Azimi, p. 349; IATH, X, 73–4; SJ, XII, 34, 42–4.
20. Beihammer, *Byzantium*, pp. 151–5; El-Azhari, *Saljuqs*, pp. 31–4; Zakkar, *Emirate*, pp. 176–1; Cobb, *Race for Paradise*, pp. 78–81.
21. The switch of the *khutba* in Aleppo by Ridwan b. Alp Arslan in 490/1096 is discussed in Chapter 2.

22. Bianquis, *Damas*, II, 590.
23. The importance of *Khidma* ties are discussed in the Introduction to Part I. For *khidma* in a Seljuq context, see Paul, 'Khidma', pp. 408–11; Peacock, *Empire*, p. 158.
24. Mahmud's campaign against Ba'albek in 463/1071 is discussed briefly above in Chapter 2.
25. The details of these tributary agreements and are outlined in Chapters 1 and 2. On their wider significance, see Wilson, 'The Ransom of High-ranking Captives', pp. 23–8.
26. SJ, XII, 479–80.
27. Beihammer has also discussed the difficulties that Alp Arslan's army experienced prior to their arrival at Aleppo, see Beihammer, *Byzantium*, pp. 151–5.
28. SJ, XII, 479. With the exception of Bar Habraeus and the compilers of the *History of the Patriarchs of the Egyptian Church*, the other chroniclers only briefly mention an unsuccessful siege, with no reference to any diplomatic negotiations. Sawirus ibn al-Muqaffa', *History of the Patriarchs of the Egyptian Church*, II/III, 200–2, 304–7; IATH, X, 64; IAD ZH, II, 19; ME, pp. 131–2; Bar Habraeus, *Chronography*, p. 219.
29. SJ, XII, 479–80.
30. The proclivity of Türkmen troops for plunder and battle is a common theme in much of the medieval literary sources. Peacock has argued convincingly that Türkmen troops were particularly opposed to any extended campaigning in northern Syria, due to a dearth of suitable grazing lands, see Peacock, *Empire*, p. 224.
31. SJ, XII, 254.
32. Peacock, *Empire*, pp. 58, 69
33. The request was reportedly made by the chief of the *ahdath* (local urban militia) of Aleppo, Abu 'Ali al-Hasan b. Hibat Allah al-Hutayti. IQ, p. 195; IATH, X, 148; IAD ZH, II, 20–4.
34. According to Usama ibn Munqidh, his father made a seperate visit to the sultan's court at Isfahan during Malik Shah's reign. See Usama ibn Munqidh, *Kitab al-I'tibar*, p. 49.
35. The dates given here are again taken from Ibn al-'Adim's *Zubdat al-halab*. IQ, pp. 195–6; al- 'Azimi, pp. 353–4; IATH, X, 148–50; SJ, XIII, 178–9; IAD ZH, II, 100–3; IAD BH, IV, 1954–62; MS, p. 615; Bar Habraeus, *Chronography*, p. 231.
36. IQ, p. 191; IATH, X, 134–8; IAD ZH, II, 103.
37. The impact of this campaign on Malik Shah's brother, Tutush b. Alp Arslan,

and the wider policy the sultan adopted towards his brother are discussed in detail below.
38. SJ, XIII, 178–9.
39. According to William of Tyre, Nur al-Din conducted a similar ritual at the same location following his victory against the Antiochene forces at the battle of Inab in 544/1149. WT, II, 704; WT trans., II, 196–200.
40. al-'Azimi, p. 354.
41. This calculation is made on the basis that Alp Arslan was sultan between 443 and 455/1051 and 1063 and spent approximately 120 days in northern Syria, while Malik Shah was sultan between 465 and 485/1072 and 1092 and spent approximately 34 days in northern Syria. This section has been heavily influenced by Durand-Guédy's research on Seljuq-era Isfahan, from where the figures relating to the percentage of each sultans' reign spent in Isfahan are taken. See Durand-Guédy, *Iranian Elites*, pp. 75–6, 208, 321–3.
42. IAD ZH, II, 55–6.
43. IAD ZH, II, 56.
44. IQ, pp. 181–2; al-'Azimi, p. 350; IATH, X, 111; SJ, XIII, 114; IAD ZH, II, 57–63. Sharaf al-Dawla, Muslim b. Quraysh and his position in the Seljuq political hierarchy is discussed in more detail later in this chapter.
45. IQ, pp. 182–3; al-'Azimi, p. 350; IATH, X, 111; SJ, XIII, 119–20; IAD ZH, II, 62, 65–7; IM, pp. 45–6.
46. IQ, pp. 183, 188; al-'Azimi, pp. 350–2; IATH X, 114–15; SJ, XII, 121–2; IAD ZH, II, 73, 75; MS, p. 615.
47. SJ, XIII, 186.
48. IQ, p. 197; al-'Azimi, p. 355; SJ, XIII, 195; IM, p. 50.
49. IQ, p. 198; al-'Azimi, p. 355; IATH, X, 202–3; SJ, XIII, 197; IAD ZH, II, 106.
50. The omission of these events by Ibn al-Qalanisi and Ibn al-'Adim is somewhat problematic, and places some doubt on whether this siege occurred at all. IATH, X, 202–3; SJ, XIII, 203.
51. Hillenbrand, 'The First Crusade', p. 131.
52. al-Qifti, *Ikhbar al-Ulama Bi Akhbar al-Hukama'*, pp. 110–11; Zakkar, *Emirate*, p. 34.
53. IAD ZH, II, 55–6.
54. Ibn al-Athir famously referred to Nizam al-Mulk's reign as vizier as '*al-dawla al-nizamiyya*' (the state of Nizam or Nizam's state). IATH, X, 33. The extent of his power was perhaps unparalleled in the Seljuq political world. This must be tempered by the knowledge that the concept of an all-powerful vizier from

the traditional Persian bureaucracy guiding the most successful Seljuq sultan through his reign would have been an appealing image for those from a *katib* background, who wrote much of the surviving source material. For more discussion on the extent of Nizam al-Mulk's authority as vizier, see Peacock, *Empire*, pp. 68–71; Hillenbrand, 'Nizam al-Mulk', pp. 28–40.

55. Peacock, *Empire*, p. 68.
56. SJ, XIII, 114. Atsiz's ties to the Seljuq sultans Alp Arslan and Malik Shah are discussed later in this chapter in a section dedicated to Syrian-based Türkmen rulers.
57. IQ, pp. 182–3; al-'Azimi, p. 350; IATH, X, 111; SJ, XIII, 119–20; IAD ZH, II, 65; IM, pp. 45, 61; MS, p. 615.
58. For more background on the career of Muslim b. Quraysh Sharaf al-Dawla and the Uqaylid dynasty, see Moritz Sobernheim, 'Muslim b. Kuraysh', in *Encyclopaedia of Islam*, 2nd edn, Peri Bearman et al. (2012), available at Brill online, last accessed 30 March 2022; Clifford E. Bosworth, "Ukaylids', in *Encyclopaedia of Islam*, 2nd edn, ed. Peri Bearman et al. (2012), available at Brill online, last accessed 30 March 2022; Heidemann, 'Arab Nomads and the Saljuq Military', pp. 285, 292–4; Morton and France, 'Arab Muslim Reactions', XV, pp. 20–3.
59. IATH, X, 51.
60. This was before Alp Arslan's death and Malik Shah's ascension to the sultanate. This means that Sharaf al-Dawla's wife was also one of the sultan's daughters when they married. IATH, X, 61.
61. IATH, X, 78–9.
62. IQ, pp. 183, 188; al-'Azimi, pp. 350–2; IATH, X, 114–15; SJ, III, 121–2.
63. Peacock, *Empire*, pp. 126–34.
64. SJ, XIII, 139–41. Ibn al-'Adim outlines the nature of the conflict between Sharaf al-Dawla's forces and Tutush's coalition in the most detail, but made no reference to any correspondence between Tutush and the Sultan Malik Shah. IQ, pp. 185–6, 188; al-'Azimi, p. 352; IAD ZH, II, 79–82, 86.
65. Philaretos Brachamios, who was of Armenian descent, was in the process of integrating himself into the Seljuq political sphere. His other attempts to ingratiate himself with the Sultan Malik Shah are discussed in Chapter 1.
66. Muslim b. Quraysh reportedly claimed: 'if there were letters from me sent to the lord of Egypt, you can arrest me', see SJ, XIII, p. 139.
67. IQ, pp. 186–7; al-'Azimi, p. 352; IATH, X, 126–7; SJ, XII 146–8; IAD ZH, II, 81–2.
68. Ibn al-Qalanisi claimed that 'Sharaf al-Dawla had relied upon the assistance of

an Egyptian army ... but nothing came of his plans and agreements'. Ibn al-Athir asserted that Sharaf al-Dawla 'sent messages to the Caliph in Egypt, requesting the sending of reinforcements to besiege Damascus. Having received promises of that, he himself marched against the city'. Ibn al-'Adim stated that Sharaf al-Dawla 'had thought that he would be supported by an Egyptian army'. IQ, pp. 186–7; IATH, X, 126–7; IAD ZH, II, 81–2.

69. IAD ZH, II, 84–5. Ibn al-Athir made no reference to an appeal to the Fatimids in 477/1084–5, but did indicate that Muslim b. Quraysh had to win back the sultan's favour at this time following the events at Amid. In order to do so, Muslim b. Quraysh gave Malik Shah a racehorse who was 'a champion without rival' as part of a diplomatic charm offensive. IATH, X, 136.

70. IAD ZH, II, 86.

71. IAD ZH, II, 99.

72. Sulayman b. Qutlumush, and his dual role in the political spheres of the Great Seljuq Sultanate and the Byzantine Empire are discussed in Chapter 1.

73. For more detail on Sulayman's standing among Türkmen tribal leaders, see Peacock, *Empire*, pp. 65–6.

74. IQ, p. 192; al-'Azimi, pp. 352–3; IATH, X, 138–41; SJ, XIII, 158–9, 165; IAD ZH, II, 86–7, 96–7; Bar Habraeus, *Chronography*, pp. 229–30. For the River 'Afrin, see Yaqut, *Mu'ajam al-Buldan*, IV, 132; Dussaud, *Topographie historique*, pp. 223, 240; Cahen, *Syrie*, pp. 105, 107, 115, 117.

75. IQ, pp. 194–5; al-'Azimi, pp. 353–4; IATH, X, 147–8; SJ, XIII, 182; IAD ZH, II, 96–7; MS, p. 618; Bar Habraeus, *Chronography*, p. 230. For 'Ayn Silim, see Yaqut, *Mu'ajam al-Buldan*, IV, 178.

76. Sibt b. al-Jawzi provided the dates for Malik Shah's departure from Isfahan, while the date of the sultan's arrival in Aleppo are taken from Ibn al-'Adim's *Zubdat al-halab*. SJ, XIII, 176; IAD ZH, II, 98–101.

77. These reports, and other details concerning Malik Shah's campaign in northern Syria during the winter months of 479/1086–7 are discussed in detail in an earlier part of this chapter.

78. SJ, XIII, 178.

79. IQ, p. 196; al-'Azimi, p. 354; IAD ZH, II, 102–3; IAD BH, IV, 1954–62.

80. This point has been made by Michael Köhler and Taef El-Azhari, with Köhler identifying how in this instance, Malik Shah created an 'equilibrium between lordships of approximately equal strength' to constrain Tutush's power, see Köhler, *Alliances*, pp. 13–17; El-Azhari, *Saljuqs*, pp. 68–9.

81. Ibn al-Athir, *al-Ta'rikh al-bahir*, p. 4. Aqsunqur was the father of the famous

sixth/twelfth century-jihad warrior Imad al-Din Zangi. As one of the principal themes of Ibn al-Athir's *al-Ta'rikh al-bahir fi'l-dawlat al-atabakiyya* was to praise members of Zangid dynasty, it seems probable that the notion of the all-powerful Seljuq Vizier Nizam al-Mulk viewing Aqsunqur as a rival would have been appealing for Ibn al-Athir. For a more detailed consideration of whether Ibn al-Athir's political leanings influenced his historical writing, see Donald S. Richards, 'The Early History of Saladin', in *The Crusades, vol. 2: Crusading and the Crusader States, 1095–1197*, ed. Andrew Jotischky (Abingdon: Routledge, 2008), pp. 432–53.

82. IQ, p. 196; IATH, X, 162; SJ, XIII, 192; IAD ZH, II, 105; IAD BH, IV, 1954, 1960–1.
83. Köhler, *Alliances*, pp. 13–16.
84. IAD ZH, II, 109–10; Cobb, *Race for Paradise*, pp. 86–8.
85. IQ, pp. 207–8; al-'Azimi, p. 356; IATH, X, 232–3; SJ, XIII, 226; IAD ZH, II, 110–13.
86. IQ, pp. 211–12; al-'Azimi, p. 358; IATH, X, 244–5; SJ, XIII, 237–8; IAD ZH, II, 118–19.
87. For more detail on this conflict between Ridwan and Duqaq, and contrasting views on Ridwan's career, see El-Azhari, *Saljuqs*, pp. 79–90; Robert Crawford, 'Ridwan the Maligned', in *The World of Islam: Studies in Honour of Philip K. Hitti*, ed. James Kritzeck and R. Bayly Winder (London: Macmillan, 1959), pp. 135–44. Anne-Marie Eddé, 'Ridwan, Prince D'Alep de 1095 à 1113', *Revue de études Islamiques* 54 (1986): 101–25.
88. For Malik Shah and Nizam al-Mulk, see Hillenbrand, *Crusades*, pp. 31–50. For Tutush, see Köhler, *Alliances*, pp. 15–16.
89. IQ, p. 212; al-'Azimi, pp. 356, 359; IAD ZH, II, 117–18, 120–1, 124–5.
90. The campaigns against Homs and Tripoli are discussed in detail earlier in this chapter.
91. Köhler, *Alliances*, pp. 31–75; Hillenbrand, 'The First Crusade', pp. 130–41; Hillenbrand, *Crusades*, pp. 38–50; El-Azhari, *Saljuqs*, pp. 24–113; Beihammer, *Byzantium*, pp. 133–98, 244–65.
92. The Seljuq campaigns of 505/1111 and 509/1115 are discussed in Chapter 4.
93. For more on these events see the detailed accounts of Lambton, 'The Internal Structure', pp. 203–82; Clifford E. Bosworth, 'The Political and Dynastic History of the Iranian World A.D. 1100–1217', *The Cambridge History of Iran, vol. V*, ed. John A. Boyle (Cambridge: Cambridge University Press, 1968), pp. 112–20; Durand-Guédy, *Iranian Elites*, pp. 153–81; El-Azhari, *Saljuqs* pp. 24–113;

Köhler, *Alliances*, pp. 7–20; Hillenbrand, *Crusades*, pp. 31–75; Hillenbrand, 'The First Crusade', pp. 130–41; Cobb, *Race for Paradise*, pp. 70–94; Peacock, *Empire*, pp. 72–82; Heidemann, *Die Renaissance der Städte*, pp. 173–205.

94. IQ, pp. 241, 257–8; al-'Azimi, pp. 363–4; IATH, X, 452–4; SJ, XIII, 317–18; IM, p. 76.
95. IQ, pp. 265–6.
96. The 509/1115 campaign is discussed in detail in Chapter 4.
97. Ibn al-Qalanisi included a copy of the document of investiture that Tughtegin brought back to Damascus from Baghdad, which exemplifies how Ibn al-Qalanisi's chronicle was based upon documentary evidence. IQ, pp. 308–13; IATH, X, 514.
98. According to Ibn al-'Adim's *Zubdat al-halab*, the letter was fairly explicit: 'you are my son and I would like you to kill them'. IAD ZH, II, 164, 168–1; IAD BH, IV, 1984–7.
99. While Ibn al-Qalanisi, al-'Azimi and Ibn al-Athir all mention the attack on the Nizari Isma'ili Assassins in Aleppo, Ibn al-'Adim is the only source who refers to contacts between Alp Arslan b. Ridwan and the Sultan Muhammad. The move against the Nizari Isma'ili Assassins was also supported by the prominent Aleppan notable Abu al-Qasim b. Badi'a, indicating that the sultan's request was not the only motivation for Alp Arslan b. Ridwan. IQ, pp. 301–3; al-'Azimi, p. 366; IATH, X, 499; SJ, XIII, 347–8.
100. Carole Hillenbrand has provided the most in-depth analysis of Il-ghazi's career. See Carole Hillenbrand, 'The Career of Najm al-Din Il-ghazi', *Der Islam* 58 (1981): 250–92.
101. al-Fariqi, *Ta'rikh al-Fariqi*, pp. 34, 149; IATH, X, 592.
102. Mallett, 'Aq-Sunqur al-Bursuqi', pp. 39–56, 53–4. For more detail on Aqsunqur al-Bursuqi's career, see Paul Cobb, 'Aq-Sunqur al-Bursuqi', in *Encyclopaedia of Islam: THREE*, ed. Kate Fleet et al. (2010), available at Brill online, last accessed 27 April 2019.
103. IAD ZH, II, 177; IAD BH, IV, 1963–70.
104. IATH, X, 563–4; SJ, XIII, 3967.
105. IATH, X, 588.
106. IATH, X, 622.
107. IQ, pp. 341–2; al-'Azimi, p. 376; IATH, X, 633–5; SJ, XIII, 439; IAD ZH, II, 234–5; ME, pp. 234–6.
108. David Durand-Guédy, 'The Türkmen–Saljuq Relationship in Twelfth-century Iran: New Elements based on a Contrastive Analysis of Three Insa' Documents',

Eurasian Studies 9 (2011): 11–66; David Durand-Guédy, 'Goodbye to the Türkmen? The Military Role of Nomads in Iran after the Saljuq Conquest', in *Nomadic Military Power: Iran and the Adjacent Areas in the Islamic Period*, ed. Kurt Franz and Wolfgang Holzwarth (Wiesbaden: Reichert Verlag, 2015), pp. 107–36; Andrew C. S. Peacock, 'From the Balkhan-Kuhiyan to the Nawakiya: Nomadic Politics and the Foundation of Seljuq Rule in Anatolia', in *Nomad Aristocracies in a World of Empires*, ed. Jürgen Paul (Wiesbaden: Reichert Verlag, 2013), pp. 55–80; Peacock, *Empire*, pp. 59, 221–8. See also Alexander Beihammer, 'Patterns of Turkish Migration and Expansion in Byzantine Asia Minor in the 11th and 12th Centuries', in *Migration Histories of the Medieval Afroeurasion Transition Zone*, ed. Johannes Preiser-Kapeller, Lucian Reinfandt and Yannis Stouraitis (Leiden: Brill, 2020), pp. 166–92; Morton, *The Crusader States*, pp. 14–19.

109. The works of Vladimir Barthold and Ann Lambton formed the historiographical foundations for the conceptualisation of the Türkmen as disruptive nomadic raiders and herders who held no interest in adopting a settled lifestyle. See Vladimir Barthold, *Turkestan down to the Mongol invasion* (London: Luzac, 1928), p. 309; Ann Lambton, 'Aspects of Saljuq Ghuzz Settlement in Persia', in *Islamic Civilisation 950–1150*, ed. Donald S. Richards (Oxford: Cassirer, 1973), pp. 105–25, 109–10; Hillenbrand, *Crusades*, pp. 441–3. In relation to the Türkmen in *bilad al-sham*, Steven Tibble, building on the research of Ronnie Ellenblum, has argued that the presence of nomadic warriors from the Eurasian Steppe from 463/1064 onwards triggered a 'primal social war' in Syria and Palestine. Tibble, *Crusader Armies*, pp. 3–22, 88–160; Ellenblum, *The Collapse of the Eastern Mediterranean*, pp. 3–12, 88–160.

110. For more background on the transhumant Arab tribal groups that played an integral role in Syrian political and martial affairs during the fourth/tenth and fifth/eleventh centuries, see Hugh Kennedy, 'Nomads and Settled People in Bilad al-Sham in the Third/Ninth and Fourth/Tenth Centuries', in *Bilad al-Sham during the Abbasid Period: Proceedings of the Fifth International Conference on the History of Bilad al-Sham*, ed. Muhammad A. Bakhit and Robert Schick (Amman: History of the Bilad al-Sham Committee, 1991), pp. 105–13; Heidemann, 'Arab Nomads', pp. 289–305; Morton and France, 'Arab Muslim Reactions', XV, pp. 1–38.

111. For a brief overview of nomads in the medieval Islamic world, see Rudi P. Linder, 'What Was a Nomadic Tribe?' *Comparative Studies in Society and History* 24 (1982): 689–711; Hugh Kennedy, 'The City and the Nomad', ed. Robert Irwin,

The New Cambridge History of Islam, vol. 4 (Cambridge; Cambridge University Press, 2010), pp. 274–89; Nol, *Settlement and Urbanization in Early Islamic Palestine*, pp. 29–30. For detailed analysis of how the writings of Ibn Khaldun (d. 808/1406), and the colonialist era interpretation of Ibn Khaldun's work, have influenced thinking surrounding the nomadic Bedouin groups of north Africa, see Michael Brett, 'The Way of the Nomad', *Bulletin of the School of Oriental and African Studies* 58 (1995): 251–69, 256–9.

112. Michael Rowton, 'Enclosed Nomadism', *Journal of the Economic and Social History of the Orient* 17 (1974): 1–30, 1–7. Stefan Heidemann has situated these Arab tribes within the framework of 'enclosed nomadism', see Heidemann, 'Arab Nomads', pp. 290–1.

113. For instance, Mirdasid succession was often decided by tribal leaders of the Banu Kilab. For the fullest account of these Arab tribal groups and the territories they occupied along the River Euphrates, see IAD, BH, I, 527–68.

114. Michael Rowton, 'Urban Autonomy in a Nomadic Environment', *Journal of Near Eastern Studies* 32 (1973): 201–15, 202–4; Stefan Heidemann, 'Numayrid ar-Raqqa Archaeological and Historical Evidence for a "Dimorphic State" in the Bedouin Dominated Fringes of the Fatimid Empire', in *Egypt and Syria in the Fatimid, Ayyubid and Mamluk Eras*, 9 vols, ed. Urbain Vermeulen and Jo Van Steenbergen (Leuven: Peeters, 2005), IV, pp. 85–109. It should be noted that the Mirdasids of Aleppo, and their Türkmen and Seljuq successors, also relied upon the *ahdath* (local urban militia) who were recruited from the local population.

115. The topographical and climatic factors that made *bilad al-sham* unsuited to extended Türkmen campaigns are discussed earlier in this chapter. For an explanation of the need for caution when dealing with Eurasian Steppe tribal groups and their negative impact upon the sedentary societies they interacted with, see Anatoly M. Khazanov, 'The Eurasian Steppe Nomads in World Military History', in *Nomad Aristocracies in a World of Empires*, ed. Jürgen Paul (Wiesbaden: Reichert Verlag, 2013), pp. 187–207; Linder, 'What Was a Nomadic Tribe?' pp. 689–711.

116. The most commonly used term by the chroniclers is Türkmen (*turkuman*), but *ghuzz* and the Turks *(al-atrak)* are also employed by some authors.

117. See, e.g., al-'Azimi, p. 345; IAD ZH, II, 16, 18, 47, 55.

118. Before attacking their encampment outside the city walls, Nasr had detained the Türkmen group's leader, Ahmad Shah. IQ, p. 175; al-'Azimi, p. 349; IAD ZH, II, 49; IAD BH, III, 1298–9.

119. SJ, XIII, 72–3; IAD ZH, II, 16; IAD BH, IX, 4078. In 461/1069–70, the Türkmen raided Ma'rrat al-Nu'man and Kafartab, which were both historically seen as part of the *bilad halab* (region of Aleppo, see Chapter 5 for further discussion on the frontiers of Aleppo). According to Sibt b. al-Jawzi, the 467/1075 attack led to the city of Aleppo being placed under siege, with the Mirdasid ruler Nasr b. Mahmud making an unspecified tribute payment.
120. Andrew Peacock has outlined how the Türkmen were reliant upon settled populations to earn revenue from their pastoralist lifestyles, see Peacock, *Empire*, pp. 293–7. See also: Jean-Luc Krawczyk, 'The Relationship between Pastoral Nomadism and Agriculture: Northern Syria and the Jazira in the Eleventh Century', *JRUR* 1 (1985): 1–22, 15–20; Claude Cahen, 'Nomades et sedentaries dans la monde muslaman du milieu de moyen age', in *Islamic Civilisation 950–1150*, ed. Donald S. Richards (Oxford: Cassirer, 1973), pp. 93–104, 102–3.
121. Mahmud b. Nasr granted Ibn Khan Ma'rrat al-Nu'man as an *iqta'* in 458/1066, while Ahmed Shah and his Türkmen followers were residing in 'Hisn al-Jisr' in 471/1069–70. According to Ibn al-'Adim, Hisn al-Jisr was close to Shayzar. IAD ZH, II, 9, 56.
122. Some Türkmen brought their herds to the pasturelands around the River Euphrates. On one occasion in the winter of 517/1123–4, Joscelyn of Edessa raided a joint Kurdish and Türkmen encampment near the Euphrates, where 10,000 horses and sheep were grazing. IAD ZH, II, 216.
123. IAD, ZH, II, 11–12.
124. There were, of course, some exceptions, such as the Türkmen raids conducted against Aleppo during the 505/1111 campaign ordered by the Seljuq Sultan Muhammad (discussed in Chapter 4), and in Antiochene territory in the aftermath of the battle of the Field of Blood in 513/1119.
125. For more detail on Crusader settlement and the Principality of Antioch's strategy of retaining control of key sites, see Ronnie Ellenblum, *Frankish Rural Settlement in the Latin Kingdom of Jerusalem* (Cambridge: Cambridge University Press, 2002); Ellenblum, 'Were there Borders', pp. 105–19; Asbridge, *Creation*, pp. 45–91; Asbridge, 'Crusader Community at Antioch', pp. 305–25; Thomas S. Asbridge, 'Jabal as-Summaq', in *The First Crusade: Origins and Impact*, ed. Jonathan Phillips (Manchester: Manchester University Press, 1997), pp. 142–52; Buck, *The Principality of Antioch*, pp. 1–20, 164–88; Andrew D. Buck, 'The Castle and Lordship of Harim and the Frankish–Muslim Frontier of Northern Syria in the Twelfth Century', *al-Masaq* 28 (2016): 113–31.
126. On Türkmen involvement in the ransom of Frankish captives. See Wilson,

'The Ransom of High-ranking Captives', pp. 13–23. For detailed discussion of captivity, ransom and the taking of hostages during the Crusading era, see Yvonne Friedman, *Encounter between Enemies: Captivity and Ransom in the Latin Kingdom of Jerusalem* (Leiden: Brill, 2002), pp. 148–55; Philippe Goridis, *Gefangen im Heiligen Land Verarbeitung und Bewältigung christlicher Gefangenschaft zur Zeit der Kreuzzüge* (Ostfildern: Thorbecke, 2015); Yaacov Lev, 'Prisoners of War during the Fatimid–Ayyubid Wars with the Crusaders', in *Tolerance and Intolerance: Social Conflict in the Age of the Crusades*, ed. Michael Gervers and James M. Powell (Syracuse: Syracuse University Press 2001), pp. 11–27; Adam Kosto, 'Hostages during the First Century of the Crusades', *Medieval Encounters* 9 (2003): 3–31.

127. Sedentary rulers in Syria frequently sent messengers to request assistance from Türkmen troops in preparation for offensive actions, or at times of crisis. See, e.g., IQ, pp. 218, 221; SJ, XIII, 130, 306, 378, 388, 438; IAD ZH, II, 130, 154, 186–7, 195.

128. IAD BH, III, 1300. Ahmed Shah's Türkmen troops had secured Sabiq's rise to power in Aleppo earlier in 468/1076 by defeating the Bedouin armies of the Banu Kilab, who backed a rival claimant.

129. Rowton, 'Urban Autonomy', pp. 202–4; Rowton, 'Enclosed Nomadism', pp. 1–7; Tibble, *Crusader Armies*, pp. 3–22, 88–160.

130. SJ, XIII, 22. For an overview of the archaeological evidence for the villages of northern Syria during this period, see Anne-Marie Eddé and Jean-Pierre Sodini, 'Les Villages de Syrie du Nord du VIIe au XIIIe Siecle', in *Les Villages dans l'Empire byzantine (IVe–XVe siècle)*, ed. Jacques Lefort, Cécile Morrisson and Jean-Pierre Sodini (Paris: Lethielleux, 2005), pp. 465–83.

131. For more detail on the *Waqf* endowment system, see Astrid Meier, 'Wakf II. In the Arab Lands', in *Encyclopaedia of Islam*, 2nd edn, ed. Peri Bearman et al. (2012), available at Brill online, last accessed 3 January 2021; Stefan Heidemann, 'Charity and Piety for the Transformation of the City: the New Direction in Taxation and Waqf Policy in Mid-Twelfth Century Syria and Northern Meopotamia', in *Charity and Giving in Monotheistic Religions*, ed. Miriam Frenkel and Yaacov Lev (Berlin: De Gruyter, 2009), pp. 154–74, 164; Heidemann, *Die Renaissance der Städte*, pp. 315–16; Peacock, *Empire*, pp. 260–1, 302–8; Burns, *Aleppo*, pp. 103–4; Yasser Tabbaa, 'Survivals and Archaisms in the Architecture of Northern Syria, ca. 1080–ca. 1150', *Muqarnas* 10 (1993): 29–41, 32–3. For Seljuq contributions to military architecture in Aleppo and Damascus, see Chapter 5.

132. IQ, pp. 183, 235–6, 347–8; Ibn 'Asakir, *Ta'rikh madinat Dimashq*, XI, 35; IAD ZH, II, 103–4; IAD BH, IV, 1954–62; Ahmad b. Muhammad Ibn Khallikan, *Kitab Wafaat al-'ayan wa anba' abna' al-zaman*, 8 vols, ed. Ihsan Abbas (Beirut: Dar Sadir, 1977–8), I, pp. 295–7, II, pp. 523–5. For context, see Mallett, 'Islamic Historians of the Ayyubid Era', pp. 241–52.
133. Heidemann, *Die Renaissance der Städte*, pp. 97–353, 315–18.
134. Beihammer, *Byzantium*, pp. 180–1.
135. The influence wielded by urban political elites (notables) during this period is discussed in Chapter 5.
136. Beihammer portrayed Atsiz as a prototypical Türkmen ruler, who managed to integrate himself into the Seljuq political infrastructure before developing into a dangerous threat that required the intervention of the sultan. El-Azhari presented a different viewpoint, pointing to evidence of support from the Sultan Malik Shah, see Beihammer, *Byzantium*, pp. 179–88; El-Azhari, *Saljuqs*, pp. 34–50.
137. IAD, II, 31.
138. It should be noted that the Seljuq court (*dargah*) often moved with the sultan. See David Durand-Guédy, 'The Tents of the Saljuqs', in *Turko-Mongol Rulers, Cities and City Life*, ed. David Durand-Guédy (Leiden: Brill, 2013), pp. 149–89.
139. Accounts of the Türkmen conquest of Palestine in 463/1071, see IQ, pp. 166–7; IATH, X, 68; SJ, XII, 486. Account of Atsiz's message to Baghdad in 466/1073–4, see Ibn al-Jawzi, *al-Muntazam fi ta'rikh*, XVI, 154; SJ, XIII, 50.
140. Peacock cited Atsiz's retention of the Fatimid caliph in the *khutba* at Tyre as support for what he viewed as occasional 'Saljuq tolerance' of Shi'ism. See Peacock, *Early Saljuq History*, p. 119.
141. Atsiz's willingness to retain the *khutba* in the name of the Fatimid caliph can be compared with one of his near contemporaries in Egypt, Nasir al-Dawla Husayn b. Hamdan, who kept the *khutba* in Cairo for the Fatimid caliph between 466 and 467/1072 and 1073 despite having received financial backing from the Abbasid caliph and Seljuq sultan. See IM, p. 38. Nasir al-Dawla did eventually change the *khutba* in Alexandria to the Abbasids. Saladin also showed similar pragmatism when he kept the *khutba* in the name of the Fatimid caliph when he first gained control of Cairo between 564–7/1169–71.
142. SJ, XIII, 73; El-Azhari, *Saljuqs*, p. 38; Peacock, *Early Saljuq History*, pp. 119–21.
143. SJ, XIII, 114. According to al-'Azimi, who is quoted by Ibn al-'Adim, Zengi paid the Seljuq sultan a sum of 120,000 dinars in 523/1129 in exchange for a tughra (sultanate grant) for Jazira, and *bilad al-sham*. See IAD, BH, VII, 3847.

PART II
COUNTERING THE CRUSADES?

Part II Introduction

The armies of the First Crusade arrived outside Antioch on 5 Dhu 'l-Qaʿda 490/20 October 1097. Within less than two years, 'Crusader states' had been established at Antioch, Jerusalem and Edessa. Tripoli fell to Frankish dominion in 502/1109, while Tyre was captured in 518/1124. The following chapters reassess the diverse reactions from the Islamic Near East to this unprecedented series of events.

Chapter 4 re-examines the responses that the Crusaders' arrival provoked from the Great Seljuq Sultanate, the Fatimid Caliphate, and local Syrian-based elites. By carefully scrutinising the various military campaigns and alliances formed during the first three decades of Frankish settlement, it questions whether the 'counter-Crusade' and '*la maqam*' paradigms can be applied to the early Crusading period.

Chapter 5 details the largely overlooked role played by the notables of Aleppo and Damascus in Syrian political phenomena between 442 and 522/1050 and 1128. Through detailed analysis of siege events and calls for assistance, it outlines how urban elites exploited periods of crisis to elevate rulers that would help to preserve their own autonomous status. It then considers the physical frontiers of *bilad halab* (the region of Aleppo) throughout this time frame, before revisiting Baldwin II of Jerusalem's failed attempt to capture Aleppo in the winter months of 518/1124–5.

4

The Reactions of Seljuq, Fatimid and Syrian Elites

The 'Counter-Crusade' and *'la maqam'* Paradigms

There are two seemingly contradictory, but interlocking historiographical frameworks through which historians have approached the Islamic Near East's responses to the onset of the Crusades. The first is the 'counter-Crusade' movement, which is generally applied to nearly all Muslim military, social and cultural reactions to Frankish entanglements in the eastern Mediterranean.¹ The second is Michael Köhler's *'la maqam'* or 'no place' theory, which contends that the Frankish polities established in the Levant were almost directly integrated into the Syrian political milieu by local autonomous rulers, who prioritised mutual survival over the religious obligations of *jihad* against the Franks.²

The term 'counter-Crusade' (*contre-croisade*) was first coined in the 1930s by the French Orientalist René Grousset.³ According to Grousset, the counter-Crusade encompassed any attempt by Muslim peoples to combat the Crusaders, from 491/1098 onwards.⁴ Just one year after the publication of the first volume of a three-volume history of the Kingdom of Jerusalem, Grousset's 'false conception' of the Muslim counter-Crusade was strongly disputed by Hamilton A. R. Gibb. For Gibb, Grousset's interpretation of the 'counter-Crusade' was far too broad, as there was no Muslim 'mass movement ... swept forward by a wave of emotion' until the time of Nur al-Din 'at the earliest'.⁵

Gibb's assertion that there was no organised opposition to the Crusaders during the first fifty years of the sixth/twelfth century was built upon by the Israeli scholar Emmanuel Sivan, who charted the development of an anti-Frankish *jihad* or counter-Crusade movement around the 'pivot' of Nur al-Din's career.⁶ As such, Sivan was the first to conflate the counter-Crusade with medieval Islamic conceptualisations of *jihad*, placing great emphasis on the writings of the early sixth/twelfth-century Damascene *hadith* scholar 'Ali ibn Tahir al-Sulami (d. 500/1106).⁷ Recent scholarship, based upon a broader range of source materials including religious *hadith* literature and *jihad* poetry, has corroborated much of Sivan's thesis.⁸

However, some historians have drawn a distinction between counter-Crusade activity by Syrian and Egyptian political elites and non-elites, and *jihad* sentiment among the religious classes.⁹ There are also ongoing debates about the chronology underpinning the counter-Crusade movement. Carole Hillenbrand has proposed the battle of the Field of Blood in 513/1119 as the starting point of the counter-Crusade movement, while Mallett has drawn a distinction between the motivations behind the morally pure 'anti-Frankish *jihad*' and more prosaic 'counter-Crusade' activity. Kenneth Goudie also differentiated between the theological underpinnings of *jihad* ideology in sixth/twelfth century Syria, and the counter-Crusade paradigm.¹⁰

Divergent views on the meaning and chronology of the counter-Crusade has resulted in unique definitions and applications of the term in almost every single study that employs it. Often, the terms anti-Frankish *jihad* and counter-Crusade are used synonymously. This is also partly a natural consequence of intense historical discussions surrounding the polysemy of the term Crusade, and how these distinctions should be applied to the process of Frankish settlement.¹¹ Yet if we accept that there are fundamental questions about the term Crusade when applied solely to the Latin Christian participants in this conflict, then we should also acknowledge that it is incredibly problematic to characterise all Islamic reactions to the onset of the Crusades as a 'counter-Crusade' movement.

Leaving aside concerns about the nomenclature of Crusader studies, deeper problems surround how broadly the counter-Crusade paradigm has been applied within modern historiography. The most strident criticisms of the notion of an Islamic counter-Crusade paradigm have been made by Paul Cobb, who adopted a broader pan-Mediterranean approach to Muslim perspectives on Frankish entanglements in the Levant. Cobb states that 'there was no such thing as the "counter Crusade", in the sense of a coherent movement against the Franks that shared the same motivations and goals'.¹²

Another consequence of Sivan's conclusion that there was very little active military resistance to the Franks in the first fifty years of Crusader settlement has meant that much of the existing scholarship has concentrated on the sixth/twelfth century as a whole. As a result, the careers the charismatic 'counter-Crusade' leaders Imad al-Din Zangi, Nur al-Din and Saladin have received disproportionally more attention than the first three decades of the sixth/twelfth century.

A notable exception to this is the hugely influential and innovative work of Michael Köhler on cross-cultural diplomatic interactions. Köhler's '*la maqam*', or 'no place theory', postulates that the Frankish Crusader polities were almost instantly assimilated in the system of autonomous lordships in Syria through a series of defensive alliances made between Christian and Muslim rulers, which superseded any concerted attempt to collaborate against the newly arrived Latin settlers. Köhler identified threats such as Seljuq 'eastern armies', the Byzantine Empire, the Zangid dynasty and Saladin as the key drivers of the '*la maqam*' principle in the sixth/twelfth century.[13]

These collaborative military operations disrupted efforts to infiltrate the region by external actors and factions who had the potential to take control of both Aleppo and Damascus. Köhler contends that these alliances were driven by a collective desire to maintain the balance of power within *bilad al-sham*. Based upon the evidence of these alliances, Köhler demonstrated how during the sixth/twelfth century, political pragmatism transcended the religious demands of 'holy war' or *jihad* among the military elite of Syria and Palestine.

While Hillenbrand provided convincing evidence that *jihad* sentiments were observable among the religious classes and in the funerary inscriptions for the Artuqid ruler of Aleppo, Nur al-Dawla Balak b. Bahram, she largely subscribes to Köhler's viewpoint concerning the majority of Seljuq amirs in Syria. Köhler and Hillenbrand both agree that the initial Syrian military response was attenuated by rulers in the region placing local interest above any sense of joint responsibility to combat the Franks, while also arguing that Seljuq and Fatimid rulers were broadly in favour of a Frankish buffer state between Egypt and inland Syria. According to this viewpoint, there was evidence of what Hillenbrand labelled a 'pan-Syrian solidarity', which included the Franks, against interventions from the east.[14] The discernment of references or allusions to a collective Syrian sensibility in the medieval Arabic sources dates back to the work of Cahen, although Hillenbrand and particularly Köhler took this further, viewing the Frankish polities as an assimilated component of this collective '*al-sham*' opposition to eastern intrusion.[15]

This chapter reconsiders whether the counter-Crusade and *la maqam* paradigms can be applied to the political and military interactions in *bilad al-sham* prior to 522/1128. In doing so, it not only aims to improve our understanding of the impact that the foundation of Frankish polities had upon conflict in the region, it also provides important context for the careers of the *jihad* leaders Zangi, Nur al-Din and Saladin later in the sixth/twelfth century.

Discussion begins by placing the Fatimid and Seljuq 'counter-Crusade' movements within the context of similar campaigns that took place in the fifth/eleventh century. There will then be an analysis of the alliance networks formed by local rulers in Syria during the early sixth/twelfth century, outlining how the Franks' arrival triggered a clear military response from the Muslim political elite of *bilad al-sham*.

The Seljuq Counter-Crusade

The 'Asakir al-sham *at Antioch: 491/1098*

According to Grousset, the counter-Crusade began during the First Crusade with the relief force that ultimately failed to dislodge the Crusader armies from Antioch in Rajab 491/ June 1098.[16] The link between the Syrian coalition force, labelled the *'asakir al-sham* (army of *al-sham*) by some Arabic chroniclers, and the Seljuq sultan is quite ambiguous.[17] There is a suggestion in the chronicle of Ibn al-Jawzi that the Sultan Berkyaruq 'assembled an army of his Amirs for *jihad* to expel' the Crusaders, but most of the Arabic accounts of the siege and battle of Antioch attribute the assembly of the relief force to successful appeals for aid from Yaghi-Siyan, the besieged ruler of Antioch.[18]

Whatever the underlying cause of the coalition's formation, it is clear that many of the difficulties that hindered Seljuq campaigns into northern Syria during the late fifth/eleventh century, such as disaffection among Türkmen troops or an inability among senior amirs to effectively cooperate against external enemies, are discernible in the medieval Arabic accounts of events at Antioch in the summer of 491/1098.[19]

The Failed Seljuq Campaigns of 505/1111 and 509/1115

The Seljuq campaigns into northern Syria in 505/1111 and 509/1115 have been analysed repeatedly by generations of historians, with their failures generally attributed to two factors.[20] The first was the inability or unwillingness of the Sultan Muhammad b. Malik Shah to lead the campaigns in person. The second was a lack of support from Seljuq rulers based in *bilad al-sham*, who actively impeded the efforts of the sultan's armies. This non-cooperation was at least partly motivated by a belief that these '*jihad*' expeditions against the newly formed Frankish polities were a pretence for wider efforts to curtail the autonomy of the Syrian amirs. Both of these issues have usually been attributed to the collapse of centralised Seljuq rule following the death of the Sultan Malik Shah in 485/1092.[21]

The purpose of this section is not to recreate or dispute the narratives surrounding these events, rather it is to place these campaigns in the context of the Seljuq expeditions of the fifth/eleventh century.[22] In doing so, it becomes clear that many of issues that hampered efforts to expand Seljuq authority in northern Syria in the decades preceding the First Crusade, persisted into the sixth/twelfth century.

For instance, there are signs that the sultan's armies suffered from supply problems in the accounts of the 505/1111 campaign. The Latin chronicler Albert of Aachen, who wrote his chronicle in Germany based upon eyewitness testimony from those who had returned from the Latin east, described how after the siege of Tell Bashir in 505/1111, a significant portion of the sultan's army had to return east as 'vital supplies were running out'.[23] An army encountering issues with provisions only shortly after arriving in *bilad al-sham* from the east corresponds well with the campaign led by Malik Shah in 479/1086–7. However, it is worth noting that Ibn al-Qalanisi, Ibn al-Athir and Ibn al-'Adim claimed that many of the eastern amirs departed due to tensions with other rulers within the coalition, following their failed siege of Aleppo.

After the amirs commanding the expedition of 505/1111 moved away from Tell Bashir, they raided the territory around Aleppo and Ma'rrat al-Nu'man, providing further indications of supply problems. Ibn al-Qalanisi described how the leaders of the sultan's army, infuriated by Ridwan of

Aleppo's refusal to assist them 'encamped before the city, ravaged its territories, and created worse devastation than the Franks had done'.[24] Additionally, Ibn al-'Adim reported that during the siege of Aleppo, Ridwan sent thieves and brigands to prevent provisions from reaching the sultan's army, which would have exacerbated any supply difficulties.[25] Following their failed siege of Aleppo, the sultan's army moved on to Ma'rrat al-Nu'man at the end of Safar 505/September 1111, where they 'plundered the region' according to Ibn al-Qalanisi and Ibn al-'Adim, again hinting at continuing issues.[26]

The earliest example of personal gain taking precedence over the collective goals of the expedition also occurred during the 505/1111 campaign. Ibn al-Qalanisi claimed that during the siege of Tell Bashir, the ruler of the settlement, Joscelyn, paid the Amir Ahmadil 'with money and gifts' to lift the siege. Ahmadil agreed to do so 'in spite of the disapproval of the other Amirs'.[27] The Latin source material made no reference to this payment, although the Armenian chronicler Matthew of Edessa alluded to dialogue between the two rulers, claiming that Ahmadil and Joscelyn 'made peace … and both men became brothers'.[28] It is possible to compare Ahmadil's actions to events at Tripoli in 484/1091. As discussed in Chapter 3, the ruler of Aleppo Qasim al-Dawla Aqsunqur agreed to accept a payment from the besieged governor of Tripoli in order to lift the siege, despite the protestations of the ruler of Damascus Tutush b. Alp Arslan.

Another instance of amiral defiance of the sultan's orders can be found in Ridwan b. Tutush of Aleppo's refusal to assist the eastern amirs during the 505/1111 campaign. According to Ibn al-'Adim's account, Ridwan appealed for assistance to the amirs leading the campaign, only to close the gates of the city upon their arrival at Aleppo. Although Ibn al-'Adim claimed that Ridwan's decision to refuse entry to the sultan's army cost him support in the city due to resulting deprivation caused by the siege, he failed to offer a reason for Ridwan's hasty volte-face.

Albert of Aachen provided the most convincing explanation, as he claimed that the killing of an unnamed son of Ridwan drove the ruler of Aleppo into open resistance against the sultan's army. According to the Latin chronicler, Ridwan endeavoured to remain a neutral party in 505/1111 in what he considered to be a conflict between the sultan's army and the Franks, due to his ongoing treaty with Tancred of Antioch. Ridwan therefore offered an unnamed son as a hostage to the sultan's army, but the leading amirs of the eastern armies executed the son when Ridwan persevered in his refusal to open the gates of Aleppo. This turn of events forced Ridwan into complete resistance against the 505/1111 expedition.[29]

Albert of Aachen's account has generally been discounted by historians, largely due to Albert's distance from the events he described, but also because there is no corroboration in the Arabic source material, with the omission of these events from Ibn al-'Adim's detailed chronicle of Aleppo being particularly problematic. However, the method of taking hostage a son of an uncooperative Seljuq ruler was repeated during a later campaign by the leader of one of the sultan's armies. According to Ibn al-Athir, the amir of Mosul Aqsunqur al-Bursuqi took Ayaz, one of the sons of Najm al-Din Il-ghazi b. Artuq of Mardin, captive in Dhu 'l-Hijja 508/late April 1115 after Il-ghazi initially refused to send troops on the campaign.[30] Because of this later precedent, Albert of Aachen's version of events should perhaps not be dismissed out of hand, especially as it provides the best justification for Ridwan's actions.

Another parallel can be drawn between the apparent collaboration between Syrian Seljuq rulers and the Franks against the sultan's armies in 509/1115, and Sharaf al-Dawla Muslim b. Quraysh's disruption of Tutush b. Alp Arslan's attempt to capture Aleppo in 471/1079. There is some disagreement in the source material as to the extent of the alliance that was formed by figures such as Tughtegin of Damascus, Il-ghazi of Mardin and Lu'lu' and Shams al-Khawass of Aleppo with the Frankish rulers Roger of Antioch, Baldwin I of Jerusalem and their Armenian allies. Although Ibn al-Qalanisi omitted any reference to these events, the Arabic chronicles of Ibn al-Athir, Sibt b. al-Jawzi and Ibn al-'Adim all describe a coalition between Frankish and Syrian-based Seljuq potentates.[31] Further corroboration was provided by Albert of Aachen and Fulcher of Chartres, who both claimed that Tughtegin fought alongside the Frankish troops.[32] Walter the Chancellor stated that Damascene troops were present in the Frankish camp, but asserted that they left before the battle against the sultan's army.[33]

Again, the overt opposition of Seljuq Syrian amirs to the 509/1115 campaign is widely considered to be the strongest indicator of the decline in Seljuq influence in *bilad al-sham*. However, the coalition that the Seljuq amirs of

Syria entered into with Frankish and Armenian rulers was not dissimilar to the Uqaylid ruler Sharaf al-Dawla Muslim b. Quraysh's collaborations with the Arab tribes of the Banu Numayr, Qushayri and Kilab during Tutush's campaign in 471/1079.

Seljuq Campaign Issues and the Counter-Crusade Narrative

The failed Seljuq military operations against the Franks in the early sixth/ twelfth century are generally deemed to have been a highly decisive factor in the formation of the Crusader states. Yet by placing these campaigns within the counter-Crusade framework, historians have tended to overlook issues encountered by almost all Seljuq expeditions into *bilad al-sham* between 463 and 522/1071 and 1128. While the armies dispatched to northern Syria by the sultan in 505/1111 and 509/1115 were at least partly intended to combat the Frankish polities in the Levant, non-cooperation from Syrian-based Seljuq rulers, the general inability of Seljuq amirs to collaborate, disaffection among Türkmen troops and supply problems were not exclusive features of the sixth/ twelfth-century Seljuq counter-Crusade movement.

The Fatimid Counter-Crusade

The arrival of the First Crusaders led to the removal of nearly all Fatimid territorial dominions in the region. Jerusalem fell to the Franks in 492/1099, Acre in 497/1103–4, Tripoli in 502/1109 and Tyre in 518/1124. Rather than sparking a counter-Crusade movement, the onset of the Crusades saw the continuation of the Fatimid's previous strategy of targeted military campaigns combined with active diplomatic measures in Syria and Palestine.[34]

Like their Seljuq contemporaries, most of the military actions launched in response to these events have been debated by generations of historians in nearly every book that has covered this period from the Crusader, Damascene or Fatimid perspective.[35]

Yet disagreement persists about the driving forces behind the decline in Fatimid fortunes between 492 and 518/1099 and 1124. Traditionally, the Fatimid failures against the Franks have been attributed to criticism of their military capabilities, stemming from a poorly trained army led by incompetent military leaders.[36] Carole Hillenbrand placed more emphasis on the deaths of the Fatimid Caliph al-Mustansir and his Vizier Badr al-Jamali in 487/1094.[37]

While Badr al-Jamali was the more influential of these two figures, the transition to his son and successor al-Afdal was relatively smooth. Instead, it was a dispute over who would succeed al-Mustansir which triggered the Nizari schism, leading to the fracture of the Isma'ili movement and the establishment of the Nizari Isma'ili faction, better known as the Assassins in western Europe.[38]

In addition to internal problems, Hillenbrand asserted that the ideologically based conflict between the Fatimids and the Great Seljuq Sultanate made any potential cooperative action against the emergent Crusader polities impossible. This estrangement greatly aided Frankish efforts to seize Egyptian territorial possessions in the Levant. Köhler took this argument further and has contended that the Fatimids were content to have the Franks as a buffer state against the threat posed by the Seljuqs in *bilad al-sham*.[39] Only recent work by Brett has looked to re-evaluate the qualified success of the Fatimid military policy in the early sixth/twelfth century and the motivations underpinning this activity.[40] Brett has argued that the threat posed to Fatimid dominions by the Franks forced the ruling hierarchy in Cairo to ally themselves with Seljuq rulers in what he viewed as a clear shift in Egyptian diplomatic and military policy in *bilad al-sham*.

The following section reframes the Fatimid reactions to the establishment of Frankish polities in the context of their fifth/eleventh-century endeavours in the region. It begins with the notion that the Fatimids sought to derive benefit from the First Crusade, and scrutinises the evidence surrounding Fatimid communications with the Crusader armies. Discussion then moves onto Fatimid policy in the early sixth/twelfth, namely the protection of Ramla and Ascalon, and retaining some level of influence in Tyre and Tripoli, before examining Cairo's diplomatic contacts with Tughtegin of Damascus.

Did the Fatimids Derive Benefit from the First Crusade?

The arrival of the First Crusaders in Palestine had an almost immediate impact on Fatimid interests in the region. The western European Crusader forces captured Jerusalem after a month-and-a-half-long siege on 17 Sha'ban 492/15 July 1099.[41] The response from Egypt was almost instantaneous, with the Fatimid Vizier al-Afdal leading an army to confront the Franks. On 16 Ramadan/12 August 1099, the Egyptian army was defeated at Ramla following a surprise attack by the Crusading forces at dawn, and the Fatimid survivors fled to Ascalon. Subsequently, the Franks besieged Ascalon, and negotiated a payment of 20,000 dinars with the inhabitants to withdraw.[42] The initial military reaction to the Franks can therefore be summarised as disastrous, with the loss of Jerusalem, secured only twelve months previously, and a catastrophic military defeat, which placed the southernmost Fatimid dominions in *bilad al-sham* under threat.

Yet despite the negative implications of the expedition for Egyptian interests in the eastern Mediterranean, some medieval Arabic chroniclers intimated that the Shi'i Fatimid Caliphate was complicit in the success of the First Crusade. Ibn Zafir al-Azdi wrote that, for the Fatimids, it was better for the Franks to occupy the Syrian coastline 'so that they could prevent the spread of the influence of the Turks to the lands of Egypt'.[43] Ibn al-Athir was more unequivocal, writing that:

> it is said that the 'Alid rulers of Egypt, when they saw the power of the Seljuq state and their strength and their conquering of the lands of Syria as far as Gaza, there remaining between them and Egypt no province to hold them back, and when Atsiz entered Egypt and blockaded it, they were afraid and sent messages to the Franks inviting them to *al-sham* to conquer it, so that they (the Franks) would be between them and the Muslims, but Allah knows best.[44]

In addition, Ibn Muyassar wrote that when al-Afdal learnt of the fall of Jerusalem, he 'sent an envoy to the Franks rebuking them for what they had done'.[45] Hillenbrand and Köhler have used these accounts, in addition to evidence in the Latin sources of diplomatic interactions between the leadership of the Crusading armies and Egyptian envoys, to suggest that the Fatimids were open to collaborating with the First Crusaders in the hope of establishing a 'Frankish buffer state' in Palestine, which would protect Egypt from the Seljuq polities of Syria.[46] While some evidence suggests that diplomatic negotiations and potentially even military collaboration between Fatimid envoys and the leadership of the First Crusade took place, there are several problems with this argument.[47]

The first is the inherent bias against the Fatimids within the Arabic source base, written largely by Sunni Muslim authors. To begin with, the employment of the common formulaic qualifier of 'it is said' by Ibn al-Athir in the passage quoted above hints that he was less confident in the veracity of this information. Additionally, Ibn al-Athir's impartiality when it came to the Fatimids has been called into question by historians for some time. Among other similar examples, Gibb pointed to Ibn al-Athir's coverage of the fall of Tripoli in 502/1109, where the chronicler blamed disagreement among Fatimid military leaders for the fleet arriving late, just eight days after the fall of Tripoli.[48] Ibn al-Athir claimed that even after the fleet 'was ready and everything needed had been supplied' its departure was delayed after the Fatimids 'argued about it for more than a year'.[49] The obvious implication here was that if the Fatimids had not been engaged in 'infighting' for a year, they would easily have been able to save Tripoli from falling under Frankish control. Ibn al-Athir's judgements on Fatimid interactions with the Franks should therefore be regarded with some circumspection, as his account could be construed as an attempt to apportion blame for the establishment of Frankish polities in the eastern Mediterranean on the Fatimid Caliphate.

The second issue relates to chronology. Atsiz's attack upon Egypt occurred in 469/1077.[50] As it took place some twenty years before the arrival of the First Crusaders outside Antioch, it seems unlikely that this would have triggered a Fatimid appeal to Frankish rulers. Instead, Ibn al-Athir's inclusion of Atsiz's short-lived failed invasion of Egypt was little more than an attempt to conflate two unconnected events, separated by two decades, in order to place culpability upon the Egyptian Caliphate for the success of the First Crusade.

Also, the notion that the Fatimids captured Jerusalem in the hope of using it to negotiate with the Franks becomes problematic once the timing of events is scrutinised in close detail. According to the dates provided by Ibn al-Qalanisi, the Fatimid army departed Egypt in Shaʿban 491/4 July–1 August 1098, and survivors fleeing Jerusalem arrived in Damascus after the fall of the town in the first ten days of Shawwal 491/1–10 September 1098.[51] Al-Maqrizi agreed that the Egyptian forces left Cairo in Shaʿban 491/July 1098, with Jerusalem falling to Fatimid forces in the last five days of Ramadan 491/26–31 August 1098 after a siege of '40 days', indicating that the town was first besieged between 7 and 12 Shaʿban 491/16 and 21 July 1098.[52] This chronology is confirmed by the more contemporaneous Latin sources.[53] This means that there is broad agreement across Latin, Syrian and Egyptian historiographical traditions that Cairene-based elements of the Fatimid army departed Cairo in early Shaʿban 491/July 1098, and that the town fell under Egyptian control in Ramadan 491/August 1098.

We can also assume that this expedition, described as 'large' by Ibn al-Qalanisi and equipped with some '40 catapults' that destroyed a section of Jerusalem's exterior walls according to al-Maqrizi, would have required some degree of prior planning and preparation. Although al-Afdal's decision to besiege Jerusalem can probably be categorised as an opportunistic attack prompted by the siege of Antioch by the armies of the First Crusade, it seems highly unlikely that the Fatimids were not already planning to campaign in *bilad al-sham* before they learnt of the outcome of the Crusaders' battle against the *'asakir al-sham*' at Antioch on 19 Rajab 491/28 June 1098.

Conversely, Ibn al-Athir, who dated the surrender of Jerusalem to Shaʿban 489/July 1096, lends support to Köhler's assertions.[54] Yet the problematic nature of Ibn al-Athir's coverage of the Fatimids, coupled with the author's decision to place his account of the Egyptian conquest of Jerusalem under the Hirji year 492/1099 rather than 489/1096, conspicuously linking it to his account of the Crusader's siege, suggests the author's dating of the Fatimid siege to 489/1096 was little more than an extension of his efforts to make the Shiʿi dynasty appear responsible for the success of the First Crusade.[55]

If the Fatimids had used their foreknowledge of the impending arrival of the Crusaders to capture Jerusalem in 489/1096, rather than 491/1098, then it would lend credence to Ibn al-Athir's claim that the Egyptians had invited the Franks to the Levant. It should also be noted that accounts of invitations being sent to invading forces by dissenting or rival groups or individuals are a common feature in medieval Arabic accounts of comparable contemporaneous events, such as the Almohad invasion of Spain or the Norman conquest of Sicily.[56] Even when discussion is confined to the First Crusade, Ibn al-ʿAdim accused Shiʿi Arab rulers in northern Syria of communicating with the Franks during his account of events at Antioch.[57]

Köhler also asserted that Jerusalem was of limited strategic value to the Fatimid Caliphate, particularly when compared to Damascus, which had been the target of their policy in *bilad al-sham* for the previous fifteen years.

While it is correct that control of Jerusalem provided little strategic benefit to the Fatimids, it did develop into a more viable target for the Egyptian Caliphate towards the end of the fifth/eleventh century.[58]

The Fatimids would also have been aware of the precedent set by Atsiz b. Uwaq al-Khwarizmi, who had used Jerusalem to wrestle Damascus from Egyptian dominion in the 460s/1070s. Atsiz seized control of Jerusalem and a string coastal settlements in 463/1071, and used these areas as a base to launch continuous attacks upon Damascus, until the inhabitants surrendered to him in 468/1076.[59] When looked at in this context, control of Jerusalem, in conjunction with other coastal settlements, would have been attractive to the Fatimids in Sha'ban 491/4 July–1 August 1098 as a possible route to the future conquest of Damascus. This would have been the case irrespective of the presence and objectives of the armies of the First Crusade. This would also not have precluded them from offering the Franks control of Jerusalem in exchange for a joint military attack upon Damascus in the spring of 492/1099, as was claimed by Raymond of Aguillers.[60] Indeed, the late fifth/eleventh century had seen the Fatimids discuss joint military ventures against Damascus with both the Uqaylid ruler of Aleppo and Mosul Muslim b. Quraysh, and the Seljuq Ridwan of Aleppo.

The final difficulty with this argument is that it is based almost entirely on the notion of irreconcilable hostility between 'Fatimid' and 'Seljuq' rulers grounded in doctrinal divergence. While it is possible that the Fatimids may have preferred the Franks to occupy Palestine over their Sunni Seljuq adversaries, there is also evidence of sustained diplomatic contact and military alliances between figures from the Seljuq and Fatimid spheres, both prior to and following the arrival of the Franks in the Levant.[61] This raises questions about the extent to which a 'buffer-state' against the Seljuqs would have been a desired outcome for the ruling hierarchy in Cairo.[62]

The Collapse of Fatimid Power along the Syrian Littoral

The defeat at Ramla on 16 Ramadan 492/12 August 1099, signalled the beginning of further Fatimid territorial losses in Palestine. Godfrey and Baldwin I, the first rulers of the newly founded Frankish kingdom of Jerusalem, targeted coastal settlements, capturing Haifa and Caesarea and Arsuf in 494/1100–1.[63] The First Crusade veteran Raymond St. Gilles placed Tripoli under siege in 495/1101–2, whilst there were also failed Frankish siege attempts against Beirut and Acre.[64]

In response, several Fatimid armies marched north into Palestine. The first was defeated between Ramla and Ascalon by the army of Jerusalem, led by Baldwin I, in early Dhu 'l-Qaʿda 494/early September 1101.[65] A second Egyptian force marched north into Palestine in Rajab 495/21 April–20 March 1102, and defeated the army of Jerusalem, again led by King Baldwin I, at Ascalon. A subsequent Fatimid siege of the port of Jaffa was curtailed by a recently arrived fleet from Europe and a second attack by Baldwin I, who had managed to escape the first battlefield and receive reinforcements.[66]

A third expedition was sent into *bilad al-sham* from Egypt to combat the Franks in 496/1103, leading to a battle at Yazur, near Ramla, from which the Fatimid forces again emerged victorious.[67] As part of the preparations for the 496/1103 campaign, al-Afdal's son Sharaf al-Maʿali sent to Duqaq of Damascus asking for assistance and received a 'favourable reply', but Damascene reinforcements were 'prevented by certain circumstances which arose and accidents which intervened', according to Ibn al-Qalanisi's account.[68]

Duqaq died in 497/1104, a year in which his *atabeg* and successor as ruler of Damascus, Tughtegin, failed in attempts to impede Frankish sieges of Jubayl and Acre, which were subsumed into the burgeoning kingdom of Jerusalem.[69] In Dhu 'l-Hijja 498/August–September 1105, another battle took place between Egyptian and Frankish forces between Ascalon and Jaffa. The Egyptian forces were led by a different son of al-Afdal, Sanaʾ al-Mulk Husayn, and on this occasion Tughtegin sent some Damascene troops to reinforce the Fatimid army.[70] This was the first of several alliances between the rulers of Damascus and Egypt against the Frankish forces.[71]

For much of the early years of the sixth/twelfth century, the Fatimids largely managed to keep Frankish troops away from Ascalon. Yet the Fatimids were markedly less successful in the coastal settlements. After an intermittent eight-year siege, 502/1109 saw the fall of Tripoli, while Banyas also succumbed to Frankish control.[72] Beirut and Sidon fell to the Franks in 504/1110.[73] Tyre was again placed under siege by Baldwin I between 25 Jumada I and 10 Shawwal 505/29 November 1111 and 10 April 1112, but the city was relieved by Tughtegin of Damascus, who was offered financial incentive to do so by the governor 'Izz al-Mulk al-A'zz.[74] A detachment from the Egyptian navy was dispatched to Tyre with supplies in 516/1122, but was then defeated by a Venetian fleet at Ascalon in 517/1123, following another failed Egyptian attempt to retake Jaffa.[75] Tyre finally fell to Frankish forces on 23 Jumada I 518/8 July 1124 after being besieged for a third time.[76]

The Fatimids did conduct aggressive military activity against the Franks between 492 and 498/1099 and 1105, particularly in comparison with the insouciant response from the Great Seljuq Sultanate during this same period. Yet this policy of targeted Egyptian military campaigns into Palestine and Syria was not new. Many of the methods and objectives pursued by the Fatimid ruling hierarchy were carried over from the fifth/eleventh century, particularly the retention of key settlements in the interior of *bilad al-sham* to protect Egypt from overland invasion. The only expedition into mainland Egypt prior to 522/1128 occurred in 512/1118, when Baldwin I launched a campaign into Egypt that reached Tinnis before returning north.[77] Although it should be acknowledged that the Frankish polities prioritised expansion along the coastline and northern Syria during the first three decades of the sixth/twelfth century.

As Fatimid influence declined throughout 442–522/1050–1128, their strategic focus shifted from Aleppo and Damascus, to Jerusalem and Ascalon. While Fatimid military activity certainly intensified in the six-year-period that followed the First Crusade, their overarching strategy and the methods they employed did not alter significantly in the early years of the Crusading period. The main difference was the limited success enjoyed by these military operations, not the underlying policy. As a consequence, it is not accurate to view the Egyptian military activity against the Franks as distinct manifestations of a Fatimid 'counter-Crusade' movement.

Fatimid Contacts with Tughtegin of Damascus

The interactions between Tughtegin of Damascus and the Fatimid court has been the subject of some debate in modern historiography. Michael Brett viewed the Fatimid alliance with Tughtegin as representing an 'ideological shift away from the confrontational approach ... towards a more oecumenical appeal to the generality of Islam'.[78] In contrast, Köhler downplayed its importance, arguing that Tughtegin entered into alliances with Cairo only when it benefited him strategically.⁷⁹ Certainly, there is evidence in the source material that points to a deeper relationship than Köhler allowed for. Aside from the above-mentioned alliances with the Fatimids against the Franks at Ascalon in 498/1105, Sidon in 501/1107–8 and Tyre in 505/1111–12, there were repeated instances of meaningful contact and collaboration between Tughtegin and the Egyptian Caliphate prior to the former's death in 522/1128.

One of the clearest manifestations of this relationship can be seen in the fluid power-sharing dynamics in Tripoli and Tyre during the early sixth/twelfth century. When the Fatimids installed Sharaf al-Dawla b. Abi al-Tayyib as the new governor of Tripoli in 501/1108, in place of Ibn 'Ammar, a close ally of Tughtegin, Tughtegin could have taken such a development badly.⁸⁰ But he remained willing to maintain a dialogue with the Fatimids. So, five years later, when Tughtegin appointed a new governor in Tyre named Mas'ud to replace his Fatimid-appointed predecessor in 506/1112–13, it caused no problems with the caliph's court in Cairo. Tughtegin reportedly sent a messenger to the Fatimid Vizier al-Afdal, informing him that he had taken control of Tyre only at the behest of its residents, who had threatened to surrender the city to the Franks if he had not done so. He also told the Fatimid vizier that the *khutba* in the town remained in the name of the Fatimid caliph. This flexibility is reminiscent of Atsiz's retention of the *khutba* in the name of the Fatimid Caliph al-Mustansir in Jerusalem during the early 460s/1070s. Al-Afdal replied, stating that he approved of Tughtegin's actions.⁸¹

The situation reversed itself again in 516/1122–3, when the Fatimid Caliph al-Amir bi-Ahkam Allah sent a fleet to remove Tughtegin's deputy Mas'ud, and replace him with a Fatimid governor. This was once more a result of complaints made about Mas'ud's conduct. Ibn al-Athir claimed that the new Fatimid governor of Tyre then contacted Tughtegin informing him of these developments, to which Tughtegin responded positively, offering to provide military aid to Tyre in future.⁸²

Perhaps the most revealing insight into the Fatimid relationship with Tughtegin was provided by Ibn al-Athir, who claimed that Tughtegin was placed in command of Egyptian troops during a collaborative military expedition near Ascalon in 512/1118–19. Upon his arrival at Ascalon, the commander of 7,000 Egyptian cavalry informed Tughtegin that 'their Caliph had ordered him to follow Tughtegin's plans and to act in accordance with his decisions'.[83] Although none of the sources refer to any substantial battle taking place at this time, the supposed placement of Fatimid troops under the command of a 'Seljuq' ruler of Damascus was unprecedented.

The diplomatic relationship survived the fall of Tyre in 518/1124. In 519/1125–6, Tughtegin sent 'Ali b. Hamid to act as his envoy to the Fatimid court at Cairo.[84] Ibn Muyassar placed this event in the year 520/1126–7, and claimed that the ruler of Aleppo and Mosul, Aqsunqur al-Bursuqi, also sent a messenger who arrived at the same time as Tughtegin's representative.[85] In response, Amir al-Dawla Gumushtagin, governor of Bosra, and Amir al-Muntadi b. Musafir al-Ghanawi, messenger of al-Amir lord of Egypt, travelled to Damascus in Sha'ban 520/August 1126 'bringing magnificent robes of honour and costly Egyptian presents'.[86] This strongly suggests that interactions between Cairo and Damascus were ongoing in 520/1126 and serves to illustrate the enduring nature of the alliance, which by this point had spanned two decades. Additionally, claims that Tughtegin was able to bring another prominent Seljuq amir into these discussions in the form of Aqsunqur al-Bursuqi further underlined the strength of his ties to the Fatimids.

The diplomatic relationship between the Fatimid Caliphate and Tughtegin of Damascus seems to have been a deep, long-standing alliance, almost unparalleled by Fatimid standards, both in terms of time and the degree of trust implied between the two parties. The longevity of the alliance was partly a consequence of Tughtegin's twenty-year reign, and his willingness to collaborate with multiple rulers operating in the Levant throughout this period.

However, it also needs to be stressed that Fatimid alliances with 'Seljuq' rulers were not a novel development provoked by the establishment of the Latin east. The late fifth/eleventh century had seen the Fatimids make similar approaches to members of the Seljuq dynasty, such as Tutush of Damascus and Ridwan of Aleppo. The alliance with Tughtegin was certainly not evidence of an 'ideological shift' in Fatimid policy, provoked by the onset of the Crusades. Rather, it was a logical extension of their former policy, one necessitated by the realities of political interactions in *bilad al-sham* throughout this period. Even evidence of shared rule in Tripoli and Tyre was not new. The Fatimids lost absolute control of these settlements in the late fifth/eleventh century, requiring the careful fostering of close diplomatic ties with local rulers for several decades prior to the Franks' arrival in the Levant.

Alliance Networks among Syrian Elites in the Early Crusading Era

A key foundational point of Michael Köhler's *la maqam* or no place theory is that at the time of the establishment of Frankish polities in *bilad al-sham*, the region was divided into what he labelled the 'Syrian system of autonomous lordships', with the Great Seljuq Sultanate having little or no influence in the region. The Franks were therefore allowed to follow a policy of 'integration' assimilating themselves into this fractured political climate, swiftly establishing an understanding with the other local rulers to maintain the balance of power in the *bilad al-sham*. For Köhler, the *la maqam* principle was a prominent feature of Syrian political interactions from 502/1108–9, when Ridwan of Aleppo formed an alliance with Tancred of Antioch, and endured until Saladin's capture of Aleppo in 579/1183.[87]

The following section will re-examine two key elements of Köhler's thesis as applied to the first three decades of the sixth/twelfth century. These are the circumstances surrounding Ridwan of Aleppo's alliance with Tancred of Antioch in 502/1108–9, and the identification of inflamed tensions between the major Syrian urban centres of Damascus and Aleppo.

Ridwan's Alliance with Tancred

The most prominent example of a Syrian-based Seljuq amir entering into an alliance with a Frankish ruler during the early sixth/twelfth century is that made by Ridwan of Aleppo with Tancred of Antioch in 502/1108–9.[88] Köhler viewed this collaborative military action as 'the first instance of common strategic thinking of the Syrian local states'.[89] Yet certain features of this coalition, and the events of 502/1108–9, indicate the exceptional circumstances that enabled this cooperation between various Frankish, Turkish and Armenian potentates.

First, it should be clarified that the source material relating to the coalitions formed between Ridwan of Aleppo and Tancred of Antioch against Jawli Saqoa of Mosul, Baldwin of Edessa and the Armenian ruler Kogh Vasil contain discrepancies relating to the nature of the alliance and the chronology surrounding its formation.[90]

Beginning with the Arabic accounts, Ibn al-Athir claimed that after an initial battle between Edessan and Antiochene forces, a second battle took place with Ridwan in coalition with Tancred against Baldwin of Edessa, Joscelyn of Tell Bashir and Jawli Saqoa of Mosul at some point in Safar 502/10 September–8 October 1108.[91] Ibn al-ʿAdim also referred to a battle in 501/1107–8 or 502/1108–9 with Joscelyn of Tell Bashir and Jawli Saqoa allied against Ridwan and Tancred.[92]

In terms of Armenian sources, Matthew of Edessa wrote that there was initially a battle between Tancred and a combined force led by Baldwin of Edessa, Joscelyn of Tell Bashir and Jawli Saqoa of Mosul in addition to the Armenian ruler Kogh Vasil. According to Matthew's account, a second battle took place between 'Arabs and Turks' after which, the Arab forces marched to Aleppo 'intending to place themselves under the protection of Tancred', hinting at Antiochene involvement in two separate military engagements.[93] Michael the Syrian described an alliance between Ridwan and Tancred against Jawli, but the Anonymous Syriac Chronicle of 1234 made no reference to Muslim involvement in a battle between the Antiochene and Edessan armies.[94]

The Latin sources are also more circumspect about any active involvement by Muslim troops in this dispute. Albert of Aachen claimed that there was a battle between forces from Antioch and Edessa, which the Antiochene forces won. Baldwin then fled to Duluk, where Tancred besieged him but was forced to withdraw following the advance of a relief force led by Jokermesh of Mosul and Joscelyn of Tell Bashir.[95] Albert's reference to Jokermesh was probably an error, as Jokermesh was Jawli's predecessor as ruler of Mosul and had died in 500/1106–7.[96] Fulcher of Chartres made no reference to Baldwin, and stated that Joscelyn allied himself to '7,000 Turks' and engaged Tancred in battle, from which Tancred emerged victorious.[97] Although there is little consensus in the source material, it is generally accepted that there was some form of alliance between Ridwan of Aleppo and Tancred of Antioch at some point during 502/1108–9.

Jawli's decision to ransom Baldwin of Edessa, combined with the personal animosity between Tancred and Baldwin, helped to create the correct conditions for collaboration between various Seljuq and Frankish rulers.[98]

Ibn al-Athir's depiction of events is central to Köhler's argument. According to Ibn al-Athir, Ridwan persuaded Tancred to enter into an alliance by claiming that if Jawli were to capture Aleppo then there would be 'no place (*la maqam*)' for the Franks in *bilad al-sham*.⁹⁹ Köhler placed great emphasis upon these purported messages between Ridwan and Tancred, overlooking several factors which help to explain Ridwan's willingness to ally himself to Tancred at this time.

For instance, one of Jawli's first actions after he crossed the Euphrates was to attack and capture the town of Balis, a strategically important crossing point on the River Euphrates, making it an important site on Aleppo's eastern frontier.¹⁰⁰ For his part, Jawli had been forced to hastily flee Mosul before it was besieged by a rival amir named Madwdud, who was acting on the Seljuq Sultan Muhammad's orders. This meant that upon his arrival in *bilad al-sham*, Jawli was desperate for new territory to use as a power base. Ridwan also had a problematic relationship with Jawli, which dated back to a joint military campaign against Rahba in 500/1107. According to Ibn al-Qalanisi, Ridwan returned to Aleppo 'afraid' of Jawli following this expedition.¹⁰¹ Ridwan's troubled past with Jawli, and indications that Jawli made the first offensive move by attacking Aleppan territory at Balis, left Ridwan with no option but to defend his position by whatever means possible.

Ridwan also had little choice but to turn to Tancred when Jawli arrived in northern Syria in 502/1108–9, as he had either alienated his potential allies or they were engaged in conflict elsewhere. During a campaign against Nisibis in Ramadan 499/May–June 1106, Ridwan had taken Il-ghazi captive at the request of the then ruler of Mosul, Jokermesh.¹⁰² While Ridwan's relationship with Il-ghazi dated back to the fifth/eleventh century, and they later participated together in Jawli's attacks on Rahba and Mosul between Rajab and 19 Shuwal 500/February and 13 June 1107 without any issues, it seems doubtful that Il-ghazi or other members of the Artuqid dynasty would have rushed to Ridwan's assistance in 502/1108.¹⁰³

Further south, Tughtegin of Damascus would have been pre-occupied with the ongoing Frankish siege of Tripoli. Damascene forces were involved in a battle against Gervase of Tiberias in Ramadan 501/May 1108, and Tughtegin was subsequently forced to withdraw from 'Arqa to Damascus after a failed attempt to relieve Tripoli in Sha'ban 502/March 1109.¹⁰⁴ After the latter engagement, Ibn al-Qalanisi informs us that the Franks had captured a large number of 'horses and other animals' and described the Damascene army that reached Homs as being in 'the most pitiable condition'.¹⁰⁵ It is therefore unlikely that Tughtegin would have had the time or resources to assist Ridwan in 502/1108–9. Finally, the ongoing siege of Mosul by Mawdud prevented Ridwan from calling for aid from Mosul, the last source of support that rulers of Aleppo had relied upon in the late fifth/eleventh and early sixth/twelfth centuries.[106]

While the events of 502/1108–9 indicate that at this point in time Antiochene and Aleppan interests were aligned, this alignment was driven by a set of highly unique circumstances. First, it is far from certain that Tancred would have allied himself to Ridwan if Jawli had not been in alliance with Baldwin, with whom Tancred had long-standing personal issues. Secondly, Ridwan had little choice but to turn to Tancred due to the scarcity of other prospective allies, while his previous history with Jawli suggests that there was more personal animosity involved in his decision-making than a desire to maintain the balance of power in the region. These factors formed the backdrop to the alliance between Ridwan and Tancred in 502/1108–9, indicating that it should not be viewed as indicative of a wider trend. Indeed, hostages and captives of war had been used to build alliances that bridged ethno-cultural and ideological boundaries in *bilad al-sham* on multiple occasions between 442 and 522/1050 and 1128.[107]

Heightened Hostility between Damascus and Aleppo?

Increased animosity between the Syrian cities of Damascus and Aleppo, especially during Ridwan's reign in Aleppo, is the second element that Köhler cites to support the application of *la maqam* theory to the early sixth/twelfth century. As a result of this rising sense of antipathy, the rulers of these cities were pushed into coalitions with the Latin polities of the Levant, rather than cooperating together against the Franks. However, it is far from clear that the rivalry between city-states of Aleppo and Damascus intensified during the early sixth/twelfth century.

Although Köhler depicted Tughtegin as Ridwan's 'arch rival', there is little reliable evidence for this.[108] Much of Köhler's claims centre around 488–90/1095–7, when Ridwan of Aleppo and Duqaq of Damascus were engaged in a series of military engagements that followed the death of their father Tutush in 488/1095. While this struggle did trigger at least two battles, at Marj Dabiq in 488/1095–6 and Qinnasrin in 490/1097–8, and a failed siege of Damascus in 488/1095–6, Ibn al-Athir claimed that the two sides came to an agreement after the latter battle that 'Ridwan's name should be mentioned in the *khutba* at Damascus and Antioch before Duqaq's'.[109]

After this settlement, there were no battles in which the rulers of Damascus and Aleppo were on opposite sides prior to 522/1128. Indeed, the scarcity of open conflict between Aleppo and Damascus in the thirty years between 490 and 522/1098 and 1128 represented a marked change from the situation in the late fifth/eleventh century, when the two most important settlements in Syria regularly engaged in open conflict with each other. Damascus had been the central hub of Fatimid attempts to conquer Aleppo between 440 and 452/1048 and 1060, while conflict broke out between Tutush of Damascus and the Aleppan amirs Sharaf al-Dawla Muslim b. Quraysh and Qasim al-Dawla Aqsunqur during the period of Seljuq predominance between 472 and 488/1080 and 1095.

Although there are suggestions of ongoing tensions between the brothers during their participation in the coalition that confronted the armies of the First Crusade at Antioch in 491/1098, it did not preclude the amirs who had supported both sides in the dispute between Ridwan and Duqaq from entering into the alliance in the first place.[110] Although Tughtegin participated in two separate sieges of Aleppo, first, with the Seljuq army dispatched to northern Syria in 505/1111 by the Sultan Muhammad, and, second, in 510/1116–17 with Aqsunqur al-Bursuqi, these attacks on Aleppo were instigated by the eastern amirs involved, not Tughtegin.[111] Indeed, Tughtegin's support for the latter siege indicated that he was in favour of Aqsunqur al-Bursuqi, then ruler of Rahba, assuming control over Aleppo, which would have severely disrupted the balance of power in *bilad al-sham*. Even the reports that Ridwan had plotted with eastern amirs to assassinate Tughtegin during the Seljuq sultan's campaign into northern Syria in 505/1111 should be viewed with scepticism, as the chroniclers employed the common formulaic qualifier of 'it is said' to indicate their uncertainty about the veracity of this information.[112]

There is also a good deal of evidence that contradicts the notion that there was a long-standing rivalry between Ridwan and Tughtegin. In 488/1095, Ridwan negotiated Tughtegin's release from captivity with the Sultan Berkyaruq.[113] Additionally, in the aftermath of Duqaq's death in Ramadan

497/May–June 1104, Tughtegin initially made the *khutba* in Damascus in the name of Ridwan, according to Ibn al-'Adim.[114] The *khutba* was again made in Damascus in Ridwan's name in 506/1113 when Tughtegin and Ridwan entered into an alliance with Mawdud of Mosul against the Franks. Ridwan subsequently reneged on the agreement, sending only 100 troops from Aleppo to support Mawdud and Tughtegin after they had already defeated the Franks in battle.[115] In retaliation, Tughtegin removed Ridwan's name from the *khutba* in Damascus. While the outcome of the 506/1113 agreement exposed a certain level of distrust between the parties involved, the initial terms settled between Mawdud, Tughtegin and Ridwan indicated a mutual willingness to cooperate.

Tughtegin also attempted to forge alliances with nearly all of Ridwan's successors in Aleppo. Following Ridwan's death, his son Alp Arslan was invited to Damascus, where Ibn al-Qalanisi related that he was seated upon his uncle Duqaq's throne. Subsequently, Tughtegin was invited to Aleppo, but when Alp Arslan refused to heed Tughtegin's advice, the latter returned to Damascus.[116] Tughtegin also allied himself with Il-ghazi, when he was ruler of Aleppo, against the Franks in 513/1119, assisting him in the skirmishes and raiding that followed the battle of the Field of Blood.[117] Another less successful joint campaign with Balak b. Bahram was launched against the Franks at Zardana and al-Atharib 516/1122.[118] Finally, Damascene contingents led by Tughtegin were involved in attacks on the Frankish held settlement of 'Azaz in 517/1124 and 519/1125–6 with the Aleppan rulers Balak and Aqsunqur al-Bursuqi.[119]

In total, Damascene troops were involved in thirteen alliances to attack Frankish territories or armies between 491 and 522/1098 and 1128. Four were with Aleppo, four with the ruler of Mosul or Rahba, and five with the Fatimid Caliphate.[120] Tughtegin entered into only one alliance with the Franks in this period, during the 509/1115 Seljuq campaign into the region.[121] Of the various alliances Aleppo was involved in between 491 and 522/1098 and 1128, four targeted the Franks. All four involved an alliance with Damascus, one of which also included Mawdud of Mosul. These numbers indicate that alliances with the Franks were actually a pretty rare occurrence during this period. Indeed, the Franks were more often than not the target of alliances formed between members of the Syrian political elite during the early sixth/twelfth century.

Can Köhler's la maqam *Theory be Applied before 522/1128?*

While it is accurate to say that the military reaction to the foundation of the Latin-Christian polities in the Levant by the rulers of *bilad al-sham* was largely unsuccessful, there clearly was a reaction. It cannot be denied that the Aleppan alliance with Antioch in 502/1108–9 indicated that the Franks were able to assimilate themselves into the fluid alliance structures of the region. However, this was a highly unique event and should not be viewed as representative of the wider political dynamics.

From the *'asakir al-sham* that fought at Antioch in 491/1098, through to the large number of coalitions forged against the Franks in the following three decades, there was a clearly perceptible reaction to the creation of Frankish polities.[122] Indeed, the Franks elicited the most overt and widespread military reaction from the region's Islamic political elite between 442 and 522/1050 and 1128. It is also probable that this collective sensibility laid the groundwork for the political and military successes enjoyed by Zangi, Nur al-Din and Saladin later in the sixth/twelfth century.

Notes

1. Similarly, much of modern Crusade historiography, has viewed the responses of the rulers of *bilad al-sham* through the context of wider Muslim 'disunity', see Runciman, *Crusades*, II, pp. 3–139, 143–77; Asbridge, *Creation*, pp. 47–91, 104–27; Asbridge, *Crusades*, pp. 115–221; Barber, *Crusader States*, pp. 111–16.
2. Köhler, *Alliances*, pp. 59–127, 162, 179–212, 244–7, 262, 267–8. The term '*la maqam*' is taken directly from Ibn al-Athir's, *al-Kamil fi'l ta'rikh*, see IATH, X, 464, XI, 324.
3. René Grousset, *Histoire des croisades et du royaume franc de Jérusalem*, 3 vols (Paris: Perrin, 1934–6), *L'Anarchie Musulmane et la Monarchie Franque* (1934), I, p. 162.
4. Aziz Atiya had an even broader interpretation, as he viewed the Crusades as the driving force behind the formation of the Ottoman Empire. Aziz S. Atiya, *Crusade, Commerce and Culture* (Bloomington: Indiana University Press, 1962), pp. 120–61. See also Hadia Dajani-Shakeel, 'A Reassessment of Some Medieval and Modern Perceptions of the Counter-Crusade', in *The Jihad and its Times*, ed. Hadia Dajani-Shakeel, Ronald A. Messier and Andrew S. Ehrenkreutz

(Ann Arbor, MI: Center for Near Eastern and North African Studies, 1991), pp. 41–70.

5. Hamilton A. R. Gibb, 'Notes on the Arabic Materials for the History of the Early Crusades', *Bulletin of the School of Oriental Studies* 7 (1935): 739–54, 741–3. Interestingly, these criticisms of the 'counter-Crusade' are not included in his review of the first volume, included in the same issue of this journal. See Hamilton A. R. Gibb, 'Review of Histoire des Croisades et du Royaume Franc de Jérusalem. I. L'Anarchie Musulmane et la Monarchie Franque by René Grousset', *Bulletin of the School of Oriental Studies* 7 (1935): 981–3. For wider critiques of Grousset's work, particularly his 'colonialist' interpretation of the Crusading movement, see Christopher Tyerman, *The Debate on the Crusades* (Manchester: Manchester University Press, 2011), pp. 149–50, 155–7.

6. Sivan, *L'Islam et la Croisade*, p. 59.

7. For more detail on development of medieval Islamic *jihad* theory, see David Cook, *Understanding Jihad* (Oakland: University of California Press), pp. 49–72.

8. Niall Christie and Deborah Gerish, 'Parallel Preachings: Urban II and al-Sulami', *al-Masaq* 15 (2003): 139–48; Niall Christie, 'Motivating Listeners in the *Kitab al-Jihad* of 'Ali ibn Tahir al-Sulami', *Crusades* 6 (2007): 1–14; Mourad and Lindsay, *Intensification and Reorientation of Sunni Jihad Ideology*; Hadia Dajani-Shakeel, 'Jihad in Twelfth-Century Arabic Poetry: a Moral and Religious Force to Counter the Crusades', *Muslim World* 66 (1976): 96–113; Carole Hillenbrand, 'Jihad Poetry in the Age of the Crusades', in *Crusades: Medieval Worlds in Conflict*, ed. Thomas F. Madden, James L. Naus and Vincent Ryan (London: Routledge, 2010), pp. 9–23; Latiff, *The Cutting Edge of the Poet's Sword*.

9. See, e.g., Hillenbrand, *Crusades*, pp. 150–61; Christie, *Muslim and Crusaders*; Mallett, *Popular Muslim Reactions*, pp. 14, 144–5.

10. Hillenbrand, *Crusades*, pp. 108–10; Mallett, *Popular Muslim Reactions*, pp. 14, 60, 89, 144–5; Goudie, *Reinventing Jihad*, pp. 4–9, 161, 194–5. For a dissenting view, see Yaacov Lev, 'The "Jihad" of Sultan Nur al-Din of Syria (1146–1174): History and Discourse', *Jerusalem Studies in Arabic and Islam* 35 (2008): 227–84.

11. For an overview of the polysemy of the term Crusade, see Jotischky, *Crusading*, pp. 7–22; Phillips, *Crusades*, pp. 1–9. For discussion of the historical validity of the term 'Crusader states', see Christopher MacEvitt, 'What was Crusader about the Crusader States?', *Al-Masaq* 30 (2018): 317–30; Andrew D. Buck, 'Settlement, Identity and Memory in the Latin East: An Examination of the Term "Crusader States"', *English Historical Review* 135 (2020): 271–302.

12. Cobb, *Race for Paradise*, p. 274. See also Jay Rubenstein, 'Saladin and the Problem of the Counter-Crusade in the Middle Ages', *Historically Speaking* 13 (2012): 2–5.
13. Köhler's '*la maqam*' theory has been broadly accepted within the field, although Nicholas Morton has argued that it 'fits rather more awkwardly in conflicts where the aggressor was driven by ambition and aspiration', see Morton, *The Crusader States*, pp. 206–10.
14. Köhler, *Alliances*, pp. 59–127, 162; Hillenbrand, *Crusades*, pp. 56–9, 81–8, 108–12.
15. Cahen, *Syrie*, p. 241.
16. Grousset, *Histoire des croisades*, I, p. 162. The most detailed analysis of events at Antioch in 491/1098 are Runciman, *Crusades*, I, pp. 213–52; Smail, *Crusading Warfare*, pp. 170–4; John France, *Victory in the East* (Cambridge: Cambridge University Press, 1995), pp. 197–296; Asbridge, *The First Crusade*, pp. 202–40.
17. The phrase '*asakir al-sham* is employed by both Ibn al-Qalanisi and Ibn al-Athir, see IQ, pp. 218–21; IATH: X, 274–8. For a detailed overview of the Arabic accounts of events at Antioch, see James Wilson, 'The "*asakir al-Sham*": Medieval Arabic Historiography of the Siege, Capture and Battle of Antioch During the First Crusade', *al-Masaq* 33 (2021): 300–36.
18. Ibn al-Jawzi, *al-Muntazam fi ta'rikh*, XVII, 43. This claim is then repeated in the chronicle of Sibt b. al-Jawzi, who was Ibn al-Jawzi's grandson. See SJ, XIII, 258; Cahen, *Syrie*, p. 215; Heidemann, *Die Renaissance der Städte*, pp. 184–6, 189–90. On the successful calls for aid by Yaghi-Siyan, see Cobb, *Race for Paradise*, pp. 88–94.
19. For more detailed discussion of these factors, see Wilson, 'The "*asakir al-Sham*"', pp. 316–20.
20. IQ, pp. 278–83; al-'Azimi, pp. 365, 367; Usama b. Munqidh, *Kitab al-I'tibar*, pp. 73–7; IATH, X, 485–8, 509–11; SJ, XIII, 332–3, 355–6; IAD ZH, II, 158–61, 174–7; AA, pp. 810–19, 853–7; FC, pp. 549–57, 580–92; FC trans., pp. 201–3, 210–15; WC, pp. 61–77; WC trans., pp. 77–108; Bar Habraeus, *Chronography*, pp. 244, 247–8; Anonymous Syriac Chronicle, pt. 1, p. 86; MS, pp. 627, 631; ME, p. 207. See also Stevenson, *Crusaders*, pp. 59–62, 87–101; Smail, *Crusading Warfare*, pp. 140–48; Runciman, *Crusades*, II, pp. 115–33; Asbridge, *Creation*, pp. 67–73; Asbridge, *Crusades*, pp. 62–103, 111–14, 128–62; Barber, *Crusader States*, pp. 100–4; Jotischky, *Crusading*, pp. 114–15; Susan B. Edgington, *Baldwin I of Jerusalem, 1100–1118* (London: Routledge,

2019), pp. 184–8; Tibble, *Crusader Armies*, pp. 252–71; Morton, *The Crusader States*, pp. 20–49, 62–78.

21. Hillenbrand, *Crusades*, pp. 78–81. This is the prevailing view in much of the historiography, see Köhler, *Alliances*, pp. 90–105; Heidemann, *Die Renaissance der Städte*, pp. 212–24; Peacock, *Empire*, pp. 82–9.
22. For detailed discussion of the issues surrounding Seljuq campaigns into northern Syria during the fifth/eleventh century, see Chapter 3.
23. There is some discrepancy in the source material around the dating of this siege. Ibn al-Qalanisi claimed that the siege began on 19 Muharram 505/28 July 1111, while Fulcher of Chartres asserted that the siege lasted a month, Albert of Aachen two months and Ibn al-Athir forty-five days. IQ, p. 259; IATH, X, 485–8; AA, pp. 810–13; FC, pp. 549–52; FC trans., p. 201.
24. IQ, p. 279; IAD ZH, II, 160.
25. IAD ZH, II, 160.
26. IQ, pp. 270–3; al-'Azimi, p. 365; IATH, X, 485–8; SJ, XIII, 328; IAD ZH, II, 154–6; ME, p. 207; Bar Habraeus, *Chronography*, p. 244.
27. IQ, p. 259.
28. ME, p. 207.
29. AA, pp. 812–15.
30. IATH, X, 501–2.
31. IQ, pp. 278–83; al-'Azimi, p. 367; IATH, X, 509–11; SJ, XIII, 355–6; IAD ZH, II, 176–7.
32. AA, pp. 852–5; FC, pp. 582–4; FC trans., p. 211. See also Anonymous Syriac Chronicle, pt. 1, p. 86; Bar Habraeus, *Chronography*, pp. 247–8. Bar Habraeus reported that Antiochene troops sent Ridwan the 'spoils of war' after defeating a detachment from Seljuq army.
33. WC, p. 70; WC trans., p. 95.
34. For an overview of Fatimid policy in *bilad al-sham* during the fifth/eleventh century, see Chapter 2.
35. Stevenson, *Crusaders*, pp. 33–68, 113–16; Smail, *Crusading Warfare*, pp. 85–7, 174–7; Runciman, *Crusades*, II, pp. 3–17, 71–106, 143–87; Barber, *Crusader States*, pp. 26–65, 121–73; Phillips, *Crusades*, pp. 39–41, 44–5; Asbridge, *Crusades*, pp. 121–38, 147–51, 159–62; Jotischky, *Crusading*, pp. 49–80, 111–18; Edgington, *Baldwin I of Jerusalem*, pp. 132–73; Bramoullé, 'Les populations littorals', pp. 303–4; Halm, *Kalifen und Assassinen*, pp. 92–114, 158–60; Tibble, *Crusader Armies*, pp. 211–51; Morton, *The Crusader States*, pp. 50–62; Mathew Barber, 'Al-Afdal b. Badr Al-Jamali:

The Vizierate and the Fatimid Response to the First Crusade: Masculinity in Historical Memory', in *Crusading and Masculinities*, ed. Natasha R. Hodgson, Katherine J. Lewis and Matthew M. Mesley (London: Routledge, 2019), pp. 53–71.

36. Grousset, *Histoire des Croisades*, I, pp. 224–45; Runciman, *Crusades*, II, pp. 74–91; Smail, *Crusading Warfare*, pp. 83–7; Lev, *State and Society*, pp. 93–121; William Hamblin, 'To Wage Jihad or Not: Fatimid Egypt during the Early Crusades', in *The Jihad and its Times*, ed. Hadia Dajani-Shakeel, Ronald A. Messier and Andrew S. Ehrenkreutz (Ann Arbor, MI: Center for Near Eastern and North African Studies, 1991), pp. 31–41.
37. Hillenbrand, *Crusades*, pp. 42–7.
38. The growth of influence of the Batinis would have wide-ranging consequences across the entire Middle East throughout the Crusading period. For more information, see Daftary, *Assassin Legends*.
39. Köhler, *Alliances*, pp. 44–57.
40. Michael Brett, 'The Battles of Ramla (1099–1105)', in *Egypt and Syria in the Fatimid, Ayyubid and Mamluk Eras*, 9 vols, ed. Urbain Vermeulen and Daniel De Smet (Leuven: Peeters, 1995), I, pp. 17–37; Michael Brett, 'The Fatimids and the Counter-Crusade, 1099–1171', in *Egypt and Syria in the Fatimid, Ayyubid and Mamluk Eras*, 9 vols, ed. Urbain Vermeulen and Daniel De Smet (Leuven: Peeters, 1998), II, pp. 15–25; Brett, *Empire*, pp. 233–6, 240–5, 256–9; Halm, *Kalifen und Assassinen*, pp. 92–114, 158–60.
41. IQ, p. 221; al-'Azimi, p. 359; IATH, X, 283–3; SJ, XIII, 247–8; IAD ZH, II, 143; IM, pp. 65–6; Shibab al-Din al-Nuwayri, *Nihayat al-arab fi funun al-adab*, 34 vols, ed. Ibrahim Shams al-Din and Mufid M. Qumayhah (Beirut: Dar al-Kutub al-'Ilmiya, 2004–5), XXVIII, pp. 156–7; al-Maqrizi, II, 23–4; GF, pp. 87–93; AA, pp. 410–37; FC, pp. 281–303; FC trans., pp. 116–22. For detailed discussion of the Arabic historiography of the First Crusaders' capture of Jerusalem, see Hirschler, 'The Jerusalem Conquest of 492/1099', pp. 37–76.
42. Ibn al-Qalanisi stated that the Franks ultimately did not receive the money due to disagreement among the army leadership. IQ, p. 233; al-'Azimi, p. 360; IATH, X, 286; SJ, XIII, 264–5; IM, p. 67; al-Nuwayri, *Nihayat al-arab*, XXVIII, pp. 166–7; al-Maqrizi, II, 23–4. GF, pp. 95–7; AA, pp. 463–75; RC, p. 703; RC trans., pp. 154–5; FC, pp. 311–18; FC trans., pp. 125–8.
43. 'Ali Ibn Zafir al-Azdi, *Akhbar al-Duwal al-munqati'a*, ed. André Ferré (Cairo: Al-Ma'had al-'Ilmial-Faransi lil-Athar al-Sharqiya, 1972), p. 82.

44. IATH, X, 273.
45. IM, p. 67.
46. Michael A. Köhler, 'Al-Afdal and Jerusalem. Was versprach sich Ägypten vom ersten Kreuzzug?' *Saeculum*, 37 (1986): 228–39; Köhler, *Alliances*, pp. 44–54; Hillenbrand, *Crusades*, pp. 42–7.
47. The most detailed account of these negotiations is provided by the Latin chronicler Raymond of Aguilers, see Raymond of Aguilers, *Le 'Liber' de Raymond D'Aguilers*, ed. and trans. John H. Hill and Laurita L. Hill (Paris: P. Geuthner, 1969), pp. 58, 109–10.
48. Gibb, 'Notes on Arabic Materials', pp. 743–9.
49. IATH, X, 476–7.
50. Atsiz's failed campaign into Egypt is discussed in Chapter 2.
51. IQ, p. 221. Al-'Azimi also dated the Fatimid capture of Jerusalem to Shawwal 491/September 1098, while Ibn Muyassar stated that the Fatimid army departed Egypt in Sha'ban 491/July 1098, see al-'Azimi, p. 359; IM, pp. 65–6.
52. al-Maqrizi, III, 22. Ibn al-Athir also stated that the siege lasted '40 days', see IATH, X, 282–3.
53. Raymond of Aguilers, *Le 'Liber'*, pp. 58, 109–10. See also Morton, *Encountering Islam*, pp. 141–9.
54. IATH, X, 282–3. Sibt b. al-Jawzi, who provided only a brief account with no dates, also placed the Fatimid siege of Jerusalem under the year 489/1096–7: SJ, XIII, 247–8.
55. The way in which information is framed is vital to understanding the motive of the author, see Hirschler, *Medieval Arabic Historiography*, pp. 63–114.
56. Cobb, *Race for Paradise*, pp. 49–57, 146–56.
57. IAD ZH, II, 133.
58. The argument for urban decline in Jerusalem and Palestine in general during the fifth/eleventh century has been made most earnestly by Ronnie Ellenblum, and with slightly more circumspection by Gideon Anvi. See Ellenblum, *The Collapse of the Eastern Mediterranean*, pp. 163–95; Anvi, '"From Polis to Madina" Revisited', pp. 301–29.
59. IQ, pp. 174–5; al-'Azimi, p. 349; IATH, X, 99–100; SJ, XIII, 85–6; IAD ZH, 46; IM, pp. 42–3.
60. Raymond of Aguilers, *Le 'Liber'*, pp. 109–10.
61. See Chapters 2 and 3 for a full discussion of these alliances. The Fatimid relationship with Tughtegin of Damascus is discussed below.
62. See also Morton, *Encountering Islam*, pp. 141–7.

63. IQ, pp. 224–5; al-ʿAzimi, pp. 360–1; IATH, X, 324–5; al-Nuwayri, *Nihayat al-arab*, XXVIII, pp. 167–8; al-Maqrizi, II, p. 26; AA, pp. 486–95, 498–503, 514–23, 562–7; FC, pp. 393–404; FC trans., pp. 151–5.
64. IQ, p. 228; IATH, X, 343–5; SJ, XIII, 286–7; al-Nuwayri, *Nihayat al-arab*, XXVIII, pp. 168–9; al-Maqrizi, II, 28; AA, pp. 634–5, 660–3; FC, pp. 456–7; FC trans., pp. 174–5.
65. There is some disagreement in the source material over the dating of the second battle of Ramla, with Ibn al-Qalanisi stating that it occurred in early Ramadan 494/early July 1101, while Albert of Aachen and Fulcher of Chartres assert that it occurred on either 3 or 5 Dhu 'l-Qaʿda 494/6 or 8 September 1101. IQ, p. 229; IM, p. 68; al-Maqrizi, II, 26; AA, pp. 566–85; FC, pp. 407–20; FC trans., pp. 156–61.
66. IQ, p. 229; SJ, XIII, 288–9; AA, pp. 640–53; FC pp. 424–8, 436–56; FC trans., pp. 163–4, 167–74.
67. There is again a discrepancy between the Arabic and Latin sources for the events of 496/1103. While the medieval Arabic historiography refer to both a battle and a siege, Albert of Aachen only described an attempted siege of Jaffa by the Fatimids, without providing a date. IQ, p. 231; al-ʿAzimi, p. 361; IATH, X, 364–6; SJ, XIII, 287; IM, p. 74. al-Maqrizi, II, 32–3; AA, pp. 666–71.
68. IQ, p. 231; al-ʿAzimi, p. 361; IATH, X, 364–6; SJ, XIII, 287; IM, p. 74; al-Maqrizi, II, 32–3.
69. IQ, pp. 231–3; al-ʿAzimi, p. 362; IATH, X, 372–3; IM, p. 75; al-Nuwayri, *Nihayat al-arab*, XXVIII, pp. 169–70; al-Maqrizi, II, 28; AA, pp. 670–7; FC, pp. 462–4; FC trans., p. 176.
70. IQ, pp. 240–1; al-ʿAzimi, p. 363; IATH, X, 394–5; SJ, XIII, 300; al-Maqrizi, II, 35; AA, pp. 704–17; FC, pp. 489–501; FC trans., pp. 182–7.
71. The Fatimid relationship with Tughtegin of Damascus in discussed in detail below.
72. IQ, pp. 261–3; al-ʿAzimi, p. 364; IATH, X, 475–7; SJ, XIII, 321; al-Nuwayri, *Nihayat al-arab*, XXVIII, pp. 170–2; al-Maqrizi, II, 42–4; AA, pp. 780–5; FC, pp. 526–33; FC trans., pp. 193–6.
73. IQ, pp. 268–9, 273–4; al-ʿAzimi, p. 364; SJ, XIII, 327–8; al-Nuwayri, *Nihayat al-arab*, XXVIII, pp. 172–3; al-Maqrizi, II, 45; AA, pp. 790–1; FC, pp. 534–6; FC trans., pp. 196–7.
74. IQ, pp. 284–8; al-ʿAzimi, pp. 365–6; IATH X, 488–90; SJ, XIII, 334–5; al-Maqrizi, II, 48–9; AA, pp. 826–35; FC pp. 558–62; FC trans., pp. 203–4.
75. IQ, pp. 329, 333; al-ʿAzimi, pp. 372–3; IATH, X, 617; al-Maqrizi, II, 96; FC, pp. 669–73; FC trans., pp. 243–5.

76. IQ, pp. 336–7; al-ʿAzimi, p. 374; IATH, X, 620–2; SJ, XIII, 434; IM, pp. 96–7; al-Nuwayri, *Nihayat al-arab*, XXVIII, pp. 173–5; MS, p. 643; FC, pp. 693–8, 728–30, 733–42; FC, trans., pp. 255–6, 264–9.
77. IATH, X, 543–4; AA, pp. 862–5; FC, pp. 594–6; FC trans., pp. 215–16.
78. Brett, *Empire*, pp. 237, 233–6, 240–5, 256–7, 259.
79. Köhler, *Alliances*, pp. 88–90, 105–6.
80. IQ, pp. 257–8; al-ʿAzimi, pp. 363–4; IATH, X, 452–4; SJ, XIII, 317–18; IM, p. 76.
81. IQ, pp. 290–1; IATH, X, 620; IM, p. 93.
82. IATH, X, 620–2.
83. It is slightly problematic that the sixth/twelfth century Damascene chronicler Ibn al-Qalanisi makes no reference to this campaign, let alone Tughtegin assuming command over Egyptian troops. IATH, X, 543–4.
84. Ibn al-Qalanisi placed this event under the year 517/1123–4 in his chronicle, but Gibb argued that this entry, and one concerning Tughtegin's involvement in an attempted siege of the settlement of ʿAzaz in northern Syria was an error, and should have been placed under the year 519/1125–6. See Ibn al-Qalanisi, *The Damascus Chronicle*, p. 170; IQ p. 335; al-ʿAzimi, p. 373.
85. IM, p. 105; al-Maqrizi, II, 99–100.
86. IQ, p. 342.
87. Köhler, *Alliances*, pp. 59–127, 179–212, 244–7, 262, 267–8.
88. IATH, X, 459–66; SJ, XIII, 327; IAD ZH, II, 153; AA, pp. 752–5; FC, pp. 477–81; FC trans., pp. 180–1; ME, pp. 201–2.
89. Köhler, *Alliances*, p. 66.
90. Asbridge, *Creation*, pp. 112–14.
91. IATH, X, 459–66.
92. IAD ZH, II, 153.
93. ME, pp. 201–2.
94. MS, pp. 638–9; Anonymous Syriac Chronicle, pt. 1, p. 82.
95. AA, pp. 752–5.
96. IATH, X, 424.
97. FC, pp. 480–1; FC trans., pp. 180–1.
98. For more information on the personal differences between Baldwin and Tancred, see Asbridge, *Creation*, pp. 104–23. For more detail on the ransom of Baldwin II in 502/1108–9, see Wilson, 'The Ransom of High-ranking Captives', pp. 15–17.
99. IATH, X, 464.

100. The strategic importance of Balis to the frontiers Aleppo are discussed in Chapter 5.
101. IQ, pp. 251–4; al-'Azimi, p. 362; IATH, X, 422–30; SJ, XIII, 311–13.
102. al-'Azimi, p. 362; IATH, X, 405–7.
103. IQ, pp. 251–4; al-'Azimi, p. 362; IATH, X, 422–30; SJ, XIII, 311–13.
104. The date of Ramadan 501/May 1108 for the engagement against Gervase of Tiberias is taken from Albert of Aachen's chronicle. Ibn al-Qalanisi only gave the broad description of 'in this year', which could have been any point in the year 501/22 August 1107–10 August 1108. IQ, pp. 257–8, 260–1; IATH, X, 467–9; SJ, XIII, 317–18; AA, pp. 768–71, 774–5; FC, pp. 509–11; FC trans., p. 190.
105. IQ, pp. 260–1.
106. Calls for assistance are discussed in more detail in Chapter 5.
107. Beihammer, 'Muslim Rulers Visiting the Imperial City', pp. 157–77; Wilson, 'The Ransom of High-ranking Captives', pp. 5–30.
108. Köhler, *Alliances*, p. 102.
109. IQ, p. 215; al-'Azimi, pp. 358–9; IATH, X, 247–8, 269; SJ, XIII, 237–8, 255; IAD ZH, II, 123–6.
110. Wilson, 'The "*'asakir al-Sham*"', pp. 312–14.
111. IQ, pp. 278–83, 316; al-'Azimi, pp. 365, 367; IATH, X, 486–7; SJ, XIII, 328, 332–3, 375; IAD ZH, II, 159–60, 177–8.
112. IQ, pp. 278–83; IAD ZH, II, 158–61.
113. IATH, X, 232–3, 258; IAD ZH, II, 110–13, 121–2.
114. IAD ZH, II, 150. Ibn al-'Adim also claimed that Ridwan besieged Damascus, while the absence of reference to these events in Ibn al-Qalanisi means that we should call into question whether or not they actually happened.
115. IQ, pp. 293–8; IATH, X, 495–7; SJ, XIII, 347, 353–4; IAD ZH, II, 163–4.
116. IQ, pp. 301–3; al-'Azimi, p. 366; IATH, X, 499; SJ, XIII, 347–8; IAD ZH, II, 164, 168–71.
117. IQ, pp. 319–20; IATH, X, 553–5; SJ, XIII, 388; IAD ZH, II, 186–93; FC, pp. 620–31; FC trans., pp. 225–30; WC, pp. 78–107; WC trans., pp. 109–59; MS, p. 632; ME, pp. 223–4.
118. IAD ZH, II, 204–5; FC, pp. 649–51; FC trans., pp. 236–7.
119. IQ, p. 335; al-'Azimi, p. 375; IATH, X, 628–9; IAD ZH, II, 216, 231; ME, pp. 234–6.
120. Tughtegin's relationship with the Fatimid Caliphate is discussed earlier in this chapter in relation to the Fatimid counter-Crusade movement.

121. The events of 509/1115 are discussed earlier in this chapter in relation to the Seljuq counter-Crusade movement.
122. As Paul Cobb has argued, the success of the response to Yaghi Siyan's desperate appeal for assistance cannot be disputed, see Cobb, *Race for Paradise*, pp. 88–94; Barber, *Crusader States*, p. 77; Asbridge, *Crusades*, p. 72; Morton, *The Crusader States*, p. 74.

5

The Notables and Frontiers of Aleppo

The *qadi* promised to meet with Zangi about the matter. He went to see him in the citadel and found him mounting his horse near the gate. The *qadi* said to him: 'My lord, the Khatun [Zangi's wife] came to me and complained about her situation.' Zangi did not reply, and was about to leave on the horse. My father held the mount's bridle, preventing it from moving and said: 'My lord, this is the purified Shari'a, and one cannot ignore it.' Then Zangi said: 'be my witness that she is divorced'. My father then let the bridle free and said: 'now the matter is settled'.[1]

According to Ibn al-'Adim, this was how the author's grandfather, the *qadi* Abu al-Fadl, induced Zangi into divorcing his estranged wife in 524/1130. Although Ibn al-'Adim's account of this episode should be read with a healthy degree of scepticism due to the central role played by the author's grandfather, it is representative of how, under certain circumstances, Syrian urban elites could exert power over Turkish military potentates. Indeed, support from the inhabitants of Aleppo, particularly the landowning 'notables' (*al-a'yan*), was vital prerequisite for any prospective ruler of the city.

This chapter discusses the ways in which urban notables were able to influence political developments in *bilad al-sham* throughout 442–522/1050–1128. The first part discusses the factors that led to the empowerment of Aleppan and Damascene elites, before focusing on how this power manifested itself, particularly at times of crisis or when choosing new rulers. The second part defines the physical frontiers of *bilad halab* (the country or region of Aleppo) throughout this time frame, before revisiting Baldwin II's siege of Aleppo in the winter of 518/1124–5 and what this failed venture can reveal about perceptions of the Frankish Crusaders by northern Syria's established urban elite.

The Empowerment of Syrian Notables

It is important to distinguish between 'the people of Aleppo' (*ahl halab*), usually taken to mean the general population, and the notables (*al-a'yan*), which typically refers to individuals from prominent landowning families who held leadership positions within local civic governance structures.[2]

Urban notables in the Islamic world are generally thought to have been deprived of the autonomy enjoyed by their western European counterparts, at best playing the role of middlemen between the ruler and their subjects.[3] Yet there are several aspects of the political world of *bilad al-sham* between 442 and 522/1050 and 1122 that enabled urban elites to wield a significant amount of influence. In part, this dynamic was a by-product of the fluid political environment present in Syria for much of this period, with a near constant state of conflict leading to the instalment of Arab and Turkish rulers with little or no connection to *bilad al-sham*. These newly arrived 'outsiders' were therefore partially reliant upon the notables for legitimisation.

The notables of the major urban centres were further empowered by the strong defensive fortifications of Aleppo and Damascus.[4] They also benefited greatly from control of civic institutions, such as the *ahdath* (local urban militia) of Aleppo, a unit drawn from the local population that actively fought in several major battles during this period.[5] The *ahdath* were placed under the command of the *ra'is*, who was typically selected from the leading notable families of Aleppo and Damascus during this period, providing urban elites with a battle-hardened militia to use at times of extreme crisis.[6]

Additionally, from the 450s/1060s onwards, many of the Arab and Turkish potentates who came to rule over the major urban centres of Syria became increasingly reliant upon nomadic Türkmen troops, who were unsuited to extended stays in *bilad al-sham*.[7] Unlike their Arab Bedouin predecessors, who had tended to occupy grazing areas along the River Euphrates, many Türkmen groups only came to Syria for short periods, meaning that a large segment of these rulers' military forces were not based within striking distance of Aleppo for much of the year. Indeed, multiple rulers of Aleppo, including the Uqaylid ruler Muslim b. Quraysh and the members of the Artuqid dynasty, had to return east at least once a year to govern other dominions or recruit Türkmen troops for future campaigns.[8] These absences provided further opportunities for the notables to expand their influence within the urban centres.

Indicators of notable power in Aleppo are particularly apparent in the medieval Arabic historiography at times of transition or crisis. For instance, one Aleppan notable fought off an assassination attempt in 512/1118, while an individual from a different family gave a dramatic speech to nomadic Türkmen troops before the battle of the Field of Blood in 513/1119.[9] However, it should also be noted that many of the more authoritative chroniclers for this period were members of this Syrian urban elite, and it is therefore quite probable that they would have wanted to depict the notables of Aleppo and Damascus as significant and influential figures, particularly when writing about their ancestors. Caution is therefore required when gauging the degree of autonomy exercised by the Syrian notables of this era.

Land, Commerce and Legitimisation

The power of the urban notables is best demonstrated by the uninterrupted occupation of prominent civic and religious posts in Damascus and Aleppo by certain aristocratic families.[10] Some of these notable families, such as the Banu al-Khashshab and Banu Abi Jarada of Aleppo, played prominent roles in the governance of the city for nearly three hundred years, dating from the third/ninth century until the Mongol conquest of Aleppo in 658/1260.[11] This longevity suggests that the notables were far better at navigating the troubled political currents of northern Syria than the short-lived Turkish dynasts of the fifth/eleventh and sixth/twelfth centuries, who typically struggled to survive longer than one or two generations.

The influence of this Syrian urban elite was rooted in their possession of much of the farmland surrounding these cities, which in turn granted them a monopoly over mercantile activity. Partial or complete control of entire villages passed down from generation to generation, taking the form of '*milk*' or personal property, rather than *iqtaʿ* grants, making it more difficult for the ruler to remove them from the family's control.[12] In 508/1114, the notables actually purchased extensive tracts of land from the ruler of Aleppo.[13] While amirs did seize territories from certain individuals as a form punishment, the collective wealth and landholdings of each major family provided a cushion for future generations to fall back on.[14]

Long-standing control over local rural communities and the influence this granted them over commercial trade enabled the notable families of Syria to influence almost any potentate when acting in a coordinated manner. This landed wealth, combined with control of most urban civic institutions meant 'alien' military leaders were reliant upon what David Morray termed the 'legitimising acquiescence of the indigenous aristocracy'.[15] Protection of these landholdings, and the associated revenue streams, was a vital part of gaining or retaining the support of Syrian notables. It is no coincidence that when these territories were placed under threat, there was an uptick in political instability in Syrian urban centres.[16]

The Defensibility of Aleppo and Damascus

The influence of the notables was further bolstered by the strong defences of Aleppo and Damascus. As Figure 5.1 demonstrates, most attempts to capture Aleppo or Damascus by force in the late fifth/eleventh and early sixth/twelfth centuries were unsuccessful.

Using Ian Wilson's definition of siege warfare in the early decades of Crusader settlement, 'any hostile attack against a walled stronghold', as a starting point, the years 439–522/1047–1128 saw Aleppo placed under siege on an extraordinary twenty-three different occasions, of which just five resulted in the capture of the city.[17] Damascus was besieged on eight occasions, of which just one was successful. It should be noted that there is some disagreement in the sources about the severity of the sieges of Aleppo in the years 495/1102–3, 513/1119 and 522/1128.[18] Additionally, in 478/1085–6, 479/1086–7 and 511/1117–18 the attacking armies seemingly camped outside the city walls

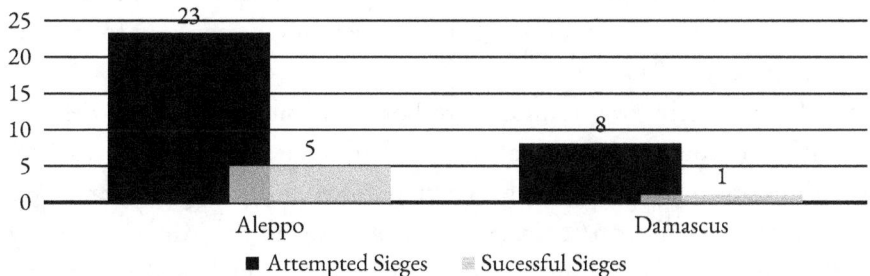

Figure 5.1 Occasions Aleppo and Damascus were besieged: 439–522/1047–1128[19]

and requested that the inhabitants surrender control of Aleppo to them.[20] Once these events are removed, the siege success rate of the respective settlements is five out of twenty-two for Aleppo and one out of eight for Damascus. This strongly suggests that both Aleppo and Damascus were incredibly difficult to capture by force throughout this period.

Of course, each of these siege events occurred in a unique temporal context, with different besieging armies that could have employed varying tactics or techniques.[21] Moreover, political leaders would have had distinct motivations or objectives they hoped to achieve by placing these settlements under siege. Outright occupation would not always have been the goal, with some of these sieges resulting in the establishment or modification of tributary arrangements and other symbolic forms of 'conquest'.

In order to circumvent these issues, key words used by the medieval Arabic chroniclers have been selected to determine what constituted a siege event. These Arabic terms include 'to surround or blockade' (*hasara*), 'to harass' (*al-mudayaqah*), 'to attack or raid' (*aghara*) and 'to plunder or loot' (*nahaba*).[22] Although each siege event was unique, this is the best means of quantifying them in a way that is suitable for the analysis conducted above. References to siege events in 'independent' sources, written in Latin, Armenian or Syriac by a party with no obvious interest in the outcome of the engagement, are also important components of the methodology.[23]

The results presented in Figure 5.1 correspond well with the admittedly limited archaeological and literary evidence we have for the defensive architecture of Aleppo and Damascus during this time frame. Nasir-i Khusraw, a famous poet and Isma'ili philosopher, who travelled through Aleppo in 3–11 Rajab 438/3–11 January 1047 on route to Cairo, provided a detailed description of Aleppo's imposing defences. 'It has a huge rampart, twenty-five cubits (37.5–50 feet or 11–15 metres) high, I estimated, and an enormous fortress, as large as the one at Balkh, set on rock.'[24]

Unfortunately, we cannot corroborate Nasir-i Khusraw's description of the citadel and defences of Aleppo from architectural research, as there is little extant evidence of the pre-Ayyubid citadel.[25] The original citadel was present from the fourth/tenth century onwards, and the Mirdasid dynasty converted this structure into a palace and governmental residence during the fifth/eleventh century.[26] The fortifications of Aleppo underwent some improvement during the early sixth/twelfth century. Ibn al-'Adim claimed that the *atabeg* Lu'lu' made improvements to 'the citadel, the army and the city' between 508 and 510/1114 and 1117, while an earthquake in 508/1114 caused damage to 'towers on the northern gates of Aleppo' which needed to be repaired.[27]

Additionally, in 514/1120–1, Il-ghazi ordered his son, Sulayman b. Il-ghazi, to begin renovating the *qal'at al-sharif*.[28] The *qal'at al-sharif*, or citadel *al-sharif*, is the term used to refer to a supposed second smaller citadel, constructed on the southern edge of Aleppo. Heinz Gaube and Eugen Wirth were unconvinced that this southern citadel ever existed, but the *qal'at al-sharif* is referenced sporadically by both of the Aleppan chroniclers al-'Azimi and Ibn al-'Adim throughout their coverage of the late fifth/eleventh and early sixth/twelfth century.[29] The main citadel received further investment during the reigns of Zangi and Nur al-Din later in the sixth/twelfth century.[30]

Construction of the citadel of Damascus began in 478/1085–6 under Tutush b. Alp Arslan.[31] Damascus was also protected by orchards, villages and agricultural land almost up to the city walls, which were used by the inhabitants to ambush besiegers, as happened during the Second Crusade.[32] Evidence of construction or repair work on citadels in both Aleppo and Damascus during the time frame implies that these settlements had strong defensive capabilities and that their secular rulers and inhabitants prioritised investment in military architecture.

It is possible to discern a disparity in the rate at which these settlements were placed under siege in the period prior to and after the establishment of Frankish polities in the eastern Mediterranean. Sixteen out of twenty-four sieges of Aleppo occurred between 439 and 491/1047 and 1098, at a rate of a siege every 3.18 years. During the early Crusading period, eight sieges of Aleppo took place between 492 and 522/1099 and 1128, a siege every 3.625 years. All of the eight attempts to capture Damascus by force happened during the latter half of the fifth/eleventh century, with no siege of the city occurring during the early sixth/twelfth century. If one excludes the siege events of Aleppo about which there are doubts, those in 457/1064–5, 495/1102–3, 509/1115, 513/1119 and 522/1128, then the number of sieges would reduce to eighteen. Consequently, the siege rate of Aleppo would be one every 2.83 years between

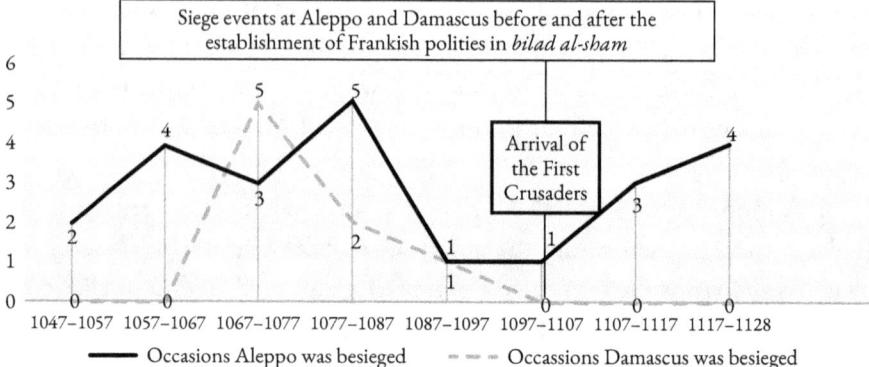

Figure 5.2 Siege events at Aleppo and Damascus: 439–522/1047–1128

439 and 491/1047 and 1098, and drop to one every 7.25 years between 492 and 522/1099 and 1128, denoting a substantial disparity between the two periods.

Of course, there are factors that could explain this discrepancy in the rate at which the two settlements were besieged between 439 and 491/1047 and 1098 and 492 and 522/1099 and 1128. For instance, the early Frankish rulers of Antioch and Jerusalem spent much of their first three decades in the Levant attempting to expand their influence along the Syrian and Palestinian coastline and into Cilicia. Yet the numbers outlined above indicate that in comparison with the fifth/eleventh century, the early Crusading period actually resulted in a more stable situation for the inhabitants of Aleppo and Damascus, at least in terms of substantive attacks on the polities themselves. This is in contrast to the perception in modern historiography, which has often portrayed the establishment of Frankish lordships as having a hugely disruptive impact upon the major Syrian urban centres.

Circumventing and Conspiring with Syrian Notables

The strong fortifications at Aleppo and Damascus forced many besieging armies to develop bespoke tactics in the hope of capturing these settlements. The approaches that met with the most success included besieging a settlement repeatedly over consecutive years in an attempt to provoke supply shortages, and the use of subterfuge.

Typically, in medieval western warfare, the inimical act of besieging a settlement revolved around a blockade of long duration. This was intended to not only deplete the defender's provisions, such as food supplies or military equipment, but also to grind down their resolve to resist the besieging army.[33] However, sieges of major settlements that lasted longer than six months were quite rare in fifth/eleventh- and early sixth/twelfth-century *bilad al-sham*, and none occurred at Aleppo or Damascus during this period.[34] Instead of drawn-out encirclements, individual Syrian cities were besieged in successive years. By adopting this approach, the resources of a town or fortress were diminished over several years, rather than months.

The first time this strategy was employed during the years 442–522/1050–1128 was during the Mirdasid succession crisis that followed the death of Thimal b. Salih in 454/1062. Mahmud b. Nasr besieged his uncle 'Atiyya b. Salih in Aleppo three times between 455 and 457/1063 and 1065, with the last attempt culminating in 'Atiyya's surrender.[35]

The second such instance occurred during the years 470–3/1077–81, when Aleppo came under attack from Tutush b. Alp Arslan, brother of the Seljuq Sultan Malik Shah, and Sharaf al-Dawla Muslim b. Quraysh, the Uqaylid ruler of Mosul, in quick succession.[36] Tutush also captured the fortifications of Buza'a (approximately 46 km northeast of Aleppo), Bira (approximately 92 km southwest of Aleppo), and besieged and burned the suburbs of 'Azaz (47 km north of Aleppo) during this period. This was part of a broader attempt to intimidate the general populace, while also intensifying food shortages in the city. Any supply problems would have been exacerbated by a raid in northern Syria led by one of Tutush's Türkmen deputies, Afshin, in 472/1079.[37] Yet when Tutush moved south to answer a call for assistance from the ruler of Damascus, it was Muslim b. Quraysh who besieged Aleppo and captured it in 473/1081.[38] Tutush's earlier attacks undoubtedly contributed to Muslim b. Quraysh's capture of the city, as Ibn al-'Adim tells us that the 'people of Aleppo' surrendered in Rabi'I 473/May 1081 due to widespread famine among the urban populace.

The third and final example involving Aleppo transpired in 478–9/1085–6, when Sulayman b. Qutlumush and Tutush b. Alp Arslan besieged the city on three or four separate occasions in a short fourteen-month period. It was a point of high confusion in the city, following the death of the Uqaylid ruler Sharaf al-Dawla Muslim b. Quraysh in 478/1085. News of an approaching army led by the Seljuq Sultan Malik Shah forced his brother Tutush b. Alp

Arslan to retreat from Aleppo, and the city then swiftly surrendered to Malik Shah without resistance.[39] While the inhabitants submitted to Malik Shah without his army resorting to military action, it is probable that the cumulative effects of the preceding months strongly influenced their decision to offer no resistance to the sultan's forces.

Possibly the best example of the effect of consecutive years of siege upon one settlement can be seen in Atsiz b. Uwaq al-Khwarizmi's attempts to capture Damascus between 463 and 468/1071 and 1075.[40] According to Ibn al-Qalanisi, Atsiz 'raided Damascus and continued the attacks on it and the surrounding area', until the situation in the city deteriorated to the point that the people were forced 'to eat carrion, whilst some ate each other', with inhabitants subsequently surrendering the city to Atsiz's army in Dhu 'l-Qa'da 468/6 June–5 July 1076.[41] Ibn al-Qalanisi made multiple references to Atsiz's unpopularity with the inhabitants of Damascus, which serves to underline just how effective a strategy five years of continual attacks on the city proved to be.[42]

These examples demonstrate how one of the only ways to capture Aleppo or Damascus by force without support from among the inhabitants was to besiege them repeatedly over a period of several years. The one exception to this seems to have been the Artuqid ruler Balak b. Bahram's capture of Aleppo in 517/1123.[43] Balak besieged Aleppo for around thirty days before he secured the city's surrender from his cousin Sulayman b. Il-ghazi. However, Balak had spent the preceding months leading intense raids on the rural areas surrounding Aleppo, while the Franks of Antioch and Edessa had been pursuing a similar policy in the years leading up to Balak's attack.[44]

Gaining entry to a city or citadel via cooperation with persons residing inside the fortifications was another potential route for rulers hoping to gain control of Damascus and Aleppo.[45] An early example of this form of subterfuge occurred in 452/1060 when Mahmud b. Nasr and the troops under his command gained access to Aleppo with the assistance of his mother, al-Sayyida al-'Alawiyya.[46] According to Sibt b. al-Jawzi, Mahmud's mother 'corrupted a unit from the *ahdath* (local urban militia) of Aleppo and won their affection', so that they later 'opened the gates for them [Mahmud and his army] and displayed their symbol'.[47] Despite their assistance, Mahmud failed to seize control of the citadel and was forced to withdraw from Aleppo shortly afterwards.

Sulayman b. Qutlumush enjoyed more success using a slightly different strategy at Antioch in Sha'ban 477/December 1084. According to Ibn al-Athir, Sulayman corresponded with dissatisfied persons within the town, and arranged to take Antioch with their assistance.[48] Ibn al-'Adim's account is somewhat different, as he reported that Sulayman and his army surprised the people of Antioch after performing night marches from his dominions in Anatolia. Arriving at the settlement after nightfall, his troops 'attached ropes to the balconies and walls with their spears, and they appeared on them by the gate' which they then opened and took control of the city.[49] Sulayman's actions enabled him to capture Antioch without a prolonged siege.

Another instance where there was evidence of collaboration with rebellious townspeople occurred during Tutush b. Alp Arslan's attempts to capture Aleppo in 479/1086. Ibn al-'Adim recounts how:

> a man from the merchants of Aleppo known as Ibn 'Awni al-Halabi ... had corresponded with Taj al-Dawla [Tutush] to surrender Aleppo to him. He raised some of his companions with ropes to one of the towers on the wall with the assistance of member of the *ahdath* (local urban militia) and they swung the emblem of Taj al-Dawla at this place. The people got word of this and everyone in the city swung the emblem.[50]

Through these supporters in Aleppo, Tutush managed to briefly take control of the city, but was unable to secure the citadel. He was then forced to depart Aleppo after receiving news of the imminent arrival of his brother, the Seljuq Sultan Malik Shah.

Ultimately though, these instances of successful subterfuge and collaboration were rare exceptions rather than the norm for besieging forces attempting to capture these settlements. This further underlines the defensibility of Damascus and Aleppo during this period, granting urban notables increased status during periods of crisis.

Appeals for Assistance

One of the most obvious ways in which notables were able to exercise their power was through appeals for assistance. Often the most decisive factor in attempts to occupy Aleppo or Damascus was the extent of the support that prospective rulers could draw from political elites in these cities. To emphasise this point, aside from a male brother, son or nephew inheriting Aleppo from a recently deceased brother, father or uncle, control of the city changed nine times between 442 and 522/1050 and 1122. Yet a siege was only employed by incoming rulers during three of these nine transitions of power.

The remaining sections of this chapter will focus on Aleppo, as the situation in Damascus remained fairly stable for much of this period. This was largely due to the long reigns of Taj al-Dawla Tutush b. Alp Arslan, 471–88/1078–95, and Zahir al-Din Tughtegin, 497–522/1104–28.[51] Frequently, a change of ruler in Aleppo was initiated by an appeal for assistance from urban elites.

These appeals, particularly those made during the early sixth/twelfth century, have been studied in some detail within the context of the counter-Crusade and *la maqam* paradigms.[52] Yet it would be a mistake to view the 'notables' of Aleppo as one cohesive group acting concertedly in pursuit of the same goals, as each family had their own discrete agendas and priorities. Indeed, the chroniclers refer to instances when multiple different groups were making requests for assistance at the same time, namely, in the three years prior to the battle of the Field of Blood in 513/1119, before and during the siege of Aleppo by Baldwin II in 518/1124–5, and the period leading up to Zangi's occupation of Aleppo in 522/1128. As Claude Cahen observed, Aleppo was a 'republic of notables', and it is the dramatic episodes of 513/1119, 518/1124–5 and 522/1128 that provide the best windows through which the influence of these notables is most discernible.[53]

The following section begins with a discussion of how urban elites in Aleppo attempted to manipulate the circumstances surrounding requests for assistance to enhance their own influence within the city, before profiling the qualities that the notables of Aleppo looked for in prospective rulers during this period.

Temporary Calls for Assistance?

There were occasions when members of the Aleppan political elite made appeals for assistance to external parties, but did not have the capability or inclination to surrender the settlement to this new ruler once they arrived outside the city walls. Often these appeals came following the death of a previous amir, or when disaffected individuals wanted to dislodge the figure in command of the city with the support of a third party. Occasionally, calls for assistance were used to remove potential threats to Aleppo, after which the suppliant would rely on the city's sturdy fortifications to deny entry to their saviours. This section highlights how the strength of the fortifications of Aleppo enabled some notables to exploit these requests to maintain or expand their positions of influence and autonomy.

The earliest example of the inhabitants of Aleppo refusing to surrender control of the city after making a request for assistance came in 473/1081, when Sharaf al-Dawla Muslim b. Quraysh seized control of Aleppo following an petition made by influential figures in the city.[54] There is some dispute in the source material as to who actually made the appeal to Muslim b. Quraysh. Sibt b. al-Jawzi mentioned 'a group' from the 'people of Aleppo' as being behind the initial approach, while Ibn al-'Adim described how the Mirdasid ruler Sabiq b. Mahmud sent to Muslim b. Quraysh with the intention of relinquishing control of the city to him. Ibn al-'Adim also claimed that Sadid al-Mulk 'Ali of the Banu Munqidh of Shayzar played an important role in Muslim b. Quraysh's acquisition of Aleppo. Despite these appeals, Sibt b. al-Jawzi claimed that Muslim b. Quraysh had to defeat the *ahdath* (local urban militia) of Aleppo in battle outside the city walls, whilst Ibn al-'Adim and Sibt b. al-Jawzi agree that the Uqaylid leader had to besiege the citadel for several months before the Mirdasid rulers surrendered to him.

However, Muslim b. Quraysh entrance into the city was facilitated by this collection of influential figures, and his claim to rule was bolstered by their support. This demonstrates how appeals could be made by people who did not always have the capacity to deliver the city to a new ruler, or changed their minds during the process. It also reveals that the inhabitants of Aleppo had a history of appealing to the rulers of Mosul prior to the sixth/twelfth century. This appeal to Muslim b. Quraysh was actually made during the reign of Malik Shah, the Seljuq sultan who enjoyed the greatest degree of influence in *bilad al-sham*, suggesting that later Aleppan appeals to the rulers of Mosul were not indicators of reduced Seljuq influence in the early Crusading period.[55]

This process continued into the sixth/twelfth century. Ibn al-'Adim claimed that at some point in 510/1116–17, a group of people in *khidma* to the ruler of Aleppo Lu'lu', probably members of the military hierarchy, approached Aqsunqur al-Bursuqi of Rahba proposing that if they worked together to kill Lu'lu', 'they would retain Aleppo as an *iqta*'' operating under

Aqsunqur al-Bursuqi's dominion. Ibn al-'Adim also suggested that half of the army of Aleppo hoped to take control of the city for themselves.[56] When Lu'lu' was killed shortly afterwards by dissident members of the Aleppan army, Aqsunqur al-Bursuqi marched against Aleppo and demanded that the inhabitants surrender, but received no response. A second attempt to subjugate the people of Aleppo in 511/1117–18 also ended in failure.[57]

At some point in the same year, the temporary ruler of Aleppo, Yaruqtash al-Khadim, wrote to Najm al-Din Il-ghazi b. Artuq of Mardin, asking him to come to *bilad al-sham* and remove Aqsunqur from Aleppo.[58] However, upon his arrival at Aleppo, Il-ghazi was not granted full control of the city. Instead, Ibn al-'Adim related how Il-ghazi was given access to 'the citadel *al-sharif*' but not allowed to assume possession of the larger main citadel (*al-qal'at al-kabira*). He was also given charge of Ridwan's son, Sultan Shah, effectively making him an *atabeg*, in addition to being granted control of 'Balis and some fortresses'. Il-ghazi later withdrew from the city when he was 'deserted by the people of Aleppo and the army'.[59]

Ibn al-Qalanisi only vaguely mentions that Il-ghazi's 'plans were disrupted and he departed the city'. Ibn al-Athir claimed that he left for Mardin in the east after he found the treasury of Aleppo empty, with the intention of returning to the city once he had raised additional troops. Interestingly, Sibt b. al-Jawzi mentions that Il-ghazi 'was appointed to manage the situation for a period of a month' after which he departed the city.[60]

This seems to be another example of partial control of Aleppo being offered in return for removing an enemy force, in this case Aqsunqur al-Bursuqi. By not granting Il-ghazi control over both citadels in Aleppo, the notables were then able to force him out of the city after the threat posed to their chance of independent rule had been removed.

On some of these occasions, it seems clear that individuals who did not have the influence to deliver control of the city were making appeals for assistance from external rulers. This was evidence of the range of factions vying for influence in the city, Cahen's 'republic of notables' in action.[61] However, on other occasions, it appears that these appeals were made to remove threats to the city, before then relying on the strong defences of Aleppo to thwart any attempt to take the settlement by force by the snubbed saviour. It also seems that this strategy dates back to at least the late fifth/eleventh century, and therefore should not be attributed to the establishment of Frankish polities in the Levant or the decline of Seljuq influence in the region.

Outmanoeuvring Suppliant Notables of Aleppo

In order to negate the risk of answering calls for assistance from Aleppo without later taking control of the city, individual rulers attempted to secure their position within Aleppo prior to their arrival. This approach was adopted by Tutush in 487/1095. When given a second opportunity to take control of Aleppo, he took no chances. After defeating the combined armies of Aqsunqur, Buzan and Kerbogha near Qinnasrin, he immediately sent Wathab b. Mahmud, the son of the previous Mirdasid ruler, to secure Aleppo with the vanguard of his army before Tutush arrived.[62] The success Tutush experienced using the son of a former ruler also suggests that the inhabitants of Aleppo placed significance on a family history of leadership in Aleppo.[63]

Similarly, when Il-ghazi was offered control of Aleppo for a second time in 512/1118–19, he also tried to establish himself firmly in control of the city before his arrival. He would possibly have been aware that other approaches had been made to Khir Khan of Homs, Tughtegin of Damascus and the Amir Jayush Beg of Mosul in the period since Il-ghazi had received his first appeal in 511/1117–18. The failed first attempt also meant that Il-ghazi would have known that he was far from a popular choice with some of the factions within the city, although Ibn al-'Adim reported that the notables who made the second approach to the Artuqid leader 'guaranteed him money that they would pay him in instalments at Aleppo if he diverted his army' to northern Syria. In order to avoid a repetition of the events of 511/1117–18, the same chronicler tell us that Il-ghazi 'dispatched some servants to organise his entrance into the city. The *qadi* Abu'l Fadl b. al-Kashshab, who wanted to preserve the city ... refused to let them [Il-ghazi's servants] enter the city.' Eventually, the city and the main citadel were later surrendered to him without further complaint upon his arrival in Aleppo, probably due to the growing threat posed by the Franks to the city at this time.[64]

Likewise, when Aqsunqur al-Bursuqi took control of Aleppo in 518/1125 he took comparable precautions. On receiving the delegation led by Ibn al-'Adim's great grandfather Aba Ghanam Muhammad b. Habah Allah b. 'Abi Jaradah, Aqsunqur al-Bursuqi demanded that the inhabitants would have to surrender the citadel to him in advance. The notables acquiesced to this and handed over the citadel to his deputies. Aqsunqur al-Bursuqi's army advanced into northern Syria only once he knew that his people were established in the citadel.[65] Zangi followed a similar procedure in Muharram 522/January 1128. According to Ibn al-'Adim:

> the *atabeg* sent troops to the city with the Amir Sankur Daraz and the Amir al-Hajib Salah al-Din Hasan. The Amir Salah al-Din entered the city and improved the situation and he was successful until he summoned the *atabeg* Zangi from Mosul, and so he approached Aleppo with his army.[66]

These examples illustrate how support of some factions within Aleppo was not always enough to secure control of the city, as the strength of the fortifications enabled different groups to reject rulers they refused to accept. Although some potentates managed to find ways around these issues, widespread support or desperation caused by a genuine threat to the city was often required for new rulers to secure control of Aleppo.

The level of influence wielded by Aleppan notables throughout 442–522/1050–1128 provides important context for the early Crusading period. Generally speaking, Aleppo is viewed by modern historians as a debilitated and chaotic polity during the first three decades of the sixth/twelfth century, and territorially this is accurate, as will be outlined in detail below.[67] However, the manipulation of calls for assistance for political benefit by Aleppo's urban elite was common practice throughout both the late fifth/eleventh and early sixth/twelfth century, indicating that Cahen's 'republic of notables' long pre-dated the arrival of the armies of the First Crusade.

'Born and Raised in Aleppo': Profiling Potential Potentates

If the support of the urban notables of Aleppo was vital to any prospective ruler of the settlement, what type of ruler did they want to have? Although each *malik* or amir of Aleppo took control of the city under unique circumstances, a personal or familial history of political activity in Aleppo, or even *bilad al-sham*, enhanced the chance of a more positive reception from the city's more affluent residents.

This predilection for individuals with links to the city was exemplified by Michael the Syrian's account of Zangi's acquisition of Aleppo. According to

Michael's chronicle, when Zangi approached Aleppo in 522/1128, those in control of the city closed the gates against him. However, as the 'people' remembered his father Qasim al-Dawla Aqsunqur, who had ruled Aleppo in the late fifth/eleventh century, and because Zangi was 'born and raised in Aleppo', the inhabitants opened the gates for him.[68] A similar account of Zangi's entrance to Aleppo was provided by the sixth/twelfth-century Aleppan historian Ibn Abi Tayyi', which was preserved in the seventh/fifteenth-century chronicle of Ibn al-Furat:

> he (Zangi) marched to Aleppo and descended on the Iraqi gate, which was shut in his face. He (Zangi) intended to fight, but the Aleppans (*al-halabiyun*) conferred together and opened the Iraqi gate for the *atabeg* Zanki. The *atabeg* had been born in Aleppo, and therefore the Aleppans inclined towards and loved him, so they opened the gate and he took possession of Aleppo.[69]

Ibn al-Athir also claimed that upon Zangi's arrival, the 'people of Aleppo came out to welcome him and were delighted at his coming'.[70] Moreover, in his account of the Seljuq campaign of 508/1111, Ibn al-Athir claimed the Zangi was known in Seljuq military circles as 'Zangi *al-shami*', suggesting that his Syrian ties were recognised by his contemporaries.[71] These accounts are of a similar texture to Baha' al-Din Ibn Shaddad's account of Saladin's visit to his father's house upon his arrival in Damascus in Rabi'I 570/November 1174, indicating that an emphasis on rulers with ties to individual cities extended beyond the Aleppan notables of this period.[72]

Further evidence of the legitimising impact that prior involvement in Syrian affairs could have for future rulers of Aleppo came in 510/1116–17. This was when Aqsunqur al-Bursuqi launched his first failed bid for power in Aleppo. After the siege failed, he then went to Homs and Damascus and, according to Ibn al-'Adim, 'returned with his status increased to Aleppo'.[73] The implication here is that by forging or renewing alliances with Khir Khan of Homs and Tughtegin of Damascus, Aqsunqur al-Bursuqi had improved his standing in Aleppo. However, even the presence of Tughtegin assisting Aqsunqur al-Bursuqi's second attempt to secure Aleppo in 511/1117–18 did not earn him enough support to take the city. Ibn al-'Adim wrote that the inhabitants rejected Aqsunqur's second call to surrender, reportedly telling him that 'we do not want someone from the east' before appealing to the 'Franks of Antioch' to dislodge him from the vicinity of Aleppo.[74]

A comparable proclivity for rulers with local ties to Aleppo or Syria has been identified during the Ayyubid period. Konrad Hirschler has demonstrated how young Syrian rulers were frequently elevated to power because they could be manipulated to prioritise local interests, chief among which was avoiding the danger of 'centralised' Egyptian rule.[75] It is probable that a similar dynamic motivated the decision-making of prominent Aleppan political figures in the late fifth/eleventh and early sixth/twelfth century, as they hoped rulers with ties to Aleppo or *bilad al-sham* would place the city's interests ahead of those of the Great Seljuq Sultanate.[76]

This apparent preference is also borne out when considering the broader picture. Between 491 and 522/1099 and 1128, with the exception of Aqsunqur al-Bursuqi, all of the long-term rulers of Aleppo, those whose reigns lasted longer than three years, had ancestors who had been active in *al-sham* politics during the fifth/eleventh century. Ridwan and his son Alp Arslan could rely upon their ties to Tutush b. Alp Arslan, while as noted above Zangi's father Qasim al-Dawla Aqsunqur had also ruled Aleppo. Il-ghazi and his Artuqid successors in Aleppo, Balak, Sulayman and Timurtash, could all point to Artuq b. Aksab, who had governed Jerusalem for Tutush, in addition to the short period when Il-ghazi and his brother Suqman had ruled over Jerusalem and Manbij after Artuq's death.

However, the Artuqid ancestry was seemingly not sufficient for the notables of Aleppo, as Il-ghazi and Balak thought it necessary to enter into marriage alliances with the daughter of a former ruler. Il-ghazi married an unnamed daughter of Ridwan b. Tutush in 515/1121–2, following the repression of a rebellion instigated by some notables in Aleppo.[77] Ibn al-'Adim also mentioned that following Il-ghazi's marriage to Ridwan's daughter, 'the *khutba* was made for the daughter of the Malik Ridwan', even though Ridwan's surviving sons had returned to Aleppo, having been moved to Qal'at Ja'bar during the rebellion mentioned above. The timing of this marriage, in the immediate aftermath of a revolt, points to an obvious attempt to further legitimise his rule of Aleppo. Similarly, Balak married Ridwan's daughter, the Lady Farkhanha, on 23 Dhu al-Hajja 517/11 February 1124, in the immediate aftermath of his capture of Aleppo.[78] Even Zangi, who was born in Aleppo, married one of Ridwan's daughters, the Lady Zumurrud in 524/1030.[79]

It could be argued that these marriages to Ridwan's daughters were a logical extension of the policy of *atabeg*, where legitimisation was derived through the wife, rather than a son-in-law. The practice of new rulers using marriage alliances to the daughters of former amirs of Aleppo dated back to the late fifth/eleventh century, as the daughter of the Mirdasid ruler of Aleppo, Mahmud b. Nasr, Mani'a b. Mahmud, married both Muslim b. Quraysh and Sulayman b. Qutlumush in the 470s/1080s.[80]

Modern historians have viewed these marriages as a way of deriving legitimisation by forging familial ties to previous rulers.[81] It is not coincidental that Mahmud and Ridwan were the rulers who enjoyed the longest periods in control of the city, that is, eleven and twenty years, respectively. This made them the only two amirs of Aleppo whose reigns lasted longer than seven years between 442 and 522/1050 and 1128. In particular, the children of Ridwan seem to have retained value as subjects for legitimisation long after their father's death in 507/1113. One of his sons, Sultan Shah b. Ridwan, was part of the Frankish-led coalition that besieged Aleppo in 518/1124–5, whilst another, Ibrahim b. Ridwan, attempted to assert his claims in Aleppo shortly before Zangi assumed control of the city in 522/1128.[82] Both of these attempts ended in failure, perhaps indicating that their appeal to the notables was not absolute.

Seemingly, Ridwan's daughters had more success in earning the trust of the political elite of Aleppo. In 510/1116–17, Ridwan's daughter Yumin supposedly took control of the citadel of Aleppo for a short period of time. According to Ibn al-'Adim, following Lu'lu''s demise, 'the citadel of Aleppo was placed in the safe hands of the Lady daughter of Ridwan, Yumin, until Yaruqtash al-Khadim Mubadaran arrived and entered Aleppo'.[83] The short period when Yumin was in command of the citadel in 510/1116–17 and the placing of the *khutba* in Farkhanha's name in 515/1121–2 indicates that their father was still held in high esteem within Aleppo nearly a decade after his death. These examples also suggest that a certain amount of trust was placed in the women themselves by the notables.

This points to another important reason behind these marriage alliances, the integration of new rulers into the Aleppan network of notables. The 'republic of notables' in Aleppo was made up of numerous factions. The children of Mahmud in the late fifth/eleventh century and Ridwan in the early sixth/twelfth century grew up in the city and understood this complicated patchwork of elite Aleppan political society, and occupied an established place within it. The need for their new husbands to understand and integrate themselves into this network would have been just as important a motivation for these marriage alliances as legitimisation.

Another way that new rulers sought to secure the support of the Aleppan notables was through the lowering of taxes. In 514/1120–1, Il-ghazi was forced to lower taxes in the city in order to foster a more positive opinion of his rule following a failed campaign against ʿAzaz. Ibn al-ʿAdim noted that:

> the people of Aleppo had made complaints to him about the renewal of a tax which had been levied against them in the days of Ridwan, which was not a custom in the Arab state [under the Mirdasid dynasty], Egyptian state [the Fatimids], nor in the days of Aqsunqur.[84]

Il-ghazi then ordered a report of the amounts involved, and after being informed that it amounted to '12,000 dinars every year' he removed the tax. Ibn al-Qalanisi, al-ʿAzimi and Sibt b. al-Jawzi also mentioned that Il-ghazi lowered the taxes in Aleppo, and in the words of Ibn al-Qalanisi 'this action was received with gratitude, praise, appreciation and blessings'.[85]

Aqsunqur al-Bursuqi also lowered taxes in Aleppo in 518/1125, immediately after assuming control of the city. According to Ibn al-ʿAdim 'he (Aqsunqur) wrote to the people of Aleppo signing the removal of the unjust taxes, of which there is an existing copy'.[86] Both of these decisions were taken following direct requests by the notables of Aleppo.

In summary, a history or ancestry of political leadership in Aleppo or *bilad al-sham* was viewed as a positive by Aleppan notables when deciding upon potential rulers between 442 and 522/1050 and 1128. It is likely that this inclination towards political figures with ties to the city or region was motivated by the hope that they would place the interests of Aleppo ahead of those of the Great Seljuq Sultanate. Although each ruler of Aleppo rose to power under unique circumstances, the strong fortifications of the city often enabled the notables to accept those rulers who met these criteria and reject those who did not. Individuals who managed to establish themselves as ruler of Aleppo without the sufficient Aleppan or Syrian bona fides, such as Muslim b. Quraysh, Il-ghazi or Balak, had to marry women who did possess them. The one exception to this was Aqsunqur al-Bursuqi, who gained control of the city by answering a call for assistance made in response to Baldwin II's siege of Aleppo in 518/1124–5, the point at which the Frankish threat was at its zenith.

The Frontiers of *Bilad halab*

The toponym *bilad halab* is used sporadically in medieval Arabic historiography, and can loosely be translated as the country or region of Aleppo.[87] *Bilad halab* generally refers to a collection of settlements and territories traditionally viewed to have fallen under the control of the city of Aleppo, therefore making up the region of Aleppo. The first volume of Ibn al-'Adim's biographical dictionary consists of entries extolling the virtues and characteristics of different towns and settlements, and offers a clear indication of what he viewed as *bilad halab* in the mid-seventh/thirteenth century.[88] However, Ibn al-'Adim's definition should be read in the knowledge that he was writing over a century after the events covered in his book, and with Zayde Antrim's conclusions that the biographical dictionaries of Ibn 'Asakir and Ibn al-'Adim exaggerated the limits of these cities' dominions in order to bolster their geopolitical footprints.[89]

The situation on the frontiers of *bilad halab* had a great deal of influence on the internal politics of the city. For the general populace, a failure to protect key strategic sites in the rural hinterlands of Aleppo from the raiding activities of Byzantine, Frankish or Türkmen troops could lead to severe food shortages. For the notables, these territories were a long-standing source of financial revenue and political power. An amir's capacity to defend these outlying farmlands was therefore an essential criterion for gaining or retaining the support of the urban elite.

In broad terms, most historians have viewed the city of Aleppo as enduring a period of decline during the late fifth/eleventh and early sixth/twelfth century. The highly influential work of Jean Sauvaget identified the catastrophic sack of Aleppo by the Byzantine Emperor Nicephorus Phocas in 351/962 as the starting point of this deterioration, with the reigns of the Mirdasid dynasty and petty Seljuq rulers indicative of Aleppo's reduced importance.[90] However, it was between 442 and 522/1050 and 1128 that the polity of Aleppo developed the territorial dimensions it retained during the Ayyubid and Mamluk periods. The years between 442 and 522/1050 and 1128 also saw Aleppo grow into a distinct lordship, as prior to 452/1060 it had been just one of a triumvirate of cities, alongside Rahba and Raqqa, which formed the dominions of

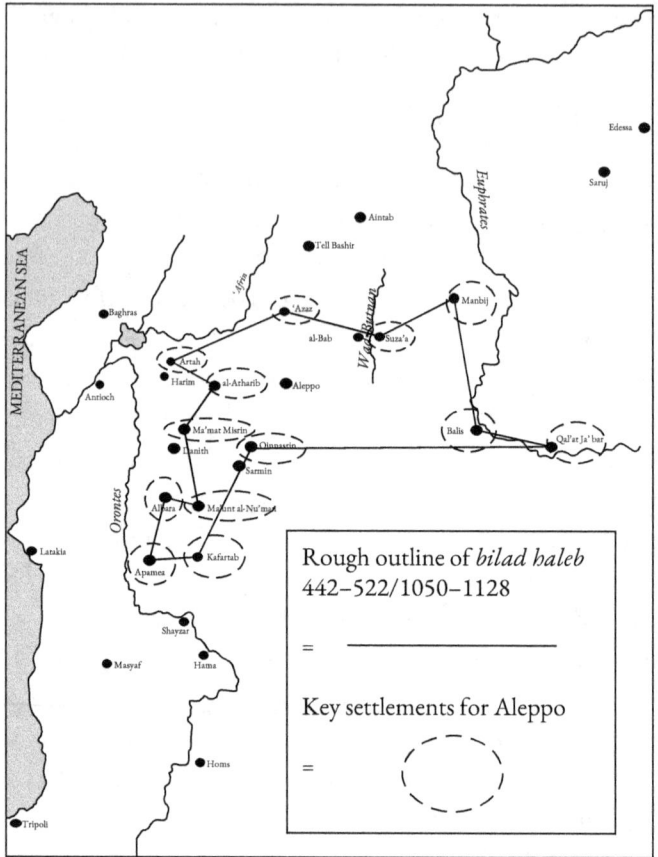

Figure 5.3 Frontiers of *bilad halab*: 442–522/1050–1128

the Mirdasids.[91] Essentially, the alterations that Aleppo underwent territorially and politically between 442 and 522/1050 and 1128 defined the meaning of *bilad halab* for at least the next two centuries.

Recent historical research has demonstrated how difficult it is to apply the concept of fixed frontiers in a medieval context.[92] Thomas Asbridge and Andrew Buck have analysed the western frontier of Aleppan dominions during the sixth/twelfth century in reference to the Frankish 'Principality of Antioch', while most research on Aleppan political history during this period has touched on the importance of individual settlements.[93] Asbridge and Buck identified Ma'rrat al-Nu'man, Apamea, Kafartab, al-Atharib, 'Azaz, Zadarna and Harim as what the latter referred to as 'strategic hotspots' in northern Syria.[94]

The following section examines this complex conflict zone from the Aleppan perspective. In order to understand the extent of the threat the Franks posed to Aleppo between 512 and 522/1118 and 1128, it is first necessary to outline the settlements that made up the amirate of Aleppo or *bilad halab* in the years 442–522/1050–1128. This outline is divided into the western, northern, southern and eastern frontiers, with particular emphasis placed on the strategic importance of the town of 'Azaz, to the north of Aleppo.

The Western Frontier of Bilad halab

As Asbridge and Buck have outlined in detail, the geographical and topographical features of the territory between Antioch and Aleppo were hugely decisive factors in military interactions on the eastern frontier of the 'Principality of Antioch', or Aleppo's western frontier.[95] Antioch is located approximately 90 km to the west of Aleppo. The territory between the two major settlements is bisected by a series of low-lying limestone massifs known as the Jabal al-'Ala or Belus Hills, housing rocky and barren terrain which is difficult to traverse.[96]

To the west of the Jabal al-'Ala were the settlements of Artah and Harim, which safeguarded the *jisr al-hadid* (Iron Bridge). The Iron Bridge was one of the few crossing points on the River Orontes, and it controlled any approach to Antioch from the direction of Aleppo. Artah also guarded the southern entrance to the Vale of 'Afrin to the northwest of Aleppo, and therefore blocked any potential approach from the direction of 'Azaz in the north.[97] To the east of the Jabal al-'Ala was a largely indefensible flat plain which continued to the city of Aleppo. This approach was only protected by the settlements of al-Atharib and Zardana to the west and southwest of Aleppo.[98]

This made Artah and al-Atharib vital to the defence of both Aleppo and Antioch. When Aleppan rulers controlled Artah, they could attack the city of Antioch and its environs, while when Antiochene rulers held al-Atharib, they could launch assaults upon Aleppo and the fertile areas to the southwest of the city along the River Quwayq. For much of the fifth/eleventh century Artah had been under Aleppan dominion, and rulers of Aleppo were able to extract tributary payments from Byzantine Antioch.[99] The arrival of the armies of the First Crusade changed this, with a rebellion against Aleppan control in 491/1098 by the Armenian garrison returning

Artah to Antiochene control, now under Frankish rulership.[100] Ridwan of Aleppo attempted to take advantage of another rebellion by the garrison of Artah in Sha'ban 498/April 1105, but his army was defeated in a subsequent battle against Antiochene forces.[101]

After this point, the focus of the conflict moved eastwards to al-Atharib and Zardana. Al-Atharib had mostly been under Aleppan control since 457/1065.[102] In 504/1110–11 Tancred of Antioch took both al-Atharib and Zardana by force.[103] Afterwards, Ibn al-'Adim made specific reference to how Aleppo had been weakened by the fall of al-Atharib. This was exemplified by Ridwan being forced to sell his personal provisions of grain at a third of the normal price due to food shortages provoked by Frankish raiding.[104] Although Il-ghazi retook al-Atharib and Zardana after defeating an Antiochene army at the battle of the Field of Blood in 513/1119, his nephew Sulayman later surrendered al-Atharib to the Franks in exchange for a peace treaty in 517/1123.[105]

The Northern Frontier of Bilad halab

'Azaz was probably the single most important settlement on the Aleppan frontier between 442 and 522/1050 and 1128. This is best illustrated by words attributed to Il-ghazi in the aftermath of the battle of the Field of Blood by the Latin chronicler Walter the Chancellor, who claimed that Il-ghazi lamented 'we are not yet able to hold the castle of 'Azaz, which is reckoned to be the gate of entry and exit for Aleppo'.[106] Although such examples of reported speech should be read with caution, the general sentiment of the remarks either from Il-ghazi himself, or invented by Walter the Chancellor, underscored a wider appreciation of 'Azaz's strategic value.

'Azaz guards the closest entry point into the Vale of 'Afrin from Aleppo, as a collection of limestone massifs to the northwest of Aleppo, known as the Jebel Sheykh Barakat, Jebel Semaan and Jebel Lailun, blocks off direct access to the 'Afrin valley from the city. 'Azaz is located between these massifs to the southwest and the Jabal Barisha to the north. There were other approaches to the River 'Afrin further north, at Ayntab, Tell Bashir and Ravendan, which would play an increasingly important role during the sixth/twelfth century.[107] Claude Cahen, René Dussaud, Thomas Asbridge and Andrew Buck have tended to place 'Azaz alongside Artah, al-Atharib and Zardana, as one of a

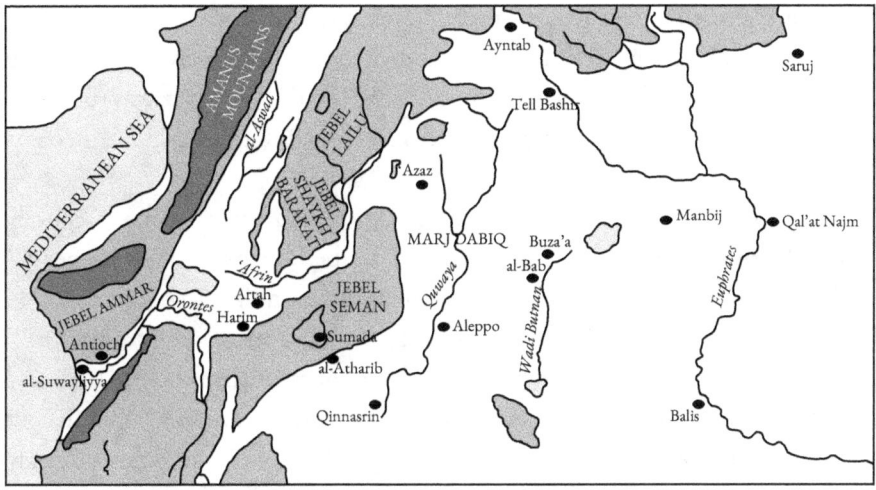

Figure 5.4 The strategic importance of 'Azaz

number of sites that could help to protect Antioch against attacks from the direction of Aleppo. However, from an Aleppan perspective control of 'Azaz was essential, as it guarded the fertile areas of Marj Dabiq and the area around the River Quwayq to the north of the city from raids originating from the direction of Tell Bashir and Antioch via the 'Afrin valley.

Archaeological evidence suggests that the areas around the River Quwayq greatly benefited from newly founded Islamic settlements in the vicinity of 'Azaz from the late first/seventh to early second/eighth century onwards. Additionally, the rural areas surrounding 'Azaz proved to be almost uniquely resistant to the decline in settlement patterns that afflicted most of Syria during the transition from Roman to Islamic control.[108] Writing in the late seventh/thirteenth century, Ibn Shaddad claimed that there were three hundred villages in the vicinity of 'Azaz, most of which belonged to 'the people of Aleppo' (*ahl halab*), and that the land tax revenues from the rural areas of the district were enough to pay for '200 horsemen'.[109]

Although there is archaeological evidence to suggest that substantial economic growth took place in rural Syria between 522/1128 and when Ibn Shaddad wrote his topographical history over a hundred years later, this entry supports the impression that 'Azaz was of significant agrarian value to the region of Aleppo. Accordingly, its defence would have been a priority for many of the notable families of the city, especially as many of the landholding elites referred to here by Ibn Shadad had ancestors who were active during the late fifth/eleventh and early sixth/twelfth centuries.[110] 'Azaz was therefore hugely significant both for Aleppo's wider strategic interests, and the incomes of the city's urban notables.

Throughout the late fifth/eleventh century, 'Azaz remained securely under Aleppan dominion. The Byzantine Emperor Romanos Diogenes IV and Tutush b. Alp Arslan raided the areas surrounding the settlement in 471/1068–9 and 472/1079, respectively, but did not manage to capture it.[111] Aside from a couple of failed rebellions by governors of 'Azaz in 491/1098 and 501/1107–8, Aleppo retained control of 'Azaz until 512/1118, when Roger of Salerno captured the settlement following a siege.[112] Ibn al-'Adim strongly lamented the loss of 'Azaz:

> this cut out the resources of the people of Aleppo because nothing remained to support Aleppo apart from 'Azaz and the territory around it. The rest of the region of Aleppo was under the control of the Franks, and to the east the land was destroyed and barren. There was very little food in Aleppo ... because half the grain did not reach Aleppo now.[113]

Various rulers of Aleppo attempted to retake 'Azaz in 513/1119, 514/1120, 517/1124 and 519/1125–6, underscoring its importance, but all of these attempts proved to be in vain.[114]

The Southern Frontier of Bilad halab

There was an important road network between Aleppo in the north and Shayzar, Homs and Damascus in the south. Augusto Palombini and Cinzia Tavaneri have completed a detailed archaeological reconstruction of the Syrian caravanserai networks between Damascus and Aleppo during the seventh/thirteenth century.[115] Although Palombini and Tavaneri focused on a later period, their work emphasised the importance of the southern route from Aleppo via Qinnasrin, Ma'rrat al-Nu'man and Hama to Damascus.[116]

Aside from this key road to the south, the valley between the Jabal Ansariyah and the Jabal al-Summaq housed an expanse of fertile lands along the River Orontes, which stretched eastwards to the settlements on the plain.[117] This meant that the whole region held great financial and agrarian value to rulers of Aleppo. The settlements of Apamea, Albara, Maʿrrat al-Nuʿman, Shayzar and Kafartab were also of great strategic importance to the balance of power in the region. Kafartab and Apamea overlooked the road to southern Syria.[118] Albara occupied an important opening in the Jabal Zawiya, providing access to Jisr al-Shugur, one of the few crossing points on the River Orontes.[119] Shayzar controlled another one of the few locations where the Orontes could be crossed, outside the major settlements of Homs and Hama.[120] Maʿrrat al-Nuʿman's significance was rooted in its location on the route between Aleppo and Damascus, and its proximity to the limestone massifs that influenced all military activity in the area.[121] As Asbridge and Buck have highlighted, the Jabal al-Summaq was vital to Antiochene interests during the sixth/twelfth century, as it controlled the southern approach to the city.[122]

For much of the fifth/eleventh century, Aleppan activity in the region was often driven by the need to confront Fatimid and Seljuq rulers of Damascus and Homs, or occasionally Byzantine forces. The occupation of Shayzar in 474/1081–2 by the Banu Munqidh introduced a new faction into the region, with whom both Antiochene and Aleppan rulers had to contend for influence in the Jabal al-Summaq. In 491/1098, the armies of the First Crusade captured Maʿrrat al-Nuʿman and Albara by siege and sacked the settlements.[123]

In the aftermath of the Antiochene and Edessan defeat at the battle of Harran in 497/1104, Kafartab, Maʿrrat al-Nuʿman and Albara were returned to Aleppan control.[124] Asbridge and Cahen have argued that Maʿrrat al-Nuʿman and Kafartab returned to Antiochene control after the battle of Artah in 498/1105, although there is no specific reference to this in the source material.[125] Armies dispatched by the sultan to *bilad al-sham* in 505/1111 and 509/1115 occupied Maʿrrat al-Nuʿman for brief periods, and in the years after this the Banu Munqidh of Shayzar occupied the settlement intermittently.[126] Apamea fell under Antiochene control in 499/1105–6 when it surrendered following a siege led by Tancred, and remained under Frankish suzerainty until 518/1125.[127] Baldwin II also captured Albara by siege in 516/1122, although Balak recaptured it a year later.[128]

The situation in the Jabal al-Summaq was more fluid than on the other frontiers of *bilad halab* during this time frame. This was largely a result of the number of different factions grappling for influence in the area. For Aleppo, the importance of the Jabal al-Summaq seems to have varied over time, and become gradually less important as the threat from Damascus receded, and that of Antioch increased in the early sixth/twelfth century. It is also notable that Aleppan influence in the area was at its lowest in 503/1111, 513/1119 and 518/1124–5, when food supplies in the city were reportedly short, reiterating the agrarian value of the Jabal al-Summaq region. Yet the situation on Aleppo's other frontiers was comparably bleak during these periods.

The Eastern Frontier of Bilad halab

Key sites on Aleppo's eastern frontier controlled access to crossing points on the River Euphrates and approaches to the city from the east. Of primary importance in this era were the settlements of Buza'a, Manbij and Qal'at Ja'bar along which ran the quickest route to Mosul. Buza'a controlled crossing points at Wadi Butnan, while Manbij had guarded the western bank of the Euphrates since Roman times.[129] With the advent of the Frankish rule at Edessa, the port settlements of Qal'at Ja'bar and Balis further to the south became increasingly important as alternate crossing points on the River Euphrates.

Initially, Buza'a only came under attack from armies arriving in *bilad al-sham* from the east. This occurred when Tutush b. Alp Arslan attempted to coerce a surrender from the inhabitants of Aleppo in 471/1078–9, while the army dispatched to the region by the Seljuq sultan in 509/1115 employed similar tactics.[130] Starting with a raid on Buza'a by Roger of Salerno in 513/1119, the Franks launched repeated attacks on the area in 514/1120–1, 516/1122 and 517/1123, with the populace swearing oaths of loyalty to Baldwin II following the second of these engagements.[131]

Manbij oscillated between Aleppan and Byzantine control in the fifth/eleventh century until 468/1075–6, when the Byzantine commander surrendered to Mirdasid forces from Aleppo.[132] Although Manbij was captured by Tutush in 471/1078–9 and Malik Shah in 479/1086, it remained part of the *bilad halab*, until a series of Frankish raids in 502/1108 and 504/1110–11 caused the inhabitants of Manbij and Balis to flee the settlements.[133]

The uncertainty these raids provoked culminated in a rebellion against the Aleppan ruler Balak by the amir of Manbij, Hassan al-Baalbeki, in Safar

518/20 March–17 April 1124. Ibn al-ʿAdim reported that Balak marched against Manbij and during the subsequent siege, Hassan's brother 'wrote to Joscelyn: "if you come and remove the army of Balak from my city I will surrender Manbij to you". And it is said that he raised the emblem of Joscelyn at Manbij'. Balak defeated the Frankish relief force which Joscelyn of Tell Bashir dispatched, but died from an arrow wound he suffered while besieging Manbij.[134] Fulcher of Chartres also mentioned contact between Joscelyn, 'the possessor' of Manbij and the relief force sent by the ruler of Tell Bashir against Balak's forces, but diverged from the Arabic sources by claiming that the Franks won the subsequent battle during which Balak was killed.[135] Whichever account is accurate, Balak's death ensured that Manbij remained outside the Aleppan sphere of influence.

Qalʿat Jaʿbar and Balis had been under the control of members of the Arab tribe the Banu Kilab for much of the fifth/eleventh century. In 479/1086–7, the Sultan Malik Shah compensated Salim b. Malik al-Uqayli for the citadel of Aleppo with the fortress of Qalʿat Jaʿbar, Raqqa and a number of villages as an *iqtaʿ*.[136] Frankish forces raided the plain of Raqqa and Qalʿat Jaʿbar in Safar 497/November 1103, but the Uqaylid rulers of Qalʿat Jaʿbar largely managed to avoid direct conflict with the Franks.[137] Their backing of Baldwin II's siege of Aleppo in 518/1124–5 provides further support for the notion that the amirs of Qalʿat Jaʿbar were slightly removed from the orbit of Aleppan control.[138] The Amir Salim b. Malik of Qalʿat Jaʿbar had played a role as an intermediary during Baldwin II's first ransom by Jawli Saqoa of Mosul in 502/1108.[139] Additionally, they housed the sons of Ridwan during Sulayman b. Il-ghazi's rebellion against his father in Aleppo in 515/1121–2.[140]

In 496/1102–3, Ridwan established Aleppan hegemony at Balis.[141] The Franks did not challenge this until 516/1122–3 when there was an unsuccessful siege of Balis by Baldwin II. Ibn al-ʿAdim mentioned that Ibn Malik was willing to negotiate, but 'his (Baldwin's) demands were excessive', and a group of Türkmen, supported by a unit of cavalry from Aleppo, then defeated the Franks in battle.[142]

The Frontiers of Bilad halab: 513/1119 and 518/1124–5

It is not coincidental that during the two periods that saw Aleppo most at risk of falling under Frankish rule, the notables of city accepted rulers whom they had previously rejected, Il-ghazi in 512/1118 and Aqsunqur al-Bursuqi in 518/1125. As Asbridge has outlined, prior to the battle of the Field of Blood in 513/1119, all of the key settlements surrounding the city of Aleppo were either in Frankish possession or had recently suffered from targeted raids.[143] To the west, Artah, al-Atharib and Zardana were all under Antiochene control, in addition to ʿAzaz in the north, while Buzaʾa had also been attacked by Roger's forces. In 513/1119, Aleppo had no controlling influence over any of the important settlements in the Jabal al-Summaq, such as Apamea, Albara, Maʿrrat al-Nuʿman, Shayzar and Kafartab. If Il-ghazi's army had not emerged victorious from the battle of the Field of Blood, Aleppo would have been at risk of falling under Frankish rule.

If anything, the Aleppan position had deteriorated even further by the time of Baldwin II's siege of the city in 518/1124–5. While the situation on the northern, southern and western frontiers remained equally as bleak for the notables of Aleppo in the winter of 518/1124–5 as in 513/1119, conditions on the eastern frontier had worsened. Qalʿat Jaʿbar and Balis remained in the hands of the Banu Uqayl, who had only a loose relationship with the amir of Aleppo. Relations with the Banu Uqayl appeared to decline further during Il-ghazi and Balak's time in control of the city. The amir of Manbij had attempted to declare for the Franks as recently as Safar 518/20 March–17 April 1124, and Buzaʾa had been subjected to Frankish raids in 516/1122 and 517/1123.

In 518/1124–5, the *bilad halab* was effectively reduced to the areas in the immediate vicinity of Aleppo. The Artuqid ruler of Aleppo, Timurtash b. Il-ghazi, had one final card to play. Baldwin II of Jerusalem was his hostage, having been captured by Balak in 517/1123.[144] In order to secure his release in 518/1124, Baldwin II pledged to 'surrender' al-Atharib, Zardana, al-Jizr, Kafartab, ʿAzaz and 80,000 dinars, with '20,000 dinars presented in advance' according to Ibn al-ʿAdim.[145] If this agreement had been complied with, it would have effectively restored the western, northern and southwestern frontiers of Aleppo and negated any immediate threat to Aleppo from Antioch. Unfortunately for Timurtash, Baldwin reneged on his promise, claiming that he had been forced to make these commitments under duress, and that he was therefore not obligated to fulfil them.[146] Shortly afterwards, Timurtash was called east to Mardin and he remained there while Aleppo was placed under siege. In 518/1124–5, the city of Aleppo had never been as isolated or as vulnerable to a siege throughout the preceding seventy-five years.

Revisiting Baldwin II's Siege of Aleppo

The case that the Crusades could have been 'won', or even prolonged, by the Frankish occupation of Aleppo in 518/1124–5 has been made convincingly by Thomas Asbridge.[147] Asbridge's focused on the overall strategy pursued by Baldwin II to capture Aleppo in 518/1124–5 or Damascus in 523/1129, outlining how their acquisition would have bolstered the long-term security of the Latin east. According to Asbridge's line of reasoning, if Baldwin II of Jerusalem had managed to capture Aleppo in 518/1124–5, it would have helped to swing the balance of power in northern Syria towards the Frankish polities, while also providing a vital link to Edessa, 'Outremer's lonely inland arm'. In addition, the Frankish occupation of either of these cities would have deprived the Zangid dynasty of the opportunity to capture Aleppo and Damascus in the following decades.

Asbridge's explanation as to why Baldwin II's attempt to capture Aleppo in 518/1124–5 failed is that it was opportunistic attack, launched with little preparation. This has some validity, particularly as Baldwin II was only released from captivity in Aleppo several months prior to the beginning of the siege. However, it is possible to view the siege of Aleppo in 518/1124–5 as the culmination of a four-year strategy to slowly erode the territorial dominions of the *bilad halab* from all sides, as has been outlined above.[148]

Once looked at in this light, significant questions surround the viability of the Frankish occupation of Aleppo in the early sixth/twelfth century. The failure of Baldwin's siege in 518/1124–5 reveals how even under the harshest of conditions, both in terms of the situation with the city and the wider territorial dominions of *bilad halab*, surrender to the Franks was not an option for the notables of Aleppo. Due to the resilient defences of Aleppo and the sway this granted the urban elites over prospective rulers, severe doubts surround the notion that Frankish rule over Aleppo was ever a realistic prospect. This also calls into question the extent to which the Frankish lordships were a fully integrated component of the Syrian political landscape.

Discussion begins with a brief outline of the various parties that made up the coalition and the approaches they took to Aleppo in the winter of

518/1124–5. Focus will then shift onto Baldwin's reported scheme to install a Muslim 'client ruler' in Aleppo, and Dubays b. Sadaqa's incompatibility with the profile typically sought by Aleppan notables during this period.

Reconstructing the Coalition Force's March against Aleppo

Asbridge provided a detailed analysis of the military aspects of the siege and the coalition that Baldwin II forged with various political figures in *bilad al-sham*.[149] The coalition Baldwin formed with the amirs from the eastern frontier of Aleppo, Malik b. Salim of Qal'at Ja'bar, 'Isa b. Salim b. Malik of Manbij, Yaghi Siyan 'Abd al-Jabbar b. Artuq of Balis, supplemented by Joscelyn of Edessa and opportunists such as Dubays b. Sadaqa, the lord of Hilla, Sultan Shah b. Ridwan and Tughrul Arslan b. Qilij Arslan, lord of Melitene, bespeaks to the success of Baldwin's strategy over the preceding four years.[150] By continuously raiding territories to the east of Aleppo, Baldwin had managed to coerce these amirs to support his efforts to subjugate Aleppo. This strongly suggests that Baldwin II was viewed as the dominant power in northern Syria at this time.

According to Ibn al-'Adim, Baldwin and his allies raided the area surrounding Aleppo as they advanced, with Baldwin marching from Artah to the River Quwayq where his forces 'destroyed all that was there'. Joscelyn and Dubays raided the areas to the east of Aleppo, including Buza'a, al-Qutun al-Dukhan and Marj Dabiq, targeting territories where the River Quwayq flowed to the northeast of Aleppo, 'taking all that was available from the people equating to 100,000 dinars'.[151] Baldwin's coalition force then established a blockade surrounding the city, with Baldwin encamped to the west, Joscelyn to the north, and the Muslim allies securing the northeastern and eastern approaches to Aleppo. Baldwin's forces then pursued a policy of encirclement combined with occasional direct assaults upon the fortifications.[152]

The decision to raid the surrounding area before encircling the walls was an extension of Baldwin's strategy over the previous four years, with the aim of further exacerbating food shortages in the city. Again, the chroniclers agree about the deprivation this strategy provoked among Aleppo's inhabitants. Ibn al-'Adim provided a fairly emotive account of the populace being forced to eat dogs, carrion and corpses, and the subsequent proliferation of disease, with ailing citizens being forced to defend the walls before collapsing into

THE NOTABLES AND FRONTIERS OF ALEPPO | 215

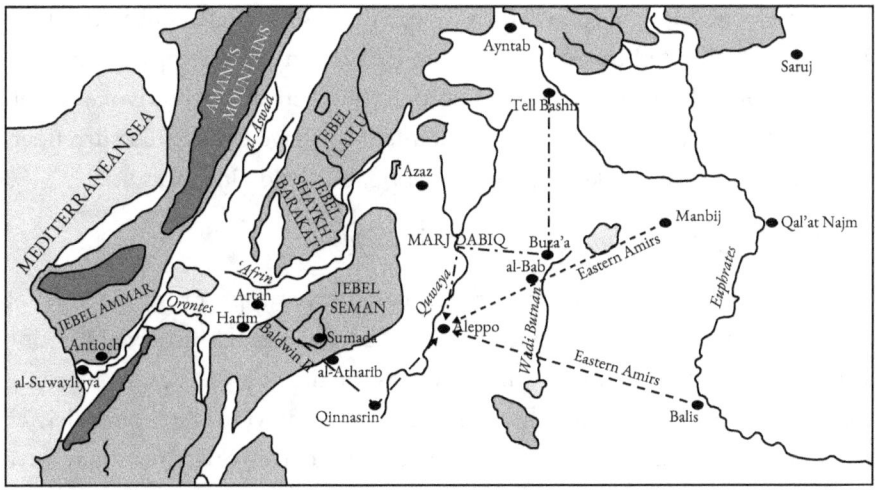

Figure 5.5 Approaches to Aleppo taken by Baldwin II's forces in 518/1124

their sick-beds once enemy assaults had been repulsed. While Ibn al-'Adim's account should be read in the knowledge that his great-grandfather led the delegations to the court of Aqsunqur al-Bursuqi, which resulted in the city being relieved and spared the potential humiliation of Frankish rule, other sources also described harsh conditions in Aleppo during the siege.[153]

Strong parallels can be drawn between Baldwin's plan of action and the template established by Balak b. Bahram when he captured Aleppo two years earlier in 517/1123. Aside from Saladin's conquest of Aleppo in 579/1183, Balak's siege was the only successful attempt to capture the city in the sixth/twelfth century. Ibn al-'Adim wrote that as Balak approached Aleppo his forces raided the surrounding areas which 'affected the planting for the harvest and … caused a great increase in prices'. Balak then besieged the city, during which his army 'shattered the gate of Antioch, and made a hole in the western gate of the Jews'. Aleppo surrendered to him on Monday at the beginning of Jumada I of the year 517/25 June 1123, with the citadel surrendering four days later on Friday, 4 Jumada I/29 June 1123. As Ibn al-'Adim gave the date of Thursday, 19 Safar 517/18 April 1123 for the battle at which Balak took Baldwin II captive, this indicates that Balak's siege of Aleppo lasted around two months.[154]

Although the time of year was vastly different, early summer for Balak, late autumn and winter for Baldwin II, the overall strategy of initially raiding the purlieus of Aleppo, followed by a siege of close encirclement with direct assaults, was adopted by both rulers. So, if Baldwin did attempt to replicate Balak's approach in 517/1123, and both armies were able to provoke conditions within Aleppo where the inhabitants must have considered surrender, why was Balak able to take control of Aleppo, but Baldwin II was not?

The Prospect of a Frankish Client Ruler in Aleppo

As discussed above, any prospective ruler had to win support from notables of the city to gain control of Aleppo. In 517/1123, Balak had a history of fighting against the Franks in *bilad al-sham* and was the nephew of Il-ghazi, meaning that he did not represent a radical departure from previous Artuqid rulers of Aleppo. Additionally, the man he forced out, his cousin Sulayman, may have lost some support in Aleppo when he surrendered the key town of al-Atharib to the Franks earlier that year.[155]

It seems highly unlikely that either the notables or the general populace would have been willing to accept a Frankish ruler. Although rulers of Aleppo had made alliances with the Franks in 502/1108–9 and 509/1115, and there is evidence of a regular diplomatic dialogue centred around peace treaties, tributary arrangements and *condominia* agreements, Claude Cahen detected a growing culture of hostility towards the Franks from the city's inhabitants during the 510s/1120s.[156] In 517/1123–4, the *qadi* of Aleppo, Abu al-Fadl b. al-Kashshab, directed with 'the agreement of the commanders of Aleppo' that all but two churches in Aleppo be closed and converted into mosques for Muslim prayer.[157] It seems probable that this was at least in part a reaction to continual raiding of *bilad halab* by Baldwin II and Joscelyn of Edessa, and the loss of al-Atharib at around the same time. Although the Anonymous Syriac Chronicle of 1234 intimated that this action was taken only after Joscelyn I of Edessa had destroyed mosques on the outskirts of Aleppo and the Christian inhabitants of the city subsequently refused to rebuild them.[158]

It is ironic that the policy Baldwin II pursued to weaken Aleppo to the point that it could be besieged effectively, increased anti-Frankish sentiments in the city to the extent that it would have been impossible for the inhabitants to accept a Frankish ruler. This perhaps suggests that early Frankish potentates had a set strategy for taking control of major settlements which differed from their Syrian, Turkish and Arab rivals. Baldwin II's attritional approach certainly fit the pattern of earlier successful Frankish attacks upon Antioch in 491/1098, Tripoli in 502/1109 and Tyre earlier in 518/1124. Yet this tactic of forced subjugation was unlikely to work at Aleppo, where the strength of the fortifications empowered notable families who had successfully navigated several generations of political upheaval.

Due to this uptick in anti-Frankish sentiment in Aleppo, and the need to provide some form of stability for the landowning urban elites, Asbridge is correct to seriously consider suggestions made in some of the sources that Baldwin considered placing a client ruler in charge of Aleppo. Although it is impossible to determine what Baldwin II's intentions would have been had he actually managed to capture Aleppo in 518/1124–5.

Yet the notion of a Muslim ruler governing territory on behalf of a Frankish ruler was largely without precedent in 518/1124–5.[159] This was in stark contrast to their Byzantine predecessors in *bilad al-sham*, who had been able to utilise diplomatic mechanisms of vassalage through the bestowal of honorific titles upon members of the Arab Mirdasid dynasty during the fifth/eleventh century. The most widely cited example of a Muslim 'vassal' of the Franks is the poet and historian Hamdan al-Atharibi (d. 542/1147–8), who, according to Ibn al-'Adim, was granted control of a small village near Ma'rrat Misrin by the Frankish lord of al-Atharib. However, Paul Cobb has questioned whether this land grant actually made Hamdan al-Atharibi a Frankish vassal.[160] There was also the example of the Seljuq *malik* Tekesh b. Alp Arslan, who arrived in *bilad al-sham* in 506/1112 and, according to Ibn al-Qalanisi, was treated with 'honour and respect' by Tancred of Antioch and he 'remained with him and a group of Turks who were with Tancred'.[161] Tekesh seems to have left Antioch at some point in the following seven years, as he reportedly moved on to Sidon and Egypt, before returning to northern Syria. Al-'Azimi claimed that after Frankish forces captured Qal'at al-Sinn in 512/1118–19 the *malik* Tekesh was reportedly given a guaranty of safety.[162]

In terms of the details of the proposed plan to install a client ruler in Aleppo in 518/1124–5, Ibn al-Athir only noted that Dubays b. Sadaqa offered to be an 'an obedient deputy' to Baldwin. Ibn al-'Adim provided more particulars in his chronicle of Aleppo, the *Zubdat al-halab min ta'rikh halab*, describing the 'basis of an alliance' between Dubays and 'the Franks', whereby

Aleppo would come under Dubays' control, with all financial assets and the attendant rural areas placed under Frankish rule.[163]

Given that these terms would have permanently stripped the Aleppan notables of lands that had been their main source of financial wealth and political power for generations, it is hardly surprising that they opposed Baldwin's attempt to capture the city. This inability or unwillingness to permit the Aleppan urban elites to retain their landed wealth differentiated Dubays and Baldwin from their Turkish rivals, who could offer a form of stability to this influential group of gatekeepers.

Ibn al-'Adim did slightly contradict this account in his biographical dictionary, the *Bughyat al-talab fi ta'rikh halab*, where he described a plan to instead elevate Sultan Shah b. Ridwan as amir of Aleppo.[164] This inconsistency can be cleared up by speculating that Dubays b. Sadaqa could have acted as Sultan Shah's *atabeg*, much like Il-ghazi had done for him initially, and Lu'lu' had for his brother Alp Arslan. Sultan Shah was sixteen or seventeen years old at the time of Baldwin II's siege, which would not have precluded the appointment of an *atabeg*.[165]

Regardless, it is far from clear that Dubays b. Sadaqa would have been viewed by the notables of Aleppo as an acceptable candidate to act as a client ruler. Dubays had seemingly harboured ambitions to rule Aleppo since his arrival in *bilad al-sham* in 515/1121–2.[166] Ibn al-'Adim wrote how Dubays b. Sadaqa offered Il-ghazi '100,000 dinars' in exchange for control of Aleppo during their campaign into Georgia that same year. Il-ghazi consented to this, while the Türkmen agreed to 'assist him until they captured Antioch'.[167] The agreement was never acted upon. Il-ghazi's defeat against the Georgians on this campaign and a subsequent rebellion against the Artuqid amir in Aleppo probably made it impossible to do so. However, as Dubays b. Sadaqa had a long-standing interest in controlling Aleppo, he could have been building support in the city in the years leading up to the Frankish siege operation in 518/1124–5.

Dubays b. Sadaqa made his first approach to the people of Aleppo just before the siege began in 518/1124–5. Ibn al-'Adim claimed that 'Dubays corresponded with representatives from the people of Aleppo, and he gave them all of his dinars, and he demanded that they surrender the city to him'. However, the *ra'is* of Aleppo Fada'il b. Sa'id b. Badi'a, found out about this and informed Timurtash b. Il-ghazi, who ordered that Dubays' supporters be 'captured' and 'tortured' after which some of them were hung and burnt, while others had property confiscated.[168]

On the one hand, this could indicate that Dubays b. Sadaqa had some measure of support in the city. On the other, many of his supporters were seemingly hunted down and punished or killed. Even if the *ra'is* and Timurtash failed to locate all of his supporters, these harsh punishments would likely have discouraged any overt support for Dubays b. Sadaqa once the siege began. It also appears as though Dubays b. Sadaqa was not even able to buy sufficient support within the city, and that he wasted some of his resources attempting to do so.

According to Ibn al-Athir, Dubays b. Sadaqa's confidence that he would be able to win the support of Aleppo's inhabitants was based upon the misguided impression that his status as a Shi'i Muslim held a special appeal for the populace. Ibn al-Athir reported that Dubays claimed 'the inhabitants are Shi'i. They lean towards me for sectarian reasons. When they see me, they will surrender the city to me.'[169] However, it is important to note that there are many different forms of Shi'ism.[170] Carole Hillenbrand has shed light on the Twelver Shi'i community of Aleppo in the late fifth/eleventh and early sixth/twelfth century, and the existence of the *mashhad al-dikka* in Aleppo, a Shi'i shrine to al-Muhassin b. Husayn, the grandson of 'Ali b. Abu Talib, and great-grandson of the Prophet Muhammad.

The presence of this Twelver Shi'i community, the recent occupation of the position of *qadi* by the Shi'i notable Abu al-Fadl b. al-Kashshab, in addition to the prominence of the Nizari Isma'ili Assassins in Aleppo during the reigns of Ridwan and Il-ghazi may all have contributed to Dubays b. Sadaqa's impression that his religious beliefs might earn him support from the inhabitants of the city. Nonetheless, his confidence evidently proved to be misplaced. Hillenbrand's research identified the presence of a subtle equilibrium in sixth/twelfth century Aleppo, where Sunni Turkish rulers actively sought acceptance and legitimisation of the Twelver Shi'i community. It was not until Nur al-Din's reign that the Twelver Shi'i's of Aleppo faced persecution from the ruler of the city. Consequently, it seems as though the followers of Shi'ism in Aleppo did not necessarily value the notion of a Shi'i ruler over other considerations, at least in the winter of 518/1124–5.

Ultimately, the notables of Aleppo elected to turn to the ruler of Mosul, Aqsunqur al-Bursuqi, a figure who they had rejected on two occasions and dismissed as 'someone from the east', rather than surrender the city to Dubays b. Sadaqa. Essentially, Dubays b. Sadaqa was of a similar profile to Aqsunqur al-Bursuqi. They were both 'someone from the east', with little personal or familial links to Aleppo or *bilad al-sham*. Although Dubays was of Arab rather than Turkish heritage, this distinction seemingly made little difference to the Aleppans. Similar to the prominent position occupied by the Arab Uqaylid ruler Muslim b. Quraysh in the Seljuq political sphere during the fifth/eleventh century, the decisions taken by the political elite in Aleppo in 518/1124–5 contradict the conceptualisation of a Syrian society divided between a Sunni Turkish ruling elite and a Shi'i Arab populace. Dubays b. Sadaqa also had a tempestuous relationship with the Abbasid Caliph al-Mustarshid, which may have counted against him.[171]

Ultimately, it is difficult to disentangle whether Dubays' reputation was damaged by his links to the Franks, or if Baldwin's attempt to capture Aleppo was impaired by Dubays' presence. The only certainty is that neither Baldwin, Dubays or the amirs from the eastern frontier had enough support among the notables or the general populace to gain control of Aleppo at this time, even when these groups were pushed to the edge of starvation and the city's territorial dominions had been steadily stripped away over the preceding three decades.

Conclusion: Aleppan Notables and the Threat of Frankish Rule

Ultimately, the failure of individuals within the coalition to garner enough support among the notables and inhabitants of the city is the reason why the siege of Aleppo in 518/1124–5 failed. Between 442 and 522/1050 and 1128, Aleppo had historically been incredibly difficult to capture by siege. With the exception of Balak b. Bahram in 517/1123, no besieging force managed to capture Aleppo without either attacking the city multiple times, or receiving support from inside the city. The siege led by Baldwin II in 518/1124–5 came at a time when Aleppo had been weakened by nearly two decades of attritional conflict, while the besieging armies provoked conditions of extreme deprivation within the city walls.

While this calls into question the appeal of the allies that Baldwin II managed to assemble, it also indicates that the Franks would likely never have been viewed as acceptable rulers for the notables of Aleppo. As Frankish rulers of Antioch were never able to maintain either a continuous siege of the settlement, or produce sustained attacks over many years, the capture of Aleppo was never a viable possibility. Despite this, the tactics Baldwin II deployed against Aleppo, namely, coercing the amirs surrounding the city to collaborate with the dominant potentate in the region using a blend of diplomacy and military force, provides important context for the tactics employed by Nur al-Din and Saladin during the later sixth/twelfth century.

Baldwin II's failed siege of Aleppo also raises doubts about the extent to which the Frankish polities of the Latin east were fully 'integrated' into the system of autonomous lordships in Syria during the early sixth/twelfth century. They were partly assimilated into the complicated patchwork of political factions, but not totally, and there remained barriers to their full integration.

Notes

1. IAD BH, VIII, 3852–3; IAD ZH, II, 244–5. An English translation of this extract was included in Appendix 1 of Taef K. El-Azhari, *Zengi and the Muslim Response to the Crusades* (London: Routledge, 2015), p. 154.
2. Ira Lapidus has discussed the meaning of term *al-aʿyan* in reference to the Mamluk period, while David Morray has outlined the influence wielded by the notables of Aleppo during the Ayyubid era. See Ira M. Lapidus, 'Muslim Urban Society in Mamluk Syria', in *The Islamic City: a Colloquium*, ed. Albert H. Hourani and Samuel M. Stern (Oxford: Cassirer, 1970), pp. 195–205; Ira M. Lapidus, *Muslim Cities in the Later Middle Ages* (Cambridge: Cambridge University Press, 1984), pp. 79–85, 116–42; Morray, *An Ayyubid Notable*, pp. 122–43. For an overview on the power wielded by urban non-elites in Syria prior to and after the onset of the Crusades, see Fukuzo Amabe, *Urban Autonomy in Medieval Islam* (Leiden: Brill, 2016), pp. 54–84; Mallett, *Popular Muslim Reactions*, pp. 31–143.
3. The line of historical thought dates back to the seminal work of Max Weber, see Max Weber, *The City*, trans. and ed. Don Martindale and Gertrud Neuwirth (London: Free Press, 1958), pp. 100, 119. See also Chamberlain, *Knowledge and Social Power*, pp. 4, 47–8; Boaz Shoshan, 'The "Politics and Notables" in Medieval Islam', *Asian and African Studies* 20 (1986): 179–215.
4. Andrew Peacock has demonstrated how similar periods of transition enabled instances of 'urban autonomy' among notables in seventh/thirteenth century

Anatolia, see Andrew C. S. Peacock, 'Urban Agency and the City Notables of Medieval Anatolia', *Medieval Worlds* 14 (2021): 22–34, 27–9.

5. For to these engagements, which occurred in 454/1062, 473/1081, 477/1084, 487/1094, 490/1097, 498/1104 and 513/1119, see al-'Azimi, p. 351; IATH, X, 114–15; SJ, XIII, 121–2, 300, 165–6; IAD ZH, I, 276–8, 287, II, 68–73, 111–12, 126, 150, 191.
6. For more detail on the *ahdath* and the position of *ra'is*, see Havemann, 'The Vizier and the Ra'is in Saljuq Syria', pp. 233–42; Abbés Zouache, *Armées et Combats en Syrie de 491/1098 à 569/1174 Analyse Comparée des Chroniques Médiévales Latines et Arabes* (Damascus: Presses de l'Ifpo, 2008), pp. 251–4 (section 2.4).
7. For further discussion on the Türkmen of Syria and the unsuitability of the region for their nomadic lifestyle, see Chapter 3.
8. For the negative impact this dynamic had upon Aleppo's diplomatic activities with the Franks in the early Crusading period, see Wilson, 'The Ransom of High-ranking Captives', pp. 30–3.
9. Abu'l Qasim b. Badi'a, then *ra'is* of Aleppo, fought off an assassination attempt whilst crossing the River Euphrates in 512/1118, see IAD ZH, II, 186–7. For the speech reportedly given by the *qadi* Abu'l Fadal b. al-Khashshab before the battle of the Field of Blood, see IAD ZH, II, 188–9; Hillenbrand, *Crusades*, pp. 108–9.
10. For more background on the notable families of Aleppo and Damascus during the sixth/twelfth and seventh/thirteenth centuries, see R. Stephen Humphreys, *From Saladin to the Mongols: the Ayyubids of Damascus 1193–1260* (New York: State University of New York Press, 1977), p. 25; Morray, *An Ayyubid Notable*, pp. 72, 122–43; James E. Lindsay, *Ibn 'Asakir and Early Islamic History* (Princeton, NJ: Darwin Press, 2001); Mourad and Lindsay, *Intensification and Reorientation of Sunni Jihad Ideology*, pp. 3–13, 47–51; Suleiman A. Mourad, *Ibn 'Asakir of Damascus: Champion of Sunni Islam in the Time of the Crusades* (Oxford: Oneworld, 2021).
11. For the Banu al-Khashshab, see Ibn Shaddad, *al-A'laq al-khatira*, I/I, pp. 35–6. For the Banu Abi Jarada, see IAD BH, IX, 3903.
12. Yaqut al-Hamawi and Ibn al-'Adim both refer to properties owned by Ibn al-'Adim's family, the Banu Abi Jarada, as *milk* or *amlak*. See Yaqut al-Hamawi, *Irshad al-udaba' fi ma'rifat al-adib*, 7 vols, ed. David S. Margoliouth (London: Luzac, 1923–31), VI, p. 26; IAD BH, VII, 3440. For more detail on this distinction between '*milk*' and *iqta'*, see Morray, *An Ayyubid Notable*, pp. 126–8.

13. See IAD, ZH, II, 173.
14. Morray, *An Ayyubid Notable*, pp. 126–9.
15. Morray, *An Ayyubid Notable*, p. 124.
16. This is discussed in more detail below in the section dealing with the frontiers of Aleppo.
17. Ian Wilson, 'By the Sword or by an Oath: Siege Warfare in the Latin East 1097–1131', in *A Military History of the Mediterranean Sea: Aspects of War, Diplomacy, and Military Elites*, ed. Georgios Theotokis and Aysel Yildiz (Leiden: Brill, 2018), pp. 235–53. See also the methodology outlined by Morton, which closely corresponds with Wilson's definition: Morton, *The Crusader States*, p. 7.
18. IQ, pp. 347–8; al-'Azimi, pp. 369–70, 377; IATH, X, 553–4, 649–51; IAD ZH, II, 240.
19. Tables with entries for all of these siege events, including references to the relevant primary sources, can be found in Appendices 3 and 4.
20. IQ, pp. 192, 194–5, 316; al-'Azimi, pp. 353–4, 367; SJ, XIII, 165–6, 169, 177; IAD ZH, II, 90–1, 95–6, 98–101, 177–8; ME, p. 154.
21. For more detail on the ways in which siege warfare was conducted during this period, see Hillenbrand, *Crusades*, pp. 523–40; John France, *Western Warfare in the Age of the Crusades 1000–1300* (Abingdon: Routledge, 1999), pp. 107–27; Zouache, *Armées et Combats en Syrie*; Nicolle, *Arms and Armour of the Crusading Period*, II, 220–40; Christie, *Muslims and Crusaders*, pp. 65–66; Tibble, *Crusader Armies*, pp. 155–207, 211–92. For the importance of undermining during the sixth/twelfth century, see Morton, *The Crusader States*, pp. 245–50. For a revisionist view on the impact of counterweight trebuchet technology upon military architecture, see Michael S. Fulton, *Artillery in the Era of the Crusades* (Leiden: Brill, 2018), pp. 39–149.
22. Arabic verbs are given in past tense, third-person, singular form. The medieval Arabic historians also used the terms 'to descend upon' (*nazala*), although this was usually mentioned in conjunction with one of the above terms when describing a siege, and 'take over or possession of' (*malaka*) when describing the occupation of settlement without a siege.
23. Using the Arabic nomenclature facilitates analysis of the entire period from 442 to 522/1050 to 1128, as most medieval Arab historians covered the entirety of this time frame.
24. Thackson defined the term 'cubit' (*arash/arsh* in Arabic) as 'the distance from the tip of the middle finger to the elbow' or between 1.5 and 2 feet. By this measurement Aleppo's walls at the start of this period would have been

somewhere between 37.5 and 50 feet or 11 and 15 metres high, according to Nasir-i Khusraw's account. See Nasir-i Khusraw, *Naser-e-Khosraw's Book of travels*, pp. 10, 119.

25. Gonnella, 'The Citadel of Aleppo', p. 169.
26. Nasser Rabbat, 'The Militarization of Taste in Medieval Bilad al-Sham', in *Muslim Military Architecture in Greater Syria: From the Coming of Islam to the Ottoman Period*, ed. Hugh Kennedy (Leiden: Brill, 2006), pp. 88–91; Yasser Tabbaa, *Constructions of Piety and Power in Medieval Aleppo* (Philadelphia: Pennsylvania State University Press, 2001), pp. 54–9; Peacock, *Empire*, p. 240; Bianquis, 'Pouvoirs arabes à Alep', p. 55.
27. IAD ZH, II, 172–4.
28. al-'Azimi, p. 370; IAD ZH, II, 199.
29. For more information on the *qal'at al-sharif* or citadel *al-sharif*, see Sauvaget, *Alep*, I, p. 103; Elisséeff, *Nur ad-Din*, I, p. 177; Gaube and Wirth, *Aleppo. Historische und geographische Beiträge*, p. 97; Jørgen S. Nielsen, 'Between Arab and Turk: Aleppo from the 11th till the 13th Centuries', in *Manzikert to Lepanto: the Byzantine World and the Turks 1071–1571*, ed. Anthony Bryer and Michael Ursinius (Amsterdam: A. M. Hakkert, 1991), pp. 323–40, 327–8.
30. Tevfik Buyukasik, 'A Survey of the Measurements of the Castles, Villages and Cities that are Situated in the Kingdom of the Just King Nur al-Din Abu al-Qasim Mahmud ibn Zangi ibn Aqsunqur in the year 564/1168–9, as described in MS Arabe 2281 (BN Paris) (Introduction, Translation and Arabic Text)', in *East and West in the Medieval Eastern Mediterranean II: Antioch from the Byzantine Reconquest Until the End of the Crusader Principality*, ed. Krijna N. Ciggaar and V. D. van Aalst (Leuven: Peeters, 2013), pp. 79–200; Elisséeff, *Nur ad-Din*, II, pp. 513–14, 710, 712.
31. Ibn Kathir, *al-Bidaya*, XII, 113; Sophie Berthier, 'La citadelle de Damas', in *Muslim Military Architecture in Greater Syria: From the Coming of Islam to the Ottoman Period*, ed. Hugh Kennedy (Leiden: Brill, 2006), pp. 151–64, 152–3.
32. Nicolle, *Crusader Warfare*, II, 233.
33. Smail, *The Crusades*, p. 120; France, *Western Warfare*, pp. 113–15.
34. There were a couple of exceptions, such as the nine-month siege of Antioch by the armies of the First Crusade between 490 and 491/1097 and 1098. For more on this siege, see Wilson, 'The "*asakir al-Sham*"', pp. 300–36.
35. IQ, pp. 154–6; al-'Azimi, pp. 345–6; IATH, X, 24; SJ XII, 414, 421, 435; IAD ZH, I, 297. See also Zakkar, *Emirate*, pp. 165–9.

36. IQ, pp. 181–3; al-ʿAzimi, pp. 181–2; SJ, XIII, 114–15; IAD ZH, II, 57, 62, 64; Zakkar, *Emirate*, pp. 191–4, 201–4; El-Azhari, *Saljuqs*, pp. 47–9; Köhler, *Alliances*, p. 11; Peacock, *Empire*, p. 64.
37. SJ, XIII, 120; IAD ZH, II, 56, 67; ME, pp. 143–4.
38. al-ʿAzimi, p. 351; IATH, X, 114–15; SJ, XIII, 121–2; IAD ZH, II, 68–73.
39. IQ, pp. 192, 194–5; al-ʿAzimi, pp. 353–4; SJ, XIII, 165–6, 169, 176–8; IAD ZH, II, 90–1, 95–6, 96–101. Zakkar, *Emirate*, pp. 212–19; El-Azhari, *Saljuqs*, pp. 62–5; Köhler, *Alliances*, p. 13; Peacock, *Empire*, pp. 65–6.
40. IQ, pp. 166–7, 174–5; al-ʿAzimi, p. 349; IATH, X, 99–100; SJ, XII, 486, XIII, 28.
41. IQ, pp. 174–5.
42. Most notably when Atsiz was defeated in battle in Egypt in 469/1076–7, Ibn al-Qalanisi wrote that: '[Atsiz] arrived in Damascus after this defeat and the population rejoiced at his misfortune and the verdict inflicted by the sword. It was hoped that this event would cause Atsiz's downfall and departure'. IQ, p. 181.
43. IQ, p. 332; al-ʿAzimi, p. 372; IATH, X, p. 611; IAD ZH, II, 211–13.
44. Frankish raiding strategy in the build-up to the battle of the Field of Blood in 513/1119 and Baldwin II of Jerusalem's siege of Aleppo in 518/1124–5 is discussed below in the section dealing with the frontiers of Aleppo.
45. For the influence that urban populations had upon siege warfare against major towns and cities, see Morton, *The Crusader States*, pp. 88–98.
46. For the prominent role that Mirdasid women, particularly al-Sayyida al-ʿAlawiyya, had upon Aleppan diplomatic interactions, see Bianquis and Shamma, 'Mirdas'; Beihammer, 'Muslim Rulers Visiting the Imperial City', pp. 168–70.
47. SJ, XII, 377–8.
48. IATH, X, 138–9.
49. IAD ZH, II, 86–7.
50. IAD ZH, II, 98–99.
51. Revolts by the inhabitants of Damascus against Fatimid governors between 453 and 463/1061 and 1071 are discussed briefly in Chapter 2.
52. Mallett, *Popular Muslim Reactions*, pp. 31–48; Köhler, *Alliances*, pp. 59–127. For general background on appeals for assistance, see Lapidus, *Muslim Cities in the Later Middle Ages*, pp. 44–85.
53. Cahen, *Syrie*, p. 269.
54. al-ʿAzimi, p. 351; IATH, X, 114–15; SJ, XIII, 121–2; IAD ZH, II, 67–73; MS, p. 615; ME, pp. 151–2.

55. For a contrary viewpoint on the importance of these later appeals, see Mallett, *Popular Muslim Reactions*, pp. 31–48.
56. IAD ZH, II, 177.
57. IAD ZH, II, 179.
58. IAD ZH, II, 179.
59. IAD ZH, II, 179–80.
60. IQ, pp. 316–17; al-'Azimi, pp. 368–9; IATH, X, 531–2; SJ, XIII, 378.
61. Cahen, *Syrie*, p. 269.
62. IQ, pp. 206–9; al-'Azimi, p. 355; IATH, X, 232–4; SJ, XIII, 226; IAD ZH, II, 117; MS, p. 640; Anonymous Syriac Chronicle, pt. 1, p. 88.
63. The importance placed on a family history of leadership in *bilad al-sham* is discussed in more detail below.
64. IAD ZH, II, 185. The situation in Aleppo at this time is discussed below on the section dealing with the frontiers of Aleppo. See also Asbridge, *Creation*, pp. 73–81; Asbridge, 'Field of Blood', pp. 309–16; Morton, *The Crusader States*, pp. 88–98.
65. IQ, pp. 337–8; IATH, X, 623–4.
66. IAD ZH, II, 241–2.
67. The weakened state of Aleppo during the early Crusading period is prominent in the work of Cahen, *Syrie*, pp. 205–95; Köhler, *Alliances*, pp. 59–127; Hillenbrand, 'Career of Najm al-Din Il-ghazi', pp. 250–92, 267–71; Asbridge, *Creation*, pp. 45–91; Asbridge, 'Field of Blood', pp. 301–16; Asbridge, 'Crusader Community at Antioch', pp. 305–25; Asbridge, 'How the Crusades Could Have Been Won', pp. 73–93; Morton, *The Crusader States*, pp. 88–98.
68. MS, p. 651.
69. M. F. Elshayyal, 'A Critical Edition of Volume II of *Ta'rikh al-duwal wa'l-muluk* by Muhammad b. 'Abd al-Rahim b. 'Ali Ibn al-Furat', unpublished PhD dissertation, University of Edinburgh, 1986, pp. 101–2.
70. IATH, X, 650.
71. Ibn al-Athir, *al-Ta'rikh al-bahir*, p. 19.
72. Baha' al-Din Ibn Shaddad, *al-Nawadir al-sultaniyya wa'l mahasin al-yusufiyya*, ed. Jamal El-Shayyal (Cairo: Al-Dar al-Misriya li'l Ta'lif wa'l Tarjama, 1964), p. 50.
73. IAD ZH, II, 179.
74. IAD ZH, II, 180–1.
75. Konrad Hirschler, '"He is a Child and this Land is a Borderland of Islam": Under-age Rule and the Quest for Political Stability in the Ayyubid Period', *al-Masaq* 19 (2007): 29–46.

76. Mallett argued that Aleppan appeals to Baghdad in the sixth/twelfth century were 'a last resort' because 'they generally detested interference in their affairs from Baghdad'. Mallett, *Popular Muslim Reactions*, p. 36.
77. IAD ZH, II, 202–3; MS, p. 640; Anonymous Syriac Chronicle, pt. 1, p. 96. There is some dispute between Ibn al-Azraq al-Fariqi and Ibn al-'Adim as to whether the marriage was consummated. Al-Fariqi asserted that it was not and that Il-ghazi never met the Lady Farkhanha, while Ibn al-'Adim claimed that they met in Aleppo when they were married. See al-Fariqi, *Ta'rikh al-Fariqi*, pp. 46, 156.
78. al-'Azimi, p. 373; al-Fariqi, *Ta'rikh al-Fariqi*, pp. 46, 156; IATH, X, 611; IAD ZH, II, 216–17.
79. According to an extract from Ibn Abi Tayyi''s non-extant chronicle, which is preserved in the *Ta'rikh al-duwal wa'l muluk* of Ibn al-Furat, it was a short marriage which ended when Zengi, supposedly in a drunken fury, divorcing Zumurrud, before ordering that she be raped, that her father Ridwan's tomb be removed from the city and that all family members and former slaves of Ridwan be killed and their wealth seized. Ibn al-'Adim and Ibn Wasil both provided briefer accounts of the short marriage and subsequent divorce. Elshayyal, 'A Critical Edition of Volume II of *Ta'rikh al-duwal wa'l-muluk*', pp. 32, 132; IAD ZH, II, 244; IAD BH, VIII, 3852–3; Muhammad b. Salim Ibn Wasil, *Mufarrij al-kurub fi akhbar bani Ayyub*, 5 vols, ed. by Jamal El-Shayyal (Cairo, 1953–77), I, p. 40. See also Carole Hillenbrand, '"Abominable Acts": the Career of Zengi', in *The Second Crusade: Scope and Consequences*, ed. Jonathan Phillips and Martin Hoch (Manchester: Manchester University Press, 2001), pp. 111–32, 115, 121.
80. IAD ZH, II, 126. Ibn al-'Adim only briefly referred to Sulayman's marriage to Mani'a in 479/1086–7, but also mentioned that she was the widow of Sharaf al-Dawla and the daughter of Mahmud.
81. Carole Hillenbrand, 'Women in the Seljuq Period', in *Women in Iran from the Rise of Islam to 1800*, ed. Guity Nashat and Lois Beck (Urbana: University of Illinois Press, 2003), pp. 103–20, 108–10; Eric Hanne, 'Women, Power, and the Eleventh and Twelfth Century Abbasid Court', *Hawwa* 3 (2005): 80–110, 87–97. For more on women in general during the Seljuq period, see Taef El-Azhari, 'The Role of Saljuqid Women in Medieval Syria', in *Egypt and Syria in the Fatimid, Ayyubid and Mamluk Eras*, 9 vols, ed. Urbain Vermeulen and Jo van Steenbergen (Leuven: Peeters, 2005), IV, pp. 111–26; Taef El-Azhari, *Queens, Eunuchs and Concubines in Islamic History, 661–1257* (Edinburgh:

Edinburgh University Press, 2019), pp. 285–348; Peacock, *Empire*, pp. 140–2, 178–81. For a general overview of marriage in the medieval Islamic world, see Jean-Michel Mouton and Dominique Sourdel, *Mariage et Séparation à Damas au Moyen Âge. Un Corpus de 62 Documents Juridiques Inédits entre 337/948 et 698/1299* (Paris: Académie des Inscriptions et Belles-Lettres, 2013), pp. 11–63; Yossef Rapoport, *Marriage, Money and Divorce in Medieval Islamic Society* (Cambridge: Cambridge University Press, 2005), pp. 12–30, 69–88; Hillenbrand, *Islam*, pp. 250–1.

82. IAD ZH, II, 223–4, 240.
83. IAD ZH, II, 178.
84. IAD ZH, II, 196.
85. IQ, p. 322; al-'Azimi, p. 370; SJ, XIII, 398.
86. IAD ZH, II, 230.
87. Occasionally, the term *bilad halab* or simply *bilad* is used to refer to the actual city of Aleppo, not the wider region. See, e.g., IQ, pp. 187, 194, 216, 221; SJ, XII, 232, 480, XIII, 248, 259; IAD ZH, I, 265, II, 90, 131.
88. IAD BH, I, 51–68. See also Morray, *An Ayyubid notable*, pp. 2–7.
89. For a more detailed discussion around conceptual representations of space in the medieval Arabic source material, see Antrim, *Routes and Realms*, pp. 1–8, 144; Antrim, 'Ibn 'Asakir's Representations', pp. 109–29; Antrim, 'Becoming Syrian', pp. 46–71.
90. Sauvaget, 'Halab'; Sauvaget, *Alep*, I, pp. 83–108; Elisséeff, *Nur ad-Din*, I, pp. 173–4. For a contrasting view on the supposed decline of Aleppo under the Mirdasid dynasty, see Bianquis, 'Pouvoirs arabes à Alep', pp. 53–5.
91. Zakkar, *Emirate*, pp. 154–5.
92. For more detail on the nuances of frontiers during the Middle Ages, see Burns, 'The Significance of the Frontier', pp. 307–30; Abulafia, 'Introduction: Seven Types of Ambiguity', pp. 1–34; Ellenblum, 'Were there Borders', pp. 105–19; Berend, 'Frontiers', pp. 148–71. For the northern Syrian frontier prior to mid fifth/eleventh century, see Eger, *The Islamic Byzantine Frontier*, pp. 1–101, 264–314.
93. Asbridge, *Creation*, pp. 45–91; Asbridge, 'Field of Blood', pp. 301–16; Asbridge, 'Crusader Community at Antioch', pp. 305–25; Asbridge, 'Jabal as-Summaq', pp. 142–52; Buck, *The Principality of Antioch*, pp. 1–20, 164–88; Buck, 'The Castle and Lordship of Harim', pp. 113–31; Denys Pringle, 'Castles and Frontiers in the Latin East', in *Norman Expansion: Connections Continuities and Contrasts*, ed. Keith Stringer and Andrew Jotischky (Farnham: Routledge, 2013), pp. 227–39; Cahen, *Syrie*, pp. 205–95; Köhler, *Alliances*, pp. 7–20,

59–73, 90–127; Burns, *Aleppo*, pp. 114–71; Ronnie Ellenblum, *Crusader Castles and Modern Histories* (Cambridge: Cambridge University Press, 2007); Ellenblum, *Frankish Rural Settlement*, p. 15.

94. Asbridge, *Creation*, pp. 45–91; Buck, *The Principality of Antioch*, pp. 34, 245. See also Morton, *The Crusader States*, pp. 211–17.
95. Asbridge, *Creation*, pp. 47–91; Asbridge, 'Field of Blood', pp. 301–16, 309–11; Buck, *The Principality of Antioch*, pp. 1–20; Buck, 'The Castle and Lordship of Harim', pp. 113–31.
96. Dussaud, *Topographie historique*, pp. 225–8; Cahen, *Syrie*, pp. 133–6; Deschamps, *Les châteaux*, III, pp. 59–61.
97. The importance of 'Azaz is discussed below in reference to the northern frontier of Aleppo.
98. The increased emphasis placed on Zardana in the sixth/twelfth century seems to have been occasioned by the arrival of the Franks. There is little or no reference in the source material to Zardana in the latter half of the fifth/eleventh century. This is similar to Harim, which, as Buck highlighted, aside from being the location of a skirmish during the Frankish siege of Antioch in 491/1098, was largely absent from the source material prior to the mid-520s/early 1130s. IAD ZH, II, 132; Buck, 'The Castle and Lordship of Harim', pp. 113–14
99. For a more detailed overview of Aleppan–Antiochene relations in the fifth/eleventh century, see Chapter 1. IQ, p. 199; al-'Azimi, p. 347; SJ, XII, 388–9; IAD ZH, II, 12–13.
100. IAD ZH, II, 131; RC, pp. 639–40; 672–3; RC trans., pp. 70–1, 112–13; AA, pp. 182–9.
101. IQ, pp. 239–40; IATH, X, 393–4; SJ, XIII, 300; IAD ZH, II, 150–2; RC, pp. 714–15; RC trans., pp. 171–2; AA, pp. 702–5; FC, pp. 484–8; FC trans., pp. 181–2.
102. IAD ZH, I, 295.
103. IQ, p. 273; al-'Azimi, pp. 364–5; IATH, X, 481; IAD ZH, II, 156–7; AA, pp. 818–23.
104. IAD ZH, II, 156–7.
105. IQ, p. 331; al-'Azimi, pp. 369–70, 372; IATH, X, 555, 610; SJ, XIII, 427; IAD ZH, II, 190–2, 210; WC, pp. 98–102; WC trans., pp. 145–52; Asbridge, 'Field of Blood', pp. 312–16.
106. WC, p. 109; WC trans., p. 162.
107. Cahen, *Syrie*, pp. 117–18, 139–40; Dussaud, *Topographie historique*, pp. 229, 240; Deschamps, *Les châteaux*, III, p. 66.

108. Eger, *The Islamic Byzantine Frontier*, pp. 87–9.
109. Ibn Shaddad, *al-A'laq al-khatira*, I/II, pp. 73, 93; Ibn Shaddad, *Description de La Syrie du Nord*, pp. 46, 50. For more detail on 'Azaz, see IAD BH, I, 267–8; Yaqut, *Mu'ajam al-Buldan*, IV, 118.
110. For more detail on the economic growth in the northern Syrian agricultural areas during the sixth/twelfth and seventh/thirteenth centuries, see Eddé and Sodini, 'Les Villages de Syrie du Nord', pp. 465–83.
111. IQ, p. 183; al-'Azimi, pp. 347, 350; SJ, XII, 461–2; IAD ZH, II, 13–14, 16; Attaleiates, *The History*, pp. 199–219.
112. al-'Azimi, p. 369; IAD ZH, II, 141, 152–3; ME, pp. 222–3.
113. IAD ZH, II, 185–6.
114. IQ, p. 335; al-'Azimi, p. 375; IATH, X, 628-9; IAD ZH, II, 187, 196, 216; FC, pp. 763-7; FC trans., pp. 277–9; MS, p. 640; ME, pp. 225-6, 234-6; Anonymous Syriac Chronicle, pt. 1, pp. 97–8. Ibn al-'Adim is the only source to mention the attempted siege of 'Azaz in 517/1124, which places significant doubt on whether or not it happened.
115. Augusto Palombini and Cinzia Tavaneri, 'On Their Way Home ... a Network Analysis of Medieval Caravanserai Distribution in the Syrian Region, according to a 1D Approach', in *CAA 2015: Proceedings of the 43rd Annual Conference on Computer Applications and Quantitative Methods in Archaeology*, ed. Stefano Campana et al. (Oxford: Archeopress, 2016), pp. 637–45.
116. Cahen, *Syrie*, pp. 155, 161–4; Dussaud, *Topographie historique*, pp. 154, 214.
117. David Kaniewski, Elise Van Campo, Etienne Paulissen, Harvey Weiss, Thierry Otto, Johan Bakker, Ingrid Rossignol and Karel Van Lerberghe, 'Medieval Coastal Syrian Vegetation Patterns in the Principality of Antioch', *The Holocene* 21 (2010): 251–62.
118. Cahen, *Syrie*, pp. 158, 161–5; Dussaud, *Topographie historique*, pp. 170, 178–94; Deschamps, *Les châteaux*, III, pp. 63–4, 87–8 135–8; Burns, *Monuments of Syria*, pp. 59–60; Philippe Dangles, 'Afamiya. Qal'at al-Mudiq, Die Mittelalterliche Wiederbefestigung der Antiken Zitadelle von Apamea am Ende des 12. bis Mitte des 13. Jahrhunderts', in *Burgen und Städte der Kreuzzugszeit*, ed. Mathias Piana (Petersberg: Imhof, 2008), pp. 221–33.
119. Cahen, *Syrie*, p. 162; Dussaud, *Topographie historique*, pp. 173, 176; Deschamps, *Les châteaux*, III, pp. 63, 84; Burns, *Monuments of Syria*, pp. 71–2; Jean-Pascal Fourdrin, 'La fortification de la seigneurie épiscopale latine d'El Bara dans le patriarcat d'Antioche (1098–1148)', in *Pèlerinages et Croisades*, ed. Léon Pressouyre (Paris: Éditions du CTHS, 1995), pp. 351–406.

120. Cahen, *Syrie*, pp. 162–3; Dussaud, *Topographie historique*, pp. 179, 181, 187–8; Deschamps, *Les châteaux*, III, p. 59; Burns, *Monuments of Syria*, pp. 282–3; Christina Tonghini and Nadia Montevecchi, 'The Castle of Shayzar: the Fortification of the Access System', in *Muslim Military Architecture in Greater Syria: From the Coming of Islam to the Ottoman Period*, ed. Hugh Kennedy (Leiden: Brill, 2006), pp. 201–24; Paul Cobb, *Usama Ibn Munqidh: Warrior-Poet of the Age of the Crusades* (London: Oneworld, 2005), pp. 1–5.
121. Cahen, *Syrie*, pp. 155, 157–8, 161; Dussaud, *Topographie historique*, pp. 188–90; Deschamps, *Les châteaux*, III, pp. 60, 63; Burns, *Monuments of Syria*, p. 194.
122. Asbridge, 'Jabal as-Summāq', pp. 142–52; Asbridge, *Creation*, pp. 42–91; Buck, *The Principality of Antioch*, pp. 1–20.
123. IQ, p. 222; al-ʿAzimi, p. 360; IATH, X, 278; SJ, XIII, 258–60; IAD ZH, II, 142–3; al-Nuwayri, *Nihayat al-arab*, XXVIII, pp. 164–5; GF, pp. 29, 35; RC, pp. 674, 679; RC trans., pp. 114–15, 121–2; AA, pp. 368–71; FC, pp. 266–8; FC trans., pp. 112–13.
124. IAD ZH, II, 148–9.
125. Asbridge, *Creation*, p. 59; Cahen, *Syrie*, p. 242.
126. IQ, pp. 270–3, 278–83; al-ʿAzimi, pp. 365, 367; Usama b. Munqidh, *Kitab al-Iʿtibar*, pp. 73–7; IATH, X, 485–8, 509–11; SJ, XIII, 328, 332–3, 355–6; IAD ZH, II, 154–6, 158–61, 174–7; ME, p. 207.
127. IQ, pp. 242–3, 335; al-ʿAzimi, p. 375; IATH, X, 408–10, 628–9; SJ, XIII, 305; IAD ZH, II, 151–2, 231; FC, p. 554; FC trans., p. 202.
128. IQ, p. 333; al-ʿAzimi, p. 373; IAD ZH, II, 209, 212–13; FC, pp. 763–7; FC trans., pp. 278–9.
129. Cahen, *Syrie*, pp. 117, 155–6; Dussaud, *Topographie historique*, p. 244; Deschamps, *Les châteaux*, III, p. 95; Burns, *Monuments of Syria*, pp. 202–3.
130. IQ, p. 183; IATH, X, 114–15, 510; SJ, XIII, 114; IAD ZH, II, 62.
131. IQ, p. 323; IATH, X, 553, 587; IAD ZH, II, 175, 198, 209, 214.
132. al-ʿAzimi, p. 349; IATH, X, 100, 148–50; SJ, XIII, 83; IAD ZH, II, 46.
133. IATH, X, 460, 482.
134. al-ʿAzimi, p. 374; IATH, X, 619; IAD ZH, II, 218–19; ME, pp. 231–2.
135. FC, pp. 721–7; FC, trans., pp. 262–4.
136. al-ʿAzimi, p. 354; IAD ZH, II, 101.
137. IATH, X, 369.
138. For more on the Uqaylid dynasty at Qalʿat Jaʿbar and their role in northern Syrian politics in the sixth/twelfth century, see Heidemann, *Die Renaissance*

der Städte, pp. 260–84; Morton and France, 'Arab Muslim Reactions', XV, pp. 20–3.
139. IATH, X, 460.
140. IAD ZH, II, 200–3.
141. IAD ZH, II, 149.
142. al-'Azimi, p. 372; IAD ZH, II, 209.
143. Asbridge, *Creation*, pp. 47–81; Asbridge, 'Field of Blood', pp. 301–16; Nicholas Morton, *The Field of Blood: the Battle for Aleppo and the Remaking of the Medieval Middle East* (New York: Basic Books, 2018), pp. 49–163.
144. IQ, p. 332; al-'Azimi, p. 372; IATH, X, 614; SJ, XIII, 427–8; IAD ZH, II, 210–12; FC, pp. 658–61; FC trans., pp. 239–40.
145. IAD ZH, II, 221.
146. Usama b. Munqidh, *Lubab al-Adab*, pp. 132–4; IAD ZH, II, 222; FC, pp. 749–51; FC trans., pp. 272–3; WT, I, 603–6; WT, trans., II, 21–3; MS, p. 643; ME, pp. 232–3.
147. Asbridge, 'How the Crusades Could Have Been Won', pp. 73–93. See also Morton, *Field of Blood*, pp. 193–9.
148. Asbridge has discussed the military activity of Baldwin II in northern Syria elsewhere, see Asbridge, *Creation*, pp. 81–9.
149. Asbridge, 'How the Crusades Could Have Been Won', pp. 73–93.
150. Dubays b. Sadaqa, the lord of Hilla, Amir Malik b. Salim lord of Qal'at Ja'bar, 'Isa b. Salim b. Malik. Yaghi Siyan 'Abd al-Jabbar b. Artuq, lord of Balis, Sultan Shah b. Ridwan are all mentioned by Ibn al-'Adim, see IAD ZH, II, 222–4. Tughrul Arslan b. Qilij Arslan, lord of Melitene, is only included in the account of Matthew of Edessa, see ME, pp. 233–4. See also MS, p. 640; Anonymous Syriac Chronicle, pt. 1, p. 96.
151. IAD ZH, II, 223–4.
152. IAD, ZH, II, 224. Ibn al-Qalanisi stated that the Franks 'set about fighting the inhabitants and besieging the city', while Ibn al-Athir noted that they besieged the city, and 'kept up fierce attacks'. IQ, pp. 337–8; IATH, X, 623–4.
153. Ibn al-Qalanisi wrote that: 'the siege continued until supplies in (Aleppo) became deficient and its people were on the brink of destruction'; Ibn al-Athir noted that: 'spirits (in the city) were weakened and they feared their situation'; and Matthew of Edessa stated that the inhabitants were 'put in dire straits for many days through famine and continual assaults'. IQ, pp. 337–8; IATH, X, 623–4; WT, I, 603; WT trans., II, 21–3; ME, p. 234.
154. IQ, p. 332; al-'Azimi, p. 372; IATH, X, 611; IAD, ZH, 211–13.

155. IQ, p. 331; al-'Azimi, p. 372; IATH, X, 610; SJ, XIII, 427; IAD, ZH, II, 210.
156. Cahen, *Syrie*, pp. 297–8. For an overview of these diplomatic interactions, see Köhler, *Alliances*, pp. 59–126, 312–20; Asbridge, *Creation*, pp. 47–62, 65–7, 69–91; Asbridge, 'Crusader Community at Antioch', pp. 305–25; Wilson, 'The Ransom of High-ranking Captives', pp. 28–34.
157. al-'Azimi, p. 373; IAD, ZH, 214–15.
158. Anonymous Syriac Chronicle, pt. 1, p. 94.
159. Michael Köhler has asserted that the First Crusade led to development of 'Muslim lordships under Frankish suzeranity' at Maraqiyya, Tripoli and Beirut, see Köhler, *Alliances*, p. 55.
160. IAD BH, VI, 2926–32. For more discussion on the curious case of Hamdan b. 'Abd al-Rahim al-Atharibi, see Cahen, *Syrie*, pp. 41–2, 343–4; Cobb, *Race for Paradise*, pp. 271–5; Cobb, 'Hamdan al-Atharibi's History of the Franks', pp. 3–9.
161. IQ, p. 292. The term *malik* is usually only applied members of the Seljuq aristocracy in the Syrian regional Arabic historiographic tradition. However, some caution is need as Ibn al-Athir claimed that Tekesh b. Alp Arslan was killed by the Sultan Berkyaruq in Rabi'I 487/21 March–19 April 1094. IQ, p. 292; IATH, X, 239.
162. al-'Azimi, p. 369; Köhler, *Alliances*, p. 70. Ibn al-'Adim referred to both the Mirdasid ruler of Aleppo Mahmud b. Nasr and Imad al-Din Zangi capturing 'Qa'lat al-Sinn' on 9 of Rabi' II 466/12 December 1073 and in the middle of Rajab 524/late June 1130, respectively, indicating that it was situated in northern Syria. IAD ZH, II, 42; IAD BH, 3847. Thierry Bianquis also stated that Qa'lat al-Sinn was located close to 'Azaz, see Thierry Bianquis, 'Wathab b. Sabik al-Numayri', in *Encyclopaedia of Islam*, 2nd edn, ed. Peri Bearman et al. (2012), available at Brill online, last accessed 28 July 2019.
163. IATH, X, 623; IAD ZH, II, 222–3.
164. IAD BH, IV, 1963–74.
165. For more details on the age at which a child ruler could begin to rule in their own right during the Ayyubid era, see Hirschler, '"He is a Child"', pp. 29–46.
166. For more on Dubays b. Sadaqa's career, see George Makdisi, 'Notes on Hilla and the Mazyadids in Medieval Islam', *Journal of the American Oriental Society* 74 (1954): 249–62; Abbés Zouache, 'Dubays b. Sadaqa (m. 529/1135), aventurier de légende. Histoire et fiction dans l'historiographie arabe médiévale (VI/XIIe–VII/XIIIe siècles)', *Bulletin d'études orientales* 58 (2008): 87–130.

167. IAD ZH, II, 200. The use of the common formulaic qualifier of 'it is said' by Ibn al-'Adim suggests that he was less confident in the veracity of this information, so it should be read with some circumspection.
168. IAD ZH, II, 221–2.
169. IATH, X, 623.
170. For a succinct overview of the various doctrinal interpretation of Shi'ism, see Hillenbrand, *Islam*, pp. 145–62.
171. In 514/1120–1, the Caliph al-Mustarshid asked Il-ghazi to dismiss Dubays b. Sadaqa from his service, see IATH, X, 568; SJ, VIII, 408. Carole Hillenbrand described Dubays b. Sadaqa as 'a thorn in the side of the Caliphs', see Hillenbrand, 'Career of Najm al-Din Il-ghazi', p. 289.

Conclusion: Situating the Crusades in Syrian History

The Crusades in the east and the protracted conflict they provoked continue to be popular subjects in public, political and academic discourse, seemingly retaining a deep significance in the western and Islamic worlds. Obvious parallels have been drawn between the notion of a religiously motivated conflict between Christianity and Islam in *bilad al-sham* during the Middle Ages and developments in the region over the past eighty years. Despite the resonance associated with these struggles, there remains a divide between Crusade historians and specialists of Middle Eastern history regarding the actual significance of Frankish entanglements in the eastern Mediterranean.

This book set out to provide a more nuanced understanding of the political world of *bilad al-sham* before and after the advent of the Crusades. In doing so, it hoped to reposition the First Crusade and the formation of the Latin east within the wider context of Syrian history. In terms of the pre-Crusading period, a new chronology has been outlined for the development the system of autonomous lordships in Syria, with 452–4/1060–2 identified as the point at which Fatimid and Byzantine influence in *bilad al-sham* underwent significant decline. Similarly, a new model for understanding the political dynasties of this period has been proposed, one which cuts across wider Byzantine, Fatimid and Seljuq polities.

There has also been a reassessment of current historical thinking surrounding the extent of Seljuq power in Syria during the late fifth/eleventh and early sixth/twelfth centuries. Two related features of Seljuq governance in Syria, namely, persistent issues surrounding military campaigns into *bilad al-sham* and the autonomy wielded by the amirs, hindered Seljuq attempts to retain and expand their influence in the region throughout 463–522/1071–1128. The notion that Seljuq potentates or nomadic Türkmen groups had a uniquely disruptive impact upon the political world of *bilad al-sham* has also been called into question.

Perhaps the most important findings relate to the nature and significance of the Crusading conflicts in the east. This may seem like a bold claim, as this book covers only some twenty-eight years of the near two hundred-year history of the Crusades in the Levant. However, conclusions pertaining to the early sixth/twelfth century underpin much of the research on the later Crusading periods, in addition to colouring wider definitions and judgements relating to Frankish activity in *bilad al-sham*.

Concerning the nature of the early Frankish 'states', it is inaccurate to say that these western European polities were swiftly 'assimilated' or 'integrated' into the patchwork of minor lordships present in *bilad al-sham* at the end of the fifth/eleventh century. Instead, the arrival of the Franks provoked a distinct and discernible military reaction from the Syrian political elite, beginning with the 'armies of *al-sham*' that confronted the First Crusaders outside Antioch in the summer of 491/1098. During the first three decades of the sixth/twelfth century, the Franks were not just another faction in *bilad al-sham*, but a distinct one, who became the target, rather than the beneficiaries, of most military alliances.

In relation to the significance of the formation of the Latin east, this book has two main seemingly contradictory conclusions. The first relates to underlying political dynamics in northern *bilad al-sham*. The establishment of Frankish potentates at Antioch and Edessa during the First Crusade largely reset political dynamics in the region from those that had existed prior to the fall of Byzantine Antioch in 477/1084. There are obvious similarities, with the Franks inhabiting former Byzantine territories, an 'autonomous lordship' at Aleppo, and intermittent attempts by the Great Seljuq Sultanate and the Fatimid Caliphate to assert their authority. This would indicate that whilst trying to explain the success of the First Crusade and early Frankish settlement, historians have perhaps placed too much importance on the polities the western Europeans established.

However, indications that the Franks were viewed as a distinct faction supports the notion that the First Crusade in the Levant occasioned a unique form of conflict in the region. Although this book has largely failed to discuss religious motivations relating to individuals and political groups, it remains possible that this distinction was drawn along ethno-cultural or devotional divides. This would support the interpretation of the Crusading conflict as a religiously based struggle over the Levant during the early sixth/twelfth century, indicating that the significance placed on the conflict in medieval history, Mediterranean history and global history is in some way justified.

Future research on this subject could place more emphasis on the views of eastern Christian and Jewish communities in the eastern Mediterranean during this tempestuous period of Syrian history. This would provide a more holistic 'Islamicate' perspective, rather than the more limited focus on elite 'Islamic' protagonists who form the focal point of this study.

Ultimately, this book sets out to refine our understanding of the political world of *bilad al-sham* encountered by the early Frankish Crusaders and settlers, thereby providing a more accurate gauge of the impact of western European incursions upon the region. In doing so, it has interrogated the current historiographical consensus on three interlocking fronts: the region's underlying political dynamics prior to the Latins' arrival; the political and military reactions to the establishment of Crusader polities; and the initial perceptions of the Franks by northern Syria's established ruling elite.

Throughout, it has been maintained that in order to better understand the nature and significance of the Crusades and the formation of the Latin east, it is first necessary to properly appreciate their place within the history of *bilad al-sham*.

Appendix I: Chronology of Events

441/1049–50: Fatimid army unsuccessfully besieged Aleppo.
444/1052–3: Mirdasid ruler Thimal b. Salih surrendered Aleppo to al-Mustansir.
447/1055–6: Fatimid occupation of Aleppo.
452/1060: Fatimid defeat at battle of al-Funaydiq.
454/1062: Thimal b. Salih died and provoked Mirdasid succession crisis.
457/1065: End of Mirdasid succession crisis.
461/1068–9: Romanus Diogenes IV's campaign into northern Syria.
463/1071: Battle of Manzikert. Alp Arslan's siege of Aleppo, which forced the Mirdasids into Seljuq allegiance. Atsiz captured Ramla, Jerusalem and most of Palestine.
468/1075–6: Atsiz captured Damascus.
471/1078–9: Failed siege of Damascus by Fatimid commander Nasr al-Dawla al-Juyushi, Tutush b. Alp Arslan took control of Damascus.
472/1080: Aleppo fell under control of the Uqaylid ruler Muslim b. Quraysh Sharaf al-Dawla.
477/1084: Sulayman b. Qutlumush captured Antioch.
478/1085: Muslim b. Quraysh Sharaf al-Dawla killed during battle against Sulayman b. Qutlumush.
479/1086: Tutush killed Sulayman b. Qutlamush in battle. Malik Shah took control of Aleppo, Edessa and Antioch, and appointed Aqsunqur, Buzan and Yaghi Siyan as governors of these settlements.
487/1095: Death of Aqsunqur and Buzan in battle against Tutush. Death of Tutush in battle against his nephew Berkyaruq at Isfahan. Ridwan and Duqaq took control of Aleppo and Damascus, respectively.

APPENDIX I | 239

491/1098: The First Crusaders defeated the 'armies of *al-sham*' and captured Antioch. The Fatimids recaptured Jerusalem.

492/1099: The First Crusaders captured Jerusalem and defeated the Fatimids at the first battle of Ascalon.

505/1111: First campaign sent into *bilad al-sham* by Sultan Muhammad.

507/1113: Death of Ridwan b. Tutush.

509/1115: Second campaign sent into *bilad al-sham* by Sultan Muhammad.

512/1118: Najm al-Din Il-ghazi took control of Aleppo.

513/1119: Antiochene defeat against Aleppan forces at the battle of the Field of Blood.

516/1122: Death of Najm al-Din Il-ghazi.

518/1124–5: Baldwin II's failed siege of Aleppo.

518/1125: Aqsunqur al-Bursuqi took control of Aleppo.

519/1126: Assassination of Aqsunqur al-Bursuqi in Mosul.

522/1128: Zangi took control of Aleppo. The death of Tughtegin.

Appendix II: Regnal Dates in *Bilad al-sham*[1]

Major Dynasties

The Abbasid Caliphate: the Caliphs

422–67/1031–75: ʿAbd Allah b. al-Qadir al-Qaʾim.
467–87/1075–94: ʿAbd Allah b. Muhammad al-Muqtadi.
487–512/1094–1118: Ahmad b. al-Muqtadi al-Mustazhir.
512–29/1118–35: al-Fadl b. al-Mustazhir al-Mustarshid.

The Great Seljuq Sultanate

431–55/1040–63: Tughrul (I) Beg, Abu Talib Muhammad b. Mikaʾil b. Seljuq.
431–52/1040–60: Chagri Beg Dawud b. Mikaʾil b. Seljuq, ruler in Khurasan.
455–65/1063–73: ʿAdud al-Dawla Abu Shuja Muahammed b. Davud Chagri Beg Alp Arslan.
465–85/1073–92: Malik Shah I b. Alp Arslan, Jalal al-Dawla Muʿizz al-Din Abu ʾl-Fath.
485–7/1092–4: Mahmud I b. Malik Shah, Nasir al-Dunya wa ʾl-Din.
487–98/1094–1105: Berkyaruk b. Malik Shah, Abu ʾl-Muzaffar Rukn al-Dunya wa ʾl-Din.
498–511/1105–18: Muhammad I Tapar b. Malik Shah, Abu Shuja Ghiyath al-Dunya wa ʾl-Din.
511–52/1118–57: Ahmad Sanjar b. Malik Shah, Aba Shujaʾ Ghiyath al-Dunya wa ʾl-Din.

Sultans in Iraq and Western Persia

511–26/1118–32: Mahmud II b. Muhammad I, Abu 'l-Qasim Mughith al-Dunya wa 'l-Din Jalal al-Dawla.

The Fatimid Caliphate: the Caliphs

427–87/1036–94: Ma'add b. al-Zahir, Abu Tamim al-Mustansir.
487–95/1094–1101: Ahmad b. al-Mustansir, Abu 'l-Qasim al-Musta'li.
495–524/1101–30: al-Mansur b. al-Musta'li, Abu 'Ali al-Amir.

The Fatimid Viziers (with Political Authority)

467–87/1074–94: Abu l-Najm Badr al-Jamali al-Mustansiri.
487–515/1094–1121: al-Afdal b. Badr al-Jamali.

Rulers of Aleppo, Damascus and Mosul

Aleppo

433–49/1042–57: Thimal b. Salih, Abu 'Ulwan Mu'izz al-Dawla (*first reign*).
449–52/1057–60: Fatimid occupation of Aleppo by Ibn Mulhim.
452–3/1060–1: Mahmud b. Nasr II, Rashid al-Dawla (*first reign*).
453–4/1061–2: Thimal b. Salih, Abu 'Ulwan Mu'izz al-Dawla (*second reign*).
454–7/1062–5: 'Atiyya b. Salih, Abu Dhu'aba.
457–68/1065–76: Mahmud b. Nasr II, Rashid al-Dawla (*second reign*).
468/1075–6: Nasr b. Mahmud, Abu 'l-Muzaffar Jalal al-Dawla.
468–72/1076–80: Sabiq b. Mahmud, Abu 'l-Fada'il.
472–80/1080–7: Muslim b. Quraysh, Abu 'l-Makarim Sharaf al-Dawla.
480–7/1087–95: Qasim al-Dawla Aqsunqur.
487/1095: Tutush b. Alp Arslan, Abu Sa'id Taj al-Dawla.
488–507/1095–1104: Ridwan b. Tutush, Fakhr al-Mulk.
507/1113: Alp Arslan al-Akhras b. Ridwan.
  – *Atabeg*: Lu'lu': 507–8/1113–14.
508–17/1114–23: Sultan Shah b. Ridwan.
  – First *atabeg*: Lu'lu': 508–10/1114–16.
  – Second *atabeg*: Il-ghazi b. Artuq, Najm al-Din: 512–16/1117–22.

516–17/1122–3: Sulayman b. ʿAbd al-Jabbar b. Artuq, Badr al-Din.
517–18/1123–4: Balak b. Bahram b. Artuq, Nur al-Dawla.
518–21/1125–7: Aqsunqur al-Bursuqi.
521–41/1128–46: Zangi b. Qasim al-Dawla Aqsunqur, ʿImad al-Din.

Damascus

463–71/1070–8: Atsiz b. Uwaq al-Khwarizmi.
471–88/1078–94: Tutush I b. Alp Arslan, Abu Saʾid Taj al-Dawla.
488–97/1095–1104: Duqaq b. Tutush, Abu Nasr Sham al-Muluk.
 – *Atabeg*: Tughtegin, Zahir al-Din Abu Mansur.
497/1104: Tutush II b. Duqaq.
 – *Atabeg*: Tughtegin, Zahir al-Din Abu Mansur.
497–522/1104–28: Tughtegin, Zahir al-Din Abu Mansur.
522–6/1128–32: Buri b. Tughtegin, Abu Saʾid Taj al-Muluk.

Mosul

442–3/1050–2: Baraka b. al-Muqallad, Abu Kamil Zaʾim al-Dawla.
443–53/1052–61: Quraysh b. Abi ʾl-Fafl Badran, Abu ʾl-Maʾali ʿAlam al-Din.
453–78/1061–85: Muslim b. Quraysh, Abu ʾl-Makarim Sharaf al-Dawla.
478–86/1085–93: Ibrahim b. Quraysh, Abu Muslim.
486–9/1093–96: ʿAli b. Muslim.
489–95/1096–1101: Abu Saʾid Kiwam al-Dawla Kerbogha.
495–500/1101–6: Jokermesh.
500/1106: Qilij Arslan I.
500–2/1106–8: Jawli Saqoa.
502–7/1108–13: Mawdud b. al-Tuntakin.
508–9/1114–15: Aqsunqur al-Bursuqi.
509–15/1115–21: Jayush Beg.
515–20/1121–6: Aqsunqur al-Bursuqi.
520–1/1126–7: ʿIzz al-Din Masud b. Aqsunqur.
521–41/1127–46: Zangi b. Qasim al-Dawla Aqsunqur, ʿImad al-Din.

Note

1. Made with reference to Clifford E. Bosworth, *The New Islamic Dynasties: a Chronological and Genealogical Manual* (Edinburgh: Edinburgh University Press, 1996), pp. 63–7, 91–2, 185–9, 194–6; El-Azhari, *Saljuqs*, pp. 357–69; Peacock, *Empire*, p. 326; Brett, *Empire*, pp. 305–7; Hillenbrand, *A Muslim Principality*, pp. 217–20.

Appendix III: Aleppo under Siege

Year of siege	Participants	Length of siege
439/1047–8[1]	Nasir al-Dawla b. Hamdan (Fatimid governor of Damascus) and Thimal b. Salih (Mirdasid).	Not mentioned.
441/1049–50[2]	Al-Mustansir's deputy Amir Rifq against the Mirdasids.	Not mentioned.
452/1060–1[3]	Mahmud b. Nasr against Ibn Mulhim.	Not mentioned.
455/1063[4]	Mahmud besieged his uncle 'Atiyya in Aleppo.	al-'Azimi gave date of Sha'ban 455/30 June–7 August 1063 for start of siege.
456/1063–4[5]	Mahmud besieged his uncle 'Atiyya in Aleppo a second time.	Date of Jumada II 456/21 April–20 May 1064 mentioned by Sibt b. al-Jawzi for start of siege.
457/1065 or 458/1065–6[6]	Mahmud with Ibn Khan's assistance besieged his uncle 'Atiyya in Aleppo a third time.	Ibn al-'Adim: 102 days.
463/1070–1[7]	Seljuq Sultan Alp Arslan besieged Mahmud.	Ibn al-Qalanisi: Tuesday 17 Jumada II–23 Rajab 463/22 March–26 April 1071.

Culmination of siege
Unsuccessful. Nasir al-Dawla withdrew from Aleppo after the battle outside the gates.
Unsuccessful. Fatimid force defeated in battle and commanders taken to Aleppo in captivity, where Rifq died.
Unsuccessful. Mahmud's mother opened the city for him through the *ahdath*, but the citadel did not fall and he had to withdraw.
Unsuccessful. Mahmud withdrew.
Unsuccessful. Mahmud forced to withdraw when defeated by Ibn Khan.
Successful. Mahmud captured the city of Aleppo and 'Atiyya surrendered the citadel in exchange for other settlements. Sibt b. al-Jawzi claimed that 'Atiyya surrendered 'due to rising costs caused by the harvest'.
Unsuccessful. Mahmud made a settlement with the sultan.

Year of siege	Participants	Length of siege
467/1074–5[8]	Türkmen besieged Sabiq b. Mahmud in Aleppo.	No date given.
470/1077–8[9]	Tutush besieged Sabiq b. Mahmud in Aleppo, possibly on two separate occasions.	No start date, end-date of Dhu 'l-Qa'da 470/16 May–14 June 1078.
471/1078–9[10]	Tutush besieged Sabiq b. in Aleppo a second or third time.	Sibt b. al-Jawzi: one month. Ibn al-'Adim: three months and twenty days.
472/1079–80 or 473/1080–1[11]	Sharaf al-Dawla besieged Sabiq b. Mahmud in Aleppo.	al-'Azimi: siege of citadel took seven months. Ibn al-'Adim: siege of citadel took four months from Dhu 'l-Hijja-Rabi'I 473/September 19–13 May 1081.
478/1085–6[12]	Sulayman b. Qutlumush besieged al-Sharif Abu 'Ala al-Hatiti al-Hashimi in Aleppo.	4 Rabi' I–5 Rabi'II 478/30 June 1085–2 August 1085.
479/1086–7[13]	Sulayman b. Qutlumush besieged Aleppo a second time.	Not mentioned.
479/1086–7[14]	Tutush besieged Aleppo, then Malik Shah arrived, causing Tutush to withdraw and the city and citadel surrendered to the sultan.	Not mentioned.
485/1092–3, 487/1094–5[15]	Tutush took possession of Aleppo.	He entered the city in Shawwal 486/25 October–23 November 1093.

Culmination of siege

Unsuccessful.
Türkmen army paid off.
Both sieges unsuccessful.

Unsuccessful.
Tutush forced to withdraw after some of his troops were defeated in battle to the east of Aleppo.

Successful.
Sharaf al-Dawla defeated the *ahdath* in battle outside the gates and gained access to the city through a plot with the *ra'is*. After besieging Sabiq in the citadel for a number of months, they negotiated the surrender of the citadel in exchange for other settlements.

Unsuccessful.
Sulayman b. Qutlumush forced to withdraw after siege made no progress.

Unsuccessful.
Sulayman withdrew to Qinnasrin.

Unsuccessful.
Sibt claimed that the people of the city 'opened the gates for him out of antipathy for Ibn al-Hatiti al-Hashimi'. Ibn al-'Adim claimed that the city did not surrender, so he withdrew from Aleppo then returned and his men entered the city via ropes from one of the towers arranged by the merchant Ibn 'Awni al-Halabi. Citadel resisted after this.

Successful.
Tutush took the city after defeating Aqsunqur, Buzan and Kerbogha in battle.

Year of siege	Participants	Length of siege
495/1102–3[16]	Bohemond and Tancred of Antioch against Ridwan of Aleppo.	Unspecified. Merely stated that it lasted for 'a day or two'.
505/1111[17]	Army of the Sultan Muhammad led by Mawdud of Mosul against Ridwan of Aleppo.	Not mentioned.
509/1115[18]	Army of the Sultan Muhammad led by Bursuq b. Bursuq, lord of Hamadhan against Lu'lu' and the commander of the *ahdath* Shams al-Khawass.	Not mentioned.
511/1117–18[19]	Aqsunqur al-Bursuqi and Tughtegin against Yaruqtash, temporary governor of Aleppo.	Not mentioned.
513/1119[20]	Roger of Salerno, lord of Antioch, besieged Timurtash b. Il-ghazi in Aleppo.	Not mentioned.
517/1123[21]	Balak b. Bahram against Badr al-Dawla Sulayman of Aleppo.	Rabi'I–Jumada I 517/29 April–27 June 1123.
518/1124–5[22]	Frankish coalition led by Baldwin II of Jerusalem with Dubays b. Sadaqa, lord of Hilla and against the inhabitants of Aleppo and Aqsunqur al-Bursuqi.	Aqsunqur al-Bursuqi took control of Aleppo in Dhu 'l-Hijja 518/9 January–6 February 1125.
522/1128[23]	Joscelyn of Edessa and Bohemond II of Antioch.	Not mentioned.

Culmination of siege

Unsuccessful.
Bohemond and Tancred learnt of an attack by Anwashtikin al-Danishmandid against some Frankish troops near Maltiyya, and they moved off to engage him.

Unsuccessful.
Ridwan locked the gates against the sultan's army, who had expected his cooperation. They then withdrew.

Unsuccessful.
Bursuq b. Bursuq asked the Aleppan's to surrender, but they instead sent to Il-ghazi and Tughtegin to request assistance, who sent reinforcements. The sultan's army then moved away to Hama.

Unsuccessful.
The notables of Aleppo refused to accept Aqsunqur al-Bursuqi as governor and his siege failed.

Unsuccessful.
The people of Aleppo came to terms with the Franks 'on the basis of sharing the produce of their estates at the gates of Aleppo'.

Successful.
Balak b. Bahram besieged the settlement closely, prevented any supplies entering the city and burnt the crops. Sulayman surrendered after one–two months.

Unsuccessful.
Aqsunqur al-Bursuqi, lord of Mosul, relieved the city after the inhabitants surrendered the city to him.

Unsuccessful.
The people of Aleppo paid Joscelyn of Edessa and Zangi arrived before Bohemond II could begin his siege.

Notes

1. IATH, IX, 549; IAD ZH, I, pp. 264–5; IM, p. 6.
2. al-ʿAzimi, p. 339; IATH, IX, 549; IAD ZH, I, 265–6; IM, pp. 9–10.
3. IQ, pp. 150–1; al-ʿAzimi, p. 344; SJ, XII, 377–8; IAD ZH, I, 276.
4. IQ, p. 154; al-ʿAzimi, p. 345; IATH, X, 24; SJ, XII, 414.
5. IQ, p. 155; al-ʿAzimi, pp. 345–6; SJ, XII, 421.
6. IQ, p. 156; al-ʿAzimi, p. 346; SJ, XII, 435; IAD ZH, I, 297.
7. IQ, pp. 167–8; al-ʿAzimi, pp. 348–9; IATH, X, 64; SJ, XII, 480–1; IAD ZH, II, 19–23; ME, pp. 131–2.
8. SJ, XIII, 72–3; IAD BH, IX, 4078.
9. IQ, pp. 181–2; al-ʿAzimi, p. 350.
10. SJ, XIII, 114–15; IAD ZH, II, 57.
11. al-ʿAzimi, p. 351; IATH, X, 114–15; SJ, XIII, 121–2; IAD ZH, II, 68–73; MS, p. 615; ME, pp. 151–2.
12. IQ, p. 192; al-ʿAzimi, p. 353; SJ, XIII, 165–6, 169; IAD ZH, II, 90–1, 95–6.
13. IQ, p. 194; al-ʿAzimi, pp. 353–4; SJ, XIII, 177; IAD ZH, II, 96.
14. IQ, pp. 194–5; al-ʿAzimi, pp. 353–4; SJ, XIII, 177; IAD ZH, II, 98–101; ME, p. 154.
15. IQ, pp. 206–9; al-ʿAzimi, p. 355; IATH, X, 232–4; SJ, XIII, 226; IAD ZH, II, 110.
16. IAD ZH, II, 144–5.
17. al-ʿAzimi, p. 365; IATH, X, 486–7; SJ, XIII, 328, 332–3; IAD ZH, II 159–60; AA, pp. 812–15.
18. al-ʿAzimi, p. 367; IATH, X, 509–10; SJ, XIII, 375.
19. IQ, p. 316; al-ʿAzimi, p. 367.
20. al-ʿAzimi, pp. 369–7; IATH, X, 553–4.
21. IQ, p. 332; al-ʿAzimi, p. 372; IATH, X, 611; IAD ZH, II, 211–13.
22. IQ, pp. 337–8; al-ʿAzimi, pp. 374–5; IATH, X, 623–4; IAD ZH, II, 221–8; MS, p. 640; FC, pp. 749–51; FC trans., pp. 272–3; WT, I, p. 603; WT trans., II, pp. 21–3.
23. IQ, pp. 347–8; al-ʿAzimi, p. 377; IATH, X, 649–51; IAD ZH, II, 240; MS, p. 651; Bar Habraeus, *Chronography*, p. 253.

Appendix IV: Damascus under Siege

Year of siege	Participants	Length of siege	Outcome of siege
463/1070–1[1]	Atsiz b. Uvaq against unnamed deputy.	Ibn al-Qalanisi: 'He did this for several years every spring.'	Unsuccessful.
464/1071–2[2]	Nawakiya Türkmen against unnamed deputy.	Not mentioned.	Unsuccessful.
467/1074–5 or 468/1075–6[3]	Atsiz takes Damascus from Amir Razin al-Dawla.	Not mentioned.	Successful. The city surrendered following successive sieges.
470/1077–8 or 471/1078–9[4]	Nasr al-Dawla al-Juyushi against Atsiz.	Not mentioned.	Unsuccessful. The city was relived by Tutush, who then took control of it.
475/1082–3, 476/1083–4[5]	Sharaf al-Dawla against Tutush.	Not mentioned.	Unsuccessful.
478/1085–6[6]	Egyptian army against Tutush.	Not mentioned.	Unsuccessful.

Year of siege	Participants	Length of siege	Outcome of siege
488/1096[7]	Ridwan against Duqaq.	Ibn al-Qalanisi: siege ended in Dhu 'l-Hijja 489/ December 1096.	Unsuccessful.

Notes

1. IQ, pp. 166–7; SJ, XII, 486.
2. SJ, XIII, 28.
3. IQ, pp. 174–5; al-ʿAzimi, p. 349; IATH, X, 99–100; SJ, XIII, 85–6; IAD ZH, II, 46; IM, pp. 42–3.
4. IQ, p. 174; al-ʿAzimi, p. 350; IATH, X, 111; SJ, XIII, 114; IAD ZH, II, 65; IM, p. 45; MS, p. 615.
5. IQ, pp. 187–8; al-ʿAzimi, p. 352; IATH, X, 126–7; IAD ZH, II, 81–2.
6. al-ʿAzimi, p. 353; IATH, X, 145.
7. IQ, p. 215; al-ʿAzimi, p. 358; IATH, X, 247–8; SJ, XIII, 237–8.

Bibliography

Primary Source Material

Arabic Source Material

Abu l-Fida', Isma'il, *al-Mukhtasar fi akhbar al-bashar*, 2 vols (Cairo: al-Matba'ah al-Husayniyah, 1907).

Yahya b. Sa'id al-Antaki, *Ta'rikh al-Antaki*, ed. 'Umar A. Tadmuri (Tripoli: Yarus Burs, 1990).

Muhammad b. 'Ali al-'Azimi, *Ta'rikh halab*, ed. Ibrahim Za'rur (Damascus: s.n., 1984).

Ibn al-Azraq al-Fariqi, Ahmad b. Yusuf, *Ta'rikh al-Fariqi*, ed. and trans. Carole Hillenbrand, *A Muslim Principality in Crusader Times* (Leiden: Brill, 1990).

al-Husayni, Sadr al-Din, *Akhbar al-Dawla al-Saljuqiyya*, ed. Muhammad Iqbal (Lahore: University of the Panjab, 1933).

Taqi al-Din al-Maqrizi, *Itti'az al-hunafa' bi-akhbar al-a'imma al-fatimiyyin al-khulafa'*, 3 vols (Cairo: al-Lajnat Ihya' al-Turath al-Islami, 1967–73), I, ed. Jamal al-Din al-Shayyal (1967), II and III, ed. Muhammad H. M. Ahmad (1971–3).

al-Muqaddasi, Shams al-Din Abu 'Abd Allah Muhammad b. Ahmad b. Abi Bakr al-Bana' al-Shami, *Ahsan al-taqasim fi ma'rifat al-aqalim*, ed. Michael J. de Goeje (Leiden: Brill, 2014).

al-Nuwayri, Shibab al-Dinm *Nihayat al-arab fi funun al-adab*, 34 vols, ed. Ibrahim Shams al-Din and Mufid M. Qumayhah (Beirut: Dar al-Kutub al-'Ilmiya, 2004–5).

al-Qifti, Ali b. Yusuf, *Ikhbar al-Ulama Bi Akhbar al-Hukama'*, ed. Julius Lipp (Leipzig: Dieterich'sche Verlagsbuchhandlung, 1902).

al-Safadi, Khalil b. Aybak, *Kitab al-Wafi' bi'l-wafayat*, 32 vols, ed. Sven Dedering (Weisbaden: Franz Steiner Verlag, 1974), IV.

al-Shirazi, Hibat Allah al-Mu'ayyad fi'l-Din, *Diwan al-Mu'ayyad fi'l-Din da'i al-du'ah*, ed. Muhammad K. Husayn (Cairo: Dar al-Katib al-Misri, 1949).

al-Sulami, 'Ali Ibn Tahir, *The Book of the Jihad of 'Ali ibn Tahir al-Sulami: Text Translation and Commentary*, ed. and trans. Niall Christie (Farnham: Ashgate, 2015).

Elshayyal, M. F., 'A Critical Edition of Volume II of *Ta'rikh al-duwal wa'l-muluk* by Muḥammad b. 'Abd al-Rahim b. 'Ali Ibn al-Furat', unpublished PhD dissertation (1986).

'Ali ibn al-Hasan Ibn 'Asakir, *Ta'rikh madinat Dimashq*, ed. 'Umar Gh. Al- 'Amrawi, 80 vols (Beirut, 1995–8).

Ibn al-'Adim, Kamal al-Din, *Zubdat al-halab min ta'rikh halab*, ed. Sami Dahan, 3 vols (Damascus: Institut français de Damas, 1951–68).

Ibn al-'Adim, Kamal al-Din, *Bughyat al-talab fi ta'rikh halab*, ed. Suhayl Zakkar, 12 vols (Beirut: Dar al-Fikr, 1988).

Ibn al-'Arabi, al-Nass, *al-kamil li-kitab al-'Awasim min al-qawasim*, ed. 'Ammar Talibi (Cairo: Maktabah Dar al-Turath, 1997).

Ibn al-Athir, 'Izz al-Din 'Ali, *al-Kamil fi'l ta'rikh*, ed. Carolus J. Tornberg, 12 vols (Beirut: Dar Sadir, 1965–7).

Ibn al-Athir, 'Izz al-Din 'Ali, *al-Ta'rikh al-bahir fi'l-dawlat al-atabakiyya*, ed. Abd al-Qadir A. Tulaymat (Cairo: Dar al-Kutub al-Hadithah, 1963).

Ibn al-Jawzi, 'Abd al-Rahman, *al-Muntazam fi ta'rikh al-muluk wa'l-umam*, ed. Muhammad A. Ata et al., 18 vols (Beirut: Dar al-Kutub al-'Ilmiyah, 1992).

Ibn al-Qalanisi, Abu Ya'la, *Dhayl ta'rikh Dimashq*, ed. Suhayl Zakkar (Damascus: Dar Hassan, 1983).

Ibn Hawqal, Abu'l-Qasim, *Kitab Surat al-ard*, ed. Johannes H. Kramers as *Opus Geographicum* (Frankfurt am Main: Institute for the History of Arabic-Islamic Science, 1992).

Ibn Khallikan, Ahmad b. Muhammad, *Kitab Wafaat al-'ayan wa anba' abna' al-zaman*, 8 vols, ed. Ihsan Abbas (Beirut: Dar Sadir, 1977–8).

Ibn Kathir, 'Imad al-Din, *al-Bidaya wa'l nihaya fi'l ta'rikh*, 14 vols (Beirut: Dar al-Kutub al-'Ilmiyah, 1932–77).

Ibn Muyassar, Taj al-Din, *Akhbar Misr*, ed. Ayman F. Sayyid (Cairo: Institut français d'Archéologie Orientale, 1981).

Ibn Shaddad, Baha' al-Din, *al-Nawadir al-sultaniyya wa'l mahasin al-yusufiyya*, ed. Jamal El-Shayyal (Cairo: Al-Dar al-Misriya li'l Ta'lif wa'l Tarjama, 1964).

Ibn Shaddad, 'Izz al-Din Muhammad b. 'Ali, *al-A'laq al-khatira fi dikr umara' al-Sham wa'l-Jazira*, 2 vols, I/I (Damascus: Institut Français de Damas, 1953), ed. Dominique Sourdel, I/II (Damascus: Wizarat al-Thaqafa, 1991), ed. Yahya Zakariya ʿAbbara, II (Damascus: Institut Français de Damas, 1956), ed. Sami Dahan, I/I, 15.

Ibn Taghribirdi, Abu'l Mahasin Yusuf, *al-Nujum al-zahira fi muluk Misr wa'l-Qahira*, 16 vols (Cairo: Matbaʿat Dar al-Kutub al-Misriyah, 1929–72).

Muhammad b. Salim Ibn Wasil, *Mufarrij al-kurub fi akhbar bani Ayyub*, 5 vols, ed. Jamal El-Shayyal (Cairo: s.n., 1953–77).

Ibn Zafir al-Azdi, ʿAli, *Akhbar al-Duwal al-munqatiʾa*, ed. André Ferré (Cairo: Al-Maʿhad al-ʿIlmial-Faransi lil-Athar al-Sharqiya, 1972), p. 82.

Ibn al-Muqaffaʿ, Sawirus, *History of the Patriarchs of the Egyptian Church*, vols II/III and III/I, ed. and trans. Aziz Suryal Atiya, Yassa ʿAbd al-Masih and O. H. E. Burmester (Cairo: Société d'archéologie copte, 1959–68).

Sibt b. al-Jawzi, Yusuf Qizoglu, *Miʾrat al-zaman fi taʾrikh al-aʿyan*, ed. James R. Jewett (Chicago: University of Chicago Press, 1907).

Sibt b. al-Jawzi, Yusuf Qizoglu, *Miʾrat al-zaman fi taʾrikh al-aʿyan*, ed. Ali Sevim (Ankara: Matbaʿat al-Jamʿiyat al-Tarikhiyah al-Turkiyah, 1968).

Sibt b. al-Jawzi, Yusuf Qizoglu, *Miʾrat al-zaman fi taʾrikh al-aʿyan*, ed. Kamil S. Al-Jabouri et al., 23 vols (Beirut: Dar al-Kutub al-ʿIlmiyah, 2013).

Usama b. Munqidh b. ʿAli, *Kitab al-Iʾtibar*, ed. Philip K. Hitti (Princeton, NJ: Princeton University Press, 1930).

Usama b. Munqidh b. ʿAli, *Lubab al-Adab*, ed. Ahmed M. Shakir (Cairo: Maktabat Luwis Sarkis, 1935).

Yaqut al-Hamawi, *Irshad al-udabaʾ fi maʿrifat al-adib*, 7 vols, ed. David S. Margoliouth (London: Luzac, 1923–31).

Yaqut al-Hamawi, *Kitab Muʿajam al-Buldan*, 5 vols (Beirut: Dar Sadir, 1977).

Arabic Source Material in Translation

al-Husayni, Sadr al-Din, *The History of the Seljuq State*, trans. Clifford E. Bosworth (London: Routledge, 2011).

Gabrieli, Francesco, *Arab Historians of the Crusades* (London: Routledge & Kegan Paul, 1984).

Ibn al-ʿArabi, al-Nass, 'Some Observations during a Visit to Palestine by Ibn al-ʿArabī of Seville in 1092–1094', ed. and trans. Joseph Drory, *The Crusades* 3 (2004): 101–25.

Ibn al-ʿAsakir, Thiqat al-Din, *La description de Damas d'Ibn ʿAsâkir*, trans. Nikita Elisséeff (Damascus: Institut français de Damas, 1959).

Ibn al-Athir, 'Izz al-Din 'Ali, 'Kamel al-tevarykh', in *Recueil des historiens des croisades: historiens orientaux*, 5 vols (Paris: Imprimerie Royale, 1872–1906), I (1872), pp. 189–714, II/I (1887), pp. 3–180.

Ibn al-Athir, 'Izz al-Din 'Ali, *The Chronicle of the Ibn al-Athir for the Crusading Period from al-Kamil fi'l-Ta'rikh*, trans. Donald S. Richards, 3 vols (Aldershot: Ashgate, 2005–8).

Ibn al-Furat, Nasir al-Din Muhammad, *Ta'rikh al-duwal wa'l muluk*, ed. Malcolm C. Lyons as *Ayyubids, Mamlukes and Crusaders*, 2 vols (Cambridge: Cambridge University Press, 1971).

Ibn al-Qalanisi, *The Damascus Chronicle of the Crusades*, trans. Hamilton A. R. Gibb (London: Luzac, 1932).

Ibn Shaddad, 'Izz al-Din, *Description de La Syrie du Nord*, trans. Anne-Marie Eddé-Terrasse (Damascus, Institut Français de Damas, 1984).

Le Tourneau, Roger, *Damas de 1075 à 1154* (Damascus: Institut français de Damas, 1952).

Mallett, Alex, 'Al-'Azimi's *Ta'rikh* for the Crusading Period: the Years 489–508/1095–1115', *Crusades* 19 (2020): 1–34.

Monot, Frédéric, 'La chronique abrégée d'al-'Azîmî, années 518–538/1124–1144', *Revue des Études Islamiques* 59 (1991): 101–64.

Richards, Donald S., *The Annals of the Seljuq Turks* (London: RoutledgeCurzon, 2002).

Usama b. Munqidh b. 'Ali, *The Book of Contemplation Islam and the Crusades*, ed. and trans. P. M. Cobb (London: Penguin, 2008).

Persian, Greek, Syriac and Armenian Source Material in Translation

Anonymous Syriac Chronicle, pt. 1: 'The First and Second Crusades from an Anonymous Syriac Chronicle', trans. Arthur S. Tritton and Hamilton A. R. Gibb, *Journal of the Royal Asiatic Society* 65 (1933): 69–101.

Attaleiates, Michael, *The History*, trans. Anthony Kaldellis and Dimitris Krallis (Cambridge, MA: Harvard University Press, 2012).

Bar Habraeus, *The Chronography of Gregory Abul Faraj Commonly Known as Bar Hebraeus*, trans. Ernest A. W. Budge, 2 vols (London: Oxford University Press, 1932).

Byrennios, Nikephoros, *Nicephori Byrennii Historiarum libri quattuor*, trans. Paul Gautier (Brussels: Byzantion, 1975).

Choniates, Niketas, *O City of Byzantium: Annals of Niketas Choniates*, trans Harry J. Magoulias (Detroit, MI: Wayne State University Press, 1984).

Kinnamos, John, *The deeds of John and Manuel Comnemus*, trans. Charles M. Brand (New York: Columbia University Press, 1976).

Komnene, Anna, *The Alexiad*, trans. Edgar R. A. Sewter, rev. with introduction and notes Peter Frankopan (London: Penguin, 2009).

Matthew of Edessa, *Armenia and the Crusades, Tenth to Twelfth Centuries: the Chronicle of Matthew of Edessa*, trans. Ara E. Dostourian (London: University Press of America, 1993).

Michael the Syrian, *The Syriac Chronicle of Michael Rabo (the Great): a Universal History from the Creation*, trans. Matti Moosa (Teaneck: Beth Antioch Press, 2014).

Nasir-i Khusraw, *Naser-e-Khosraw's Book of travels*, trans. Wheeler M. Thackson (New York: State University of New York Press, 1985).

Psellus, Michael, *The Chronography of Michael Psellus*, trans. E. R. A. Sewter (London: Penguin, 2011).

Zonoras, John, *The History of Zonaras: From Alexander Severus to the Death of Theodosius the Great*, ed. and trans. Thomas M. Banchich and Eugene N. Lane (Abingdon: Taylor & Francis, 2009).

Latin Source Material

Albert of Aachen, *Historia Hierosolymitana*, ed. and trans. Susan B. Edgington (Oxford: Clarendon, 2007).

Anonymous, *Gesta Francorum et aliorum Hierosolimitanorum*, ed. and trans. by Rosalind M. Hill (London: T. Nelson, 1962).

Fulcher of Chartres, *Fulcheri carnoetensis, Historia Hierosolymitana*, ed. Heinrich Hagenmeyer (Heidelberg: Carl Winters Universitatsbuchhandlung, 1913).

Ralph of Caen, 'Gesta Tancredi in Expeditione Hierosolymitana', *Recueil des historiens des croisades, Historiens occidentaux*, 5 vols (Paris: Imprimerie Royale, 1844–95), III (1866), pp. 587–716.

Raymond of Aguilers, *Le 'Liber' de Raymond D'Aguilers*, ed. and trans. John H. Hill and Laurita L. Hill (Paris: P. Geuthner, 1969).

Walter the Chancellor, *Galterii Cancelarii bella antiochena*, ed. Heinrich Hagenmeyer (Innsbruck: s.n., 1896).

William of Tyre, *Willelmi Tyremsos archiepiscopi Chronicon*, ed. Robert B. C. Huygens, Corpus Christianorum Continuatio Mediaevalis 63–63a, 2 vols (Turnhout: Brepols, 1986).

Latin Source Material in Translation

Fulcher of Chartres, *A History of the Expedition to Jerusalem*, trans. Frances R. Ryan, ed. Harold S. Fink (Knoxville: University of Tennessee Press, 1969).

Ralph of Caen, *The Gesta Tancredi of Ralph of Caen*, ed. and trans. Bernard S. Bachrach and David S. Bachrach (Farnham: Ashgate, 2005).

Walter the Chancellor, *Walter the Chancellor's The Antiochene Wars: a Translation and Commentary*, ed. and trans. Thomas Asbridge and Susan B. Edgington (Aldershot: Ashgate, 1999).

William of Tyre, *William of Tyre: a History of Deeds Done Beyond the Sea*, ed. and trans. Emily A. Babcock, and August C. Krey, 2 vols (New York: Octagon, 1976).

Secondary Source Material

Abouseada, Al-Amin, 'Modern Arabic Historical Scholarship on Medieval Europe: a Biographical Study', in *A Handbook of Modern Arabic Historical Scholarship on the Ancient and Medieval Periods*, ed. Amar S. Badaj (Leiden: Brill, 2021), pp. 595–616.

Abulafia, David, 'The Role of Trade in Muslim–Christian Contact during the Middle Ages', in *The Arab influence in Medieval Europe*, ed. Dionisius A. Agius and Richard Hitchcock (Reading: Ithaca Press, 1994), pp. 1–24.

Abulafia, David, 'Introduction: Seven Types of Ambiguity, c. 1100–1500', in *Medieval Frontiers: Concepts and Practices*, ed. David Abulafia and Nora Berend (Aldershot: Ashgate 2002), pp. 1–34.

Aceituno, Antonio J., 'The Seljuk *jihad* against Fatimid Shi'ism: an Observation on the Sunni Revival', in *Essays in Ottoman Civilization (Archiv Orientální)*, suppl. 8, 1998), pp. 173–8.

Amabe, Fukuzo, *Urban Autonomy in Medieval Islam* (Leiden: Brill, 2016).

Amitai-Preiss, Reuven, 'Northern Syria between the Mongols and Mamluks: Political Boundary, Military Frontier, and Ethnic Affinities', in *Frontiers in Question: Eurasian Borderlands, 700–1700*, ed. Daniel Power and Naomi Standen (Basingstoke: Macmillan, 1999), pp. 128–52.

Amouroux-Mourad, Monique, *Le Comté d'Edesse 1098–1150* (Paris: Librairie Orientaliste Paul Geuthner, 1988).

Anderson, Glaire D., 'Islamic Spaces and Diplomacy in Constantinople (Tenth to Thirteenth Centuries)', *Medieval Encounters* 15 (2009): 86–113.

Andrews, Tara, 'The New Age of Prophecy: the Chronicle of Matthew of Edessa and its Place in Armenian Historiography', *Medieval Chronicle* 6 (2009): 105–23.

Andrews, Tara, 'Matthew of Edessa (Matt'eos Urhayec'i)', in *Franks and Crusades in Medieval Eastern Christian Historiography*, ed. Alex Mallett (Turnhout: Brepols, 2021), pp. 153–78.

Angold, Michael, *The Byzantine Empire 1025–1204* (London: Longman, 1997).

Antrim, Zayde, 'Ibn 'Asakir's Representations of Syria and Damascus in the Introduction to the Ta'rikh Madinat Dimashq', *International Journal of Middle Eastern Studies* 38 (2006): 109–29.

Antrim, Zayde, *Routes and Realms* (Oxford: Oxford University Press, 2012).

Antrim, Zayde, *Mapping the Middle East* (Chicago: University of Chicago Press, 2018).

Antrim, Zayde, 'Becoming Syrian: Aleppo in Ibn al-'Adim's *Bughyat al-talab fi ta'rikh Halab*', in *Grounded Identities: Territory and Belonging in the Medieval and Early Modern Mediterranean and Mesopotamia*, ed. Steve Tamari (Leiden: Brill, 2019), pp. 46–71.

Anvi, Gideon, '"From Polis to Madina" Revisited: Urban Change in Byzantine and Early Islamic Palestine', *Journal of the Royal Asiatic Society* 21 (2011), 301–29.

Asbridge, Thomas S., 'The Significance and Causes of the Battle of the Field of Blood', *Journal of Medieval History* 24 (1997): 301–16.

Asbridge, Thomas S., 'Jabal as-Summaq', in *The First Crusade: Origins and Impact*, ed. Jonathan Phillips (Manchester: Manchester University Press, 1997), pp. 142–52.

Asbridge, Thomas S., 'The 'Crusader Community at Antioch: The Impact of Interaction with Byzantium and Islam', *Transactions of the Royal Historical Society* 10 (1999): 305–25.

Asbridge, Thomas S., *The Creation of the Principality of Antioch 1098–1130* (Woodbridge: Boydell, 2000).

Asbridge, Thomas S., *The First Crusade: A New History* (London: Free Press, 2004).

Asbridge, Thomas S., 'Knowing the Enemy: Latin Relations with Islam at the Time of the First Crusade', in *Knighthoods of Christ: Essays on the History of the Crusade and the Knights Templar, Presented to Malcolm Barber*, ed. Norman Housley (Aldershot: Routledge, 2007), pp. 17–38.

Asbridge, Thomas S., *The Crusades: The War for the Holy Land* (London: Simon & Schuster, 2010).

Asbridge, Thomas S., 'How the Crusades Could Have Been Won: King Baldwin II of Jerusalem's Campaigns against Aleppo 1124–5 and Damascus 1129', *Journal of Medieval Military History* 11 (2013): 73–93.

Asbridge, Thomas S., 'The Principality of Antioch and the Early History of the Latin East', in *East and West in the Medieval Eastern Mediterranean, vol. II: Antioch from the Byzantine Reconquest until the End of the Crusader Principality*, ed. Krijna N. Ciggaar and V. D. van Aalst (Leuven: Peeters, 2013), pp. 1–10.

Atiya, Aziz S., *Crusade, Commerce and Culture* (Bloomington, IN: Indiana University Press, 1962).

Attiya, Hussein M., 'Knowledge of Arabic in the Crusader States in the Twelfth and Thirteenth Centuries', *Journal of Medieval History* 25 (1999): 203–13.

Augé, Isabelle, *Byzantins, Arméniens et Francs au temps de la croisade. Politique religieuse et reconquête en Orient sous la dynastie des Comnènes (1081–1185)* (Paris: Geuthner, 2007).

Barber, Malcolm, *The Crusader States* (New Haven, CT: Yale University Press, 2012).

Barber, Mathew, 'Al-Afdal b. Badr Al-Jamali: The Vizierate and the Fatimid Response to the First Crusade: Masculinity in Historical Memory', in *Crusading and Masculinities*, ed. Natasha R. Hodgson, Katherine J. Lewis and Matthew M. Mesley (London: Routledge, 2019), pp. 53–71.

Barber, Mathew, 'Reappraising the Arabic Accounts for the Conflict of 446/1054–5: An Egyptian Perspective on Constantine IX and His Immediate Successors', in *Transmitting and Circulating the Late Antique and Byzantine World*, ed. Mirela Ivanova and Hugh Jeffrey (Leiden: Brill. 2020), pp. 170–98.

Barthold, Vladimir, *Turkestan Down to the Mongol Invasion* (London: Luzac, 1928).

Bartlett, Robert, 'Colonial Aristocracies of the High Middle Ages', in *Medieval Frontier Societies*, ed. Robert Bartlett and Angus MacKay (Oxford: Oxford University Press, 1996), pp. 23–47.

Barton, Thomas W., 'Lords, Settlers and Shifting Frontiers in Medieval Catalonia', *Journal of Medieval History* (2010): 1–49.

Basan, Aziz, *The Great Seljuqs A History* (Abingdon: Routledge, 2010).

Bauden, Frédéric, 'Taqi al-Din Ahmad ibn al-Maqrizi', in *Medieval Muslim Historians and the Franks in the Levant*, ed. Alex Mallett (Leiden: Brill, 2015), pp. 161–200.

Beech, George T., 'The Crusader Lordship of Marash in Armenian Cilicia, 1104–1149', *Viator* 27 (1996): 35–52.

Beihammer, A. D., 'Defection across the Border of Islam and Christianity: Apostasy and Cross-Cultural Interaction in Byzantine–Seljuk Relations', *Speculum* 86 (2011): 597–691.

Beihammer, Alexander D., 'Muslim Rulers Visiting the Imperial City: Building Alliances and Personal Networks between Constantinople and the Eastern Borderlands (Fourth/Tenth–Fifth/Eleventh Century)', *al-Masaq* 24 (2012): 157–77.

Beihammer, Alexander D., 'Strategies of Diplomacy and Ambassadors in Byzantine–Muslim Relations of the Tenth and Eleventh Centuries', in *Ambassades et ambas-*

sadeurs au couer de l'activité diplomatique Rome-Occident medieval-Byzance VIIe s. avant J.-C.–XIIe s. ap. J-C, ed. Audrey Becker and Nicholas Droucourt (Metz: Presses universitaires de Lorraine, 2012), pp. 371–400.

Beihammer, Alexander D., 'Christian Views of Islam in Early Seljuq Anatolia: Perceptions and Reactions', in *Islam and Christianity in Medieval Anatolia*, ed. Andrew C. S. Peacock, Bruno De Nicola and Sara Nur Yildiz (London: Routledge, 2015), pp. 51–76.

Beihammer, Alexander D., *Byzantium and the Emergence of Muslim-Turkish Anatolia ca. 1040–1130* (Abingdon: Routledge, 2017).

Beihammer, Alexander, 'Patterns of Turkish Migration and Expansion in Byzantine Asia Minor in the 11th and 12th Centuries', in *Migration Histories of the Medieval Afroeurasion Transition Zone*, ed. Johannes Preiser-Kapeller, Lucian Reinfandt and Yannis Stouraitis (Leiden: Brill, 2020), pp. 166–92.

Berend, Nora, 'Frontiers', in *Palgrave Advances in the Crusades*, ed, Helen Nicholson (Basingstoke: Palgrave Macmillan 2005), pp. 148–71.

Besançon, Jacques and Bernard Geyer, 'La cuvette du Rug (Syrie du Nord) Les conditions naturelles et les étapes de la mise en valeur', *Syria* 72 (1995): 307–55

Berthier, Sophie, 'La citadelle de Damas', in *Muslim Military Architecture in Greater Syria: From the Coming of Islam to the Ottoman Period*, ed. Hugh Kennedy (Leiden: Brill, 2006), pp. 151–64.

Bianquis, Theirry, *Damas et la Syrie sous la domination Fatimide*, 2 vols (Damascus: Institut français de Damas 1986–9).

Bianquis, Thierry, 'Pouvoirs arabes à Alep aux Xe et XIe siècles', *Revue des mondes musulmans et de la Méditerranée* 62 (1991): 49–59.

Bianquis, Thierry, 'Wathab b. Sabik al-Numayri', in *Encyclopaedia of Islam*, 2nd edn, ed. Peri Bearman et al. (2012), available online, last accessed 28 July 2019.

Bianquis, Thierry and Shamma, Samir, 'Mirdas, Banu or Mirdasids', in *Encyclopaedia of Islam*, 2nd edn, ed. Peri Bearman et al. (2012), available online, last accessed 15 June 2019.

Boas, Adrian J., *Crusader Archaeology: the Material Culture of the Latin East* (London: Routledge, 1999).

Boase, Thomas S. R., 'The History of the Kingdom', in *The Cilician Kingdom of Armenia*, ed. Thomas S. R. Boase (Edinburgh: Scottish Academic Press, 1978), pp. 1–33.

Böhme, Eric, *Die Außenbeziehungen des Königreiches Jerusalem im 12. Jahrhundert. Kontinuität und Wandel im Herrscherwechsel zwischen König Amalrich und Balduin IV* (Berlin: De Gruyter, 2019).

Bonner, Michael, 'The Naming of the Frontier: 'Awasim, Thughur, and the Arab Geographers', *Bulletin of the School of Oriental and African Studies* 57 (1994): 17–24.

Bora, Fozia, 'Did Saladin Destroy the Fatimids' Books? An Historiographical Enquiry', *Journal of the Royal Asiatic Society* 25 (2015): 21–39.

Bora, Fozia, 'Ibn Muyassar', *Encyclopaedia of Islam THREE*, ed. Kate Fleet et al. (2017), available at Brill online, last accessed 10 July 2017.

Bora, Fozia, *Writing History in the Medieval Islamic World: the Value of Chronicles as Archives* (London: Bloomsbury, 2019).

Borrut, Antoine, *Entre mémoire et pouvoir. L'espace syrien sous les derniers Omeyyades et les premiers Abbassides v. 72–193/692–809* (Leiden: Brill, 2011).

Bosworth, Clifford E., 'The Political and Dynastic History of the Iranian World A.D. 1100–1217', *The Cambridge History of Iran, vol. V*, ed. John A. Boyle (Cambridge: Cambridge University Press, 1968), pp. 1–202.

Bosworth, Clifford E., 'The Heritage of Rulership in Early Islamic Iran and the Search for Dynastic Connections with the Past', *Iran* 11 (1973): 51–62.

Bosworth, Clifford E., 'The City of Tarsus and the Arab–Byzantine Frontiers in Early and Middle Abbasid Times', *Oriens* 33 (1992): 268–86.

Bosworth, Clifford E., *The New Islamic Dynasties: a Chronological and Genealogical Manual* (Edinburgh: Edinburgh University Press, 1996).

Bosworth, Clifford E., 'Towards a Biography of Nizam al-Mulk: Three Sources from Ibn al-'Adim', in *Semetic Studies in Honour of Edward Ullendorf*, ed. Geoffrey Khan (Leiden: Brill, 2005), pp. 299–308.

Bosworth, Clifford E., 'al-Husayni', in *Encyclopaedia of Islam*, 2nd edn, ed. Peri Bearman et al. (2012), available at Brill online, last accessed 10 July 2017.

Bosworth, Clifford E., "Ukaylids', in *Encyclopaedia of Islam*, 2nd edn, ed. Peri Bearman et al. (2012), available at Beill online, last accessed 30 March 2022.

Bozoyan, Azat, 'Armenian Political Revival in Cilicia', in *Armenian Cilicia*, ed. Robert Hovannisian and Simon Payaslian (Costa Mesa, CA: Mazda, 2008), pp. 67–78.

Bramoullé, David, 'Les villes maritimes fatimides en Méditerranée orientale (969–1171)', *Histoire urbaine* 19 (2007): 93–116.

Bramoullé, David, 'Recruiting Crew in the Fatimid Navy 909–1171', *Medieval Encounters* 13 (2007): 4–31.

Bramoullé, David, 'Les populations littorals du Bilad al-Šam fatimide et la guerre', *Annales islamologiques* 43 (2009): 303–34.

Bramoullé, David, 'Tyr dans le sources de la période fatimide (969–1171)', in *Sources de l'Histoire de Tyr: Textes de l'Antiquité et du Moyen Âge*, ed. Pierre-Louis

Gaitier, Julien Aliquot and Lévon Nordiguian (Beirut: Presses de'lfpo, 2011), pp. 157–77.

Bramoullé, David, 'The Fatimids and the Red Sea (969–1171)', in *Navigated Spaces, Connected Places*, ed. Dionisius Agius, John Cooper, Athena Trakadas and Chiara Zazzaro (Oxford: Archaeopress, 2012), pp. 127–36.

Bramoullé, David, *Les Fatimides et la mer 909–1171* (Leiden: Brill, 2019).

Brauer, Ralph W., 'Boundaries and Frontiers in Medieval Muslim Geography', *Transactions of the American Philosophical Society* 85 (1995): 1–73.

Brett, Michael, 'The Battles of Ramla (1099–1105)', in *Egypt and Syria in the Fatimid, Ayyubid and Mamluk Eras*, 9 vols, ed. Urbain Vermeulen and Daniel De Smet (Leuven: Peeters, 1995), Vol. I, pp. 17–37.

Brett, Michael, 'The Way of the Nomad', in *Bulletin of the School of Oriental and African Studies* 58 (1995): 251–69, 256–9.

Brett, Michael, 'The Fatimids and the Counter-Crusade, 1099–1171', in *Egypt and Syria in the Fatimid, Ayyubid and Mamluk Eras*, 9 vols, ed. Urbain Vermeulen and Daniel De Smet (Leuven: Peeters, 1998), Vol. II, pp. 15–25.

Brett, Michael, 'Lingua France in the Mediterranean: John Wansbrough and the Historiography of Medieval Egypt', in *The Historiography of Islamic Egypt*, ed. Hugh Kennedy (Leiden: Brill, 2001), pp. 1–13.

Brett, Michael, 'Badr al-Gamali and the Fatimid Renascence', *Egypt and Syria in the Fatimid, Ayyubid and Mamluk Eras*, 9 vols, ed. Urbain Vermeulen and Kristof D'Hulster (Leuven: Peeters, 2007), V, pp. 61–79.

Brett, Michael, *The Fatimid Empire* (Edinburgh: Edinburgh University Press, 2017).

Buck, Andrew D., 'On the Frontier of Latin Christendom: The Principality of Antioch, c.a.1130–c.a.1193', unpublished PhD dissertation, Queen Mary University of London, 2015.

Buck, Andrew, 'The Castle and Lordship of Harim and the Frankish–Muslim Frontier of Northern Syria in the Twelfth Century', *al-Masaq* 28 (2016): 113–31.

Buck, Andrew D., *The Principality of Antioch and its Frontiers in the Twelfth Century* (Woodbridge: Boydell, 2017).

Buck, Andrew D., 'Settlement, Identity and Memory in the Latin East: An Examination of the Term "Crusader States"', *English Historical Review* 135 (2020): 271–302.

Bulliet, Richard W., *Cotton, Climate, and Camels in Early Islamic Iran: a Moment in Work History* (New York: Columbia University Press, 2009).

Burnett, Charles, 'Antioch as a Link between Arabic and Latin Culture in the Twelfth and Thirteenth Centuries', in *Occident et Proche-Orient. Contacts scientifiques au temps des croisades*, ed. Anne Tihon, Isabelle Draelants and Baudouin van den Abeele (Louvain-la-Neuve: Brepols, 2000), pp. 1–78.

Burns, Ross, 'The Significance of the Frontier in the Middle Ages', in *Medieval Frontier Societies*, ed. Robert Bartlett and Angus MacKay (Oxford: Clarendon, 1996), pp. 307–30.

Burns, Ross, *The Monuments of Syria: A Guide* (London: I. B. Tauris, 2009).

Burns, Ross, *Aleppo: A History* (London: Routledge, 2017).

Buyukasik, Tevfik, 'A Survey of the Measurements of the Castles, Villages and Cities that are Situated in the Kingdom of the Just King Nur al-Din Abu al-Qasim Mahmud ibn Zangi ibn Aqsunqur in the year 564/1168–9, as described in MS Arabe 2281 (BN Paris) (Introduction, Translation and Arabic Text)', in *East and West in the Medieval Eastern Mediterranean II: Antioch from the Byzantine Reconquest Until the End of the Crusader Principality*, ed. Krijna N. Ciggaar and V. D. van Aalst (Leuven: Peeters, 2013), pp. 79–200.

Cahen, Claude, *La Syrie du nord à l'époque des croisades et la Principauté Franque d'Antioche* (Paris: Librairie Orientaliste Paul Geuthner, 1940).

Cahen, Claude, 'La première pénétration turque en Asie Mineure (seconde moitié du XIe siècle)', *Byzantion* 18 (1948): 5–67.

Cahen, Claude, 'L'évolution de l'iqta du IXe au XIIe siècle' *Annales: economies, sociétés, civilization* 8 (1953): 25–52.

Cahen, Claude, 'Review of *Mir'at al-zaman fi ta'rikh al-a'yan*, tome VIII by Sibt B. al-Gawzi; *Dhayl Mir'at al-zaman* by al-Yunini', *Arabica* 4 (1957): 191–4.

Cahen, Claude, 'Qutlumush et ses fils avant l'Asie mineure', *Der Islam* 39 (1964): 14–27.

Cahen, Claude, 'Nomades et sedentaries dans le monde musulman du milieu du moyen age', in *Islamic Civilization: 950–1150*, ed. Donald S. Richards (Oxford: Cassirer, 1973), pp. 93–104.

Cahen, Claude, *Orient et Occident au temps des croisades* (Paris: Aubier Montaigne, 1983).

Cahen, Claude, *The Formation of Turkey. The Seljukid Sultanate of Rum: Eleventh to Fourteenth Century* (Harlow: Pearson, 2001).

Cahen, Claude, 'Ibn al-Kalanisi', in *Encyclopaedia of Islam*, 2nd edn, ed. Peri Bearman et al. (2012), available at Brill online, last accessed 10 July 2017.

Cahen, Claude, 'al-'Azimi', in *Encyclopaedia of Islam*, 2nd edn, ed. Peri Bearman et al. (2012), available at Brill online, last accessed 10 July 2017.

Cahen, Claude, 'Ibn al-Djawzi, Shams al-Din Abu'l-Muzaffar Yusuf b. Kizoglu, known as Sibt', in *Encyclopaedia of Islam*, 2nd edn, ed. Peri Bearman et al. (2012), available at Brill online, last accessed 10 July 2017.

Cahen, Claude, 'Ibn Muyassar', in *Encyclopaedia of Islam*, 2nd edn, ed. Peri Bearman et al. (2012), available at Brill online, last accessed 10 July 2017.

Canard, Marius, 'al-Antaki', in *Encyclopaedia of Islam*, 2nd edn, ed. Peri Bearman et al. (2012), available at Brill online, last accessed 10 July 2017.

Chamberlain, Michael, *Knowledge and Social Power in Medieval Damascus* (Cambridge: Cambridge University Press, 1994).

Chapoutot-Remadi, Mounira, 'al-Nuwayrī', in *Encyclopaedia of Islam*, 2nd edn, ed. Peri Bearman et al. (2012), available at Brill online, last accessed online 10 July 2017.

Chevedden, Paul, 'The Islamic Interpretation of the Crusades: a New (Old) Paradigm for Understanding the Crusades' *Der Islam* 83 (2006): 90–136.

Chevedden, Paul, 'The Islamic View and the Christian View of the Crusades: a New Synthesis', *History: Journal of the Historical Association* 93 (2008): 181–200.

Cheynet, Jean-Claude, 'Manzikert: un désastre militaire?', *Byzantion* 50 (1980): 410–38.

Cheynet, Jean-Claude, 'La résistance aux Turcs en Asie Mineure entre Manzikert et la Première Croisade', in *Eupsykhia: Mélanges offerts à Hélène Ahrweiler*, 2 vols (Paris: Publications de la Sorbonne, 1998), vol. I, pp. 131–47.

Cheynet, Jean-Claude, 'Les ducs d'Antioche sous Michel IV et Constantin IX', in *Novum Milennium (sic): Studies on Byzantine History and Culture Dedicated to Paul Speck*, ed. C. Sode and S. Takacs (Aldershot: Routledge, 2000), pp. 53–63.

Cheynet, Jean-Claude, 'The Duchy of Antioch during the Second Period of Byzantine Rule', in *East and West in the Medieval Eastern Mediterranean, vol. I: Antioch from the Byzantine Reconquest until the End of the Crusader Principality*, ed. Krinja Ciggaar and David M. Metcalf (Leuven: Peeters, 2006), pp. 1–16.

Chiarellia, Leonard C., *A History of Muslim Sicily* (Santa Venera: Midsea Books, 2010),

Chipman, Leigh, Gideon Anvi and Ronnie Ellenblum, 'Collapse, Affluence, and Collapse Again: Contrasting Climactic Effects in Egypt during the Prolonged Reign of al-Mustansir (1036–1094)', *Mediterranean Historical Review* 36 (2021): 199–215.

Christie, Niall, 'The Origins of Suffixed Invocations of God's Curse on the Franks in Muslim Sources for the Crusades', *Arabica* 48 (2001): 254–66.

Christie, Niall, 'Religious Campaign or War of Conquest? Muslim Views of the

Motives of the First Crusade', in *Noble Ideals and Bloody Realities: Warfare in the Middle Ages*, ed. Niall Christie and M. Yazigi (Leiden: Brill, 2006), pp. 57–72.

Christie, Niall, 'Jerusalem in the *Kitāb al-Jihād* of 'Ali ibn Tahir al-Sulami (d. 1106)', *Medieval Encounters* 13 (2007): 209–21.

Christie, Niall, 'Motivating Listeners in the *Kitab al-Jihad* of 'Ali ibn Tahir al-Sulami', *Crusades* 6 (2007): 1–14.

Christie, Niall, 'Cosmopolitan Trade Centre or Bone of Contention? Alexandria and the Crusades, 487–857/1095–1453', *Al-Masaq* 26 (2014): 49–61.

Christie, Niall, 'Ibn al-Qalanisi', in *Medieval Muslim Historians and the Franks in the Levant*, ed. Alex Mallett (Leiden: Brill, 2015), pp. 8–13.

Christie, Niall, *Muslims and Crusaders: Christianity's Wars in the Middle East 1095–1382 from the Islamic Sources*, 2nd edn (Abingdon: Routledge, 2020).

Christie, Niall and Deborah Gerish, 'Parallel Preachings: Urban II and al-Sulami', *al-Masaq* 15 (2003): 139–48.

Cobb, Paul, *White Banners: Contention in 'Abbasid Syria, 750–880* (New York: State University of New York Press, 2001).

Cobb, Paul, 'Virtual Sacrality: Making Muslim Syria Sacred before the Crusades', *Medieval Encounters* 8 (2002): 35–55.

Cobb, Paul, *Usama Ibn Munqidh: Warrior-Poet of the Age of the Crusades* (London: Oneworld, 2005).

Cobb, Paul, 'Aq-Sunqur al-Bursuqi', in *Encyclopaedia of Islam: THREE*, ed. Kate Fleet et al. (2010), available at Brill online, last accessed 27 April 2019.

Cobb, Paul M., *The Race for Paradise: An Islamic History of the Crusades* (Oxford: Oxford University Press, 2014).

Cobb, Paul M., 'Hamdan al-Atharibi's History of the Franks Revisited, Again', in *Syria in Crusader Times Conflict and Co-Existence*, ed. Carole Hillenbrand (Edinburgh: Edinburgh University Press, 2019), pp. 3–20.

Cook, David, *Understanding Jihad* (London: University of California Press, 2005).

Cook, David, 'Were the Ismaili Assassins the First Recorded Suicide Attackers? An Examination of their Recorded Assassinations', in *The Lineaments of Islam: Studies in Honour of Fred McGraw Donner*, ed. Paul Cobb (Leiden: Brill, 2012), pp. 97–117.

Crawford, Robert, 'Ridwan the Maligned', in *The World of Islam: Studies in Honour of Philip K. Hitti*, ed. James Kritzeck and R. Bayly Winder (London: Macmillan, 1959), pp. 135–44.

Crone, Patricia, *Medieval Islamic Political Thought* (Edinburgh: Edinburgh University Press, 2004).

Dadoyan, Seta B., *The Fatimid Armenians: Cultural and Political Interaction in the Near East* (Leiden: Brill, 1997).
Dadoyan, Seta B., *The Armenians in the Medieval Islamic World: Paradigms of Interaction Seventh to Fourteenth Centuries*, 2 vols (London: Routledge, 2013).
Daftary, Farhad, *The Assassin Legends: Myths of the Isma'ilis* (London: I. B. Tauris, 1994).
Daftary, Farhad, 'Hasan-i Sabbah and the Origins of the Nizari Movement', in *Medieval Isma'ili History and Thought*, ed. Farhad Daftary (Cambridge: Cambridge University Press, 1996), pp. 181–204.
Daftary, Farhad, *The Isma'ilis: Their History and Doctrines* (Cambridge: Cambridge University Press, 2007).
Daftary, Farhad, 'Ismaili–Seljuq Relations: Conflict and Stalemate', in *The Age of the Seljuqs*, ed. Edmund Herzig and Sarah Stewart (London: I. B. Tauris, 2015), pp. 41–58.
Dahan, Sami, 'The Origin and Development of the Local Histories of Syria', in *Historians of the Middle East*, ed. Bernard Lewis and Peter Holt (London: Oxford University Press, 1962), pp. 108–17.
Dajani-Shakeel, Hadia, 'Jihad in Twelfth-century Arabic Poetry: A Moral and Religious Force to Counter the Crusades', *Muslim World* 66 (1976): 96–113.
Dajani-Shakeel, Hadia, 'Al-Quds: Jerusalem in the Consciousness of the Counter-Crusader', in *The Meeting of Two Worlds: Cultural Exchange between East and West during the Period of the Crusades*, ed. Vladimir P. Goss and Christine Verzár Bornstein (Kalamazoo: Medieval Institute Publications, Western Michigan University 1986), pp. 201–21.
Dajani-Shakeel, Hadia, 'A Reassessment of Some Medieval and Modern Perceptions of the Counter-Crusade', in *The Jihad and its Times*, ed. Hadia Dajani-Shakeel, Ronald A. Messier and Andrew S. Ehrenkreutz (Ann Arbor, MI: Center for Near Eastern and North African Studies, 1991), pp. 41–70.
Dajani-Shakeel, Hadia, 'Diplomatic Relations between Muslim and Frankish Rulers 1097–1153 A.D.', in *Crusaders and Muslims in Twelfth-Century Syria*, ed. Maya Shatzmiller (Leiden: Brill, 1993), pp. 190–215.
Dangles, Philippe, 'Afamiya. Qal'at al-Mudiq, Die Mittelalterliche Wiederbefestigung der Antiken Zitadelle von Apamea am Ende des 12. bis Mitte des 13. Jahrhunderts', in *Burgen und Städte der Kreuzzugszeit*, ed. Mathias Piana (Petersberg: Imhof, 2008), pp. 221–33.
Darling, Linda T., *A History of Social Justice and Political Power in the Middle East* (London: Routledge, 2013).

Decker, Michael, 'Frontier Settlement and Economy in the Byzantine East', *Dumbarton Oaks Papers* 61 (2007): 234–8, 220.

Dédéyan, Gérard, 'Razzias "Turcomanes" et Contre-Razzias Arméniennes dans le Diyâr Bakr au Début du XIIe Siècle. Les Banoû Bôgousag de Sewawerak contre les Mamokonian de Karkar', in *Itinéraires d'Orient: Hommages à Claude Cahen*, ed. Raoul Curiel and Rika Gyselen (Bures-Sur-Yvette: Groupe pour l'Étude de la Civilisation du Moyen-Orient, 1994), pp. 49–58.

Dédéyan, Gérard, *Les arméniens entre grecs, musulmans et croisés. Étude sur les pouvoirs arméniens dans le Proche-Orient méditerranéen (1068–1150)*, 2 vols (Lisbon: Fundação Calouste Gulbenkian, 2003).

Dédéyan, Gérard, 'The Founding and Coalescence of the Rubenian Principality, 1073–1129', in *Armenian Cilicia*, ed. Robert Hovannisian and Simon Payaslian (Costa Mesa, CA: Mazda, 2008), pp. 79–92.

Deschamps, Paul, *Les châteaux des croisés. La défense du comté de Tripoli et de la principauté d'Antioche*, 3 vols (Paris: P. Geuthner, 1934–73).

Durak, Koray, 'Who are the Romans? The Definition of *Bilad al-Rum* (Land of the Romans) in Medieval Islamic Geographies', *Journal of Intercultural Studies* 31 (2010): 285–98.

Durand-Guédy, David, *Iranian Elites and Turkish Rulers: a History of Isfahahan in the Saljuq Period* (London: Routledge, 2010).

Durand-Guédy, David, 'The Türkmen–Saljuq Relationship in Twelfth-century Iran: New Elements based on a Contrastive Analysis of Three Insa' Documents', *Eurasian Studies* 9 (2011): 11–66.

Durand-Guédy, David, 'Ruling from the Outside: a New perspective on Early Turkish Kingship in Iran', in *Every Inch a King: Comparative Studies on Kings and Kingship in the Ancient and Medieval Worlds*, ed. Lynette G. Mitchell and Charles P. Melville (Leiden: Brill, 2012), pp. 325–42.

Durand-Guédy, David, 'Goodbye to the Türkmen? The Military Role of Nomads in Iran after the Saljuq Conquest', in *Nomadic Military Power: Iran and the Adjacent Areas in the Islamic Period*, ed. Kurt Franz and Wolfgang Holzwarth (Wiesbaden: Reichert Verlag, 2015), pp. 107–36.

Durand-Guédy, David, 'New Trends in the Political History of Iran Under the Great Saljuqs (11th–12th Centuries)', *History Compass* 13 (2015): 321–37.

Dussaud, René, *Topographie historique de la Syrie antique et médiévale* (Paris: P. Geuthner, 1927).

Eastmond, Antony and Lynn Jones, 'Robing, Power, and Legitimacy in Armenia and

Georgia', in *Robes and Honor: the Medieval World of Investiture*, ed. Stewart Gordon (New York: Palgrave Macmillan, 2001), pp. 147–92.

Ed., 'Ibn Zafir', in *Encyclopaedia of Islam*, 2nd edn, ed. Peri Bearman et al. (2012), available at Brill online, last accessed 10 July 2017.

Eddé, Anne-Marie, 'Ridwan, Prince D'Alep de 1095 à 1113', *Revue de études Islamiques* 54 (1986): 101–25.

Eddé, Anne-Marie, 'Sources arabes des XIIe et XIIIe siècles d'après le dictionnaire biographique d'Ibn al-'Adim (Bugyat al-Talab fi Ta'rih Halab)', in *Itinéraires d'Orient. Hommages à Claude Cahen*, ed. Raoul Curiel and Rika Gyselen (Bures-sur-Yvette: Groupe pour l'étude de la civilisation du Moyen-Orient, 1994), pp. 293–307.

Eddé, Anne-Marie, 'Francs et musulmans de Syrie au début du XIIe siècle d'après l'historien Ibn Abi Tayyi', in *Dei gesta per Francos. Études sur les croisades dédiées à Jean Richard*, ed. Michel Balard, Benjamin Kedar and Jonathan Riley-Smith (Aldershot: Routledge, 2001), pp. 159–69.

Eddé, Anne-Marie, 'Kamal al-Din 'Umar Ibn al-'Adim', in *Medieval Muslim Historians and the Franks in the Levant*, ed. Alex Mallett (Leiden: Brill, 2015), pp. 109–35

Eddé, Anne-Marie, 'Ibn al-'Adim, Kamal al-Din', in *Encyclopaedia of Islam: THREE*, ed. Kate Fleet et al. (2017), available at Brill online, last accessed 10 July 2017.

Eddé, Anne-Marie and Jean-Pierre Sodini, 'Les Villages de Syrie du Nord du VIIe au XIIIe Siecle', in *Les Villages dans l'Empire byzantine (IVe–XVe siècle)*, ed. Jaques Lefort, Cécile Morrisson and Jean-Pierre Sodini (Paris: Lethielleux, 2005), pp. 465–83.

Edgington, Susan B., 'Antioch: Medieval City of Culture', in *East and West in the Medieval Eastern Mediterranean, vol. I: Antioch from the Byzantine Reconquest until the End of the Crusader Principality*, ed. K Krinja Ciggaar and David M. Metcalf (Leuven: Peeters, 2006), pp. 247–59.

Eger, A. Asa, *The Islamic Byzantine Frontier* (London: Bloomsbury, 2014).

El-Azhari, Taef K., *The Saljuqs of Syria During the Crusades 463–549 A.H./1070–1154 A.D.* (Berlin: Klaus Schwarz, 1997).

El-Azhari, Taef, 'The Role of Saljuqid Women in Medieval Syria', in *Egypt and Syria in the Fatimid, Ayyubid and Mamluk Eras*, 9 vols, ed. Urbain Vermeulen and Jo van Steenbergen (Leuven: Peeters, 2005), IV, pp. 111–26.

El-Azhari, Taef K., 'The Policy of Balak the Artuqid against Muslim and Crusaders: a Turkmen Identity Dilemma in the Middle East 1090–1124', *International Journal of Humanities and Social Science* 4 (2014): 286–93.

El-Azhari, Taef K., *Zengi and the Muslim Response to the Crusades* (London: Routledge, 2015).

El-Azhari, Taef, *Queens, Eunuchs and Concubines in Islamic History, 661–1257* (Edinburgh: Edinburgh University Press, 2019), pp. 285–348.

El-Azhari, Taef, 'al-'Azimi', in *Encyclopaedia of Islam: THREE*, ed. Kate Fleet et al. (2020), available at Brill online, last accessed 29 December 2021.

El-Shayyal, Gamal El-Din, 'Ibn Wasil', in *Encyclopaedia of Islam*, 2nd edn, ed. Peri Bearman et al. (2012), available at Brill online, last accessed 10 July 2017.

Elisséeff, Nikita, *Nur ad-Din. Un grande prince musulman de Syrie au temps des croisades*, 3 vols (Damascus: Institut français de Damas, 1967).

Elisséeff, Nikita, 'The Reaction of the Syrian Muslims after the Foundation of the First Latin Kingdom of Jerusalem', in *The Crusades: The Essential Readings*, ed. Thomas F. Madden (Oxford: Wiley-Blackwell, 2002), pp. 221–33.

Elisséeff, Nikita, 'Ibn 'Asakir', in *Encyclopaedia of Islam*, 2nd edn, ed. Peri Bearman et al. (2012), available online, last accessed 10 July 2017.

Ellenblum, Ronnie, *Frankish Rural Settlement in the Latin Kingdom of Jerusalem* (Cambridge: Cambridge University Press, 2002).

Ellenblum, Ronnie, 'Were there Borders and Borderlines in the Middle Ages? The Example of the Latin Kingdom of Jerusalem', in *Medieval Frontiers: Concepts and Practices*, ed. David Abulafia and Nora Berend (Aldershot: Ashgate, 2002), pp. 105–19.

Ellenblum, Ronnie, *Crusader Castles and Modern Histories* (Cambridge: Cambridge University Press, 2007).

Ellenblum, Ronnie, *The Collapse of the Eastern Mediterranean: Climate Change and the Decline of the East 950–1072* (Cambridge: Cambridge University Press, 2012).

Ephrat, Dafnah, *A Learned Society in a Period of Transition: the Sunni "Ulama" of Eleventh-century Baghdad* (New York: State University of New York Press, 2000).

Ephrat, Dafnah, 'The Seljuqs and the Public Sphere in the Period of Sunni Revivalism: the View from Baghdad', in *The Seljuqs: Politics, Society and Culture*, ed. Christian Lange and Songül Mecit (Edinburgh: Edinburgh University Press, 2011), pp. 139–56.

Estevez, María de la P., 'The Development of Feudal Relations in a Post-Conquest Reality: the Experience of the Mozarab Community of Toledo (Eleventh–Thirteenth Centuries)', *Al-Masaq* 24 (2012): pp. 293–308.

Fletcher, Richard, 'Reconquest and Crusade in Spain c. 1050–1150', *Transactions of the Royal Historical Society* 37 (1987): 31–47.

Fletcher, Richard A., *Moorish Spain* (London: Phoenix, 1992).

Foss, Clive, 'The Defences of Asia Minor against the Turks', *Greek Orthodox Theological Review* 27 (1982): 145–205.

Fourdrin, Jean-Pascal, 'La fortification de la seigneurie épiscopale latine d'El Bara dans le patriarcat d'Antioche (1098–1148)', in *Pèlerinages et Croisades*, ed. Léon Pressouyre (Paris: Éditions du CTHS, 1995), pp. 351–406.

Fowden, Garth, *Empire to Commonwealth: Consequences of Monotheism in Late Antiquity* (Princeton, NJ: Princeton University, 1994).

France, John, *Victory in the East* (Cambridge: Cambridge University Press, 1995).

France, John, 'Technology and the Success of the First Crusade', in *War and Society in the Eastern Mediterranean 7th–15th Centuries*, ed. Yaacov Lev (Leiden: Brill, 1997), pp. 163–76.

France, John, *Western Warfare in the Age of the Crusades 1000–1300* (Abingdon: Routledge, 1999).

Frankopan, Peter, *The First Crusade: The Call of the East* (Cambridge, MA: Belknap Press of Harvard University Press, 2012).

Franz, Kurt, *Vom Beutezug zur Territorialherrschaft. Das lange Jahrhundert des Aufstieges von Nomaden zur Vormacht in Syrien und Mesopotamien 286–420/889–1029* (Wiesbaden: Reichert, 2007).

Franz, Kurt, 'Framing the Mongol–Mamluk Wars in Long-term History', in *Nomad Military Power in Iran and Adjacent Areas in the Islamic Period*, ed. Kurt Franz and Wolfang Holzwarth (Wiesbaden: Reichert, 2015), pp. 29–107.

Freeman-Greenville, G. S. P., 'Sikka', in *Encyclopaedia of Islam*, 2nd edn, ed. Peri Bearman et al. (2012), available at Brill online, last accessed 15 June 2019.

Frenkel, Yehoshua, 'The Impact of the Crusades on Rural Society and Religious Endowments: the Case of Medieval Syria', in *War and Society in the Eastern Mediterranean 7th–15th Centuries*, ed. Yaacov Lev (Leiden: Brill, 1997), pp. 237–48.

Frenkel, Yehoshua, 'The Turks of the Eurasian Steppes in Medieval Arabic Writing', in *Mongols, Turks and Others: Eurasian Nomads and the Sedentary World*, ed. Reuven Amitai and Michal Biran (Leiden: Brill, 2005), pp. 201–41.

Frenkel, Yehoshua, 'Muslim Responses to the Frankish Dominion in the Near East, 1098–1291', in *The Crusades and the Near East Cultural Histories*, ed. Conor Kostick (Abingdon: Routledge, 2011), pp. 27–54.

Frenkel, Yehoshua, 'The Coming of the Barbarians: Can Climate Explain the Seljuqs' Advance?' in *Socio-Environmental Dynamics along the Historical Silk Road*, ed. Liang Emlyn Yang, Hans-Rudolf Bork, Xiuqi Fang and Steffen Mischke (Cham: Springer, 2019), pp. 261–74.

Friedman, Yvonne, *Encounter between Enemies: Captivity and Ransom in the Latin Kingdom of Jerusalem* (Leiden: Brill, 2002).

Friedman, Yvonne, 'Peacemaking: Perceptions and Practices in the Medieval Latin East', in *The Crusades and the Near East: Cultural Histories*, ed. Conor Kostick (Abingdon: Routledge, 2011), pp. 229–57.

Fulton, Michael S., *Artillery in the Era of the Crusades* (Leiden: Brill, 2018), pp. 39–149.

Gaube, Heinz and Eugen Wirth, *Aleppo: historische und geographische Beiträge zur baulichen Gestaltung, zur socialen Organisation und zur wirtschaflichen Dynamic einer vorderasiatischen Fernhandelsmetropole* (Wiesbaden: Reichert, 1984).

Gelichi, Sauro, 'The Citadel of Harim', in *Muslim Military Architecture in Greater Syria: From the Coming of Islam to the Ottoman Period*, ed. Hugh Kennedy (Leiden: Brill, 2006), pp. 184–200.

Ghazarian, Jacob, *The Armenian Kingdom in Cilicia During the Crusades* (London: Curzon, 2000).

Gibb, Hamilton A. R., 'Notes on the Arabic Materials for the History of the Early Crusades', *Bulletin of the School of Oriental Studies* 7 (1935): 739–54.

Gibb, Hamilton A. R., 'Review of Histoire des Croisades et du Royaume Franc de Jérusalem. I. L'Anarchie Musulmane et la Monarchie Franque by René Grousset', *Bulletin of the School of Oriental Studies* 7 (1935): 981–3.

Gibb, Hamilton A. R., 'The Caliphate and the Arab States', in *A History of the Crusades*, 2 vols, ed. Kenneth M. Setton and Marshall Baldwin (Philadelphia: University of Pennsylvania Press, 1955), I, pp. 88–99.

Gibb, Hamilton A. R., 'Abu'l Fida', in *Encyclopaedia of Islam*, 2nd edn, ed. Peri Bearman et al. (2012), available at Brill online, last accessed 10 July 2017.

Gil, Moshe, *A History of Palestine 634–1099* (Cambridge: Cambridge University Press, 1992).

Greenwood, Tim, 'Armenian Sources', in *Byzantines and Crusaders in Non-Greek Sources 1025–1204*, ed. Mary Whitby (Oxford: Oxford University Press for the British Academy, 2007), pp. 221–41.

Goridis, Philippe, *Gefangen im Heiligen Land Verarbeitung und Bewältigung christlicher Gefangenschaft zur Zeit der Kreuzzüge* (Ostfildern: Thorbecke, 2015).

Golden, Peter B., 'Courts and Court Culture in the Proto-Urban Developments among the pre-Chingisid Turkic Peoples', in *Turko-Mongol Rulers, Cities and City Life*, ed. David Durand-Guédy (Leiden: Brill, 2013), pp. 21–73.

Gonnella, Julia, 'The Citadel of Aleppo: Recent Studies', in *Muslim Military*

Architecture in Greater Syria: From the Coming of Islam to the Ottoman Period, ed. Hugh Kennedy (Leiden: Brill, 2006), pp. 165–75.

Goudie, Kenneth A., 'Legitimate Authority in the Kitab al-Jihad of 'Ali b. Tahir al-Sulami', in *Syria in Crusader Times: Conflict and Co-Existence*, ed. Carole Hillenbrand (Edinburgh: Edinburgh University Press, 2019), pp. 21–33.

Goudie, Kenneth A., *Reinventing Jihad: Jihad Ideology from the Conquest of Jerusalem to the End of the Ayyubids* (Leiden: Brill, 2019).

Grousset, René, *Histoire des croisades et du royaume franc de Jérusalem*, 3 vols (Paris: Perrin, 1934–6).

Hagler, Aaron M., 'Unity through Omission: Literary Strategies of Recension in Ibn al-Atir's al-Kamil fi l-Ta'rikh', *Arabica* 65 (2018): 285–313.

Haider, Najam I., 'Al-Husayn b. 'Ali b. Abi Talib', in *Encyclopaedia of Islam: THREE*, ed. Kate Fleet et al. (2016), available at Brill online, last accessed 15 June 2019.

Haldon, John, 'Approaches to an Alternate Military History of the Period ca. 1025–1071', in *The Empire in Crisis(?): Byzantium in the Eleventh Century (1025–1081)*, ed. Vassiliki N. Vlyssidou (Athens: Institute for Byzantine Research, 2003), pp. 45–74.

Halm, Heinz, *Die Kalifen von Kairo: Die Fatimiden in Ägypten 973–1074* (Munich: C.H. Beck, 2003).

Halm, Heinz, 'Badr al-Gamali. Wesir oder Militärdiktator', in *Egypt and Syria in the Fatimid, Ayyubid and Mamluk Eras*, 9 vols, ed. Urbain Vermeulen and Kristof D'Hulster (Leuven: Peeters, 2007), vol. V, pp. 79–85.

Halm, Heinz, *Kalifen und Assassinen: Ägypten und der Vordere Orient zur Zeit der ersten Kreuzzüge 1074–1171* (Munich: C. H. Beck, 2014).

Hamblin, William, 'To Wage Jihad or Not: Fatimid Egypt During the Early Crusades', in *The Jihad and its Times*, ed. Hadia Dajani-Shakeel, Ronald A. Messier and Andrew S. Ehrenkreutz (Ann Arbor, MI: Center for Near Eastern and North African Studies, 1991), pp. 31–41.

Hanne, Eric J., 'Death on the Tigris: a Numismatic Analysis of the Decline of the Great Saljuqs', *American Journal of Numismatics* 16 (2004): 145–72.

Hanne, Eric, 'Women, Power, and the Eleventh and Twelfth Century Abbasid Court', *Hawwa* 3 (2005): 80–110.

Hanne, Eric, 'The Banu Jahir and Their Role in the 'Abbasid and Seljuq Administration', *Al-Masaq* 20 (2008): 29–45.

Harris, Jonathan, *Byzantium and the Crusades* (London: Bloomsbury, 2003).

Havemann, Axel, 'The Vizier and the Ra'is in Saljuq Syria: the Struggle for Urban

Self-Representation', *International Journal of Middle East Studies* 21 (1989): 233–42.

Heck, Paul L., '"Jihad" Revisited', *Journal of Religious Ethics* 32 (2004): 95–128.

Heidemann, Stefan, *Die Renaissance der Städte in Nordsyrien und Nordmesopotamien. Städtische Entwicklung und wirtschaftliche Bedingungen in ar-Raqqa und Harran von der Zeit der beduinischen Vorherrschaft bis zu den Seldschuken* (Leiden: Brill, 2002).

Heidemann, Stefan, 'Arab Nomads and the Saljuq Military', in *Shifts and Drifts in Nomad–Sedentary Relations*, ed. Stefan Leder and Bernhard Streck (Wiesbaden: Reichert, 2005), pp. 289–305.

Heidemann, Stefan, 'Numayrid ar-Raqqa Archaeological and Historical Evidence for a "Dimorphic State" in the Bedouin Dominated Fringes of the Fatimid Empire', in *Egypt and Syria in the Fatimid, Ayyubid and Mamluk Eras*, 9 vols, ed. Urbain Vermeulen and Jo Van Steenbergen (Leuven: Peeters, 2005), vol. IV, pp. 85–109.

Heidemann, Stefan, 'The Citadel of al-Raqqa and the Fortifications in the Middle Euphrates Area', in *Muslim Military Architecture in Greater Syria: From the Coming of Islam to the Ottoman Period*, ed. Hugh Kennedy (Leiden: Brill, 2006), pp. 122–50.

Heidemann, Stefan, 'Charity and Piety for the Transformation of the City: the New Direction in Taxation and Waqf Policy in Mid-Twelfth Century Syria and Northern Mesopotamia', in *Charity and Giving in Monotheistic Religions*, ed. Miriam Frenkel and Yaacov Lev (Berlin: De Gruyter, 2009), pp. 154–74, 164.

Heidemann, Stefan, 'Numismatics', in *The New Cambridge History of Islam, Volume I*, ed. Chase F. Robinson (Cambridge: Cambridge University Press, 2010), pp. 648–779, 661.

Hillenbrand, Carole, 'Some Medieval Islamic Approaches to Source Material: the Evidence of a 12th Century Chronicle', *Oriens* 27 (1981): 197–225.

Hillenbrand, Carole, 'The Career of Najm al-Din Il-ghazi', *Der Islam* 58 (1981): 250–92.

Hillenbrand, Carole, 'Jihad Propaganda in Syria from the Time of the First Crusade until the Death of Zengi: the Evidence of Monumental Inscriptions', in *The Frankish Wars and their Influence on Palestine: Selected Papers Presented at Birzeit University's International Academic Conference Held in Jerusalem*, ed. Khalil 'Athaminah and Roger Heacock (Birzeit: Birzeit University Publications, 1994), pp. 60–9.

Hillenbrand, Carole, '1092: A Murderous Year', in *Proceedings of the 14th Congress* of *Union européene des arabisants et islamisants*, ed. Alexander Fodor (Budapest: Eotvos Loránd University Chair for Arabic Studies: Csoma de Koros Society, 1995), pp. 281–96.

Hillenbrand, Carole, 'Ibn al-'Adim's Biography of the Seljuq Sultan, Alp Arslan', *Actas XVI Congreso UEAI*, ed. Maria C. Vázquez de Benito and Miguel A. Manzano Rodriguez (Salamanca: Agencia Española de Cooperación Internacional, 1995), pp. 237–42.

Hillenbrand, Carole, 'The Power Struggle between the Saljuqs and the Isma'ilis of Alamut, 478–518/1094–1125: The Saljuq Perspective', in *Medieval Isma'ili History and Thought*, ed. Farhad Daftary (Cambridge: Cambridge University Press, 1996), pp. 205–21.

Hillenbrand, Carole, 'The First Crusade: The Muslim Perspective', in *The First Crusade: Origins and Impact*, ed. Jonathan Phillips (Manchester: Manchester University Press, 1997), pp. 130–41.

Hillenbrand, Carole, *The Crusades: Islamic Perspectives* (Edinburgh: Edinburgh University Press, 1999).

Hillenbrand, Carole, '"Abominable Acts": the Career of Zengi', in *The Second Crusade: Scope and Consequences*, ed. Jonathan Phillips and Martin Hoch (Manchester: Manchester University Press, 2001), pp. 111–32.

Hillenbrand, Carole, 'Women in the Seljuq Period', in *Women in Iran from the Rise of Islam to 1800*, ed. Guity Nashat and Lois Beck (Urbana: University of Illinois Press, 2003), pp. 103–20.

Hillenbrand, Carole, 'Sources in Arabic', in *Byzantines and Crusaders in Non-Greek Sources 1025–1204*, ed. Mary Whitby (Oxford: Oxford University Press for the British Academy, 2007), pp. 283–340.

Hillenbrand, Carole, *Turkish Myth and Symbol: the Battle of Manzikert* (Edinburgh: Edinburgh University Press, 2007).

Hillenbrand, Carole, 'Jihad Poetry in the Age of the Crusades', in *Crusades: Medieval Worlds in Conflict*, ed. Thomas F. Madden, James L. Naus and Vincent Ryan (London: Routledge, 2010), pp. 9–23.

Hillenbrand, Carole, 'Aspects of the Court of the Great Seljuqs', in *The Seljuqs: Politics, Society and Culture*, ed. Christian Lange and Söngul Mecit (Edinburgh: Edinburgh, University Press, 2011), pp. 22–39.

Hillenbrand, Carole, 'What's in a Name? Tughtegin: "the Minister of the Antichrist"?' in *Fortresses of the Intellect: Ismaili and Other Islamic Studies in Honour of Farhad Daftary*, ed. Omar Alí-de-Unzaga (London: I. B. Tauris, 2011), pp. 459–71.

Hillenbrand, Carole, 'The Shi'is of Aleppo in the Zengid Period: Some Unexploited Textual and Epigraphic Evidence', in *Difference and Dynamism in Islam*, ed. Hinrich Biesterfeldt and Verena Klemm (Tübingen: Ergon, 2012), pp. 163–79.

Hillenbrand, Carole, *Islam: A New Historical Introduction* (London: Thames & Hudson, 2015).

Hillenbrand, Carole, 'Nizam al-Mulk: A Maverick Vizier?' in *The Age of the Seljuqs*, ed. Edmund Herzig and Sarah Stewart (London: I. B. Tauris, 2015), pp. 28–40.

Hinz, Walther, *Islamische Masse und Gewichte. Umgerechnet ins Metrische System* (Leiden: Brill, 1970).

Hirschler, Konrad, *Medieval Arabic Historiography: Authors as Actors* (Abingdon: Routledge, 2006).

Hirschler, Konrad, '"He is a Child and this Land is a Borderland of Islam": Under-age Rule and the Quest for Political Stability in the Ayyubid Period', *al-Masaq* 19 (2007): 29–46.

Hirschler, Konrad, *The Written Word in the Medieval Arabic Lands* (Edinburgh: Edinburgh University Press, 2012).

Hirschler, Konrad, 'Studying Mamluk Historiography: From Source-Criticism to the Cultural Turn', in *Ubi sumus? Quo vademus? Mamluk Studies-State of the Art*, ed. Stephan Conermann (Bonn: Bonn University Press, 2013), pp. 159–86.

Hirschler, Konrad, 'The Jerusalem Conquest of 492/1099 in the Medieval Arabic Historiography of the Crusades: From Regional Plurality to Islamic Narrative', *Crusades* 13 (2014): 37–76.

Hirschler, Konrad, 'Ibn Wasil: An Ayyubid Perspective on Frankish Lordships and Crusades', in *Medieval Muslim Historians and the Franks in the Levant*, ed. Alex Mallett (Leiden: Brill, 2015), pp. 142–3.

Hodgson, M. G. S., *The Order of Assassins: the Struggle of the Early Nizârî Ismâ'îlîs against the Islamic World* (Philadelphia: University of Pennsylvania Press, 2005).

Holmes, Catherine, 'Byzantium's Eastern Frontier in the Tenth and Eleventh Centuries', in *Medieval Frontiers: Concepts and Practices*, ed. David Abulafia and Nora Berend (Aldershot: Routledge, 2002), pp. 83–105.

Holt, P. M., *The Age of the Crusades: the Near East from the Eleventh Century until 1517* (London: Routledge, 2014).

Humphreys, R. Stephen, *From Saladin to the Mongols: the Ayyubids of Damascus 1193–1260* (New York: State University of New York Press, 1977).

Humphreys, R. Stephen, 'Munkidh', in *Encyclopaedia of Islam*, 2nd edn, ed. Peri Bearman et al. (2012), available at Brill online, last accessed 10 July 2017.

Humphreys, R. Stephen, 'Ta'rikh', in *Encyclopaedia of Islam*, 2nd edn, ed. Peri Bearman et al. (2012), available at Brill online, last accessed 10 July 2017.

Imad, Leila S., *The Fatimid Vizierate: 969–1172* (Berlin: Shwarz, 1990).

Inalcik, Halil, 'Resm', in *Encyclopaedia of Islam*, 2nd edn, ed. Peri Bearman et al. (2012), available at Brill online, last accessed 15 June 2019.

Irwin, Robert, 'Islam and the Crusades 1096–1699' in *The Oxford Illustrated History of the Crusades*, ed. by Jonathan Riley-Smith (Oxford: Oxford University Press, 1995), pp. 217–59.

Irwin, Robert, 'Usama ibn Munqidh: an Arab-Syrian Gentleman at the time of the Crusades Reconsidered', in *The Crusades and their Sources*, ed. John France and William G. Zajac (Aldershot: Routledge, 1998), pp. 71–87.

Jiménez, Manuel G., 'Frontier and Settlement in the Kingdom of Castile (1085–1350)', in *Medieval Frontier Societies*, ed. Robert Bartlett and Agnus MacKay (Oxford: Oxford University Press, 1996), pp. 49–76.

Jiwa, Shainool, *The Fatimids, vol. 1: The Rise of a Muslim Empire* (London: Bloomsbury, 2017).

Jotischky, Andrew, 'The Christians of Jerusalem, the Holy Sepulchre and the Origins of the First Crusade', *Crusades* 7 (2008): 35–57.

Jotischky, Andrew, *Crusading and the Crusader States* (Abingdon: Routledge, 2017).

Jotischky, Andrew, 'Ethnic and Religious Categories in the Treatment of Jews and Muslims in the Crusader States', in *Antisemitism and Islamophobia in Europe: a Shared Story?* ed. James Renton and Ben Gidley (London: Palgrave Macmillan, 2017), pp. 25–49.

Kaegi, Walter E., 'The Contribution of Archery to the Turkish Conquest of Anatolia', *Speculum* 39 (1969): 96–108.

Kaniewski, David, Van Campo, Elise, Paulissen, Etienne, Weiss, Harvey, Otto, Thierry, Bakker, Johan, Rossignol, Ingrid and Van Lerberghe, Karel, 'Medieval Coastal Syrian Vegetation Patterns in the Principality of Antioch', *The Holocene* 21 (2010): 251–62.

Khazanov, Anatoly M., 'The Eurasian Steppe Nomads in World Military History', in *Nomad Aristocracies in a World of Empires*, ed. Jürgen Paul (Wiesbaden: Reichert Verlag, 2013), pp. 187–207.

Kedar, Benjamin Z., 'The Subjected Muslims of the Frankish Levant', in *Muslims under Latin Rule 1100–1300*, ed. James M. Powell (Princeton, NJ: Princeton University Press, 1990).

Kedar, Benjamin Z., 'Some New Sources on Palestinian Muslims Before and During the Crusades', in *Die Kreuzfahrerstaaten als multikulturelle Gesellschaft:*

Einwanderer und Minderheiten im 12. und 13. Jahrhundert, ed. Hans E. Mayer and Elisabeth Müller-Luckner (Munich: Oldenbourg, 1997), pp. 129–40.

Kedar, Benjamin Z., 'The Jerusalem Massacre of July 1099 in the Western Historiography of the Crusades', *Crusades* 3 (2004): 15–75.

Kedar, Benjamin Z., 'Studying the "Shared Sacred Spaces" of the Medieval Levant: Where Historians May Meet Anthropologists', *Al-Masaq* 34 (2022): 111–26.

Kennedy, Hugh, 'From Polis to Madina: Urban Change in Late Antique and Early Islamic Syria', *Past and Present* 106 (1985): 3–27.

Kennedy, Hugh, 'Nomads and Settled People in Bilad al-Sham in the Third/Ninth and Fourth/Tenth Centuries', in *Bilad al-Sham during the Abbasid Period: Proceedings of the Fifth International Conference on the History of Bilad al-Sham*, ed. Muhammad A. Bakhit and Robert Schick (Amman: History of the Bilad al-Sham Committee, 1991), pp. 105–13.

Kennedy, Hugh, *Crusader Castles* (Cambridge: Cambridge University Press, 1994).

Kennedy, Hugh, *Muslim Spain and Portugal: a Political History of al-Andalus* (London: Longman, 1996).

Kennedy, Hugh, *The Court of the Caliphs: When Baghdad Ruled the Muslim World* (London: Phoenix, 2004).

Kennedy, Hugh, 'The City and the Nomad', *The New Cambridge History of Islam, Volume Four*, ed. Robert Irwin (Cambridge: Cambridge University Press, 2010), pp. 274–89.

Kennedy, Hugh, *The Prophet and the Age of the Caliphates. The Islamic Near East from the Sixth to the Eleventh Century* (London: Routledge, 2015).

Klausner, Carla L., *The Seljuk Vezirate: a Study of Civil Administration 1055–1194* (Cambridge, MA: Harvard University Press, 1973).

Klemm, Verena, *Memoirs of a Mission: the Islamic Scholar, Statesman and Poet al-Mu'ayyad fi'l-Din al-Shirazi* (London: I. B. Tauris, 2003).

Köhler, Michael A., 'Al-Afdal and Jerusalem – was versprach sich Ägypten vom ersten Kreuzzug?' *Saeculum* 37 (1986): 228–39.

Köhler, Michael A., *Allianzen und Verträge zwischen fränkischen und islamischen Herrschern im Vorderen Orient* (Berlin: De Gruyter, 1991, repr. 2014).

Köhler, Michael A., 'Munasafa', in *Encyclopaedia of Islam*, 2nd edn, ed. Peri Bearman et al. (2012), available online, last accessed 19 March 2019.

Köhler, Michael A., *Alliances and Treaties between Frankish and Muslim Rulers in the Middle East* (Leiden: Brill, 2013).

König, Daniel, *Arabic-Islamic Views of the West* (Oxford: Oxford University Press, 2015).

Korn, Lorenz, 'The Sultan Stopped at Halab: Artistic Exchange between Syria and Iran in the 5th/11th Century', in *Die Grenzen der Welt. Arabica et Iranica ad honore, Heinz Gaube*, ed. Lorenz Korn, Eva Orthmann and Florian Schwarz (Wiesbaden: Reichert, 2008), pp. 105–21.

Korobenikov, Dimitri, '"The King of the East and the West": the Seljuk Dynastic Concept and Titles in Muslim and Christian Sources', in *The Seljuks of Anatolia: Court and Society in the Medieval Middle East*, ed. Andrew C. S. Peacock and Sara N. Yildiz (London: I. B. Tauris, 2013), pp. 68–90.

Kostick, Conor, *The Social Structure of the First Crusade* (Leiden: Brill, 2008).

Kostick, Conor, *The Siege of Jerusalem: Crusades and Conquest in 1099* (London: Continuum, 2009).

Kosto, Adam, 'Hostages during the First Century of the Crusades', *Medieval Encounters* 9 (2003): 3–31.

Krallis, Dimitrios, 'The Army that Crossed Two Frontiers and Established a Third: The Uses of the Frontier in an Eleventh-century Author (and Some Implications on Modern Scholarship)', in *Frontiers in the Middle Ages*, ed. Outi Merisalo and Paivi Pahta (Louvain-La-Neuve: Federation internationale des instituts d'etudes medievales, 2006), pp. 335–48.

Krawczyk, Jean-Luc, 'The Relationship between Pastoral Nomadism and Agriculture: Northern Syria and the Jazira in the Eleventh Century', *JRŪR* 1 (1985): 1–22, 15–20.

Lambton, Ann K. S., 'The Internal Structure of the Saljuq Empire', in *The Cambridge History of Iran, vol. V: The Saljuq and Mongol Periods*, ed. John A. Boyle (Cambridge: Cambridge University Press, 1968), pp. 203–82.

Lambton, Ann K. S., 'Aspects of Saljuq Ghuzz Settlement in Persia', in *Islamic Civilisation 950–1150*, ed. Donald S. Richards (Oxford: Cassirer, 1973), pp. 105–25.

Lambton, Ann K. S., *Continuity and Change in Medieval Persia: Aspects of Administrative, Economic and Social History* (Albany, NY: Bibliotheca Persica, 1988).

Lambton, Ann K. S., *State and Government in Medieval Islam: An Introduction to the Study of Islamic Political Theory: The Jursits* (London, RoutledgeCurzon, 2014).

La Monte, John L., *The Feudal Monarchy in the Latin Kingdom of Jerusalem 1100 to 1291* (Cambridge, MA: Mediaeval Academy of America, 1932).

Laoust, Henri, 'Ibn al-Djawzi', in *Encyclopaedia of Islam*, 2nd edn, ed. Peri Bearman et al. (2012), available at Brill online, last accessed 10 July 2017.

Laoust, Henri, 'Ibn Kathir', in *Encyclopaedia of Islam*, 2nd edn, ed. Peri Bearman et al. (2012), available at Brill online, last accessed 10 July 2017.

Latiff, Osman, *The Cutting Edge of the Poet's Sword: Muslim Poetic Responses to the Crusades* (Leiden: Brill, 2017).

Lapidus, Ira M., *Muslim Cities in the Later Middle Ages* (Cambridge: Cambridge University Press, 1984).

Laurent, Vitalien, 'La Chronologie des Gouverneurs d'Antioche sous la seconde Domination Byzantine', *Mélanges de l'Université Saint-Joseph* 38 (1962): 221–54.

Lawrence, Thomas E., *Crusader Castles* (London: The Folio Society, 1992).

Le Strange, Guy, *Palestine Under the Moslems: a Description of Syria and the Holy Land from A.D. 650–1500* (London: Alexander P. Watt, 1890).

Lev, Yaacov, *State and Society in Fatimid Egypt* (Leiden: Brill, 1990).

Lev, Yaacov, 'Prisoners of War during the Fatimid–Ayyubid Wars with the Crusaders', in *Tolerance and Intolerance: Social Conflict in the Age of the Crusades*, ed. Michael Gervers and James M. Powell (Syracuse: Syracuse University Press 2001), pp. 11–27.

Lev, Yaacov, 'The Social and Economic Policies of Nur al-Din (1146–1174) Sultan of Syria', *Der Islam* 81 (2004): 218–42.

Lev, Yaacov, 'The "Jihad" of Sultan Nur al-Din of Syria (1146–1174): History and Discourse', *Jerusalem Studies in Arabic and Islam* 35 (2008): 227–84.

Lewis, Bernard, *The Assassins: a Radical Sect in Islam* (London: Weidenfeld & Nicolson, 1967).

Lewis, Kevin, *The Counts of Tripoli and Lebanon in the Twelfth Century: Sons of St Gilles* (Abingdon: Routledge, 2017).

Lille, Ralph-Johannes, *Byzantium and the Crusader States 1096–1204* (Oxford: Clarendon, 1993).

Lindsay, James E., *Ibn 'Asakir and Early Islamic History* (Princeton NJ: Darwin Press, 2001).

Lyons, M. C. and D. E. P. Jackson, *Saladin: the Politics of the Holy War* (Cambridge: Cambridge University Press, 1982).

Maalouf, Amin, *The Crusades through Arab Eyes* (London: Al Saqi, 1984).

MacEvitt, Christopher, *The Crusades and the Christian World of the East: Rough Tolerance* (Philadelphia: University of Pennsylvania Press, 2008).

MacEvitt, Christopher, 'What was Crusader about the Crusader States?', *Al-Masaq* 30 (2018): 317–30.

Major, Balazs, 'Observations on Crusader Settlements between the Nahr al-Kabir and the Nahr as-Sinn', in *Le comté de Tripoli. État multiculturel et multiconfession-*

nel (1102–1289), ed. Gérard Dédéyan and Karam Rizk (Paris: Geuthner 2010), pp. 119–52.

Major, Balazs, *Medieval Rural Settlements in the Syrian Coastal Region* (Oxford, Archeopress, 2015).

Makdisi, George, 'Notes on Hilla and the Mazyadids in Medieval Islam', *Journal of the American Oriental Society* 74 (1954): 249–62.

Mallett, Alex, 'The "Other" in the Crusading Period: Walter the Chancellor's Presentation of Najm al-Din Il-Ghazi', *Al-Masaq* 22 (2010): 113–28.

Mallett, Alex, 'The Life of Aq-Sunqur al-Bursuqi: Some Notes on Twelfth-Century Islamic History and Thirteenth-Century Muslim Historiography', *Turkish Historical Review* 2 (2011): 39–56.

Mallett, Alex, 'Ibn al-Azraq', in *Christian–Muslim Relations: a Biographical History, vol. 3: 1050–1200*, ed. David Thomas and Alex Mallett (Leiden: Brill, 2011), pp. 690–4.

Mallett, Alex, 'Ibn Nazif al-Hamawi', in *Christian–Muslim Relations: a Biographical History, vol. 4: 1200–1350*, ed. David Thomas and Alex Mallett (Leiden: Brill, 2012), pp. 245–7.

Mallett, Alex, 'Islamic Historians of the Ayyubid Era and Muslim Rulers from the Early Crusading Period: a Study in the Use of History', *Al-Masaq* 24 (2012): 241–52.

Mallett, Alex, 'The Battle of Inab', *Journal of Medieval History* 39 (2013): 48–60.

Mallett, Alex, *Popular Muslim Reactions to the Frankish Presence in the Levant: 1097–1291* (Farnham: Ashgate, 2014).

Mallett, Alex, 'Sibt Ibn al-Jawzi', in *Medieval Muslim Historians and the Franks in the Levant*, ed. Alex Mallett (Leiden: Brill, 2015), pp. 84–108.

Mallett, Alex, 'A Neglected Piece of Evidence for Early Muslim Reactions to the Frankish Crusader Presence in the Levant: the "Jihad Chapter" from Tuhfat al-muluk', in *The Character of Christian–Muslim Encounter*, ed. Douglas Pratt, Jan Hoover, John Davies and John Chesworth (Leiden: Brill, 2015), pp. 95–110.

Mallett, Alex, '"Ammar, Banu (Syria)', in *Encyclopaedia of Islam: THREE*, ed. Kate Fleet et al. (2019), available at Brill online, last accessed 2 July 2019.

Manzano Moreno, Eduardo, 'Christian–Muslim Frontier in Al-Andalus: Idea and Reality', in *The Arab Influence in Medieval Europe*, ed. Dionisius Agius and Richard Hitchcock (Reading: Ithaca Press, 1994), pp. 83–99.

Manzano Moreno, Eduardo, 'The Creation of a Medieval Frontier: Islam and Christianity in the Iberian Peninsula, Eighth to Eleventh Centuries', in *Frontiers in Question: Eurasian Borderlands, 700–1700*, ed. Daniel Power and Naomi Standen (London: Bloomsbury, 1999), pp. 32–54.

Mayer, Hans E., *The Crusades*, trans. J. Gillingham (Oxford: Oxford University Press, 1988).

Mazzola, Marianna, 'Gregory Abu l-Faraj Bar 'Ebroyo (Bar Hebraeus)', in *Franks and Crusades in Medieval Eastern Christian Historiography*, ed. Alex Mallett (Turnhout: Brepols, 2021), pp. 257–81.

Mecit, Söngul, *The Rum Seljuqs: Evolution of a Dynasty* (London: Routledge, 2013).

Meisami, Julie S., *Persian Historiography* (Edinburgh: Edinburgh University Press, 1999).

Meier, Astrid, 'Wakf II. In the Arab Lands', in *Encyclopaedia of Islam*, 2nd edn, ed. Peri Bearman et al. (2012), available at Brill online, last accessed 3 January 2021.

Metcalfe, Alex, *Muslims and Christians in Norman Sicily: Arabic Speakers and the End of Islam* (London: RoutledgeCurzon, 2003).

Metcalfe, Alex, *The Muslims of Medieval Italy* (Edinburgh: Edinburgh University Press, 2009).

Micheau, Françoise, 'Ibn al-Athir', *Medieval Muslim Historians and the Franks in the Levant*, ed. Alex Mallett (Leiden: Brill, 2015), pp. 52–83.

Miquel, André, 'al-Mukaddasi', *Encyclopaedia of Islam*, 2nd edn, ed. Peri Bearman et al. (2012), available at Brill online, last accessed 10 July 2017.

Miquel, André, 'Ibn Hawkal', *Encyclopaedia of Islam*, 2nd edn, ed. Peri Bearman et al. (2012), available at Brill online, last accessed 10 July 2017.

Morgan, David, *Medieval Persia 1040–1797* (London: Routledge, 2016).

Morray, David, *An Ayyubid Notable and His World* (Leiden: Brill, 1994).

Morrisson Cécile and Jean-Claude Cheynet, 'Prices and Wages in the Byzantine World', in *The Economic History of Byzantium: From the Seventh through the Fifteenth Century*, ed. Angeliki E. Laiou (Washington, DC: Dumbarton Oaks Research Library and Collection, 2002), pp. 815–78.

Morton, Nicholas, 'The Saljuq Turks' Conversion to Islam: the Crusading Sources', *al-Masaq* 27 (2015): 109–18.

Morton, Nicholas, *Encountering Islam on the First Crusade* (Cambridge: Cambridge University Press, 2016).

Morton, Nicholas, *The Field of Blood: The Battle for Aleppo and the Remaking of the Medieval Middle East* (New York: Basic Books, 2018).

Morton, Nicholas, 'Walter the Chancellor on Ilghazi and Tughtakin: a Prisoner's Perspective', *Journal of Medieval History* 44 (2018): 170–86.

Morton, Nicholas, *The Crusader States and their Neighbours: a Military History, 1099–1187* (Oxford: Oxford University Press, 2020).

Morton, Nicholas and John France, 'Arab Muslim Reactions to Turkish Authority in Northern Syria, 1085–1128', in *Warfare, Crusade and Conquest in the Middle Ages*, ed. John France (Farnham: Ashgate 2014), XV, pp. 1–38.

Mouton, Jean-Michel, *Damas et sa principauté sous les Saljoukides et les Bourides 468–549/1076–1154* (Cairo: Institut français d'archéologie orientale, 1997).

Mouton, Jean-Michel and Dominique Sourdel, *Mariage et Séparation à Damas au Moyen Âge: un Corpus de 62 Documents Juridiques Inédits entre 337/948 et 698/1299* (Paris: Académie des Inscriptions et Belles-Lettres, 2013).

Mourad, Suleiman A., *Ibn 'Asakir of Damascus: Champion of Sunni Islam in the Time of the Crusades* (Oxford: Oneworld, 2021).

Mourad, Suleiman A. and James E. Lindsay, 'Rescuing Syria from the Infidels: the Contribution of Ibn 'Asakir of Damascus to the *Jihad* Campaign of Sultan Nur al-Din', *Crusades* 6 (2007): 37–55.

Mourad, Suleiman A. and James E. Lindsay, *The Intensification and Reorientation of Sunni Jihad Ideology in the Crusader Period* (Leiden: Brill, 2013).

Mottahedeh, Roy P., *Loyalty and Leadership in an Early Islamic Society* (London: I. B. Tauris, 2001).

Murray, Alan V., *The Crusader Kingdom of Jerusalem: a Dynastic History 1099–1125* (Oxford: Linacre College, Oxford, 2000).

Murray, Alan V., 'The Franks and Indigenous Communities in Palestine and Syria (1099–1187): a Hierarchical Model of Social Interaction in the Principalities of Outremer', in *East Meets West in the Middle Ages and Early Modern Times: Transcultural Experiences in the Premodern World*, ed. Albrecht Classen (Berlin: De Gruyter, 2013), pp. 291–309.

Murray, Alan V., 'The Siege and Capture of Jerusalem in Western Narrative Sources of the First Crusade', in *Jerusalem the Golden: The Origins and Impact of the First Crusade*, ed. Susan B. Edgington (London: Brepols, 2014), pp. 191–215.

Mutafian, Claude, *Le royaume arménien de Cilicie, XIIe–XIVe siècle* (Paris: CNRS éditions 2001).

Mutafian, Claude, 'The Brilliant Diplomacy of Cilician Armenia', in *Armenian Cilicia*, ed. Robert Hovannisian and Simon Payaslian (Costa Mesa, CA: Mazda, 2008), pp. 93–110.

Nanji, Azim, 'Nasir-i Khusraw', in *Encyclopaedia of Islam*, 2nd edn, ed. Peri Bearman et al. (2012), available at Brill online, last accessed 10 July 2017.

Nicolle, D., *Arms and Armour of the Crusading Period: 1050–1350*, 2 vols (New York: Kraus International, 1988).

Nicolle, D., *Crusader Warfare*, 2 vols (London: MPG Books, 2007).

Nielsen, Jørgen S., 'Between Arab and Turk: Aleppo from the 11th till the 13th Centuries', in *Manzikert to Lepanto: the Byzantine World and the Turks 1071–1571*, ed. Anthony Bryer and Michael Ursinius (Amsterdam: A. M. Hakkert, 1991), pp. 323–40, 327–8.

Nol, Hagit, *Settlement and Urbanization in Early Islamic Palestine, 7th–11th Centuries* (London: Routledge, 2022).

Palombini, Augusto and Cinzia Tavaneri, 'On Their Way Home … a Network Analysis of Medieval Caravanserai Distribution in the Syrian Region, According to a 1D Approach', in *CAA 2015: Proceedings of the 43rd Annual Conference on Computer Applications and Quantitative Methods in Archaeology*, ed. Stefano Campana, Roberto Scopigno, Gabriella Carpentiero and Marianna Cirillo (Oxford: Archeopress, 2016), pp. 637–45.

Paul, Jürgen, '*Khidma* in the Social History of Pre-Mongol Iran', *Journal of Economic and Social History of the Orient* 57 (2014): 392–422.

Paul, Jürgen, 'Abbasid Legacy in the Seljuq World', *ERC Project. The Early Islamic Empire at Work: the View from the Regions Toward the Center*, Working Paper 01 (2015): 1–24.

Peacock, Andrew C. S., 'Nomadic Society and the Seljuq Campaigns in Caucasia', *Iran and Caucasus* 9 (2005): 205–30.

Peacock, Andrew C. S., *Early Saljuq History* (London: Routledge, 2010).

Peacock, Andrew C. S., 'Seljuq Legitimacy in Islamic History', in *The Seljuqs: Politics, Society and Culture*, ed. Christian Lange and Songul Mecit (Edinburgh: Edinburgh, University Press, 2011), pp. 79–95.

Peacock, Andrew C. S., 'From the Balkhan-Kuhiyan to the Nawakiya: Nomadic Politics and the Foundation of Seljuq Rule in Anatolia', in *Nomad Aristocracies in a World of Empires*, ed. Jürgen Paul (Wiesbaden: Reichert Verlag, 2013), pp. 55–80.

Peacock, Andrew C. S., *The Great Seljuk Empire* (Edinburgh: Edinburgh University Press, 2015).

Peacock, Andrew C. S., 'Urban Agency and the City Notables of Medieval Anatolia', *Medieval Worlds* 14 (2021): 22–34.

Phillips, Jonathan, *The Crusades: 1095–1204* (Abingdon: Routledge, 2014).

Popper, William, 'Ibn Taghribirdi', in *Encyclopaedia of Islam*, 2nd edn, ed. Peri Bearman et al. (2012), available at Brill online, last accessed 10 July 2017.

Poonawala, Ismail, 'Al-Mu'ayyad fi'l-Din', in *Encyclopaedia of Islam*, 2nd edn, ed. Peri Bearman et al. (2012), available at Brill online, last accessed 10 July 2017.

Power, Daniel, *The Norman Frontier in the Twelfth and Early Thirteenth Centuries* (Cambridge: Cambridge University Press, 2004).

Prawer, Joshua, *The Latin Kingdom of Jerusalem* (London: Weidenfeld & Nicolson, 1972).

Preiser-Kapeller, Johannes, 'A Collapse of the Eastern Mediterranean: New Results and Theories on Interplay between Climate and Societies in Byzantium and the Near East, ca. 1000–1200 AD', *Jahrbuch der Österteichischen Byzantinistik* 65 (2015): 195–242.

Pringle, Denys, 'Castles and Frontiers in the Latin East', in *Norman Expansion: Connections Continuities and Contrasts*, ed. Keith Stringer and Andrew Jotischky (Farnham: Ashgate, 2013), pp. 227–39.

Pryor, John H. and Michael J. Jeffreys, 'Alexius, Bohemond and Byzantium's Euphrates Frontier: a Tale of Two Cretans', *Crusades* 11 (2012): 31–86.

Pruitt, Jennifer, 'The Fatimid Holy City: Rebuilding Jerusalem in the Eleventh Century', *Medieval Globe* 3 (2017): 35–58.

Rabbat, Nasser, 'The Militarization of Taste in Medieval Bilad al-Sham', in *Muslim Military Architecture in Greater Syria: From the Coming of Islam to the Ottoman Period*, ed. Hugh Kennedy (Leiden: Brill, 2006), pp. 88–91.

Raphael, Kate, *Muslim Fortresses in the Levant: Between Crusaders and Mongols* (London: Routledge, 2011).

Rapoport, Yossef, *Marriage, Money and Divorce in Medieval Islamic Society* (Cambridge: Cambridge University Press, 2005).

Rapoport, Yossef, *Rural Economy and Tribal Society in Islamic Egypt: a Study of al-Nabulusi's 'Villages of the Fayyum'* (Turnhout: Brepols, 2018), pp. 143–70.

Redford, Scott, 'Trade and Economy in Antioch and Cilicia in the Twelfth and Thirteenth Centuries', in *Trade and Markets in Byzantium*, ed. Cécile Morrisson (Washington, DC: Dumbarton Oaks Research Library and Collection, 2012), pp. 297–309.

Richard, Jean, *La Comté de Tripoli sous la dynastie toulousaine 1102–1187* (Paris: Librairie orientaliste Paul Geuthner, 1945).

Richard, Jean, *The Crusades c. 1071–c. 1291* (Cambridge: Cambridge University Press, 1999).

Richards, Donald S., 'A Consideration of Two Sources for the life of Saladin', *Journal of Semitic Studies* 25 (1980): 44–65.

Richards, Donald S., 'The Early History of Saladin', in *The Crusades, vol. 2: Crusading and the Crusader states, 1095–1197*, ed. Andrew Jotischky (Abingdon: Routledge, 2008), pp. 432–53.

Riley-Smith, Jonathan, 'The Survival in Latin Palestine of Muslim Administration', in *The Eastern Mediterranean Lands in the Period of the Crusades*, ed. Peter M. Holt (Warminster: Aris & Phillips, 1977), pp. 9–22.

Riley-Smith, Jonathan, *The Crusades: a Short History* (London: Athlone, 2001).

Riley-Smith, Jonathan, *The Crusades, Christianity, and Islam* (New York: Columbia University Press, 2008).

Roche, Jason T., 'In the Wake of Mantzikert: the First Crusade and the Alexian Reconquest of Western Anatolia', *History* 94 (2009): 135–53.

Rosenthal, Franz, 'Al-Makrizi', in *Encyclopaedia of Islam*, 2nd edn, ed. Peri Bearman et al. (2012), available at Brill online, last accessed 10 July 2017.

Rosenthal, Franz, 'Ibn al-Athir', in *Encyclopaedia of Islam*, 2nd edn, ed. Peri Bearman et al. (2012), available at Brill online, last accessed 10 July 2017.

Rowton, Michael, 'Urban Autonomy in a Nomadic Environment', *Journal of Near Eastern Studies* 32 (1973): 201–15.

Rowton, Michael, 'Enclosed Nomadism', *Journal of the Economic and Social History of the Orient* 17 (1974): 1–30.

Rubenstein, Jay, *Armies of Heaven: The First Crusade and the Quest for Apocalypse* (New York: Basic Books, 2011).

Rubenstein, Jay, 'Saladin and the Problem of the Counter-Crusade in the Middle Ages', *Historically Speaking*, 13 (2012), 2–5.

Rubin, Uri, 'Muhammad's Night Journey (*isra'*) to al-Masjid al-Aqsa: Aspects of the Earliest Origins of the Islamic Sanctity of Jerusalem', *Al-Qanṭara* 29 (2008): 147–64.

Runciman, Steven, 'The Byzantine "Protectorate" in the Holy Land in the Eleventh Century', *Byzantion* 18 (1948): 207–15.

Runciman, Steven, *A History of the Crusades*, 3 vols (London: Penguin, 1965).

Safi, Omar, *The Politics of Knowledge in Premodern Islam* (Chapel Hill: University of North Carolina Press, 2006).

Sanders, Paula, 'Robes of Honor in Fatimid Egypt', in *Robes and Honor: the Medieval World of Investiture*, ed. Stewart Gordon (New York: Palgrave Macmillan, 2001), pp. 225–39.

Sato, Tsugitaka, *State and Rural Society in Medieval Islam: Sultans, Muqta's and Fallahun* (Leiden: Brill, 1997).

Sauvaget, Jean, *Alep Essai sur le développement d'une grande ville Syrienne, des origins au milieu du XIXe siècle*, 2 vols (Paris: Geuthner, 1941).

Sauvaget, Jean, 'Halab', *Encyclopaedia of Islam*, 2nd edn, ed. Peri Bearman et al (2012), available at Brill online, last accessed 31 July 2019.

Schrieke, Bentram, Josef Horovitz, J. E. Bencheikh, Jan Knappert and B. W. Robinson, 'Mi'radj', in *Encyclopaedia of Islam*, 2nd edn, ed. Peri Bearman et al. (2012), available at Brill online, last accessed 15 June 2019.

Shatzmiller, Maya, *Labour in the Medieval Islamic World* (Leiden: Brill, 1995).

Sheir, Ahmed M., 'Between Peace and War: the Peaceful Memory of the Crusades between the Middle Ages and the Modern Arabic-Egyptian Writings', in *Studies in Peace-building History between East and West through the Middle Ages and Modern Era*, ed. Ali Elsayed, Abdallah Al-Naggar and Ahmed Sheir (Cairo: Sanabil Bookshop, 2019), pp. 145–64.

Shoshan, Boaz, 'The 'Politics and Notables' in Medieval Islam', *Asian and African Studies* 20 (1986): 179–215.

Simeonova, Liliana, 'In the Depths of Tenth-century Byzantine Ceremonial: the Treatment of Arab Prisoners of War at Imperial Banquets', *Byzantine and Modern Greek Studies* 22 (1998): 75–104.

Sivan, Emmanuel, *L'Islam et la Croisade. Idéologie et Propagande dans les Réactions Musulmanes aux Croisades* (Paris: Librairie d'Amérique et d'Orient, 1968).

Sivan, Emmanuel, 'Modern Arab Historiography of the Crusades', *Asian and African Studies* 8 (1972): 109–49.

Sobernheim, Moritz, 'Muslim b. Kuraysh', in *Encyclopaedia of Islam*, 2nd edn, ed. Peri Bearman et al. (2012), available at Brill online, last accessed 30 March 2022.

Smail, R. C., *Crusading Warfare 1097–1193* (Cambridge: Cambridge University Press, 1956).

Smarandache, B., 'The Franks and the Nizari Isma'ilis in the Early Crusader Period', *Al-Masaq* 24(3) (2012): 221–40.

Smit, Timothy, 'Pagans and Infidels, Saracens and Sicilians: Identifying Muslims in the Eleventh-century Chronicles of Norman Italy', *Haskins Society Journal* 21 (2009): 67–86.

Sourdel, Dominique, 'Robes of Honor in 'Abbasid Baghdad during the Eighth to Eleventh Centuries', in *Robes and Honor: the Medieval World of Investiture*, ed. Stewart Gordon (New York: Palgrave Macmillan, 2001), pp. 137–46.

Stevenson, William B., *The Crusaders in the East: a Brief History of the Wars of Islam with the Latins in Syria during the Twelfth and Thirteenth Centuries* (Cambridge: Cambridge University Press, 1907).

Stern, Samuel M., *Fatimid Decrees: Original Documents from the Fatimid Chancery* (London: Faber & Faber, 1964).

Stouraitis, Yannis, 'Trapped in the Imperial Narrative? Some Reflections on Warfare and the Provincial Masses in Byzantium (600–1204)', *Byzantine and Modern Greek Studies* 44 (2020): 1–20.

Swanson, Mark N., 'Yahya ibn Sa'id al-Antaki', in *Christian–Muslim Relations 600–1500*, ed. David Thomas (2010), available online, last accessed 19 August 2022.

Tabbaa, Yasser, 'Monuments with a Message: Propagation of *Jihad* under Nur al-Din 1146–74', in *The Meeting of Two Worlds: Cultural Exchange between East and West during the Period of the Crusades*, ed. Vladimir P. Goss and Christine V. Bornstein (Kalamazoo: Medieval Institute Publications, 1986), pp. 233–40.

Tabbaa, Yasser, 'Survivals and Archaisms in the Architecture of Northern Syria, ca. 1080–ca. 1150', *Muqarnas* 10 (1993): 29–41.

Tabbaa, Yasser, *Constructions of Piety and Power in Medieval Aleppo* (Philadelphia: Pennsylvania State University Press, 2001).

Tabbaa, Yasser, 'Defending Ayyubid Aleppo: the Fortifications of al-Zahir Ghazi (1186–1216)', in *Muslim Military Architecture in Greater Syria: From the Coming of Islam to the Ottoman Period*, ed. Hugh Kennedy (Leiden: Brill, 2006), pp. 176–83.

Taeko, Nakamura, 'Territorial Disputes between Syrian Cities and the Early Crusaders: the Struggle for Economic and Political Dominance', in *The Concept of Territory in Islamic Law and Thought*, ed. Hiroyuki Yanagihashi (Abingdon: Routledge, 2000), pp. 101–24.

Talmon-Heller, Daniella, 'Arabic Sources on Muslim Villagers under Frankish Rule', in *From Clermont to Jerusalem: the Crusades and Crusader Societies 1095–1500*, ed. Alan V. Murray (Turnhout: Brepols, 1998), pp. 103–17.

Talmon-Heller, Daniella, *Islamic Piety in Medieval Syria: Mosques, Cemeteries and Sermons under the Zengids and Ayyubids 1146–1260* (Leiden: Brill, 2007).

Talmon-Heller, Daniella, 'Islamic Preaching in Syria during the Counter-Crusade Twelfth–Thirteenth Centuries', in *In Laudem Hierosolymitani: Studies in Crusades and Medieval Culture in Honour of Benjamin Z. Kedar*, ed. Iris Shagrir, Ronnie Ellenblum and Jonathan Riley-Smith (Aldershot: Routledge, 2016).

Teule, Herman G. B., 'The Anonymous Syriac Chronicle to the Year 1234', in *Franks and Crusades in Medieval Eastern Christian Historiography*, ed. Alex Mallett (Turnhout: Brepols, 2021), pp. 243–57.

Thomson, Kristen, *Politics and Power in Late Fatimid Egypt: the Reign of the Caliph al-Mustansir* (London: I. B. Tauris, 2016).

Tibbetts, Gerald R., 'The Balkhi School of Geographers', in *The History of Islamic Cartography, Vol. Two, Book One*, ed. J. B. Harley and David Woodward (Chicago: University of Chicago Press, 1992), pp. 108–36.

Tibble, Steven, *The Crusader Armies 1099–1187* (New Haven, CT: Yale University Press, 2018).

Tonghini, Christina and Nadia Montevecchi, 'The Castle of Shayzar: the Fortification of the Access System', in *Muslim Military Architecture in Greater Syria: From the Coming of Islam to the Ottoman Period*, ed. Hugh Kennedy (Leiden: Brill, 2006), pp. 201–24.

Tor, Deborah, *Violent Order: Religious Warfare, Chivalry and the 'Ayyar Phenomenon in the Medieval Islamic World* (Wurzburg: Ergon, 2007).

Tor, Deborah, '"Sovereign and Pious": The Religious Life of the Great Seljuq Sultans' in *The Saljuqs: Society, Politics and Culture*, ed. by Christian Lange and Songul Mecit (Edinburgh: Edinburgh University Press, 2011), pp. 39–62.

Tyerman, Christopher, *God's War: a New History of the Crusades* (London: Allen Lane, 2006).

Tyerman, Christopher, *The Debate on the Crusades* (Manchester: Manchester University Press, 2011).

Van Den Bossche, Gowaart, 'Narrative Construction, Ideal Rule, and Emotional Discourse in the Biographies of Salah al-Din and Louis IX by Baha' al-Din b. Shaddad and Jean Sire de Joinville', *Al-Masaq* 30 (2018): 133–47.

Vorderstrasse, Tasha, 'Archaeology of the Antiochene Region in the Crusader Period', in *East and West in the Medieval Eastern Mediterranean, vol. I: Antioch from the Byzantine Reconquest until the End of the Crusader Principality*, ed. Krinja Ciggaar and David M. Metcalf (Leuven: Peeters, 2006), pp. 319–36.

Vorderstrasse, Tasha, 'Medieval Encounters between China, Mongolia, Antioch and Cilicia', in *East and West in the Medieval Eastern Mediterranean, vol. II: Antioch from the Byzantine Reconquest Until the End of the Crusader Principality*, ed. Krijna N. Ciggaar and V. D. van Aalst (Leuven: Peeters, 2013), pp. 345–66.

Vryonis, Speros, *The Decline of Medieval Hellenism in Asia Minor and the Process of Islamization from Eleventh through Fifteenth Century* (Berkeley: University California Press, 1971).

Vryonis, Speros, 'The Greek and the Arabic Sources on the Eight-day Captivity of the Emperor Romanus IV in the Camp of the Sultan Alp Arslan after the Battle of Manzikert', in *Novum Millennium: Studies on Byzantine History and*

Culture Dedicated to Paul Speck, ed. Claudia Sode and Sarolta Takacs (Aldershot: Routledge, 2000), pp. 439–50.

Vryonis, Speros, 'The Decline of Medieval Hellenism in Asia Minor and the Process of Islamization from Eleventh through Fifteenth Century: the Book in Light of Subsequent Scholarship, 1971–1998', in *Eastern Approaches to Byzantium: Papers from the Thirty-Third Spring Symposium of Byzantine Studies, University of Warwick, Coventry March 1999*, ed. Anthony Eastmond (Aldershot: Routledge, 2001), pp. 1–15.

Walker, Paul E., *Exploring an Islamic Empire: Fatimid History and its Sources* (London: I. B. Tauris, 2001).

Walker, Paul E., *Fatimid History and Ismaili Doctrine* (Aldershot: Ashgate, 2008).

Walker, Paul E., 'The Abbasid–Fatimid Rivalry for Control of the Holy Cities and the Hijazi Response', in *Difference and Dynamism in Islam*, ed. Hinrich Biesterfeldt and Verena Klemm (Tübingen: Ergon, 2012), pp. 145–63.

Walker, Paul E., 'Was the *Amir al-Jayush* actually a *Wazir*?' in *The Fatimid Caliphate: Diversity of Traditions*, ed. Farhad Daftary and Shainool Jiwa (London: I. B. Tauris, 2018), pp. 80–93.

Wasserstein, David, *The Rise and Fall of the Party-Kings: Politics and Society in Islamic Spain 1002–1086* (Princeton, NJ: Princeton University Press, 1985).

Weber, Max, *The City*, trans. and ed. Don Martindale and Gertrud Neuwirth (London: Free Press, 1958).

Weigert, G., 'A Note on Hudna: Peace Making in Islam', in *War and Society in the Eastern Mediterranean 7th–15th Centuries*, ed. Yaacov Lev (Leiden: Brill, 1997) pp. 399–405.

Weltecke, Dorothea, 'Originality and Function of Formal Structures in the Chronicle of Michael the Great', *Hugoye: Journal of Syriac Studies* 3 (2000): 173–202.

Weltecke, Dorothea, 'Michael the Great', in *Franks and Crusades in Medieval Eastern Christian Historiography*, ed. Alex Mallett (Turnhout: Brepols, 2021), pp. 213–43.

Wilson, Ian, 'By the Sword or by an Oath: Siege Warfare in the Latin East 1097–1131', in *A Military History of the Mediterranean Sea: Aspects of War, Diplomacy, and Military Elites*, ed. Georgios Theotokis and Aysel Yildiz (Leiden: Brill, 2018), pp. 235–53.

Wilson, James, 'The "*asakir al-Sham*": Medieval Arabic Historiography of the Siege, Capture and Battle of Antioch during the First Crusade', *al-Masaq* 33 (2021): 300–36.

Wilson, James, 'The Ransom of High-Ranking Captives, Tributary Relationships and the Practice of Diplomacy in Northern Syria 442–522/1050–1128', *Journal of the Royal Asiatic Society* 32 (2022): 635–69.

Witakowski, Witold, 'Syriac Historiographical Sources', in *Byzantines and Crusaders in Non-Greek Sources 1025–1204*, ed. Mary Whitby (Oxford: Oxford University Press for the British Academy, 2007), pp. 255–61.

Woodhead, Christine, 'Fethiname', in *Encyclopaedia of Islam THREE*, ed. Kate Fleet et al. (2014), available online, last accessed 29 December 2021.

Yarbrough, Luke, 'History of the Patriarchs of Alexandria', in *Encyclopedia of the Medieval Chronicle*, ed. Graeme Dunphy and Cristian Bratu (2016), available online, last accessed 20 August 2022.

Yared-Riachi, Mariam, *La politique extérieure de la principauté de Damas 468–549/1076–1154* (Damascus: Institut français d'études arabes de Damas, 1997).

Yarnley C. J., 'Philaretos: Armenian Bandit or Byzantine General?' *Revue des études arméniennes* 9 (1972): 331–53.

Zakkar, Suhayl, *The Emirate of Aleppo 1004–1094* (Beirut: Dar al-Amanah, 1971).

Zouache, Abbés, 'Dubays b. Ṣadaqa (m. 529/1135), aventurier de légende. Histoire et fiction dans l'historiographie arabe médiévale (VI/XIIe–VII/XIIIe siècles)', *Bulletin d'études orientales* 58 (2008): 87–130.

Zouache, Abbés, *Armées et Combats en Syrie de 491/1098 à 569/1174. Analyse Comparée des Chroniques Médiévales Latines et Arabes* (Damascus: Presses de l'Ifpo, 2008).

Index

ahdath, xiii, 81, 185, 192, 193, 195
ahl haleb (people of Aleppo), 130, 185–6, 191, 195, 196, 199, 202, 207, 208, 218
Ahmed Shah, 93n, 128, 129
al-a'yan (notables), xvii, 184–5
   female influence, 200–2
   source of power, 186–7
   tax policy, 202
   the value placed on regional ties, 198–200
al-Basasiri, 73–4
al-Funaydiq, battle of, 75–9
al-Mustansir, 7, 44, 73, 75–6, 78–80, 82, 84, 159–9, 166
al-Mu'ayyad fi'l-Din al-Shirazi, 7, 73–4
al-Sulami, 8, 152
al-Atharib, 77, 173, 204, 211–12, 216
   strategic value of, 205–6
al-'Azimi, xiii, 8–9, 44, 57, 79, 107, 189, 202, 217
Aleppo, 2–4 203–5
   anti-Frankish sentiment, 216–17
   Twelver Shi'i community, 3, 219
   see also bilad haleb
alliance networks, 165–74
   alliances against the Franks, 173–4
   Byantine–Mirdasid alliances, 54 –5
   Muslim–Frankish alliances, 157, 168–71
   Seljuq–Fatimid alliances, 86–9, 116–18
Alp Arslan, 98–100

   in Syria, 102–5
   leadership style, 102–3, 105, 107
amiral autonomy, 101–2
amiral rivalry, 107–11, 154–8
Antioch, 2, 39–60, 205–6
   prestige of, 39–40
   territorial footprint, 41–2
appeals for assistance, 84, 193–7
Aqsunqur, Qasim al-Dawla, 84, 106, 109–10, 199, 200
Aqsunqur al-Bursuqi, 115, 125–6, 157, 167, 172, 173, 195–200, 202, 212, 215, 220
'asakir al-sham, 154, 162, 174
Asbridge, Thomas, 6, 42, 204, 206, 213
Artah, 42, 45–6, 48, 55, 209, 212, 214
   strategic importance of, 45, 205–6
Atsiz b. Uvaq, 82–3, 86, 109, 127, 131–2, 160–1
   arrival in Palestine, 82
   campaign in Egypt, 82–3, 86
   capture of Damascus, 192
   relationship with Malik Shah, 113–14, 125, 131–2
'Azaz, 48, 51, 108, 173, 191, 202, 204, 205, 212
   strategic importance of, 206–8

Badr al-Jamali, 70, 72, 85, 158–9
   approach to Tutush, 86–7

INDEX | 293

in Egypt, 80
in Syria, 81–2
Baghdad, 3, 9–14, 35, 36, 39, 58, 72–4, 76, 79–80, 88, 89, 101, 112, 113, 124, 131
Banu Kilab, 36, 48, 55, 73, 74, 75, 86, 108, 127, 155, 211
Banu Kalb, 36, 73, 127
Banu Munqidh, 9–10, 52, 53, 195, 209
Banu Numayr, 36, 43, 74, 108, 127, 158
Banu Uqayl, 108, 114, 127, 212
Baldwin I, 15, 157, 163–4, 165
Baldwin II, 149, 168–71, 184, 194, 203, 209–12
    siege of Aleppo, 213–21
Bedouin, 40, 73, 75, 116, 127, 185
Bilad al-sham, 1–7, 39, 55, 59, 71, 100, 112, 122, 127, 185, 235–7
    definition, 1–3
Bilad haleb
    definition, 2–4, 203–5
    see also Aleppo
Byzantine Empire, 6, 7, 35, 43, 55–6
    diplomacy, 55–8
    mechanisms of governance, 33–6, 41–5
    priorities in northern Syria, 41–3
    support in the provinces, 51–4

Cahen, Claude, 4, 6, 11, 154, 206, 209, 216
    republic of notables, 194, 196, 198
Cairo, 6, 7, 33–6, 44, 54, 58, 70–80, 83, 87–90, 116, 118, 122, 159, 161–3, 165–7, 188
calls for assistance, 193–7; *see also* appeals for assistance
Cobb, Paul, 13, 152, 217
Constantinople, 6, 33–6, 39, 40, 42–3, 44–5, 47, 51, 53–5, 57, 58, 72, 78
counter-Crusade, 17, 149, 194
    Fatimid counter-Crusade, 158–68

origins, definitions and criticisms, 151–4
    Seljuq counter-Crusade, 154–8
Crusades, 1, 4, 8, 14, 16, 35, 121, 126, 151–2, 158, 167
    crusader states, 1, 6, 16, 129, 133, 149, 158
    historiography, 6
    significance of, 235–7

dimorphic states, 127, 129
diplomacy, 5, 42, 58, 221
    cross-cultural approaches, 5, 35, 42, 89, 99, 153
Duqaq b. Tutush, 88, 98, 121, 123, 164, 171–3

Egypt, 2, 7, 8, 10, 12–14, 35, 44, 45, 70–90, 101, 102, 109, 114, 117, 131, 152, 153, 159–67, 200, 202, 217
    civil war, 80–2
ethno-cultural identities, 55–8, 85–9
    criticisms, 55–6, 115, 85–6

Fatimid Caliphate, 3, 6, 35, 40, 43, 45, 50, 70–3, 75, 79, 82, 84, 86–7, 89–90, 100, 102, 117, 122, 132, 149, 160–2, 167, 173, 236
    civil war, 80–2
    in northern Syria, 73–80
    in Palestine, 80–5, 158–68
    the Fatimid 'other' (?), 89–90
female influence, 192, 200–1
    marriage alliances, 86–7, 114–15, 200–2
Field of Blood, battle of, 15, 78, 129, 152, 173, 186, 194, 206, 212
First Crusade, 1, 5, 10, 11, 14, 15, 16, 33, 36, 49, 60, 84, 98, 111, 121, 129, 149, 154, 155, 158–9, 163, 165, 172, 198, 205, 209, 235–6
    Fatimid benefits (?), 159–63

Franks, 8, 11, 15, 21, 111, 124, 151–4, 156–67, 168, 170, 171, 173–4, 192, 197, 199, 205, 206, 208, 210–13, 216–17, 220, 236–7
  degree of integration, 5, 16, 151, 213, 168, 201, 220–1
  Frankish buffer state, 153, 160
  methods of conquest, 216–20
frontiers, 1, 2, 6, 13, 17, 47, 49, 129, 149, 184
  conceptualisation of, 42
  frontiers of Aleppo, 203–13
  in Arabic geography, 1–2
  see also bilad haleb

Gibb, Hamilton A. R., 89–90, 151–2, 161

Hamdan al-Atharibi, 13, 217
Hillenbrand, Carole, 5, 6, 11, 14, 111, 152–4, 158–60, 219
hudna, xvi, 35

Ibn Abi Tayyi', 199
Ibn al-'Adim, 43, 45, 55, 73, 77–9, 88, 108, 110, 112–13, 117, 120–1, 125, 155–7, 162, 169, 173, 189, 191, 193, 195–203, 206, 208, 211, 212, 214–15, 217–18
  ancestors, 184–6
  lifetime, 12–13
Ibn al-Athir, 87, 110, 115, 120, 125, 126, 155, 157, 166, 168, 169, 172, 193, 196, 199, 217, 219
  lifetime, 10–11
  on the Fatimid Caliphate, 160–3
Ibn al-Furat, 199
Ibn al-Qalanisi, 88, 89, 116, 124, 155, 156, 157, 161, 162, 164, 170, 173, 192, 196, 202, 217
  lifetime, 8
Ibn Hawqal, 1–2

Ibn Khan, 46, 55, 56, 76, 78, 93n, 128, 131
Ibn Shaddad, 'Izz al-Din Muhammad b. 'Ali, 207
Il-ghazi, 84, 125, 157, 170, 173, 189, 192, 196, 197, 200, 202, 206, 211, 212, 216, 218, 219
iqta', xvi, 87, 113–16, 119–20, 124, 125, 132, 186, 195, 211
  Seljuq application, 100–2
Isfahan, 14, 33, 36, 99, 101, 103, 106, 107, 113, 118, 119, 122

Joscelyn I of Tell Bashir and Edessa, 156, 169, 211, 214, 216

khidma, xvi, 50, 74, 79, 104, 117, 123, 195
  definition, 34–5
khutba, xvi, 44, 50, 57, 70, 74, 79, 82, 84, 88, 103, 131, 132, 166, 172, 173, 200, 201
  definition, 34–5
Köhler, Michael, 5, 6, 33, 151–4, 159, 160, 162, 165, 166, 168–74; *see also la maqam*
Komnenos, Isaac, 51

la maqam or no place theory, 151–4, 168–74; *see also* Köhler, Michael

Mahmud b. Nasr, 13, 43, 46, 48–51, 55, 75, 103, 104, 131, 191, 201
Malik Shah, 53, 56, 58, 98–100, 102, 103, 107–11, 123, 125, 126, 132–3, 155, 191–3, 195, 210, 211
  in Syria, 105–7
  leadership style, 107
  relationship with Tutush, 107–23
Ma'rrat al-Nu'man, 48, 52, 55, 76, 77, 106, 204, 212
  strategic importance of, 208–10
marriage alliances, 86–7, 114–15, 200–2

medieval Arabic historiography, 186, 203
  regional traditions, 14–15
milk, 186–7
Mirdasid dynasty, 36, 39, 43, 45, 54, 55, 70, 72, 74, 75, 103, 108, 113, 129, 188, 202, 203, 217
Muslim b. Quraysh, Sharaf al-Dawla, 53, 58, 108–9, 122, 124, 126, 157, 158, 163, 172, 185, 191, 195, 201, 202, 220
  links to the Fatimids, 87, 116–19
  links to the Seljuqs, 112, 114–19

Nizam al-Mulk, 98, 104, 113, 116–18, 120–3
nomadism, 127–31
  enclosed nomadism, 127–8
  external nomadism, 127–8
Nur al-Din, 9, 10, 89, 130, 151–4, 174, 189, 219, 221

Philaretos Brachamios, 52, 53, 85, 116
  conversion, 56–8

ransom, 40, 51, 129, 169, 211
Ridwan b. Tutush, 13, 88, 156, 200
robes of honour, 34, 46, 116, 124, 167
Roger of Salerno, 208, 210
Romanos Diogenes IV, 16, 40, 47, 103, 208

Saladin, 9, 153, 154, 168, 174, 215, 221
  entry into Damascus, 199
Seljuq Sultanate, 6, 35, 56, 58, 82, 85, 89, 90, 98, 99, 101, 110, 111, 114, 121, 123, 126, 131, 149, 159, 165, 168, 200, 202, 236
  campaigning in northern Syria, 102–11, 154–5
  centralised authority, 36, 121–2, 155
  governance mechanisms, 100–2
  shared family rule, 100, 113
Shayzar, 9, 42, 52, 53, 106, 195, 208–9, 212

Sibt b. al-Jawzi, 10, 45, 51, 52, 53, 58, 74, 75, 76, 79, 86, 87, 104, 105, 106, 109, 110, 112, 113, 116, 117, 119, 130, 132, 157, 192, 195, 196, 202
  lifetime, 11–12
siege warfare, 34
  definition, 187
  frequency of, 187–90
Sivan, Emmanuel, 6, 152, 153
Sulayman b. Qutlumush, 50, 53, 54, 57, 59, 118–19, 125, 191, 193, 201
  links to Byzantines, 56
system of autonomous lordships in Syria, 100, 126, 133, 221
  definition, 33–6
  Seljuq perpetuation of, 111–23
Syria
  geographical definition, 1–2
  historical context, 3–4
  pan Syrian sensibility, 153
  see also bilad al-sham

Tancred of Antioch, 15, 156, 168, 169, 206, 217
tributary agreements, 35, 49, 70, 76, 78, 79, 205
  annual payments, 35, 39, 43–4, 50, 51, 53–4, 59, 73
  one-off payments, 35, 46, 104, 110, 156, 160
Tughril Beg, 44, 102
Tughtegin, 16, 123–5, 130, 157, 170–3, 194, 197, 199
  links to Faimids, 165–7
Türkmen, 36, 40, 44–52, 55–6, 59, 76, 78, 81–2, 86–7, 89, 100, 104, 108, 126–33, 154, 158, 185, 186, 191, 203, 211, 218, 235
  First Türkmen in northern Syria, 46
  influence in Mirdasid Aleppo, 93n
  relations with urban centres, 126–31

Türkmen (*cont.*)
    raids in northern Syria, 46, 47, 48, 52
    Türkmen reluctance to campaign in Syria, 105
Tutush b. Alp Arslan, 52, 84, 86, 98, 130, 132, 156, 157, 189, 191, 193, 194, 200, 208, 210
    in Syria, 108–11
    relationship with Malik Shah, 111–23

Usama b. Munqidh, 9–10

Walter the Chancellor, 15, 157, 206
William of Tyre, 15

Zangi, 10, 16, 115, 126, 153, 154, 174, 184, 189, 194
    arrival in Aleppo, 198
    ties to Aleppo, 198–203

EU representative:
Easy Access System Europe
Mustamäe tee 50, 10621 Tallinn, Estonia
Gpsr.requests@easproject.com

www.ingramcontent.com/pod-product-compliance
Lightning Source LLC
Chambersburg PA
CBHW050203240426
43671CB00013B/2233